GED

PREPARATION FOR THE
HIGH SCHOOL EQUIVALENCY EXAMINATION

WRITING SKILLS

NEW GED TEST 1

SUSAN BREEMER WICKHAM

Consultant and Field Tester
Carol Nelson
Illinois Central College

Project Editor
Karin Evans

CONTEMPORARY
BOOKS, INC.
CHICAGO ▪ NEW YORK

Library of Congress Cataloging-in-Publication Data

Wickham, Susan Breemer.
    Contemporary's new GED test 1, writing skills.

    1. General educational developmental tests—Study
guides.   2. High school equivalency examination—Study
guides.   3. English language—Composition and exercises
—Examinations, questions, etc.   I. Evans, Karin.
II. Title.
LB3060.33.G45W53   1987   373.12'62   86-32958
ISBN 0-8092-5038-1

Published by Contemporary Books, Inc.
180 North Michigan Avenue, Chicago, Illinois 60601
Manufactured in the United States of America
International Standard Book Number: 0-8092-5038-1

Published simultaneously in Canada by
Beaverbooks, Ltd.
195 Allstate Parkway
Valleywood Business Park
Markham, Ontario L3R 4T8
Canada

Editorial
Ann Upperco
Sarah Schmidt
Christine M. Benton

Senior Editor
Ellen Carley Frechette

Editorial Director
Caren Van Slyke

Production Editor
Patricia Reid

Typography
Lisa A. Waitrovich

Art Director
Georgene G. Sainati

Art & Production
Lynn Rozycki
Princess Louise El
Arvid Carlson
Lois Koehler

Cover photo © Image Bank

CONTENTS

TO THE STUDENT

Introducing the Writing Skills Test

Part of preparing for a test is working through the doubts and questions that you have. Perhaps it has been a long time since you took an important test. Maybe you are not sure what is required to pass the GED Writing Skills Test, or you are nervous about the test-taking situation. You also may have heard that you will have to actually write an essay in order to pass the test, and this may concern you.

This book has been designed so that you can succeed on the test. It will provide you with instruction in the grammar and usage skills you need to pass the test, and it will provide plenty of GED-type practice. In addition, this book will give you plenty of opportunities to write as you learn useful techniques for composing an essay in a test situation. If you work carefully through this book, you should do well. The material on pages xi–xii will give you advice on how to use this book.

What Kind of Test Is This?

The GED Writing Skills Test consists of two parts; Part 1 is a multiple-choice test. In this part, several passages will be followed by questions about the sentences within the passage. Some questions will ask you to locate errors, while other questions may ask you to restate an idea in different words. These questions will check your knowledge of sentence structure, standard usage, punctuation, capitalization, and spelling. Chapter 7 of this book will provide you with many more specifics about the types of questions asked and the skills tested.

In Part 2 of the GED Writing Skills Test, you will be given forty-five minutes to write an essay on a topic provided for you. You will not be given a choice of topics, but you will not need any special information or knowledge in order to write the essay. In addition, the topic will draw on your general knowledge and ask you to explain something about a common issue or problem. In this part of the GED Writing Skills Test, an understanding of grammar and usage will not be enough to succeed. In addition, to be successful on Part 2, you should be able to plan and organize your thinking on a given issue, and you should be able to communicate these thoughts clearly on paper.

What Does the Test Look Like?

On Part 1, there are fifty-five multiple-choice questions based on six or seven short passages, each ten to twelve sentences long. You will be given seventy-five minutes to complete the test. Part 2 of the test consists of a single topic on which you will be given forty-five minutes to write. To get an idea of what the test is like, look at the posttest at the end of this book. This posttest was based on the real GED Test.

What's on the Test?

Part 1 of the GED Writing Skills Test can be broken down into the following content areas:

Sentence Structure: 35%
Usage: 35%
Mechanics (spelling, punctuation, and capitalization): 30%

All three of the areas listed above will contain questions of the following types:

Sentence Correction: 50%
Sentence Revision: 35%
Construction Shift: 15%

Chapter 7 of this book discusses these three types of questions and how you can best approach each kind.

The Five GED Tests

The following section answers some of the questions asked most frequently about the GED Tests.

Can I Take the Test?

Each year, more than 700,000 people take the GED Test. In the United States, Canada, and many territories, people who have not graduated from high school and who meet specific eligibility requirements (age, residency, etc.) may take the test. Since eligibility requirements vary, it would be useful to contact your local GED testing center or the director of adult education in your state, province, or territory for specific information.

What Should I Know to Pass the Test?

The test consists of five examinations in the areas of writing skills, social studies, science, literature and the arts, and mathematics. The chart below outlines the main content areas, the breakdown of questions, and the time allowed per test.

The GED Tests

Test	Minutes	Questions	Percentage
Writing Skills			
Part 1	75	55	Sentence Structure 35% Usage 35% Mechanics 30%
Part 2	45	1 topic	
Social Studies	85	64	History 25% Economics 20% Political Science 20% Geography 15%* Behavioral Science 20%
Science	95	66	Biology 50% Physical Sciences 50%
Literature and the Arts	65	45	Popular Literature 50% Classical Literature 25% Commentary 25%
Mathematics	90	56	Arithmetic 50% Algebra 30% Geometry 20%

On all five tests, you are expected to demonstrate the ability to think about many issues. You are also tested on knowledge and skills you have acquired from life experiences, television, radio, books and newspapers, consumer products, and advertising.

In addition to the above information, keep these facts in mind:

1. Three of the five tests—Literature, Science, and Social Studies—require that you answer questions based on reading passages or interpreting illustrations in these content areas. Developing strong reading and thinking skills is the key to succeeding on these tests.

*In Canada, 20% of the test is based on geography and 15% on behavioral science.

2. The Writing Skills Test requires you to be able to detect and correct errors in sentence structure, grammar, punctuation, and spelling. You will also have to write a composition of approximately 200 words on a topic familiar to most adults.

3. The Mathematics Test consists mainly of word problems to be solved. Therefore, you must be able to combine your ability to perform computations with problem-solving skills.

Someone once said that an education is what remains after you've forgotten everything else. In many ways, this is what the GED measures.

What Is a Passing Score on the GED?

Again, this varies from area to area. To find out what you need to pass the test, contact your local GED testing center. However, you must keep two scores in mind. One score represents the minimum score you must get on each test. For example, if your state requires minimum scores of 40, you must get at least 40 points on every test. Additionally, you must meet the requirements of a minimum average score on all five tests. For example, if your state requires a minimum average score of 45, you must get a total of 225 points to pass. The two scores together, the minimum score and the minimum average score, determine whether you pass or fail the GED.

To understand this better, look at the scores of three people who took the test in a state that requires a minimum score of 40 and a minimum average score of 45 (225 total). Ann and Sarah did not pass, but Mark did. See if you can tell why.

	Ann	Sarah	Mark
Test 1	44	42	43
Test 2	43	43	48
Test 3	38	42	47
Test 4	50	40	52
Test 5	50	40	49
	225	207	239

Ann made the total of 225 points but fell below the minimum score on Test 3. Sarah passed each test but failed to get the 225 points needed; just passing the individual tests was not enough. Mark passed all the tests and exceeded the minimum average score.

Generally, to receive a GED credential, you must correctly answer half or a little more than half of the questions on each test.

What Happens If I Don't Pass the Test?

You are allowed to retake some or all of the tests. Again, the number of times that you may retake the tests and the time you must wait before retaking them are governed by your state, province, or territory. Some states require you to take a review class or to study on your own for a certain amount of time before taking the test again.

How Can I Best Prepare for the Test?

Many libraries, community colleges, adult education centers, churches, and other institutions offer GED preparation classes. Some television stations broadcast classes to prepare people for the test. If you cannot find a GED preparation class locally, contact the director of adult education in your state, province, or territory.

Are There Other Materials Available to Help Prepare for the Other Tests?

Contemporary Books publishes a wide range of materials to help you prepare for the tests. These books are designed for home study or class use. Contemporary's GED preparation books are available through schools and bookstores and directly from the publisher, at Contemporary Books, 180 N. Michigan Ave., Chicago, IL 60601.

Test-Taking Tips

Now let's focus on some useful test-taking tips. As you read this section, you should feel more confident about your ability to succeed on the Writing Skills Test.

1. **Prepare physically.** Get plenty of rest and eat a well-balanced meal before the test so that you will have energy and will be able to think clearly. Last-minute cramming will probably not help as much as a relaxed and rested mind.

2. **Arrive early.** Be at the testing center at least fifteen to twenty minutes before the starting time. Make sure you have time to find the room and to get situated. Keep in mind that many testing centers refuse to admit latecomers.

3. **Think positively.** Tell yourself you will do well. If you have studied and prepared for the test, you should succeed.

4. **Relax during the test.** Take half a minute several times during the test to stretch and breathe deeply, especially if you are feeling anxious or confused.

5. **Read the test directions carefully.** Be sure you understand how to answer the questions. If you have any questions about the test or about filling in the answer form, ask before the test begins.

6. **Know the time limit for each test.** Part 1 of the Writing Skills Test is seventy-five minutes long; Part 2 is forty-five minutes.

Some testing centers allow extra time, while others do not. It's always best to work according to the official time limit. If you have extra time, go back and check your work.

For Part 1 of the Writing Skills Test, which has fifty-five items, you will have a little more than one minute per question.

7. **Have a strategy for answering multiple-choice questions.** Read each passage carefully, and refer back to the passage to confirm your answer choices. On the Writing Skills Test, the best answer for multiple-choice questions must be consistent with the passage as a whole.

    Have a strategy for approaching the essay as well. Be sure to take a few minutes to plan your essay. You should also save a few minutes at the end for revising and editing your writing.

8. **Don't spend a lot of time on difficult questions.** If you're not sure of an answer, go on to the next question. Answer easier questions first and then go back to the harder questions. However, when you skip a question, be sure that you have skipped the same number on your answer sheet. Although skipping difficult questions is a good strategy for making the most of your time, it is very easy to get confused and throw off your whole answer key.

    Lightly mark the margin of your answer sheet next to the numbers of the questions you did not answer so that you know what to go back to. To prevent confusion when your test is graded, be sure to erase these marks completely after you answer the questions.

9. **Answer every question on the test.** If you're not sure of an answer, take an educated guess. When you leave a question unanswered, you will *always* lose points, but you can possibly gain points if you make a correct guess.

    If you must guess, try to eliminate one or more answers that you are sure are not correct. Then choose from the remaining answers. Remember, you greatly increase your chances if you can eliminate one or two answers before guessing. Of course, guessing should be used only when all else has failed.

10. **Clearly fill in the circle for each answer choice.** If you erase something, erase it completely. Be sure that you give only one answer per question; otherwise no answer will count.

Practice Test Taking

Use the exercises, reviews, and especially the posttest in this book to better understand your test-taking habits and weaknesses. Use them to practice different strategies such as skimming questions first or skipping hard questions until the end. Knowing your own personal test-taking style is important to success on the GED.

HOW TO USE THIS BOOK

If you are a student about to prepare for the GED Tests, you are to be admired. You have decided to resume an education that had been cut short. It is never easy to get back on track after you have been derailed. While it may not be easy, it will not be impossible. It will require determination and a lot of hard work.

Each chapter of this book is divided into two sections: a **"Conventions of English"** section in which you will practice skills for Part 1 of the test, and a **"Writing Process"** section in which you will practice skills for Part 2 of the test. It is important that you work through **both** sections of each chapter in order to prepare most effectively for the Writing Skills Test. You'll find that editing practice in standard written English improves the quality of your writing and that writing practice provides a setting in which editing makes sense.

Contemporary's GED Writing Skills book has been designed to take into account the wide range of writing abilities that students have. Perhaps you have not actually written anything for many years, and you feel that you just "can't write." Or perhaps you have experience writing letters and notes but are not sure how this applies to writing an essay. Or perhaps you are comfortable with the process of writing but worry about the time limit given for the test.

The writing instruction and exercises in this book were created so that you can build upon your strengths as a writer in order to succeed on an essay test. The first writing activities you encounter in this book will not even require you to write complete sentences. Instead, you will learn about, and practice, a **writing process** that can help you get organized and overcome any "writer's block."

Here are some things to note before you begin working in this book:

1. Before beginning this book, you should take the pretest. This will give you a preview of what the Writing Skills Test includes, but more importantly, it will help you identify which areas you need to concentrate on most. Use the chart at the end of the pretest to pinpoint the types of questions you answered incorrectly and to determine what skills you need special work in. You may decide to concentrate on specific areas or to work through the entire book. We strongly suggest that you do work through the whole book to prepare yourself best for the actual test.

   If you would like to get a little practice putting pencil to paper and see examples of GED-type multiple-choice questions before you take the pretest, you can work through Chapter 1 first. Then take the pretest before you begin Chapters 2–7.

2. As you work through this book, you will see a number of features designed to help make the task of test preparation easier, as well as effective and enjoyable. These features include

   - "Focus on Punctuation" sections that appear throughout the second section of each chapter; these sections offer instruction for using commas, semicolons, apostrophes, and endmarks whenever they apply to a particular grammar or usage problem

- journal activities that encourage writing beyond the topics that appear in exercises; journal writing often helps beginning writers "warm up" to the process of writing
- plenty of GED-type multiple-choice exercises; each chapter ends with a review in GED format, and a cumulative review in GED format follows Chapters 3, 4, 5, and 6
- a GED-type essay topic that appears in Chapters 3, 4, 5, and 6; in addition, a list of GED-type topics to provide extra practice appears in Chapter 7
- a master spelling list from which all misspelled words on the GED are taken; this list appears on page 268
- a complete "Test-Taking Strategies" chapter that keys into the common areas of difficulty and offers helpful hints for success on the GED Writing Skills Test
- an answer key for each chapter that explains the correct answers for the exercises; if you make a mistake, you can learn from it by reading the explanation that follows the answer and then review the question to analyze the error

3. After you have worked through **both** sections of each chapter of the book, you should take the posttest. The posttest is a simulated GED Test that presents questions in the format, level of difficulty, and percentages found on the actual test. The posttest will help you determine whether or not you are ready for the test and, if not, what areas of the book need to be reviewed. The posttest evaluation chart is especially helpful in making this decision.

4. Keep a folder of all the writing you do in this book. Many assignments will ask you to rework earlier papers, so you'll need to keep them where you can find them easily. In addition, reviewing your writing will show you how much you improve through practice!

Each "Writing Process" section is indicated by the symbol .

Each "Conventions of English" section is indicated by the symbol **2:** .

WRITING SKILLS PRETEST, PART 1

Directions: The following items are based on a paragraph which contains numbered sentences. Some of the sentences may contain errors in sentence structure, usage, or mechanics. A few sentences, however, may be correct as written. Read the paragraph and then answer the items based on it. For each item, choose the answer that would result in the most effective writing of the sentence or sentences. The best answer must be consistent with the meaning and tone of the rest of the paragraph.

Pretest Answer Grid

1 ① ② ③ ④ ⑤	20 ① ② ③ ④ ⑤	38 ① ② ③ ④ ⑤
2 ① ② ③ ④ ⑤	21 ① ② ③ ④ ⑤	39 ① ② ③ ④ ⑤
3 ① ② ③ ④ ⑤	22 ① ② ③ ④ ⑤	40 ① ② ③ ④ ⑤
4 ① ② ③ ④ ⑤	23 ① ② ③ ④ ⑤	41 ① ② ③ ④ ⑤
5 ① ② ③ ④ ⑤	24 ① ② ③ ④ ⑤	42 ① ② ③ ④ ⑤
6 ① ② ③ ④ ⑤	25 ① ② ③ ④ ⑤	43 ① ② ③ ④ ⑤
7 ① ② ③ ④ ⑤	26 ① ② ③ ④ ⑤	44 ① ② ③ ④ ⑤
8 ① ② ③ ④ ⑤	27 ① ② ③ ④ ⑤	45 ① ② ③ ④ ⑤
9 ① ② ③ ④ ⑤	28 ① ② ③ ④ ⑤	46 ① ② ③ ④ ⑤
10 ① ② ③ ④ ⑤	29 ① ② ③ ④ ⑤	47 ① ② ③ ④ ⑤
11 ① ② ③ ④ ⑤	30 ① ② ③ ④ ⑤	48 ① ② ③ ④ ⑤
12 ① ② ③ ④ ⑤	31 ① ② ③ ④ ⑤	49 ① ② ③ ④ ⑤
13 ① ② ③ ④ ⑤	32 ① ② ③ ④ ⑤	50 ① ② ③ ④ ⑤
14 ① ② ③ ④ ⑤	33 ① ② ③ ④ ⑤	51 ① ② ③ ④ ⑤
15 ① ② ③ ④ ⑤	34 ① ② ③ ④ ⑤	52 ① ② ③ ④ ⑤
16 ① ② ③ ④ ⑤	35 ① ② ③ ④ ⑤	53 ① ② ③ ④ ⑤
17 ① ② ③ ④ ⑤	36 ① ② ③ ④ ⑤	54 ① ② ③ ④ ⑤
18 ① ② ③ ④ ⑤	37 ① ② ③ ④ ⑤	55 ① ② ③ ④ ⑤
19 ① ② ③ ④ ⑤		

1

(1) With new cars averaging over ten thousand dollars, buying a used car is one way to reduce transportation costs considerably. (2) However, a wise consumer shops carefully to make the best possible use of their money. (3) Before setting foot on a car lot, the type of car she wants is decided. (4) A subcompact won't accommodate a family of six. (5) A station wagon isn't necessary for a single adult. (6) With a general size and price range in mind, she searched newspaper advertisements and dealerships for likely prospects. (7) Body integrity is important. (8) She checks it by looking for signs of rust, dents, or uneven paint that might indicate a previous accident. (9) The cars interior is also important, for torn seatcovers and missing knobs indicate that it hasn't been well maintained. (10) Of course, the consumer wouldn't dream of buying a car without test-driving it to check the engine, electrical system, and how well the brakes work. (11) Finally, she takes the car to an independent mechanic for further inspection and advice before making the dealer an offer.

1. Sentence 1: **With new cars averaging over ten thousand dollars, buying a used car is one way to reduce transportation costs considerably.**

   What correction should be made to this sentence?

   (1) replace *dollars* with *dollar's*
   (2) replace *dollars, buying* with *dollars. Buying*
   (3) remove *is*
   (4) change the spelling of *considerably* to *considerabley*
   (5) no correction is necessary

2. Sentence 2: **However, a wise consumer shops carefully to make the best possible use of their money.**

   What correction should be made to this sentence?

   (1) remove the comma after *However*
   (2) change *shops* to *shop*
   (3) change the spelling of *carefully* to *carefuly*
   (4) replace *their* with *her*
   (5) no correction is necessary

3. Sentence 3: **Before setting foot on a car lot, the type of car she wants is decided.**

   Which of the following is the best way to write the underlined portion of this sentence? If you think the original is the best way, choose option (1).

   (1) the type of car she wants is decided.
   (2) deciding on the type of car she wants.
   (3) to decide on the type of car she wants.
   (4) she decides on the type of car she wants.
   (5) for her to decide on the type of car she wants.

4. Sentences 4 and 5: **A subcompact won't accommodate a family of six. A station wagon isn't necessary for a single adult.**

   The most effective combination of sentences 4 and 5 would contain which of the following groups of words?

   (1) six, nor is a station wagon
   (2) six, nor a station wagon isn't
   (3) six although a station wagon isn't
   (4) six; despite the fact that a station wagon
   (5) six unless a station wagon

5. Sentence 6: **With a general size and price range in mind, she searched newspaper advertisements and dealerships for likely prospects.**

   What correction should be made to this sentence?

   (1) insert a comma after *size*
   (2) change *searched* to *searches*
   (3) change the spelling of *advertisements* to *advertizements*
   (4) insert a comma after *dealerships*
   (5) change the spelling of *prospects* to *perspects*

6. Sentences 7 and 8: **Body integrity is important. She checks it by looking for signs of rust, dents, or uneven paint that might indicate a previous accident.**

   The most effective combination of sentences 7 and 8 would include which of the following groups of words?

   (1) She checks body integrity, and looking
   (2) Body integrity is checked because she looks
   (3) important, yet she looks
   (4) important; therefore, she looks
   (5) important when she looks

7. Sentence 9: **The cars interior is also important, for torn seatcovers and missing knobs indicate that it hasn't been well maintained.**

   What correction should be made to this sentence?

   (1) replace *cars* with *car's*
   (2) remove the comma after *important*
   (3) remove *for*
   (4) change *indicate* to *indicates*
   (5) no correction is necessary

8. Sentence 10: **Of course, the consumer wouldn't dream of buying a car without test-driving it to check the engine, electrical system, and how well the brakes work.**

   Which of the following is the best way to write the underlined portion of this sentence? If you think the original is the best way, choose option (1).

   (1) how well the brakes work.
   (2) how well does it brake.
   (3) if the brakes work well.
   (4) test the brakes.
   (5) brakes.

(1) Although people may try to divide our planet into separate states and nations, nature ignores these artificial boundaries. (2) Neither water nor wind respect manmade lines, as our problems with pollution have shown. (3) Industrial wastes and sewage dumped into a river in one city contaminate the water supply of the town downstream whether or not it's citizens pledge allegiance to the same flag. (4) Oil spills occurring in the middle of the ocean, may eventually wash ashore halfway around the world. (5) Winds carrying contaminants even faster and farther than water. (6) For instance, fumes from industrial plants in the Ohio River valley produce acid rain that damages forests and lakes in Canada. (7) Perhaps the most dramatic example of international air pollution occurred in 1986, when an accident in a nuclear plant in the Soviet Union releases a cloud of radioactive particles that circled the earth within a few days. (8) Hundreds of miles from the site of the plant, dairy cattle were kept inside for several days to prevent contamination of their milk, and some crops were destroyed. (9) For weeks after the accident, such imported products as vegetables grown in Italy and fish caught in scandinavian waters had to be tested for radioactivity. (10) This emphasized the need for global cooperation to maintain a livable environment.

9. Sentence 1: **Although people may try to divide our planet into separate states and nations, nature ignores these artificial boundaries.**

   If you rewrote sentence 1 beginning with

   People may try to divide our planet into separate states and nations

   the next word should be

   (1) and
   (2) so
   (3) moreover
   (4) therefore
   (5) however

10. Sentence 2: **Neither water nor wind respect manmade lines, as our problems with pollution have shown.**

    What correction should be made to this sentence?

    (1) change the spelling of *Neither* to *Niether*
    (2) insert a comma after *water*
    (3) change *respect* to *respects*
    (4) change *have* to *has*
    (5) no correction is necessary

11. Sentence 3: **Industrial wastes and sewage dumped into a river in one city contaminate the water supply of the town downstream whether or not it's citizens pledge allegiance to the same flag.**

    What correction should be made to this sentence?

    (1) replace *river* with *River*
    (2) change *contaminate* to *contaminates*
    (3) replace *downstream whether* with *downstream. Whether*
    (4) replace *it's* with *its*
    (5) change the spelling of *citizens* to *citazens*

12. Sentence 4: **Oil spills occurring in the middle of the ocean, may eventually wash ashore halfway around the world.**

    What correction should be made to this sentence?

    (1) change the spelling of *occurring* to *occuring*
    (2) replace *ocean* with *Ocean*
    (3) remove the comma after *ocean*
    (4) insert a comma after *ashore*
    (5) no correction is necessary

13. Sentence 5: **Winds carrying contaminants even faster and farther than water.**

    Which of the following is the best way to write the underlined portion of this sentence? If you think the original is the best way, choose option (1).

    (1) carrying
    (2) carry
    (3) carried
    (4) had carried
    (5) that are carrying

14. Sentence 6: **For instance, fumes from industrial plants in the Ohio River valley produce acid rain that damages forests and lakes in Canada.**

    What correction should be made to this sentence?

    (1) remove the comma after *instance*
    (2) replace *River* with *river*
    (3) change the spelling of *valley* to *vally*
    (4) change *produce* to *produces*
    (5) no correction is necessary

15. Sentence 7: **Perhaps the most dramatic example of international air pollution occurred in 1986, when an accident in a nuclear plant in the Soviet Union releases a cloud of radioactive particles that circled the earth within a few days.**

    Which of the following is the best way to write the underlined portion of this sentence? If you think the original is the best way, choose option (1).

    (1) releases
    (2) has released
    (3) is released
    (4) was released
    (5) released

16. Sentence 8: **Hundreds of miles from the site of the plant, dairy cattle were kept inside for several days to prevent contamination of their milk, and some crops were destroyed.**

    Which of the following is the best way to write the underlined portion of this sentence? If you think the original is the best way, choose option (1).

    (1) milk, and some
    (2) milk, also some
    (3) milk, in addition, some
    (4) milk, some
    (5) milk some

17. Sentence 9: **For weeks after the accident, such imported products as vegetables grown in Italy and fish caught in scandinavian waters had to be tested for radioactivity.**

    What correction should be made to this sentence?

    (1) remove the comma after *accident*
    (2) change the spelling of *vegetables* to *vegtables*
    (3) change *caught* to *catched*
    (4) change *scandinavian* to *Scandinavian*
    (5) change *had* to *have*

18. Sentence 10: **This emphasized the need for global cooperation to maintain a livable environment.**

    Which of the following is the best way to write the underlined portion of this sentence? If you think the original is the best way, choose option (1).

    (1) This
    (2) This incident
    (3) This more than anything else
    (4) It
    (5) They

(1) For several decades, Americans seen dieting as an avenue to social success. (2) They firmly believe that slim equals beautiful. (3) Therefore, they have spent millions of dollars on diet books and programs. (4) In the past several years, Doctors' studies linking obesity with increased risk of heart disease and diabetes have added new members to the ranks of dieters. (5) Unfortunatly, too many of these weight-conscious people are looking for a quick, painless way to shed extra pounds. (6) They're attracted to ads promising pills and diets that melt away fat while eating all they want. (7) What they refuse to realize is that there is no miracle cure for being overweight. (8) The only solution to the problem is a permanent change in lifestyle. (9) This change includes reducing intake of sweets and fatty red meat. (10) In addition, a regular program of exercise will help keep excess weight off improve muscle tone, and provide a general feeling of attractiveness and good health. (11) This new lifestyle requires neither books nor pills, but it does demand self-discipline.

19. Sentence 1: **For several decades, Americans seen dieting as an avenue to social success.**

    What correction should be made to this sentence?

    (1) replace *Americans* with *americans*
    (2) insert *have* after *Americans*
    (3) replace *avenue* with *Avenue*
    (4) change the spelling of *success* to *sucess*
    (5) no correction is necessary

20. Sentences 2 and 3: **They firmly believe that slim equals beautiful. Therefore, they have spent millions of dollars on diet books and programs.**

    The most effective combination of sentences 2 and 3 would contain which of the following groups of words?

    (1) If they firmly believe that slim equals beautiful, they
    (2) Firmly believing that slim equals beautiful, they have
    (3) By spending millions of dollars on diet books and programs, they firmly
    (4) Spending millions of dollars on diet books and programs because they
    (5) Slim equals beautiful so they

21. Sentence 4: **In the past several years, Doctors' studies linking obesity with increased risk of heart disease and diabetes have added new members to the ranks of dieters.**

    What correction should be made to this sentence?

    (1) change *Doctors'* to *doctors'*
    (2) change *studies* to *study's*
    (3) change the spelling of *disease* to *desese*
    (4) change *have* to *has*
    (5) insert a comma after *members*

22. Sentence 5: **Unfortunatly, too many of these weight-conscious people are looking for a quick, painless way to shed extra pounds.**

    What correction should be made to this sentence?

    (1) change the spelling of *Unfortunatly* to *Unfortunately*
    (2) change the spelling of *too* to *to*
    (3) change the spelling of *conscious* to *consious*
    (4) insert a comma after *people*
    (5) insert a comma after *way*

23. Sentence 6: **They're attracted to ads promising pills and diets that melt away fat while <u>eating all they want.</u>**

    Which of the following is the best way to write the underlined portion of this sentence? If you think the original is the best way, choose option (1).

    (1) eating all they want.
    (2) eating all you want.
    (3) eating all he wants.
    (4) you eat all you want.
    (5) the dieters eat all they want.

24. Sentences 8 and 9: **The only solution to this problem is a permanent change in lifestyle. This change includes reducing intake of sweets and fatty red meat.**

    The most effective combination of sentences 8 and 9 would include which of the following groups of words?

    (1) lifestyle, and which
    (2) lifestyle, and including
    (3) lifestyle, or this includes
    (4) lifestyle, which includes
    (5) lifestyle, but this includes

25. Sentence 10: **In addition, a regular program of exercise will help keep excess weight off improve muscle tone, and provide a general feeling of attractiveness and good health.**

    What correction should be made to this sentence?

    (1) change the spelling of *exercise* to *exersize*
    (2) insert a comma after *off*
    (3) change the spelling of *muscle* to *mussel*
    (4) insert a comma after *attractiveness*
    (5) no correction is necessary

26. Sentence 11: **This new lifestyle requires neither books nor pills, but it does demand self-discipline.**

    What correction should be made to this sentence?

    (1) change *requires* to *require*
    (2) insert a comma after *books*
    (3) remove the comma after *pills*
    (4) replace *but* with *or*
    (5) no correction is necessary

(1) A fortune-teller adressing any teenager in the United States today could probably say, "I see a computer in your future," and be right. (2) One of the hottest careers available in terms of salaries and number of job openings are computer programming. (3) Both large and small businesses are computerizing their recordkeeping systems and they need people who can develop programs to meet their companies' needs. (4) However, only a small fraction of the workers of tomorrow will actually write computer programs millions more will be operating computers daily on the job. (5) Automated offices have been equipped with word processors and microcomputers, and they are replacing the traditional typewriters and filing cabinets. (6) As a result, many secretaries are taking additional training to meet the new job requirements. (7) Computers were becoming valuable tools in the drafting field, too. (8) A drafter draws a diagram of a three-dimensional object. (9) Then the computer rotates the diagram to any view the operator desires. (10) Artists are using computers to explore colors, lines, and forms more easily. (11) With a single keystroke, you can change a beige background to brilliant orange or magnify a small section of a drawing in order to do more precise detail work. (12) In the near future, even semitrailer trucks will have computers on board to monitor weight, fuel consumption, and check movement of the carriers.

27. Sentence 1: **A fortune-teller adressing any teenager in the United States today could probably say, "I see a computer in your future," and be right.**

    What correction should be made to this sentence?

    (1) insert a comma after *fortune-teller*
    (2) change the spelling of *adressing* to *addressing*
    (3) replace *United States* with *united states*
    (4) insert a comma after *today*
    (5) change the spelling of *probably* to *probly*

28. Sentence 2: **One of the hottest careers available in terms of salaries and number of job openings are computer programming.**

    What correction should be made to this sentence?

    (1) change the spelling of *available* to *avalable*
    (2) change the spelling of *careers* to *carreers*
    (3) replace *salaries* with *salary's*
    (4) change *are* to *is*
    (5) no correction is necessary

29. Sentence 3: **Both large and small businesses are computerizing their recordkeeping systems and they need people who can develop programs to meet their companies' needs.**

    What correction should be made to this sentence?

    (1) change the spelling of *businesses* to *busnesses*
    (2) change *are* to *is*
    (3) insert a comma after *systems*
    (4) replace *who* with *which*
    (5) replace *companies'* with *companys'*

30. Sentence 4: **However, only a small fraction of the workers of tomorrow will actually write computer <u>programs millions</u> more will be operating computers daily on the job.**

    Which of the following is the best way to write the underlined portion of this sentence? If you think the original is the best way, choose option (1).

    (1) programs millions
    (2) programs, millions
    (3) programs, so millions
    (4) programs, furthermore millions
    (5) programs. Millions

31. Sentence 5: **Automated offices have been equipped with word processors and microcomputers, and they are replacing the traditional typewriters and filing cabinets.**

    If you rewrote sentence 5 beginning with

    In automated offices, word processors and microcomputers

    the next word should be

    (1) they
    (2) so
    (3) and
    (4) are
    (5) replacing

32. Sentence 7: **Computers <u>were becoming</u> valuable tools in the drafting field, too.**

    Which of the following is the best way to write the underlined portion of this sentence? If you think the original is the best way, choose option (1).

    (1) were becoming
    (2) have become
    (3) had become
    (4) have became
    (5) becoming

33. Sentences 8 and 9: **A drafter draws a diagram of a three-dimensional object. Then the computer rotates the diagram to any view the operator desires.**

    The most effective combination of sentences 8 and 9 would contain which of the following groups of words?

    (1) After a drafter draws
    (2) Because a drafter draws
    (3) By drawing a diagram, the computer
    (4) object, so the computer
    (5) Rotated by the computer, a diagram is drawn

34. Sentence 11: **With a single keystroke, you can change a beige background to brilliant orange or magnify a small section of a drawing in order to do more precise detail work.**

    What correction should be made to this sentence?

    (1) remove the comma after *keystroke*
    (2) replace *you* with *they*
    (3) change the spelling of *brilliant* to *briliant*
    (4) insert a comma after *orange*
    (5) replace *drawing in* with *drawing. In*

35. Sentence 12: **In the near future, even semitrailer trucks will have computers on board to monitor weight, fuel consumption, and <u>check movement of the carriers.</u>**

    Which of the following is the best way to write the underlined portion of this sentence? If you think the original is the best way, choose option (1).

    (1) check movement of the carriers.
    (2) check carrier movement.
    (3) they can check movement of the carriers.
    (4) check if the carriers are moving.
    (5) movement of the carriers.

(1) The phrase "mans best friend" has special meaning for the owners of service and hearing dogs. (2) These dogs are similar to seeing-eye dogs. (3) The canines are specially trained to aid people with specific disabilities. (4) Service dogs may turn light switches on and and off, pick up dropped items, and carrying purses in backpacks for people in wheelchairs. (5) If their owners are able to walk but need help maintaining their balance, the dogs accompanied them to provide the necessary support. (6) Hearing dogs serve as their owners' ears by alerting him to sounds such as a ringing telephone. (7) The dogs warn the owners by touch, and then they lead their masters to the source of the sound. (8) There taught to use special signals for important sounds such as fire alarms. (9) Training for both service and hearing dogs, is time-consuming and expensive; in fact, the average cost for training a single hearing dog is approximately three thousand dollars. (10) In most cases, however, recipients are not required to pay for the dogs although donations are accepted. (11) All costs are usually cover by a sponsoring community organization.

36. Sentence 1: **The phrase "mans best friend" has special meaning for the owners of service and hearing dogs.**

    What correction should be made to this sentence?

    (1) replace *mans* with *man's*
    (2) change the spelling of *friend* to *freind*
    (3) insert a comma after *meaning*
    (4) replace *owners* with *owner's*
    (5) no correction is necessary

37. Sentences 2 and 3: **These dogs are similar to seeing-eye dogs. The canines are specially trained to aid people with specific disabilities.**

    The most effective combination of sentences 2 and 3 would contain which of the following groups of words?

    (1) Although these dogs are similar
    (2) Like seeing-eye dogs, the canines
    (3) These canines, they are like seeing-eye dogs
    (4) seeing-eye dogs, so these canines
    (5) seeing-eye dogs, which these canines are

38. Sentence 4: **Service dogs may turn light switches on and off, pick up dropped items, and <u>carrying</u> purses in backpacks for people in wheelchairs.**

    Which of the following is the best way to write the underlined portion of this sentence? If you think the original is the best way, choose option (1).

    (1) carrying
    (2) carried
    (3) carry
    (4) have carried
    (5) they have carried

39. Sentence 5: **If their owners are able to walk but need help maintaining their balance, the dogs accompanied them to provide the necessary support.**

    What correction should be made to this sentence?

    (1) insert a comma after *walk*
    (2) change the spelling of *balance* to *ballance*
    (3) insert *so* after *balance,*
    (4) change *accompanied* to *accompany*
    (5) change the spelling of *necessary* to *neccesary*

40. Sentence 6: **Hearing dogs serve as their owners' ears by alerting him to sounds such as a ringing telephone.**

What correction should be made to this sentence?

(1) change *serve* to *served*
(2) change *owners'* to *owners*
(3) replace *ears by* with *ears. By*
(4) replace *him* with *them*
(5) change the spelling of *telephone* to *telaphone*

41. Sentence 7: **The dogs warn the owners by touch, and then they lead their masters to the source of the sound.**

If you rewrote the sentence beginning with

After the dogs warn the owners by touch,

the next word should be

(1) then
(2) and
(3) they
(4) which
(5) next

42. Sentence 8: **There taught to use special signals for important sounds such as fire alarms.**

What correction should be made to this sentence?

(1) replace *There* with *They're*
(2) replace *taught* with *teach*
(3) insert a comma after *signals*
(4) replace *sounds such* with *sounds; such*
(5) no correction is necessary

43. Sentence 9: **Training for both service and hearing dogs, is time-consuming and expensive; in fact, the average cost for training a single hearing dog is approximately three thousand dollars.**

What correction should be made to this sentence?

(1) insert a comma after *service*
(2) remove the comma after *dogs*
(3) remove the comma after *fact*
(4) change the spelling of *approximately* to *aproximately*
(5) no correction is necessary

44. Sentence 10: **In most cases, however, recipients are not required to pay for the dogs <u>although</u> donations are accepted.**

Which of the following is the best way to write the underlined portion of this sentence? If you think the original is the best way, choose option (1).

(1) although
(2) unless
(3) as though
(4) and
(5) therefore

45. Sentence 11: **All costs <u>are usually cover</u> by a sponsoring community organization.**

Which of the following is the best way to write the underlined portion of this sentence? If you think the original is the best way, choose option (1).

(1) are usually cover
(2) is usually cover
(3) are usually covering
(4) is usually covered
(5) are usually covered

(1) In the war between humans and cockroaches, they have been winning for centuries. (2) They can survive extremes of tempature, pressure, and altitude far better than humans, and they can live without food or water for two weeks. (3) Their diet, in addition to the foods humans consume, include cardboard, paper, glue, and toothpaste; therefore, they can almost always find something to eat. (4) Furthermore, they reproduce rapidly. (5) Every three weeks, the female german cockroach produces about forty offspring. (6) Until recently, attempts to eradicate roaches from homes and apartments meet with only limited success. (7) Insecticides were often ineffective. (8) The roaches either adapted to the chemicals or avoided the areas that had been sprayed. (9) Now however, scientists are testing a new technique. (10) Carl Djerassi, which is a professor of chemistry at Stanford University, has developed a hormone that keeps cockroaches in a permanently juvenile stage. (11) Sprayed as an insecticide, the roaches pick it up as they walk through it and ingest it during their normal grooming process. (12) The result is a break in the insects' reproductive cycle, leading to fewer and fewer unwelcome encounters with the scurrying creatures in the kitchen at midnight.

46. Sentence 1: **In the war between humans and cockroaches, they have been winning for centuries.**

    What correction should be made to this sentence?

    (1) insert a comma after *war*
    (2) remove the comma after *cockroaches*
    (3) replace *they* with *the roaches*
    (4) replace *have been* with *are*
    (5) change the spelling of *winning* to *wining*

47. Sentence 2: **They can survive extremes of tempature, pressure, and altitude far better than humans, and they can live without food or water for two weeks.**

    What correction should be made to this sentence?

    (1) replace *They* with *It*
    (2) change the spelling of *tempature* to *temperature*
    (3) remove the comma after *humans*
    (4) insert a comma after *food*
    (5) replace *weeks* with *week's*

48. Sentence 3: **Their diet, in addition to the foods humans consume, include cardboard, paper, glue and toothpaste; therefore, they can almost always find something to eat.**

    What correction should be made to this sentence?

    (1) replace *Their* with *There*
    (2) change *include* to *includes*
    (3) remove the comma after *cardboard*
    (4) replace *therefore* with *nevertheless*
    (5) remove the comma after *therefore*

49. Sentence 5: **Every three weeks, the female german cockroach produces about forty offspring.**

    What correction should be made to this sentence?

    (1) remove the comma after *weeks*
    (2) change *german* to *German*
    (3) insert a comma after *cockroach*
    (4) change *produces* to *produced*
    (5) no correction is necessary

50. Sentence 6: **Until recently, attempts to eradicate roaches from homes and apartments meet with only limited success.**

Which of the following is the best way to write the underlined portion of this sentence? If you think the original is the best way, choose option (1).

(1) meet
(2) meets
(3) meeted
(4) meeting
(5) had met

51. Sentences 7 and 8: **Insecticides were often ineffective. The roaches either adapted to the chemicals or avoided the areas that had been sprayed.**

The most effective combination of sentences 7 and 8 would include which of the following groups of words?

(1) ineffective, the roaches
(2) ineffective, but the roaches
(3) ineffective; therefore, the roaches
(4) ineffective although the roaches
(5) ineffective because the roaches

52. Sentence 9: **Now however, scientists are testing a new technique.**

What correction should be made to this sentence?

(1) insert a comma after *Now*
(2) remove the comma after *however*
(3) change *scientists* to *Scientists*
(4) change *are* to *is*
(5) no correction is necessary

53. Sentence 10: **Carl Djerassi, which is a professor of chemistry at Stanford University, has developed a hormone that keeps cockroaches in a permanently juvenile stage.**

Which of the following is the best way to write the underlined portion of this sentence? If you think the original is the best way, choose option (1).

(1) which is a professor of chemistry at Stanford University
(2) which is a Professor of chemistry at Stanford University
(3) which is a professor of chemistry at Stanford university
(4) who is a professor of chemistry at Stanford University
(5) who is a Professor of chemistry at Stanford University

54. Sentence 11: **Sprayed as an insecticide, the roaches pick it up as they walk through it and ingest it during their normal grooming process.**

Which of the following is the best way to write the underlined portion of this sentence? If you think the original is the best way, choose option (1).

(1) Sprayed as an insecticide,
(2) After being sprayed as an insecticide,
(3) When sprayed as an insecticide,
(4) When it is sprayed as an insecticide,
(5) Spraying as an insecticide,

55. Sentence 12: **The result is a break in the insects' reproductive cycle, leading to fewer and fewer unwelcome encounters with the scurrying creatures in the kitchen at midnight.**

Which of the following is the best way to write the underlined portion of this sentence? If you think the original is the best way, choose option (1).

(1) result is
(2) result, is
(3) result
(4) result being
(5) result, being

ANSWERS ARE ON PAGE 15.

WRITING SKILLS PRETEST, PART 2

Directions: This part of the test is designed to find out how well you write. In preparing your answer for this question, you should take the following steps:

1. Read all of the information accompanying the question.
2. Plan your answer carefully before you write. Use scratch paper to jot down notes and ideas you want to include.
3. Write your answer on a separate sheet of paper.
4. Revise. Read carefully what you have written and make any changes that will improve your writing.
5. Edit. Check your paragraphing, sentence structure, spelling, punctuation, capitalization, and usage and make any necessary corrections.

Take forty-five minutes to write on the following topic. When forty-five minutes have passed, stop writing.

Topic

We all play many roles in life. For instance, you might be a parent, a construction worker, an Italian-American, a political party member, and a student, among other things.

If you were asked to describe your role as parent, you might discuss how you feel about your children and what your relationships with them are like. You might even talk about your involvement in making the community a safe place for children.

Think of the roles that you play in your own life; then choose one role that is important to you and describe it.

INFORMATION ON EVALUATING YOUR ESSAY IS ON PAGE 16.

PRETEST ANSWER KEY

PART 1

1. (5) This sentence is correct as written.
2. (4) This pronoun refers to the singular word *consumer*. *Her* agrees with *consumer* because *her* is singular. *Their* is plural.
3. (4) The sentence does not make clear what the phrase *Before setting foot on a car lot* is referring to. Choice (4) tells you that the phrase refers to *she*.
4. (1) The new sentence would read, *A subcompact won't accommodate a family of six, nor is a station wagon necessary for a single adult.* The word *nor* connects two original sentences in a way that makes sense.
5. (2) This passage is written in the present, but the verb *searched* puts sentence 6 in the past. Changing the verb to *searches* puts the sentence in the present.
6. (4) The new sentence would read, "Body integrity is important; therefore, she looks for signs of rust, dents, or uneven paint that might indicate a previous accident." The connecting word *therefore* tells you that the idea in the first part of the sentence causes the action in the second part.
7. (1) The possessive ending *'s* shows that *car's interior* means "interior of the car."
8. (5) The three parts of the sentence that are separated by commas should all be in the same single-item form: *engine, electrical system,* and *brakes*. The phrase *how well the brakes work* is not in this form.
9. (5) The word *however* expresses the contrast between the two parts of the sentence. The rewritten sentence would read, "People may try to divide our planet into separate states and nations; however, nature ignores these artificial boundaries."
10. (3) Because the two parts of the subject, *water* and *wind*, are separated by *nor*, the verb must agree with the closer part of the subject: *wind respects. Respects* agrees with a singular subject.
11. (4) Test *it's* by replacing it with *it is . . . whether or not it is citizens . . .* makes no sense, so the contraction must be wrong. Change the contraction *it's* to the possessive pronoun *its*.
12. (3) Never separate the main parts of a sentence, the subject and predicate, with a comma.
13. (2) This word group is not a complete sentence because the verb *carrying* requires a helping verb. Choice (2) substitutes the verb *carry*, which does not require a helping verb.
14. (5) This sentence is correct as written.
15. (5) The past tense verb *occurred* and the date *1986* tell you that the event took place in the past. *Released* is the correct past tense to use instead of the present-tense *releases*.
16. (1) This sentence is correct as written.
17. (4) *Scandinavian* is a word derived from a specific region of the world, so it should always be capitalized no matter where it appears in a sentence.
18. (2) The original sentence does not make clear what the pronoun *This* refers to. Adding the word *incident* makes the subject of the sentence clear.
19. (2) The verb form *seen* is not complete without a helping verb. The correct form is *have seen*.
20. (2) This combination turns the first sentence into an introductory phrase. The new sentence reads, "Firmly believing that slim equals beautiful, they have spent millions of dollars on diet books and programs." If you test the other choices, you will find that they do not keep the meaning of the original sentences.
21. (1) In this sentence, *doctors'* is used in a general sense, not as the title or name of a specific doctor. Therefore, it should not be capitalized.
22. (1) When adding a suffix (ending) beginning with a consonant to a word ending in a silent *e*, do not drop the *e*.
23. (5) This sentence implies that the pills and diets are eating all they want; however, common sense tells you that the dieters must be the eaters. Choice (5) makes clear who is doing the eating.
24. (4) This choice both shows the relationship between the ideas in the original sentences and is worded correctly. The new sentence would read, "The only solution to this problem is a permanent change in lifestyle, which includes reducing intake of sweets and fatty red meat.
25. (2) Always separate three or more items in a series with commas: *keep excess weight off, improve muscle tone,* and *provide a general feeling*.
26. (5) This sentence is correct as written.
27. (2) You may need to memorize the spelling of this tricky word.
28. (4) The subject of the verb is *One*, so a singular verb is needed: *One is*. The phrases *of the hottest careers available in terms of salaries and number of job openings* are interrupters.
29. (3) Always use a comma between two complete thoughts joined by the conjunction *and*.
30. (5) The original sentence contains two complete thoughts run together. Choice (5) correctly divides the two complete thoughts into separate sentences.
31. (4) The new sentence would read, "In automated offices, word processors and microcomputers are replacing the traditional typewriters and filing cabinets." If you test the other choices, you'll find that none make a clear sentence.
32. (2) This passage is written in the present. In the original sentence, the verb *were becoming* is in the past. The new verb, *have become*, is a correct present form.
33. (1) The original sentences have a time order relationship. Starting the new sentence with *After* expresses this relationship. The new sentence would read, "After a drafter draws a diagram of a three-dimensional object, the computer rotates the diagram to any view the operator desires."

34. (2) The previous sentence is about artists. The pronoun *they* can refer to *artists*. The pronoun *you* does not fit.

35. (5) The three items in this series should all be in the same form, all nouns: *weight, fuel consumption*, and *movement*. In the original sentence, the third item starts with a verb.

36. (1) Use the ending *'s* to show possession: man has a best friend = man's best friend.

37. (2) The new sentence would read, "Like seeing-eye dogs, the canines are specially trained to aid people with specific disabilities." The word *Like* picks up the idea expressed by the word *similar* in the original sentence.

38. (3) The three items in this series should all be in the same form, starting with a verb in the present tense: *turn, pick*, and *carry*.

39. (4) The verb in the first part of the sentence is in the present tense, and both parts are happening at the same time. Therefore, the verb in the second part of the sentence should also be in the present tense.

40. (4) The pronoun refers to the word *owners'*, which is plural. Therefore, the plural pronoun *them* is needed.

41. (3) The original sentences are related by time order. Starting the new sentence with *after* shows that relationship. No other time clue word (such as *then* or *next*) should be used in addition to *after*. The new sentence would read, "After the dogs warn the owners by touch, they lead their masters to the source of the sound."

42. (1) Substitute the words *They are* for *There* in the sentence. *They are taught* makes sense, so the contraction *They're* is needed.

43. (2) This comma incorrectly separates the main parts (subject and predicate) of the complete thought.

44. (1) This sentence is correct as written.

45. (5) This verb should be written in the present passive form, *are covered*. This verb form shows that the action in the sentence is performed by the sponsoring community organization.

46. (3) In the original sentence, the pronoun *they* could refer to either humans or cockroaches. Choice (3) makes the meaning clear.

47. (2) This word is hard to spell if you don't pronounce all the syllables carefully: *tem-per-a-ture*.

48. (2) Removing the interrupting phrase *in addition to the foods humans consume*, you should see that the subject of the sentence is *diet*, a singular word. *Includes* is the correct singular verb form: *diet includes*.

49. (2) The word *German* is derived from the name of a specific country, Germany, so it should always be capitalized.

50. (5) Because the action in the sentence ended before a specific time in the past, the past perfect tense is needed: *had met*.

51. (5) The new sentence would read, "Insecticides were often ineffective because the roaches either adapted to the chemicals or avoided the areas that had been sprayed." The word *because* shows that the second part of the sentence is the cause of the first part.

52. (1) When words like *however* are used as transition words, they should be set off by commas.

53. (4) The relative pronoun *who* is always used to refer to humans. The word *professor* should not be capitalized in this sentence because it is not used as a title.

54. (4) The original sentence implies that the roaches themselves are sprayed as an insecticide. Choice (4) uses the pronoun *it* to refer to *hormone* in sentence 10.

55. (1) This sentence is correct as written.

PART 2

If at all possible, give your essay to an instructor to evaluate. You'll find his or her objective opinion helpful in deciding whether you're ready for the actual GED Writing Skills Test or whether you need some study and practice.

Thinking about your own reactions during each stage of your writing will also help evaluate your readiness. How would you answer the following questions?

1. As you read the topic and planned your answer, did you find it easy to jot down ideas for your essay? Were you able to look over your notes and decide which points to include and which to discard? If this planning stage gave you trouble, pay particular attention to pages 26–29 in Chapter 2 and pages 169–74 in Chapter 5.

2. As you were writing your essay, were you able to compose paragraphs that stated a main point and supported it with plenty of logically organized details? For more work on this aspect of writing, study pages 63–70 and 113–26 in Chapters 3 and 4.

3. Were you able to write a clear introduction, body, and conclusion for your essay? Were these parts linked logically and smoothly? You'll find the structure of an essay discussed on pages 168–81 of Chapter 5.

4. Did you know how to revise your essay by adding more specific details where necessary, using words to link sentences and paragraphs, and cutting out repetitive or unnecessary sections? Suggestions and practice in revising are included on pages 218–36 of Chapter 6.

5. Did you know how to edit your writing for correct sentence structure, punctuation, usage, spelling, and capitalization? The second section of each of Chapters 2 through 6 will help you polish your editing skills.

If possible, talk to your instructor about your feelings as you wrote. Together, you'll be able to identify your current writing strengths as well as any weaknesses. Based on this combined evaluation, you can locate the sections of your textbook that you'll need to study thoroughly and the parts that you can skim lightly.

Pretest Evaluation Chart

Skill Area	Item Number	Review Pages	Number Correct
Complete sentences and fragments	13, 55	30–35	/2
Parts of a sentence	12, 25, 43	35–43	/3
Nouns	7, 36	44–50	/2
Pronouns	11, 42	50–57	/2
Verb tense	5, 15, 19, 32, 39, 45, 50	71–91	/7
Subject-verb agreement	10, 28, 48	92–105	/3
Independent clauses	4, 6, 9, 16, 29, 30	127–39	/6
Dependent clauses	33, 41, 44, 51	139–48	/4
Modifiers	3, 20, 23, 31, 37, 54	183–92	/6
Parallel structure	8, 35, 38	191–95	/3
Pronoun reference	2, 18, 24, 34, 40, 46, 53	195–205	/7
Sentence and paragraph links	52	226–28	/1
Capitalization	17, 21, 49	237–41	/3
Spelling	22, 27, 47	241–58	/3
No error	1, 14, 26		/3

1

◨ PREPARING FOR THE WRITING SAMPLE

Congratulations! Opening this book means that you've made one of the most important decisions of your life: you're going to finish your high school education. You may have dropped out to get a job, to take care of a baby, or to avoid more discouragement in the classroom. But you're back now, and whatever your age, whatever your reasons for returning to school, you want to succeed this time.

One step toward your goal of earning a high school equivalency diploma is passing the GED Writing Skills Test. This test consists of two parts: Part 1 is a multiple-choice section covering sentence structure, usage, punctuation, capitalization, and spelling; and Part 2 is an essay section in which you'll be asked to write approximately two hundred words on a specified topic.

To pass the test, you'll need to know how to express yourself clearly on paper: how to make a point, support it with specific examples, organize your ideas logically, and link them smoothly. You'll also need a good command of standard written English—knowledge of the rules that good writers use to decide what makes a complete sentence, where commas belong, which words to capitalize, and when to use a particular word form.

By sharpening these writing skills, you'll accomplish far more than passing a test. You'll give yourself a gift that you can use for the rest of your life. Think about it. You may be able to go from day to day without writing a word, but when you do need to write something, you want it to be good. Do you plan to apply for a job? You may need to compose a letter of application. Put yourself in the place of an employer looking for a new worker. Which of the following statements would impress you more?

I done alot of Restrant work, so I wants to be a Manger.

After ten years as a waitress, cook, and bookkeeper in a restaurant, I feel qualified to become a manager.

As you can see, the quality of your writing reflects on you. Improving your writing will help you present yourself as a careful, thoughtful, well-educated person.

What to Expect on the GED Essay Test

As part of the GED Writing Skills Test, you'll be given forty-five minutes to write an essay. The topic will require you to explain something, such as your opinion about a common issue or the causes or effects of an everyday problem. Since this essay topic will draw on your general knowledge, you won't have to know any special information in order to write on it.

Although you won't need special knowledge, you will need to know how to plan and develop your ideas in writing. In order to write an effective essay for the writing sample, you will need to be able to state the main point of your essay and back it up with supporting ideas, evidence, and examples from your own knowledge and experience. Don't worry if you're not sure right now how to go about writing an essay. You will learn a lot about it in this book—starting in this chapter.

Getting Started

Write Regularly

What can you do to improve your writing skills? You can read this book, of course, but that won't be enough. Reading a car repair manual isn't the same as actually pulling an engine apart. Reading a book about basketball isn't the same as spending a half hour experimenting to find just the right angle for a bank shot. In the same way, reading a book about writing is no substitute for actual writing practice. It can provide helpful suggestions, but you'll best learn to write by writing. So read the book, but don't stop there. Do the writing assignments as well.

Don't shy away from writing practice because you think you can't do it. Nobody expects you to start your career as a pro. And don't worry about writing full essays at first. You can work up to that.

If you stop to think about it, you'll find plenty of opportunities to do some writing. You can make daily "to do" lists of things you want to accomplish or, even better, "to do" lists for someone else in your family! How about a short note to a relative or a friend who lives out of town? Don't just grumble about the defective appliance you bought; write a letter of complaint to the manufacturer. Letters to the editor or a representative in Congress are still other possibilities.

Journals

One form of writing practice that both professional writers and beginners find especially useful is keeping a journal. A journal is a record of a writer's observations and ideas. It might contain writings about anything—memories, events, thoughts, anything the writer wanted to write down. Entries might range in length from a few lines to a page or more. Here are three samples of the ways in which a writer might use a journal:

May 9

Tornado season again. The sky blackened, and the warning siren sounded yesterday. Headed for the basement but couldn't stand to miss the excitement of the storm, so I periodically ran back upstairs to look outside. The wind ripped a big branch from our mulberry tree and nearly tore the metal awning from our front porch. But the twister missed us. What drives people to live on the edge of danger? I could have stayed safely underground but chose to gamble instead.

June 8

An article in today's paper said that scientists are trying to develop computers that could assess a situation and react to it much as people do. Will humans not even be needed some day?

August 4

Architectural drafting might be an interesting career for me. I've done framing and finish carpentry, and I can read blueprints well. Art used to be my favorite subject in school. Maybe I can put those skills together. But how well does it pay? Is the job market good? What training would I need?
To do—

1. Talk to an architectural drafter in a construction firm.

2. Read the *Occupational Outlook Handbook* entry on drafting.

3. Talk to a counselor at the community college.

The beauty of a journal is that you don't have to share it with anyone else unless you want to. That means you don't have to worry about spelling or sentence structure—just put your ideas down.

You can use your journal in several ways. First, it's a great writing ice-breaker—a way to develop the habit of putting your ideas on paper. Second, it's a way of discovering what you really think about a topic. The act of writing something on paper forces you to take a hazy idea and give it some form. Third, you can use the material in your journal as the basis for letters or essays you want to write later. And finally, your journal will provide interesting reading in a year or two—or more—just as a record of your thoughts.

Experiment with journal writing as you prepare for the Writing Skills Test. Get a notebook and make a habit of writing in it for ten to fifteen minutes a few times each week. Topic possibilities are endless. You can write about personal experiences, neighborhood happenings, daily routines, friends, relatives, pets, work, hobbies, news stories of interest to you, career plans, class work—whatever concerns you at the moment. Journal writing will be a regular activity in this book.

Make your first entry now on any topic that interests you. If you don't have your notebook yet, use any sheet of paper for writing. Remember, no one needs to read this but you.

Freewriting

In addition to keeping a journal, you may want to experiment with a second way writers get started: freewriting. This technique is especially useful to thaw writer's block—when you can't decide how to begin or how to continue a piece of writing. When freewriting, force yourself to keep your pen or pencil moving—no matter what—by writing whatever comes into your mind. If you can't think what to write next, simply write, "I can't think what to write I can't think what to write" until you get bored and something else pops into your mind. Don't let spelling or sentence structure questions of any kind slow you down. Just write. Try ten minutes of freewriting right now.

The Writing Process

The Four Steps

By writing a journal entry and freewriting, you've discovered that you can put words on paper—ideas that make sense to you. Now, how can you write so that others understand what you mean and react the way you want them to? Most writers can't accomplish this goal in a single step, no matter how good they are. Words simply don't pour from mind to paper in a steady stream of well-organized, clearly worded sentences. Although no two writers use precisely the same process as they write, all are concerned at some point with four basic activities: (1) planning, (2) drafting, (3) revising, and (4) editing.

Planning

Planning is the phase in which a writer develops and organizes ideas. Although this is essentially a thinking stage, you'll find that it helps to think on paper. Identify a topic. Then jot down notes about what you may want to include. A simple list of words and phrases is often an effective planning aid. Much as in freewriting, you make a list of whatever comes to mind about your topic. To expand your list, you could look in your journal for additional ideas. Or you could do some reading, make observations, or talk to people about your topic.

Here's a sample list for a letter to a friend describing a bad day one writer had recently. Picture yourself in a similar situation, and add a few ideas of your own in the spaces at the end. What else might have gone wrong?

> **Rotten Day**
> woke up with headache and sore throat
> out of breakfast cereal
> car had flat—late to work
> collection agency called about car payment
> boss chewed me out
>
> _____
>
> _____

Drafting

In the drafting stage, the writer puts the fragments of ideas developed during the planning phase into sentence and paragraph form. For instance, the "rotten day" list might turn into a paragraph like the one below. Notice that there are some mistakes in grammar and spelling. Don't worry too much about these—there will be time to fix errors later. Include a sentence or two of your own based on the items you added to the planning list.

> I still can't believe what a rotten day I had yesterday! I knew when I woke up that I was comming down with a cold. I had a headache and soar throat. When I walked into the kitchen, I discovered I was out of breakfast cereal, so all I had was a glass of milk. My car had a flat tire. Taking care of the flat meant that I was half an hour late for work. Just before lunch a collection agency called threatening to reposess my car if I didn't catch up on my payments. My boss yelled at me for being late. _____
>
> _____
>
> _____

Revising

In the revising stage, the writer can add, remove, replace, and rearrange material to improve the draft. After rereading the "rotten day" paragraph, the writer decided to change the wording of a few sentences. She also added a couple of details to make the writing more lively and moved one sentence so that it fit more logically into the time sequence of the paragraph. Are there any changes you would like to make in the sentences you added? If so, rewrite them on the blank lines.

yesterday was! When the alarm

I still can't believe what a rotten day ~~I had yesterday! I knew when I~~

blared at six A.M., a headache and soar throat announced that I

~~woke up that I was comming down with a cold. I had a headache and~~

was comming down with a cold. Stumbling) *reach for the Cheerios*

~~soar throat. When I walked into the kitchen, I~~ ~~discovered I was out of~~

Only to discover an empty box, *then my*

~~breakfast cereal,~~ so all I had was a glass of milk. ~~My~~ car had a flat tire.

made me *naturally, my boss*

Taking care of the flat ~~meant that I was~~ half an hour late for work, *yelled at me.*

Just before lunch a collection agency called threatening to repossess my

car if I didn't catch up on my payments. ~~My boss yelled at me for being~~

~~late.~~ _____

_____

_____

Editing

Editing, the final phase of the writing process, is making corrections to eliminate errors that might distract the reader from the writer's ideas. These corrections include changes in sentence structure, word choice, spelling, punctuation, and capitalization.

Editing changes in the "rotten day" paragraph have been written in for you. Are there any corrections that you need to make in your section?

I still can't believe what a rotten day yesterday was. When the

sore

alarm blared at 6:00 A.M. a headache and ~~soar~~ throat announced that I

coming

was ~~comming~~ down with a cold. Stumbling groggily into the kitchen, I

reached *only*

~~reach~~ for the Cheerios, ~~Only~~ to discover an empty box, so all I had was

a glass of milk. Then my car had a flat tire. Taking care of the flat

made me half an hour late for work. Naturally, my boss yelled at me.

repossess

Just before lunch a collection agency called threatening to ~~reposess~~ my

car if I didn't catch up on my payments. _____

_____

_____

Throughout the rest of this book, you'll be studying and practicing these four phases—planning, drafting, revising, and editing—until they become a part of your own writing process, ready to be used on Part 2 of the GED Writing Skills Test and in any other writing situation you encounter.

2 THE MULTIPLE-CHOICE SECTION

What to Expect

In addition to writing an essay, you'll be taking a multiple-choice test on editing skills. This part of the test will consist of several paragraphs followed by questions about the sentences they contain. Some questions will require you to locate errors, while others will ask you to restate the same idea in different words. It's important to read the passage as a whole before you answer any of the questions, because some items will require you to think about how a sentence should fit into the paragraph.

Here's part of a typical passage followed by some sample questions. Don't worry if they seem hard now. Just read through them to get an idea of how they're constructed.

(1) Motorcycles has become a popular means of transportation in this country. (2) They are much less expensive to buy than cars, but they use much less gas. (3) Lack of safety was their one major disadvantage. (4) Riders have no surrounding structure to protect them. (5) They are more likely than passengers in cars or trucks to be badly hurt or killed in an accident.

Some questions will require you to find and correct an error in a sentence, as in the following:

1. Sentence 1: **Motorcycles has become a popular means of transportation in this country.**

   What correction should be made to this sentence?

   (1) replace *Motorcycles* with *Motorcycle's*
   (2) change *has* to *have*
   (3) change *become* to *became*
   (4) insert a comma after *transportation*
   (5) no correction is necessary

Some questions will require you to choose the most effective way of writing one section of a sentence, like this one:

2. Sentence 2: **They are much less expensive to buy than <u>cars, but</u> they use much less gas.**

Which of the following is the best way to write the underlined part of this sentence? If you think the original is the best way to write the sentence, choose option (1).

(1) cars, but
(2) cars, so
(3) cars, and
(4) cars if
(5) cars or

To answer some questions, you'll need to think of the sentence in the context of the whole passage.

3. Sentence 3: **Lack of safety <u>was</u> their one major disadvantage.**

Which of the following is the best way to write the underlined part of this sentence? If you think the original is the best way to write the sentence, choose option (1).

(1) was
(2) will be
(3) being
(4) been
(5) is

Some questions will ask you to combine two sentences or to restate a sentence in other words. In these questions, the original sentences have no errors in them. You must identify a correct way to rewrite the same ideas.

4. Sentences 4 and 5: **Riders have no surrounding structure to protect them. They are more likely than passengers in cars or trucks to be badly hurt or killed in an accident.**

The most effective combination of sentences 4 and 5 would include which of the following groups of words?

(1) Because riders have no
(2) Although riders have no
(3) Unless riders have no
(4) protect them, but they
(5) protect them, or they

Do you know what the correct answers are? Reread the passage and circle the choices that you think are right.

Answers: 1. (2)   **2.** (3)   **3.** (5)   **4.** (1)

If you had trouble answering these questions, don't worry. This book will give you plenty of skill-building and test-taking practice to prepare you for the multiple-choice part of the test.

2

 PLANNING YOUR WRITING

Thinking on Paper

The Planning Steps

A clean sheet of paper is lying in front of you, and you have to fill it up. Suddenly your mind may seem as blank as the paper. You may wonder how on earth a writer ever gets started. What can you do to set your pen in motion?

The answer is deceptively simple: think. When you're faced with a writing task, think about what the writing is for. Think about the information that this situation calls for and jot down some notes. (See? You will already have broken the ice: your page won't be blank anymore.) Think about a logical way to organize the information. Then begin a draft of your actual writing.

Some version of this thinking and scribbling phase forms a part of every writer's routine. With a little practice, you'll soon make it part of yours.

> Planning your writing is as simple as A-B-O:
>
> **A**—Analyze the situation
> **B**—Brainstorm ideas to include
> **O**—Organize the ideas

Analyze the Situation

Writing seldom occurs in a vacuum. Whether the final product is a children's story, a letter to the editor, or a note to a friend, every writing task has a topic, an audience, and a purpose. To help you get started writing, you can ask yourself three questions: What am I writing about? Why am I writing about this? Who is going to read my piece of writing?

Perhaps your goal is to get a stop sign installed on the corner by the park. You might decide that a letter to the editor of your local newspaper will exert some pressure on the town council. So you write a letter about the situation to the local paper.

Perhaps you're writing to your Aunt Charlotte. She always likes a lot of family news, so you want to update her on your family's activities. What ideas might you decide to include? Your sister's broken arm (a rollerskating accident), a surprise visit from your cousins in Vermont, and your decision to study for your GED are examples.

Once you have an idea of what you're writing about and why as well as who you're writing to, you're ready to move on.

Brainstorm

Now that you know what you're writing about, you can jot down ideas to include in your writing. Don't worry about wording or spelling; don't bother to write complete sentences; don't stop to decide whether a particular detail will or will not work. Just write down whatever comes to mind regarding your topic.

This random listing technique, known as **brainstorming**, is helpful for several reasons. First of all, brainstorming combats blank-paper panic. It helps you get something on the page quickly. Second, brainstorming helps you concentrate on your content. You aren't distracted by questions of phrasing, punctuation, or spelling. As a result, you're less likely to forget what you wanted to write while puzzling about how to write it.

One writer made the following list by brainstorming for five minutes on the topic "A Perfect Day." She wanted to let other members of her GED class know what a perfect day would be like for her.

A Perfect Day
sleep late
sunny day
no traffic jams
spaghetti for supper
letter in the mail
friends compliment me
customers smile
catch up on paperwork

Exercise 1: Brainstorming ───────────────

Directions: Write a brainstorm list of your own ideas about *each* of the three topics below. Spend about five minutes on each topic. You will be using one of these lists as a basis for a piece of writing a little later on, so be sure to save your work.

- a perfect day (or, if you wish, a rotten day)

- a person you know well and admire

- your earliest childhood memories

Organizing

With your brainstorm list on paper, you're ready to move to the next stage of planning: organizing the list. Look at the list carefully to decide which ideas you want to include in your paper; cross out anything you want to omit. Do any items now suggest additional ideas? If so, write them down.

Finally, choose a logical order for your details. You might want to put your details in time order if they are events. Or you could put them in order of their importance to you. Or you could group related details together. Keep in mind that you want your reader to be able to follow and understand your writing. Chapters 3 and 4 will present some detailed suggestions on organizing, but for now try the simple method of numbering the ideas in the order you plan to write about them.

For an example of the organizing step, look again at the brainstorming list for "A Perfect Day." Note the changes: The writer crossed out an idea and added more details. Then she numbered the ideas to show the order in which she plans to describe each item. She numbered her ideas in time order: the order they would have happened in her day. She felt that this sequence would help her readers get a good picture of what the day would be like.

A Perfect Day
~~sleep late~~

① sunny day—*blue sky; golden, scarlet leaves*

② no traffic jams at 7:30 A.M.—*all green lights*

⑥ spaghetti for supper

⑤ letter in the mail—*from a good friend*

③ friends compliment me—*on how I look at work*

④ customers smile—*and thank me for my help*

⑦ catch up on paperwork—*checkbook balances with bank statement*

Exercise 2: Organizing Details

Directions: Choose one of your lists from Exercise 1 on page 27—the one that interests you most. Make any changes you wish in the list by adding new ideas or deleting ideas you don't want to use. Then number the ideas in the order you would want to write about them. You could put them in time order or in order of importance, or you could group related ideas.

Keep in mind that you'll be using this work later when you write, so be sure to save it.

Writing a Draft

With your organized list in hand, you're ready to begin a draft of your paper. As you write, use the list as a guide, not a dictator. If you think of something else to add or you want to change the order of your ideas, go ahead. Write your ideas as clearly as you can so others will understand you.

Look carefully at the way "A Perfect Day" has been developed from the brainstorming list. Although the framework for the draft was established in the list, a few details have been added to clarify the description. In addition, the details have been grouped into two paragraphs, one for the daytime activities, the other for the evening.

A Perfect Day

Driving to work, I admire the golden and scarlet leaves on the trees shining against a cloudless blue sky. At 7:30 there are no traffic jams, and every light turns green as my car approaches. I reach work with fifteen minutes to spare. Everyone is in a good mood at work. I get compliments on my clothes, and several customers smile and thank me for my help.

Returning home, I check the mail. I find a letter from my best friend, which I read while enjoying a delicious spaghetti dinner. Later that night I catch up on some billpaying, balance my checkbook to the penny with the bank statement, and curl up in bed with a very satisfied smile. What a perfect day it's been!

Exercise 3: Writing a Draft

Directions: Write a draft based on the list of ideas that you organized in Exercise 2. As you write, don't worry about making mistakes. You'll learn a lot about correcting mistakes as you move on in this book. At this point, just practice getting ideas on paper.

Be sure to save your paper when you are finished. You'll be working on it again in this chapter.

ANSWERS WILL VARY.

 ## Journal Writing

Have you been writing in your journal regularly? Keeping a journal is a good way to get valuable writing practice. Try writing on one of the following topics in your journal, or think of your own topic.

- Saturday nights—Whom do you like to be with? Where do you like to go? What do you like to do?

- Describe a conversation that moved you—for instance, a conversation that made you laugh, cry, or feel closer to someone.

- Write about one of your dreams for your future.

⠺ SENTENCE BASICS

Complete Sentences

What Is a Complete Sentence?

"Hungry?" "Starved!" "Want a double cheeseburger?" "With a large order of fries."

You've had many ordinary conversations like this one, in which single words and short phrases carry complete messages. Signs, too, often communicate in phrases: *No Exit. Wet Paint. One Way. Falling Rocks.* These phrases make sense because of the setting in which you see them. The words *wet paint* don't mean much on their own, but placed on a sign by a glistening park bench, they deliver a clear message.

In most written communication, however, you will find that single words or phrases are not enough to make your point clear. Without the context of a specific place or two people face to face to clarify misunderstandings, you must express your ideas in complete sentences so that your reader isn't left with unanswered questions.

A word group must pass three tests in order to be called a complete sentence. First, it must have a **subject** that tells whom or what the sentence is about. In the following complete sentence, whom or what is the sentence about?

The small boy teetered on the big bicycle.

The sentence is about *the small boy,* so *the small boy* is the subject of the sentence.

Second, a complete sentence must have a **predicate** that tells what the subject is or does. Everything in the sentence that is not part of the subject is part of the predicate. Underline the words in the example sentence above that tell what the subject is or does.

You should have underlined *teetered on the big bicycle.* This part of the sentence is the predicate.

Finally, a complete sentence must express a complete thought. That is, when you read it, you are not left with unanswered questions, such as *who did it?* or *what did she do?* The sentence *The small boy teetered on the big bicycle* expresses a complete thought. You know what happened and who was involved.

> **Tests for a Complete Sentence**
> 1. It must have a subject that tells whom or what the sentence is about.
> 2. It must have a predicate that tells what the subject is or does.
> 3. It must express a complete thought.

A group of words that does *not* pass these three tests is called a *fragment*. A fragment is a group of words that does not express a complete thought—it leaves a reader with unanswered questions about what the writer is trying to say. Study the examples below to see how a fragment is different from a complete sentence.

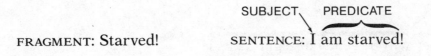

FRAGMENT: Starved!   SENTENCE: I am starved!

FRAGMENT: Wet Paint   SENTENCE: The paint on this bench is wet.

Identifying Subject and Predicate

By learning to identify the subject and predicate of a sentence, you'll be better able to avoid writing fragments that confuse your reader in the essay portion of the GED Test. You'll also need to be able to recognize and correct fragments for the multiple-choice section of the test.

Is the following word group a complete sentence or a fragment?

Sat at the kitchen table.

You're left with a question, aren't you? *Who* was sitting at the table? The word group is a fragment because the subject is missing. We can answer the question and create a complete sentence by adding a subject.

SUBJECT   PREDICATE

Mrs. Valadez sat at the kitchen table.

Let's take another example:

The man in the burgundy sports car.

Again, the word group raises a question: What about the man? This time the predicate is missing. We can complete the sentence by adding a statement about what the man is or what he does.

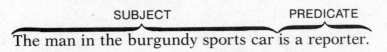

The man in the burgundy sports car is a reporter.

What question is raised by the following fragment?

>   At eight o'clock.

In this case a lot of information is missing. Who will do what at eight o'clock? In the space below, add some information to the phrase *at eight o'clock* to create a complete sentence.

_____

You may have written a sentence like one of the examples below.

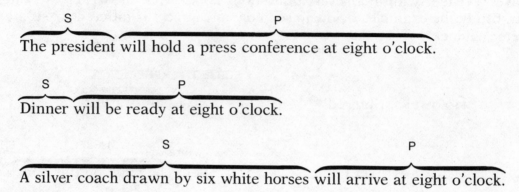

Label the subject and predicate of your own sentence just as these examples have been marked.

Correcting Fragments in a Paragraph

Fragments (incomplete sentences) are fairly easy to identify and correct when they are examined alone. It's a greater challenge to find and fix them when they're buried in a passage.

Editing hint: To locate fragments in the context of a paragraph, read the passage backward, sentence by sentence, checking for subjects and predicates. Read the last sentence first, then the next to last sentence, and so on. This technique will let you concentrate on sentence structure rather than on the meaning of the passage.

Underline the fragments in the following paragraph.

>   Simple tricks called mnemonic techniques will improve your memory. To memorize a list, you can make a word using the first letters of all the items on the list. For instance, at the grocery store. The word BADGE can help you remember to buy <u>b</u>utter, <u>a</u>pples, <u>d</u>og food, <u>g</u>rapes, and <u>e</u>ggs. A fun technique.

You should have found two fragments: *For instance, at the grocery store* (what happens there?) and *A fun technique* (*what* is a fun technique?)

Now that you've identified the fragments, how can you eliminate them? The first fragment is easy to correct because it can be attached to the sentence that follows it:

>   For instance, at the grocery store, the word BADGE can help you remember. . . .

SENTENCE BASICS   **33**

The second fragment requires more work. You need to add words to create a subject and predicate:

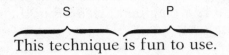

This technique is fun to use.

Two Ways to Correct Fragments

1. Attach the fragment to the sentence before or after it.

2. Reword or add words to the fragment to make a subject and predicate.

FOCUS ON PUNCTUATION

Endmarks

Once you've written a complete sentence, be sure to punctuate it correctly. All sentences begin with a capital letter and end with an endmark. The punctuation used at the end of a sentence depends on the type of sentence.

A statement ends with a period.

> Alaska has a much harsher winter than Texas.
> Eating too much salt can lead to high blood pressure.

A question ends with a question mark.

> When will the next election be held?
> Are your taxes too high?

An instruction ends with a period.

> Close the door quietly.
> Send in two boxtops and only fifty cents for your free magic ring.

An exclamation (a statement or instruction showing strong emotion) ends with an exclamation point.

> Call the fire department!
> Sandy's been hit by a car!

Exercise 4: Identifying Sentence Fragments————

Directions: Study each group of words in Parts A, B, and C. If it is a sentence, punctuate it with the correct endmark. If it is a fragment, write F in the space provided.

Examples: Stacked firewood agains the garage __F__

How kind you are __!__

Part A
1. Frantically hunted for his billfold _____
2. The teenager on the phone for hours _____
3. When will the next bus arrive _____
4. Wash the dishes _____
5. The greatest movie ever made _____
6. Pink and purple plaid _____
7. That man is choking _____
8. Caffeine is a stimulant _____

Part B
1. Do most Americans need to take vitamin pills _____ 2. Divided opinions _____ 3. Some nutritional experts say that we can easily get all the vitamins we need _____ 4. From a balanced diet _____ 5. Including several servings of bread and cereals, fruits and vegetables, dairy products, and meat _____ 6. Others feel that many Americans don't eat properly _____ 7. They skimp on vegetables _____ 8. Substitute empty calories from junk food _____ 9. Candy, cookies, and soft drinks _____ 10. Could both sides be correct _____

Part C
1. What mistakes are typical of beginning drivers _____ 2. One important error is misjudging distances _____ 3. It takes practice for a driver to estimate correctly how far his car is from the one beside him _____ 4. In the parking lot _____ 5. A related error is misjudging braking distance _____ 6. Needs to learn how to slow down smoothly _____ 7. For stop signs and traffic lights _____

ANSWERS ARE ON PAGE 307.

Exercise 5: Writing Complete Sentences

Directions: Revise all the fragments in Exercise 4, Parts A, B, and C, to make complete sentences. In Parts B and C, rewrite the entire paragraph. You may be able to correct some fragments by attaching them to previous sentences. In other cases, you will need to add words to create a complete sentence. Remember to punctuate each sentence correctly. Does each paragraph make sense?

ANSWERS ARE ON PAGE 308.

Parts of a Simple Sentence

Simple Subjects and Verbs

In this chapter, you'll be studying one kind of sentence, the simple sentence. You'll study other types of sentences later. A **simple sentence** has one subject and one predicate, as in the examples below. What do these three example sentences have in common?

The old man tripped over a skateboard on the sidewalk.
A well-dressed man tripped on his untied shoelaces.
The shy young man tripped over his girlfriend's doormat.

Although each sentence describes a different person and a different scene, the skeletons of the three sentences are identical. Reduced to barebones information, the sentences all read *man tripped*. The word *man*, from the subject part of the sentence, identifies whom the sentence is about. The word *tripped*, from the predicate, tells what the subject did. These two words are called the **simple subject** and the **verb**.

The skeleton of a sentence is the simple subject and the **verb**. The *simple subject* is the key word in the subject of the sentence that tells whom or what the sentence is about. The *verb* is the key word in the predicate that tells what the subject is or does.

In the spaces provided, write the simple subjects and verbs of the following sentences. The first one is done for you.

1. A truck loaded with cattle overturned on University Avenue.

    truck   *overturned*

2. Several confused cattle wandered through the backyards of local residents.

   _____   _____

3. The dogs in the neighborhood barked themselves hoarse.

   _____   _____

Answers:

2. _cattle_   _wandered_
3. _dogs_   _barked_

   Editing hint: If you're having trouble finding the simple subject and verb, locate the verb first by asking, "What's happening?" Once you've located the verb, find the subject by asking, "Who or what did it?" In sentence 1, for example, which word shows what's happening? _overturned_ What overturned? _truck_

   Write three sentences about a recent incident in your neighborhood. Then label the simple subject and verb in each of your sentences.

   _____

   _____

   _____

Understanding Verbs

Action Verbs

As you now know, all simple sentences have a simple subject and a verb. So far, the simple sentences you have studied contain action verbs. **Action verbs** tell what kind of action the subject is performing. Examples of action verbs are _sing, run, giggle, hit,_ and _buy._ In each of the following sentences, the verb is an action verb. Write the simple subject and verb in the spaces provided.

1. The lovers danced to the beat of the Purple Turtles.

   _____   _____

2. My mother gave me her childhood books.

   _____   _____

3. Wanda goes to work at the dog pound every day.

   _____   _____

If you have any trouble finding the simple subjects and verbs, ask yourself, "What's happening?" to find the verb. Once you have found the verb, find the subject by asking "Who or what did it?" You should have answered like this:

1. _lovers_   _danced_
2. _mother_   _gave_
3. _Wanda_   _goes_

Linking Verbs

Although all the sample sentences you've looked at so far show action, many other sentences do not. They still contain subjects and verbs, but the verbs simply link the subjects to words that describe the subjects.

Dr. Kern was the physician on duty last night.

The skeleton of this sentence is *Dr. Kern was.* The verb *was* links the subject, *Dr. Kern*, to the word *physician*.

Now try another example yourself. Write the subject and verb of the next sentence in the blanks.

He seemed pleased with your progress. _____ _____

He is the subject and *seemed* is the verb. The verb links *pleased* to *he*. Linking verbs are a little more difficult to spot than action verbs, so take time to learn the list in the box below.

Common Linking Verbs
is, am, are, was, were, be, being, been
appear, seem, remain, become

Then in the spaces provided, write the simple subjects and verbs of the following sentences.

1. The boundary between the United States and Canada is the longest unguarded border in the world.

   _____ _____

2. The two countries are strong allies.

   _____ _____

3. Their citizens appear to have similar cultures.

   _____ _____

Answers:
1. _boundary_   _is_
2. _countries_   _are_
3. _citizens_   _appear_

Use linking verbs to write three sentences about the state or province in which you live. Label the simple subject and verb in each sentence.

_____

_____

_____

FOCUS ON PUNCTUATION

Unnecessary Commas

Don't separate the subject from the verb of a simple sentence with a comma. As you write, you may recognize the boundary between subject and verb, but don't mark that boundary with a comma. If you read the sentence aloud, you'll discover that you don't pause between parts.

INCORRECT: A preschooler in torn blue overalls, was feeding mudpies to her teddy bear.

CORRECT: A preschooler in torn blue overalls was feeding mudpies to her teddy bear.

Word Order

How are the sentences in column A different from those in column B?

Column A	**Column B**
You check the oil.	Check the oil.
My billfold was in my pocket.	Where was my billfold?
The money is in the billfold.	There is money in the billfold.

All the sentences in column A follow the normal pattern of word order in English: subject before verb. The sentences in column B illustrate three common exceptions to that pattern: instructions, questions, and statements beginning with *Here* or *There*.

Instructions

When we give commands or instructions to others, we frequently omit the subject of the sentence because it's understood that the subject is *you*. For example, *Sort the laundry* means *You sort the laundry*. The skeleton is *(you) Sort*.

Please lend me fifty cents.   SKELETON: (You) lend

Questions

In questions, the verb frequently appears before the subject. To write the skeleton of the sentence, put the subject first, as in the following examples.

                             S V

Is he crazy?   SKELETON: he Is

                                  S V

Why are you so upset?   SKELETON: you are

Sometimes the verb consists of two or more words. In that case, part of the verb is placed before the subject and part is placed after it.

    V S V   S V

Where did you go last night? SKELETON: you did go

    V   S V   S V

Will the car start without a battery? SKELETON: car Will start

    V S   V   S V

Is anybody listening to me? SKELETON: anybody Is listening

Write the skeleton of this question in the blanks:

Did you buy the groceries yet?

_____ _____

The subject is *you* and the verb is *Did buy*.

Here and *There*

When a sentence begins with *Here* or *There*, the subject follows the verb. To write the skeleton, put the subject first.

    V   S

There is green fuzz on this month-old spaghetti.

       S V

SKELETON: fuzz is

Can you find the subject and verb in this sentence?

There are five people in the telephone booth.

       S   V

SKELETON: _____ _____

The subject is *people* and the verb is *are*.

Exercise 6: Identifying Sentence Parts

Directions: Write the simple subject and verb of each sentence in the spaces provided. Remember that sometimes the verb may be in two parts.

Examples: The evil empire attacked the planet Earth.

empire   *attacked*

When was the telephone invented?

telephone   *was invented*

There is a pebble in my shoe.

pebble   *is*

Turn left at the Laundromat.

(you)   *Turn*

1. This television program is boring.

   _____ _____

2. The speeding truck hit a parked car.

   _____ _____

3. A garter snake slithered through the strawberry patch.

   _____ _____

4. Please leave immediately.

   _____ _____

5. Here is today's newspaper.

   _____ _____

6. Milk is an excellent source of calcium.

   _____ _____

7. There were several bills in the mail.

   _____ _____

8. The Statue of Liberty is a symbol of freedom.

   _____ _____

9. Did you see Halley's Comet?

   _____ _____

10. The baby finally slept through the night!

    _____ _____

11. Mr. and Mrs. Garcia own the restaurant on Fourth Street.

    _____ _____

12. The New Year's Eve party lasted until two o'clock in the morning.

   _____   _____

13. When did President Roosevelt die?

   _____   _____

14. Hurricane Elsa pounded the Gulf Coast yesterday.

   _____   _____

15. Martin Luther King was a great orator.

   _____   _____

ANSWERS ARE ON PAGE 308.

Compounding Simple Sentences

What Is Compounding?

> The engine sputtered. The engine died. Joan groaned. Joan got out of the car. Joan raised the hood. Her sister settled back for a long wait. Her brother settled back for a long wait.

Although the passage above is grammatically correct and consists of complete sentences, the repetition makes it deadly boring to read. What can be done to cut the wordiness and improve the quality of the writing? Let's experiment with combining ideas from some of these sentences. How might you connect the first two?

> The engine sputtered. The engine died.

Since the subject of both sentences is the same, *engine*, they can be combined by writing the subject once and connecting the predicates with *and*:

> The engine **sputtered and died**.

Now take the next three as a set.

> Joan groaned. Joan got out of the car. Joan raised the hood.

How can you make one sentence from the three? Again, the subject is repeated. You can write it once and connect the predicates:

> Joan **groaned, got out of the car, and raised the hood.**

The final pair of sentences have different subjects but identical predicates. What can you do to combine them?

> Her sister settled back for a long wait. Her brother settled back for a long wait.

This time connect the subjects and write the predicate once.

> **Her sister and brother** settled back for a long wait.

The simple process you've just seen is called **compounding**.

> *Compounding* is connecting two or more equally important sentence parts with a conjunction: *and, or, but.*

Compounding results in smoother writing, without choppy sentences or unnecessary repetition. Note how much smoother the revised passage sounds than the original:

> The engine sputtered and died. Joan groaned, got out of the car, and raised the hood. Her sister and brother settled back for a long wait.

Sometimes compounding requires changes in the wording of a sentence. What changes must be made when the sentences below are combined?

> John Lennon was a member of the Beatles. Paul McCartney was a member of the Beatles.
> John Lennon and Paul McCartney **were members** of the Beatles.

When these sentences are compounded, *was* must be changed to *were*, and *a member* must be changed to *members*. You'll learn more about these shifts in wording in Chapter 3 when you study subject-verb agreement. For the exercises in this chapter, we'll give you a clue whenever you need to change words.

FOCUS ON PUNCTUATION

Compound Elements

If three or more compound elements are connected in a series, separate them with commas.

> The engine coughed, sputtered, and died.
> Kennedy, Johnson, and Nixon were all elected president during the 1960s.

If only two elements are connected, do not separate with commas.

> The engine coughed and sputtered.
> Kennedy and Johnson were both Democrats.

Never place a comma before or after the entire list of compound elements.

INCORRECT: Please send us, two dozen tulip bulbs, a trowel,
and a bag of bone meal, immediately.
CORRECT: Please send us two dozen tulip bulbs, a trowel,
and a bag of bone meal immediately.

Exercise 7: Using Compound Elements

Part A

Directions: Combine the following sets of sentences by compounding. Use the conjunction given and make any other necessary changes in wording. Punctuate each sentence correctly.

Example: Jim rinsed the dirty dishes. Jim stacked the dirty dishes. *(and)*

Jim rinsed and stacked the dirty dishes.

1. Do you want scrambled eggs for breakfast? Do you want oatmeal for breakfast? Do you want grits for breakfast? *(or)*

2. Torrid romances are featured in soap operas. Fatal illnesses are featured in soap operas. *(and)*

3. Sam Abramowitz is studying to become a lawyer. Donna Tatum is studying to become a lawyer. *(and; is ⟶ are; lawyer ⟶ lawyers)*

4. The batter swung blindly. The batter connected. The batter sprinted for first base. *(and)*

5. The food at Bob's Greasy Spoon is filling. The food at Bob's Greasy Spoon is tasteless. *(but)*

6. He printed his name at the top of the application form. He began to list his qualifications. *(and)*

Part B

Directions: Use compounding to answer the following questions. Make sure you write complete sentences.

Example: What three things might you buy with a million dollars?

I would buy a new house, a yacht, and a grand piano.

1. What are three things you enjoy doing on weekends?

2. What are two of your favorite television programs?

3. If you could visit any three countries in the world, where would you go?

4. Name two people who live near you.

5. What five subjects are covered on the GED tests?

ANSWERS ARE ON PAGE 308.

Nouns

What Are Nouns?

Read the following paragraph, looking carefully at the words in bold type.

> **Denver, Colorado,** has much to offer **tourists. Attractions** like the **United States Mint,** the **State Capitol,** and excellent art and science **museums** can keep a **visitor** occupied for **days** in the **city** itself. In addition, **Denver's location** near the **foothills** of the **Rocky Mountains** offers **recreation** in a **skier's, hiker's,** and **photographer's paradise.** The **beauty** of this **area** is hard to forget.

What do the words in bold type in the paragraph above have in common? They are all nouns.

Nouns are words that label people, places, things, or ideas.

PEOPLE: *tourists, visitor, skier's, hiker's, photographer's*
PLACES: *Denver, Colorado, United States Mint, State Capitol, museum, city, foothills, Rocky Mountains, paradise, location*
THINGS: *attractions, days, area*
IDEAS: *recreation, beauty*

Ideas, such as *courage, attraction, anger, unity,* and *freedom,* are sometimes hard to recognize as nouns.

Why Study Nouns?

You've already seen one way in which knowledge of nouns is related to writing: nouns are used as the simple subjects of sentences. In Chapter 6 you'll be learning when to capitalize nouns. In this chapter, you will practice identifying nouns and then study these words for three purposes: to review the spelling of plurals, to learn how to show ownership with possessive nouns, and to introduce pronouns.

Exercise 8: Recognizing Nouns

Directions: Underline all the nouns in each sentence.

Example: Jim accidentally washed his red sweater with his white shirts.

1. Three plates, two mugs, a saucepan, and an empty vase were sitting on the sink.

2. His powerful left hook ended five consecutive fights before the fourth round.

3. The earthquake reduced large sections of Mexico City to rubble and killed thousands of people.

4. The boundary between the United States and Canada is the longest unfortified frontier in the world.

5. After watching an old western, that man swaggers like John Wayne.

6. Which team won the World Series five years ago?

7. Our society rarely honors the wisdom and courage of older Americans.

8. That chilly stare warned Robert that their marriage was in deep trouble.

9. Ace Manufacturing Company has announced plans to hire twenty new employees next month.

10. Parenthood requires infinite patience and hope.

ANSWERS ARE ON PAGE 308.

Plurals

Nouns have both singular (meaning *one*) and plural (meaning *more than one*) forms. When you write nouns, sometimes you want to tell your reader that you mean more than one of something. When you mean more than one of a noun, you use the plural form. Study the passage below, especially the nouns in bold type.

1   Most major **cities** in this country are battling pollution. **Cars**,
2 **trucks**, and **buses** emit **fumes** that foul the air. **Smokestacks** on
3 **factories** also contribute to the smog. On some bad **days**, **babies** and
4 **people** with respiratory **problems** are forced to stay inside their **homes**.
5   But gray **skies** are only one part of the pollution problem. Another
6 is water contamination. Sewage, industrial **wastes**, and agricultural
7 **pesticides** are threatening our **rivers**, killing **fish**, and endangering the
8 **lives** of the **men**, **women**, and **children** who use the **rivers** for drinking
9 water. How can we clean up the **messes** we've made?

All of the bold-type nouns in the above passage are plural; that is, they refer to more than one. How does the spelling of these plural nouns differ from the singular form? Fill in the blanks on page 46 with the correct plural form. Each plural is used in the passage above, so you can look up the correct spelling if you need to.

1. Most nouns are made plural by adding *s*.

   car —→ cars *(line 2)*

   truck —→ _____ *(line 2)*

   home —→ _____ *(line 4)*

   waste —→ _____ *(line 6)*

2. Nouns ending in letters with a hissing sound (*s, sh, x,* or *z*) are made plural by adding *es*. (Note that the *es* adds an extra syllable to the pronunciation of the word.)

   church —→ churches
   bush —→ bushes

   bus —→ _____ *(line 2)*

   mess —→ _____ *(line 9)*

3. Nouns ending in *y* preceded by a vowel (*a, e, i, o, u*) are made plural by adding an *s*. Nouns ending in *y* preceded by a consonant (any letter except *a, e, i, o,* or *u*) are made plural by changing the *y* to *i* and adding *es*.

   PRECEDED BY VOWEL:
   boy —→ boys
   turkey —→ turkeys

   day —→ _____ *(line 3)*

   PRECEDED BY CONSONANT:
   thirty —→ thirties
   country —→ countries

   city —→ _____
   (line 1)

   sky —→ _____
   (line 5)

4. Many nouns ending in *f* or *fe* are made plural by changing the *f* to *v* and adding *es*.

   CHANGE:
   loaf —→ loaves
   thief —→ thieves
   wife —→ wives

   life —→ _____ *(line 8)*

   NO CHANGE:
   bluff —→ bluffs
   staff —→ staffs
   chief —→ chiefs

5. A few nouns do not change form when they are made plural.

   deer —→ deer
   sheep —→ sheep

   fish —→ _____ *(line 7)*

6. A few nouns are made plural by changing the spelling.

   foot —→ feet
   man —→ men *(line 8)*

woman ⟶ _____ *(line 8)*

child ⟶ _____ *(line 8)*

person ⟶ _____ *(line 4)*

These are the most widely used rules for spelling the plural forms of nouns, but they don't cover every case. Whenever you're unsure of the correct spelling for a plural, check a dictionary. The correct plural form will be given with the definition of the singular form.

Exercise 9: Spelling Plural Nouns

Part A
Directions: Fill the blanks in the passage below with the correct plural forms of the nouns in parentheses. Check each one to see which of the rules above applies to it.

Example: Most *nations* _____ *(nation)* couldn't survive one day without oil.

Industrialized _____ *(country)* depend on oil to fill several

_____ *(need)*. For one thing, oil is used to heat many

_____ *(home)* and _____ *(business)*. Without it our

_____ *(day)* and _____ *(night)* would be cold indeed.

Oil in some form is also used for fuel to power _____ *(car)*,

_____ *(truck)*, and machinery in _____ *(factory)*. Petro-

leum _____ *(product)* are even used in manufacturing synthetic

_____ *(fabric)* and plastic. Few _____ *(person)* would

argue that oil is not vital to our _____ *(life)*.

Part B
Directions: The following passage contains eight errors in the spelling of plural nouns. Proofread for those errors and correct them as shown in the example.

Example: Both income and income ~~taxs~~ *taxes* have increased since 1900.

Peoples born in 1900 have witnessed incredible changes during their life-

times. Travelers between citys, once dependent on horse-drawn wagones, now

speed down smooth concrete highwaies in sleek motorized coachs. Instead of

spending days on the open sea, they jet thousands of miles between countries in

a few hours. Lifes that would once have been lost to bacterial diseases are now

saved by antibiotics. In fact, the average life span for both mens and womans

has increased dramatically.

ANSWERS ARE ON PAGE 309.

Possessive Nouns

In the English language, there are several ways to show ownership. The first way is to use a complete sentence:

The farmer has a tractor.

The second way is to use a phrase beginning with *of*:

the tractor of the farmer

The third way is to use a possessive noun:

the farmer's tractor

Although all three ways are grammatically correct, the first two sometimes lead to awkward sentences. Compare the three options below.

The farmer has a tractor. The tractor overturned.
The tractor of the farmer overturned.
The farmer's tractor overturned.

All three contain the same information, and all are correct. The third, the one using a possessive noun, is most economical.

FOCUS ON PUNCTUATION

Apostrophes in Possessive Nouns

Sentences using possessive nouns are easy to write. The only trick is to learn where the apostrophe belongs.

1. If the possessive noun is singular, add an apostrophe + *s* (*'s*).

    a child's toy *(A child has a toy.)*
    Charles's house *(Charles has a house.)*

2. If the possessive noun is plural and the plural already ends in *s*, just add an apostrophe.

    the Browns' apartment *(The Browns have an apartment.)*
    the ladies' room *(The ladies have a room.)*

3. If the possessive noun is plural and the plural does not end in s, add an apostrophe + *s*.

    the children's toys *(The children have toys.)*
    three deer's hoofprints *(Three deer had hoofprints.)*

Add *'s* to all singular nouns and to plural nouns that do not end in *s*.

Add *'* to plural nouns that end in *s*.

Editing hint: To decide if a possessive noun is singular or plural, read the whole sentence for clues.

After the *(door's, doors')* hinges were oiled, they opened more quietly.

The word *they* indicates that at least two doors were oiled, so the correct punctuation is *doors'*.

Exercise 10: Using Possessive Nouns

Part A
Directions: Rewrite each pair of sentences, using a possessive noun. Be sure to place the apostrophe correctly.

Example: John has a hat. The hat is green with orange stripes.

John's hat is green with orange stripes.

1. The boy has a friend. The friend moved away.

2. James has a friend. The friend moved away.

3. The boys have a friend. The friend moved away.

4. The ladies have hats. The hats are on sale.

5. The firemen have helmets. The helmets are worn for protection.

Part B
Directions: Insert apostrophes wherever they belong in the following sentences. Remember, not all nouns ending in *s* are possessive.

1. My dogs favorite ball was out of reach behind her house.

2. In the last two seconds, the teams final chance to score appeared.

3. Chicagos skyscrapers now rival New York Citys skyline.

4. Mens coats and womens sweaters are on sale this weekend only.

5. The girls argument ended when their mothers called them for supper.

6. Lawyers and doctors fees have skyrocketed in recent years.

7. Carolines last letter arrived only yesterday.

8. The newspapers headline this morning read "Plane Crash Kills 257."

Part C

Directions: Write sentences using possessive nouns to answer the following questions. The noun that you need to make possessive is in dark type.

Example: What does your best **friend** own that you would like to borrow?

I would like to borrow my best friend's classic 1957 Chevy.

1. What clothing for **men** or **women** has been on sale recently?

2. Are fees charged by **doctors** in your local clinic reasonable?

3. What do you think is the biggest problem in this **country**?

4. In your opinion, who is the greatest athlete in the **world** right now?

5. What is the major tourist attraction of your **region**?

ANSWERS ARE ON PAGE 309.

Pronouns

What Is a Pronoun?

Imagine a language that required you to refer to a person, place, or thing by name every time. You would encounter passages like this:

> For John and Sarah, the most relaxing part of John and Sarah's vacation was spent at Leech Lake. Leech Lake is a large lake in northern Minnesota. John and Sarah stayed a week on the lake, exploring Leech Lake's reedy inlets, losing John and Sarah in the surrounding forests, and fishing from a small motorboat. John and Sarah had rented the motorboat from the owners of the cabin where John and Sarah were staying. "John would like to stay twice as long next year!" exclaimed John as John and Sarah were driving home.

Repetitious? Extremely. Boring? Definitely! Our language is saved from such dull speaking and writing by a small class of words called *pronouns*. Let's try the same passage with pronouns inserted in appropriate places. Each word in bold type is a pronoun.

> 1 For John and Sarah, the most relaxing part of **their** vacation was
> 2 spent at Leech Lake, **which** is a large lake in northern Minnesota. **They**
> 3 stayed a week on the lake, exploring **its** reedy inlets, losing **themselves**
> 4 in the surrounding forests, and fishing from the small motorboat **that**
> 5 **they** had rented from the owners of the cabin where **they** were staying.
> 6 "**I** would like to stay twice as long next year!" exclaimed John as **they**
> 7 were driving home.

A *pronoun* is a word that replaces and refers to a noun. The noun that a pronoun refers to is called its *antecedent*.

Look at the first sentence of the passage again and draw an arrow from each pronoun in bold type to its antecedent.

> For John and Sarah, the most relaxing part of **their** vacation was spent at Leech Lake, **which** is a large lake in northern Minnesota.

Did you mark *John and Sarah* as the antecedent of *their*? *Their* replaces and refers to *John and Sarah* so that the names don't have to be repeated in the sentence. You should have marked *Leech Lake* as the antecedent of *which*. Once again, the pronoun is used so that the name *Leech Lake* doesn't have to be repeated.

Exercise 11: Identifying Antecedents

Directions: Identify the rest of the antecedents for the pronouns in the passage. Ask yourself whom or what each pronoun refers to; then write the antecedent in the right column. The first two have been done for you.

Pronoun	**Antecedents**
1. their *(line 1)*	*John and Sarah*
2. which *(line 2)*	*Leech Lake*
3. They *(line 2)*	
4. its *(line 3)*	
5. themselves *(line 3)*	
6. that *(line 4)*	
7. they *(line 5)*	
8. they *(line 5)*	
9. I *(line 6)*	
10. they *(line 6)*	

ANSWERS ARE ON PAGE 309.

Pronoun Forms

Like nouns, pronouns refer to people, places, things, and ideas. Unlike nouns, however, some pronouns, called **personal pronouns**, change form depending on their use in a sentence. The forms are subject, object, and possessive. The way the pronoun is used in the sentence determines the form.

NOUN AS SUBJECT:	**The man** grasped my hand firmly.
PRONOUN AS SUBJECT:	**He** grasped my hand firmly.
NOUN AS OBJECT:	I thanked **the man** for helping me.
PRONOUN AS OBJECT:	I thanked **him** for helping me.
POSSESSIVE NOUN:	**The man's** voice silenced the crowd.
POSSESSIVE PRONOUN:	**His** voice silenced the crowd.

The following chart shows how personal pronouns change in form depending on their use in a sentence.

		Possessive	
Subject	**Object**	**1**	**2**
I	me	my	mine
you	you	your	yours
he	him	his	his
she	her	her	hers
it	it	its	its
we	us	our	ours
they	them	their	theirs
who	whom	whose	whose

Any pronoun from the subject list will fit into this sentence:

_____ felt strange.

In the sentence above, the subject pronouns act as subject of the sentence and subject of the verb *felt*.

Any pronoun from the object list will fill the blank in the following sentence:

Someone finally gave _____ some food.

In the sentence above, the object pronouns fit because they are not the subject of a verb.

Possessive pronouns from column 1 will fit in this sentence because they need a word following them to show what is owned:

That's _____ house.

Possessive pronouns from column 2 will fit here because they can stand alone:

The house is _____ .

For practice, read the sentences aloud, substituting each pronoun in turn.

Subject or Object?

It's pretty easy to tell when you need to use a possessive pronoun. You use a possessive pronoun when you want to show ownership, or possession. But sometimes you may not be sure whether to use a subject pronoun or an object pronoun.

Editing hint: If you are not sure whether to use a subject pronoun or an object pronoun, use this test:

Is the pronoun the subject of a verb? If it is, you must use a subject pronoun. If it is not the subject of a verb and it is not possessive, you must use an object pronoun.

> Sue's mother told *(she, her)* the news.

Will the pronoun be the subject of a verb? No. The only verb in the sentence is *told*, and the subject of *told* is *mother*. The correct answer is the object pronoun *her*.

> *(He, Him)* is the killer.

Will the pronoun be the subject of a verb? Yes. The only verb in the sentence is *is*, and the pronoun is the subject. The correct answer is the subject pronoun *He*.

Exercise 12: Pronoun Form

Directions: Replace the portion of each sentence in dark type with the correct pronoun. Check carefully to see whether you should choose a subject, object, or possessive pronoun.

Example: John, did ~~John~~ *you* watch *Frankenstein at the Beach Party* last night?

1. **Christine** is a lawyer and a power weightlifting champion.
2. The Russian leaders challenged **President Kennedy** by sending missiles to Cuba.
3. Susan insisted, "**Susan's** favorite vegetables really are rutabagas."
4. Dick assembled the scooter within an hour after buying **the scooter**.
5. **The senators** voted on an important appropriations bill yesterday.
6. What gave **the senators** the idea the voters would support **the senators'** action?
7. My friends, please give me **my friends'** trust.
8. Together, **you and I** can make our nation truly great.
9. Why do weddings make **that woman** sad?
10. Please give **my partner and me** a second chance.

ANSWERS ARE ON PAGES 309–10.

Pronouns in Compound Elements

It's when pronouns are used in compound elements that they cause the most problems. For instance, should you say "Please give John and **me** some pretzels" or "Please give John and **I** some pretzels"? You can answer that question with confidence by doing a simple test: Cross out *John and* and then decide what you would say if you used the pronoun alone.

> Please give ~~John and~~ me some pretzels.
> Please give ~~John and~~ I some pretzels.

Will the pronoun be the subject of a verb? *Please give John and* **me** *some pretzels* is correct. You need an object pronoun for this sentence. The only verb in the sentence is *give*, and the subject of the verb is the understood *you*.

Try another example:

> *(He, Him)* and *(I, me)* went to a great movie last night.
> **He** went to a great movie. . . .
> **Him** went to a great movie. . . .
> **I** went to a great movie. . . .
> **me** went to a great movie. . . .

Which choices are correct? *He and I* went to a great movie last night. These pronouns act as the subject of the sentence.

When the pronouns *I* and *me* appear in compound structures, they should be placed last. **He and I** (not *I and he*) went to that movie. The invitation was for **John and me** (not *me and John*).

Exercise 13: Pronoun Form in Compound Elements

Directions: Write the correct pronoun in each blank in the sentences below.

1. Keep an eye on Jeremy and _____ *(she, her)* until we get back.

2. Bob and _____ *(I, me)* plan to be married next month.

3. Please let your father and _____ *(I, me)* know when you plan to be home.

4. If the Caswells and _____ *(we, us)* will be more than fifteen minutes late, we'll call you.

5. Where did Jessica and _____ *(she, her)* go after work yesterday?

6. The flu hit _____ *(he, him)* and _____ *(I, me)* even harder than it struck Sue.

7. _____ *(They, Them)* and their cousins will hold a family reunion next month.

8. When _____ *(he, him)* and Scott passed each other at the grocery store, I thought they would at least speak.

9. The lottery winnings gave _____ *(they, them)* and their children a secure income for twenty years.

10. They met the Johnsons and _____ *(we, us)* at the union hall.

ANSWERS ARE ON PAGES 309-10.

FOCUS ON PUNCTUATION

Possessive Pronouns and Contractions

Like possessive nouns, possessive pronouns show ownership. Unlike possessive nouns, possessive pronouns use no apostrophes. Study the following examples. Notice that they all show possession, but none contains an apostrophe.

> For two hours, our cat never took **its** eyes off the parakeet.
>
> I believe this orange sock is **yours**.
>
> The house is **theirs**, but the land it stands on is **mine**.
>
> If they ever split up, the stereo is **hers** but the amplifiers are **his**.
>
> Not every neighborhood is as noisy as **ours**.
>
> **Whose** graffiti is the most artistic?

This rule—no apostrophe in possessive pronouns—should help you decide how to choose between the pronouns and contractions that sound just like them, such as *its* and *it's*. Don't confuse the word pairs shown in the following box.

Possessive pronouns	Contractions
its	it's (it is)
theirs	there's (there is)
your, yours	you're (you are)
whose	who's (who is)

Its eyes were black. *(possessive)*
It's been a long time. *(contraction)*

The house is **theirs**. *(possessive)*
There's nothing unusual about Ermentrude. *(contraction)*

Here is **your** house. *(possessive)*
You're getting bored, aren't you? *(contraction)*

Whose book is this? *(possessive)*
Who's been sleeping in my bed? *(contraction)*

Editing hint: To decide whether to use a possessive pronoun or a contraction, just try substituting the two words that the contraction stands for.

Exactly what do you think *(your, you're)* doing?

Substitute *you are*: *Exactly what do you think* **you are** *doing?* The sentence makes sense. Therefore, choose the contraction *you're*.

(Your, you're) car is in flames!

Substitute *you are*: **You are** *car is in flames!* The sentence makes no sense. Therefore, choose the possessive pronoun *your*.

Exercise 14: Possessive Pronouns and Contractions

Part A

Directions: Choose the correct word to fill each blank. Use the editing hint above to help you decide whether to choose the possessive pronoun or the contraction.

1. _____ *(Its, It's)* past time for our coffee break.

2. _____ *(Whose, Who's)* hiding behind the door?

3. _____ Although you spent *(your, you're)* childhood here,

   _____ *(your, you're)* not going to believe the changes.

4. The choice is _____ *(theirs, there's).*

5. America gets _____ *(its, it's)* name from the explorer Amerigo Vespucci.

6. The zoning commission presented _____ *(it's, its)* report to the city council.

7. Is _____ *(your, you're)* guess really as good as mine?

8. _____ *(Whose, Who's)* name is first on the list?

9. _____ *(Whose, Who's)* been stealing the chocolate chips from these cookies?

10. _____ *(Theirs, There's)* a stranger in the room; he's neither my friend nor _____ *(theirs, there's).*

Part B

Directions: Write two sentences using each of the following words. You'll need to write a total of sixteen sentences.

1. its
   it's

2. theirs
   there's

3. your
   you're

4. whose
   who's

ANSWERS ARE ON PAGE 310.

Exercise 15: Editing Practice Review

Part A

Directions: The following passage contains ten errors. Find and correct these errors, using this checklist as your proofreading guide.

☐ Are all sentences complete, or are there fragments?

☐ Does each sentence end with a period, a question mark, or an exclamation point?

☐ Are there any unnecessary commas separating the subject from the predicate of a sentence?

☐ Are commas used correctly in compound elements?

☐ Are the subject or object pronoun forms used correctly in compound elements?

☐ Are apostrophes used correctly with possessive nouns and omitted with possessive pronouns?

☐ Are plural nouns spelled correctly?

Janets bedroom, looks as though it's just been struck by a tornado. Blouses sweaters, socks, and jeans form a crazy quilt pattern on the floor A solid three-inch layer of old newspapers, and magazines covers her desk. Half-empty pop cans and candy bar wrapperes surround the overflowing wastebasket in the corner. Unmade bed. Peeping out from under it are the moldy remains of a large pepperoni pizza that her and her best friend shared. Two weeks ago. Never in my life have I seen a room as messy as her's!

ANSWERS ARE ON PAGE 311.

Part B

Directions: Using the checklist from Part A, proofread and correct the passage that you wrote in Exercise 3 on page 29.

ANSWERS WILL VARY.

Exercise 16: Sentence Basics Review

Part A

Directions: The questions in this review exercise are similar to ones that you will encounter on Part 1 of the GED Writing Skills Test. Read each question carefully; then mark the best answer in the space provided.

1. **Concrete blockes, old tires, branches, and leaves had been dumped in the vacant lot.**

    What correction should be made to this sentence?

    (1) change *blockes* to *blocks*
    (2) change *branches* to *branchs*
    (3) change *leaves* to *leafs*
    (4) insert a comma after *leaves*
    (5) no correction is necessary

2. **Dictionaries, encyclopedias, and reference manuals, are located behind the head librarian's desk.**

    What correction should be made to this sentence?

    (1) remove the comma after *Dictionaries*
    (2) remove the comma after *manuals*
    (3) insert a comma after *located*
    (4) change *librarian's* to *librarians*
    (5) no correction is necessary

3. **It's difficult to determine whether the accident was the drivers fault or the pedestrian's.**

    What correction should be made to this sentence?

    (1) change *It's* to *Its*
    (2) insert a comma after *determine*
    (3) change *drivers* to *driver's*
    (4) insert a comma after *fault*
    (5) change *pedestrian's* to *pedestrians*

4. **After supper last <u>night, John and me</u> drove along the lake front.**

    Which of the following is the best way to write the underlined portion of this sentence? If you think the original is the best way to write the sentence, choose option (1).

    (1) night, John and me
    (2) night. John and me
    (3) night, John and I
    (4) night. John and I
    (5) night me and John

5. **There's a world of difference between Harold's sloppy work and your careful attention to detail.**

   What correction should be made to this sentence?

   (1) change *There's* to *Theirs*
   (2) insert a comma after *between*
   (3) change *Harold's* to *Harolds*
   (4) change *your* to *you're*
   (5) no correction is necessary

6. **Did you mislay <u>your glasses? Or</u> lose them entirely?**

   Which of the following is the best way to write the underlined portion of these sentences? If you think the original is the best way to write the sentences, choose option (1).

   (1) your glasses? Or
   (2) you're glasses? Or
   (3) your glasses, or
   (4) you're glasses, or
   (5) your glasses or

7. **You're going to be surprised both by the monster's size and by it's incredible ugliness.**

   What correction should be made to this sentence?

   (1) change *You're* to *Your*
   (2) change *monster's* to *monsters*
   (3) insert a comma after *size*
   (4) change *it's* to *its*
   (5) no correction is necessary

8. **Antique collectors may specialize in old campaign buttons, dolls kitchen utensils, or pottery.**

   What correction should be made to this sentence?

   (1) insert a comma after *in*
   (2) remove the comma after *buttons*
   (3) insert a comma after *dolls*
   (4) change *utensils* to *utensil's*
   (5) no correction is necessary

9. **Michael glared steadily at the <u>Ballards but wouldn't tell them or us</u> what was wrong.**

   Which of the following is the best way to write the underlined portion of this sentence? If you think the original is the best way to write the sentence, choose option (1).

   (1) Ballards but wouldn't tell them or us
   (2) Ballards. But wouldn't tell them or us
   (3) Ballards. But wouldn't tell they or we
   (4) Ballards but wouldn't tell they or we
   (5) Ballards but wouldn't tell they, or we

10. <u>Toxic industrial wastes in</u> our water supply.

   Which of the following is the best way to write the underlined portion of this sentence? If you think the original is the best way to write the sentence, choose option (1).

   (1) Toxic industrial wastes in
   (2) Finding toxic industrial wastes in
   (3) Toxic industrial wastes, in
   (4) Toxic industrial wastes are contaminating
   (5) Caused by toxic industrial wastes in

Part B

Directions: Now that you are familiar with the GED question format, try answering questions about the sentences in a connected passage, as you will do on Part 1 of the GED Writing Skills Test. Read the passage completely, looking for possible errors. Then answer the questions that follow concerning individual sentences in the passage.

(1) You and me may picture the typical American family as a father, a mother, and their children. (2) An increasingly inaccurate picture. (3) Because of the high divorce rate, today more than one-fourth of all families with children, are headed by single parents. (4) Creating some problems. (5) In most cases the single parents are women. (6) Due to welfare cuts, pay inequitys, and some women's limited job skills, many families headed by females are living in poverty. (7) Father-headed households experience their own set of problems. (8) Although men's salaries are typically higher than womens, they are often less experienced at daily homemaking tasks like cooking, cleaning, and mending. (9) Regardless of whether the single parent is a man or a woman, theirs no doubt that the children are affected. (10) For a year or more after their parents' divorce, they may experience adjustment problems including academic difficulties, bedwetting, and fighting.

11. Sentence 1: **You and me may picture the typical American family as a father, a mother, and their children.**

   What correction should be made to this sentence?

   (1) change *me* to *I*
   (2) insert a comma after *as*
   (3) remove the comma after *father*
   (4) replace *You and me* with *Me and you*
   (5) no correction is necessary

12. Sentence 2: <u>**An increasingly inaccurate picture.**</u>

   Which of the following is the best way to write the underlined portion of this sentence? If you think the original is the best way to write the sentence, choose option (1).

   (1) An increasingly inaccurate picture.
   (2) A picture increasingly inaccurate.
   (3) That picture increasingly inaccurate.
   (4) That picture is increasingly inaccurate.
   (5) Is increasingly inaccurate.

13. Sentence 3: **Because of the high divorce rate, today more than one-fourth of all families with children, are headed by single parents.**

    What correction should be made to this sentence?

    (1) replace *rate, today* with *rate. Today*
    (2) change *families* to *families'*
    (3) remove the comma after *children*
    (4) change *parents* to *parents'*
    (5) no correction is necessary

14. Sentence 4: <u>**Creating some** problems.</u>

    Which of the following is the best way to write the underlined portion of this sentence? If you think the original is the best way to write the sentence, choose option (1).

    (1) Creating some
    (2) As a result creating some
    (3) Is creating some
    (4) A family pattern with significant and complex
    (5) This new family pattern is creating some

15. Sentence 6: **Due to welfare cuts, pay inequitys, and some women's limited job skills, many families headed by females are living in poverty.**

    What correction should be made to this sentence?

    (1) change *inequitys* to *inequities*
    (2) change *women's* to *womens*
    (3) change *families* to *family's*
    (4) insert a comma after *females*
    (5) no correction is necessary

16. Sentence 8: **Although men's salaries are typically higher than womens, they are often less experienced at daily homemaking tasks like cooking, cleaning, and mending.**

    What correction should be made to this sentence?

    (1) change *men's* to *mens*
    (2) change *womens* to *women's*
    (3) replace *tasks like* with *tasks. Like*
    (4) remove the comma after *cooking*
    (5) no correction is necessary

17. Sentence 9: **Regardless of whether the single parent is a man or a woman, theirs no doubt that the children are affected.**

    What correction should be made to this sentence?

    (1) insert a comma after *is*
    (2) change *theirs* to *there's*
    (3) insert a comma after *children*
    (4) insert a comma after *man*
    (5) no correction is necessary

18. Sentence 10: **For a year or more after their parents' divorce, they may experience adjustment <u>problems, including academic difficulties, bedwetting, and fighting.</u>**

   Which of the following is the best way to write the underlined portion of this sentence? If you think the original is the best way to write the sentence, choose option (1).

   (1) problems, including academic difficulties, bedwetting, and fighting.
   (2) problem's, including academic difficulties, bedwetting, and fighting.
   (3) problems. Including academic difficulties, bedwetting, and fighting.
   (4) problems, including, academic difficulties, bedwetting, and fighting.
   (5) problems, including academic difficulties bedwetting and fighting.

ANSWERS ARE ON PAGE 311.

Chapter 2 Review Evaluation Chart

Question Type	Review Pages	Question Number	Number of Questions	Number Correct
Fragments	30–41	6, 10, 12, 14	4	/4
Unnecessary commas	38	2, 13	2	/2
Compound elements	41–43	8	1	/1
Spelling of plurals	45–47	1, 15	2	/2
Possessive nouns	48–50	3, 16	2	/2
Pronoun form	50–55	4, 11	2	/2
Possessive pronouns and contractions	55–57	7, 17	2	/2
No error		5, 9, 18	3	/3

Passing score: 13 right out of 18 questions

Your score: _____ right out of 18 questions

3

WRITING PARAGRAPHS

In the section of Chapter 2 on planning a paragraph, you practiced organizing a list of details before writing a draft. You decided which details should be grouped and in what order they should appear. As you wrote the draft, how did you indicate to your reader that certain sentences belonged together?

In written English, the signal for grouped ideas is the **paragraph**.

> A *paragraph* is a set of related sentences that develop a central point or main idea.

You show the beginning of a paragraph by indenting its first line a few spaces, giving your reader a visual signal that the group of sentences develops a central point. Look at the two sets of sentences that follow. Although both have the general shape of a paragraph—several sentences together with the first line indented—only one fits the definition of a paragraph as **a set of related sentences that develop a central point**. Can you find it?

Motorists in the Snow Belt should always carry sand and a shovel during winter months. Driving on icy roads requires special techniques like pumping the brakes lightly to slow down and always steering into a spin. Wind-whipped snow blown across flat fields can reduce visibility tremendously. When the sun finally reemerges after the storm, ice-coated bushes and trees create a glittering wonderland.

From November through March, if you're planning highway travel in the Snow Belt, don't leave home without a blizzard kit in the trunk. Always carry a warm blanket, hooded jacket, snow boots, ski mask, and mittens to help conserve body heat if you're stranded in a ditch for several hours. In addition, take along some easily stored foods like peanut butter, crackers, and dried fruit. With luck, a shovel for digging out of snowdrifts and a bucket of sand for traction on ice will allow you to resume your travels soon. If not, an orange plastic pennant to attach to your aerial will signal for help.

Could you find any connections among the sentences in the first group? You may have noticed that the sentences are somewhat related: all refer to winter driving. But do they develop a central point about it? No. Each sentence discusses a different aspect of the experience. The second group, on the other hand, does qualify as a genuine paragraph. Not only do all the sentences refer to winter driving, but they also develop the central point that a traveler should carry a blizzard kit.

Parts of a Paragraph

Topic Sentences

Look again at the first sentence of the second group:

From November through March, if you're planning highway travel in the Snow Belt, don't leave home without a blizzard kit in the trunk.

This sentence is the **topic sentence** of the paragraph.

> A *topic sentence* clearly states the topic of the paragraph and the central point that the author is making about that topic.

All of the other sentences provide specific details to support the point. The topic sentence is the sentence, then, that unifies the entire paragraph.

Paragraph Building

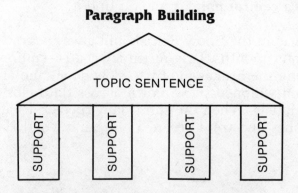

You can think of a paragraph as a building. The topic sentence is the roof that covers the rest of the material in the paragraph. The supporting sentences are like columns that support the roof. It's no coincidence that the topic sentence of the paragraph on page 64 is the first sentence. Although it may appear anywhere in a paragraph, the topic sentence most frequently occurs at the beginning, so the reader can tell right away what the entire paragraph will be about.

To be effective, a topic sentence must pass two tests. First, is it a complete sentence? A fragment like *Winter driving* or *What to put in a blizzard pack* might work as a title for the paragraph. However, a topic sentence must express a complete thought. Second, does it tell the reader the central point of the paragraph? The topic sentence *From November through March, if you're planning highway travel in the Snow Belt, don't leave home without a blizzard kit in the trunk* tells the reader what the paragraph is about—what point the writer wants to make. On the other hand, the other sentences, like "In addition, take along some easily stored foods like peanut butter, crackers, and dried fruit," have a different purpose. They expand on the topic sentence, giving the reader more details and explanation.

Tests for a Good Topic Sentence
1. Is it a complete sentence?
2. Does it tell the reader the central point of the paragraph?

Exercise 1: Matching Topic Sentences to Support——

Directions: Make each group of supporting sentences below into a complete paragraph by adding a topic sentence on the blank line. Make sure your topic sentence states the central point of the paragraph and is a complete sentence.

Here are some hints to help you develop a good topic sentence:

☐ Read through the supporting sentences.

☐ Get a general idea of what the writer is discussing.

☐ Write a sentence that summarizes the writer's main point.

Example: *Will is slacking off on the job.* Every morning Will walks into the office a half hour late. He uses work time to phone his current girlfriend. Will's lunch hours and coffee breaks last twice as long as everyone else's. He often slips away from work ten to fifteen minutes before closing time.

1. _____

_____

Some of the money from the property tax increase would be used to give police officers and firefighters a cost-of-living wage increase. New books could be added to the public library. Ten more miles of city streets could be paved. A summer employment program for teenagers could be expanded.

2. _____

_____

Situps firm stomach muscles. Leg lifts tone thighs and hips. Pushups build arm strength. Running in place strengthens legs.

3. _____

_____

Sharon consistently tailgates the car in front of her. She runs red lights, narrowly missing other cars or pedestrians in the intersection. Sharon drives at least fifteen miles an hour above the posted speed limit. She challenges other drivers to race her.

4. _____

_____

For breakfast Thomas Grosso eats three fried eggs, ten slices of bacon, and half a loaf of bread. For lunch the man downs two large pizzas and a quart of cola. Midafternoon finds him snacking on a dozen chocolate chip cookies and a gallon of ice cream. Mr. Grosso's evening meal consists of five thick pork chops, a plateful of mashed potatoes, and a chocolate cake for dessert.

5. _____

_____

Some people drink coffee because the caffeine it contains makes them feel more alert. Others drink it because they like its flavor. Some enjoy the warmth of coffee, especially on cold winter mornings. Then there are those who drink it strictly to be sociable.

SOME POSSIBLE TOPIC SENTENCES ARE ON PAGE 311.

Supporting Sentences

The following paragraph has a strong topic sentence that makes a clear point. How effective is the paragraph as a whole?

> **Mayor Campos cares about the people of this city.** She is divorced and has two children. Her reelection campaign committee raised more than five thousand dollars in donations from private businesses. Twice a week she eats lunch with the elderly people in the group meals program just so she can find out about their concerns.

Do you find the paragraph convincing? There's something wrong, isn't there? The topic sentence makes the point that the mayor cares about the people. But some of the other sentences don't seem to belong to the same central idea. Let's look at these supporting sentences to see what's wrong.

> She is divorced and has two children.
> Her reelection campaign committee raised more than five thousand dollars in donations from private businesses.

These sentences are certainly specific, but how are her personal life or campaign donations related to the point that the mayor cares about the people? These sentences are not relevant at all. Information that's not relevant to the main point of the paragraph can confuse your reader.

What about the last sentence?

> Twice a week she eats lunch with the elderly people in the group meals program just so she can find out about their concerns.

This sentence presents some solid support. It describes a specific activity of the mayor that shows she cares about elderly people in the community. Can you see that this sentence supports the writer's main point while the previous two sentences don't? Now the writer is on the right track. But is this one sentence enough to prove that the topic sentence is true? To make this into a good paragraph, the writer should add some more relevant support.

A good paragraph requires both a clear topic sentence and strong support. To test the quality of the support in a paragraph, ask these questions: Are the supporting sentences relevant? Do they actually help to prove that the topic sentence is true? Is there an adequate amount of support? One supporting sentence is rarely enough to prove a point. Usually you need at least three supporting sentences to really illustrate a point. If you aren't sure you have enough support, put yourself in the place of your reader. Will the reader understand what you have to say? Will your reader be convinced by your paragraph?

The supporting sentences in the following version of the paragraph about Mayor Campos pass these tests. What new ideas did the writer add? Do you find the revised paragraph convincing?

> Mayor Campos cares about the people of this city. Twice a week she eats lunch with the elderly people in the group meals program just so she can find out about their concerns. When the parts plant shut down last year, she immediately set up a series of meetings to inform the laid-off workers about government assistance programs and training opportunities for new jobs. She cares about young people, too. Under her leadership the city has opened fifty new summer jobs for teenagers, and preschool programs have been added in every community center.

Tests for Supporting Sentences
1. Are they relevant?
2. Is there an adequate amount of support to prove your point?

Exercise 2: Providing Supporting Details———

Part A
Directions: Each topic sentence on page 68 is followed by a list of items. Cross out the item in each list that is irrelevant to the topic sentence. Then add two more details of your own.

Example: Junk foods are common in Americans' diets.

> **a.**   sugary breakfast cereals
> ~~**b.**   poultry and fish~~
> **c.**   soft drinks
> **d.**   *candy bars*
> **e.** *greasy french fries*

1.   Many retail stores take advantage of holidays to boost sales.

> **a.**   picnic supplies promoted before the Fourth of July
> **b.**   Halloween candy displays in grocery stores
> **c.**   preinventory clearance sales
> **d.**
> **e.**

2.   Spelling in English is made difficult by pairs of words that sound alike but have different spellings and meanings.

> **a.**   smart-intelligent
> **b.**   too-to
> **c.**   pair-pear
> **d.**
> **e.**

3.   American cooking is enriched by traditional foods from many other countries.

> **a.**   sausages—Germany
> **b.**   chow mein—China
> **c.**   sweet corn—Iowa
> **d.**
> **e.**

4.   Television commercials are aimed specifically at the audience of the programs they sponsor.

> **a.**   children's cartoons—breakfast foods and toys
> **b.**   cable television—monthly fee
> **c.**   morning game shows—denture cleansers
> **d.**
> **e.**

5.   Examine a used car carefully before buying it.

> **a.**   check number of miles on odometer
> **b.**   may buy from used-car lot, new-car dealer, or private owner
> **c.**   check whether tread on tires is good
> **d.**
> **e.**

Part B

Directions: For each paragraph below, cross out the sentence that is irrelevant to the topic. Then add two specific supporting sentences of your own.

Example: The vacant house at Seventh and College is a blight on the neighborhood. Every window on the first floor has been broken by vandals. A third of the shingles on the porch roof have been blown off during storms. ~~Someone with carpentry skills should be allowed to homestead the property.~~ On the north side of the house some of the siding is hanging loose. *The unmowed yard is a tangle of dead leaves and branches. The sidewalk is crumbling.*

1. Within ten minutes I knew I didn't want to rent that apartment. The refrigerator and range were new. In the kitchen armies of cockroaches and ants were fighting over the food stuck to the floor. Chunks of plaster from the ceiling were lying in the bathtub. The carpet looked as if it hadn't been cleaned since World War I. _____

   _____

2. I've never met a more thoughtless person than my next-door neighbor. At two o'clock in the morning when I'm trying to sleep, she turns up her radio full blast. She lets her kids play in my vegetable garden, never scolding them for trampling the tomato plants. She keeps an aquarium in her living room.

   _____

   _____

3. High school dropouts return to school as adults for a variety of reasons. Some are pressured into finishing school by parents or spouses. Unfortunately, some adults are too embarrassed to admit that they never finished school. Others want to set a good example for their children. _____

   _____

   _____

SOME POSSIBLE ANSWERS ARE ON PAGES 311–12.

Chapter Highlights: Paragraphs

1. A paragraph is a set of related sentences that develop a central point.

2. The topic sentence states the subject of the paragraph and the author's point about that subject. It must also be a complete sentence.

3. The supporting sentences provide evidence to prove or explain the topic sentence. Supporting sentences should be relevant, and they should provide enough support to prove the writer's point.

Exercise 3: Writing Paragraphs

Directions: The following two writing assignments will allow you to combine the planning skills you learned in Chapter 2 with the paragraph-writing skills you have learned in this chapter: constructing a clear topic sentence and supporting it with specific details. Be sure to plan each paragraph before you write:

☐ Think about what you're writing about and who will be reading it. Be sure you understand the topic given before you write.

☐ Brainstorm ideas you could include in your paragraph. (You might want to reread the section on brainstorming on page 27 at this point.)

☐ Decide which ideas on your brainstormed list you will use in your paragraph, and number them in the order you plan to write them.

Paragraph 1

Some newspapers give a "Neighbor of the Week" award based on information provided by readers. Write a one-paragraph letter to your local paper nominating someone whom you know and respect for that award. In your topic sentence, identify the person and the quality you admire. In the supporting sentences, provide specific examples of that person's actions to prove your point.

Paragraph 2

Write a one-paragraph letter to the editor of your newspaper about a problem in your community. Identify the problem in the topic sentence and use the supporting sentences to provide several examples of the problem.

Revising Your Paragraphs

You may find you want to make some changes in your paragraphs now that you have written them. First make any changes you know now you want to make. Then check your paragraphs against this checklist and make any further revisions that would improve your writing.

☐ Is there a topic sentence?

☐ Does the topic sentence state the central point of the paragraph?

☐ Do all the other sentences support the point that it makes?

SAMPLE PARAGRAPHS APPEAR ON PAGE 312.

2▪ USING VERBS

Look carefully at the verbs in bold type in this paragraph.

> Once again the Southtown Sluggers **are** in the softball finals. Last night in the semifinal round they **played** the Midcity Maulers and easily **beat** them 10-3. Next Tuesday they **will play** their archrivals, the Westside Wasters, for this year's city championship.

In Chapter 2, you learned that, to be complete, every sentence needs a verb to tell what the subject is or does. In this chapter, you'll discover that a verb does more than make a complete sentence; it also helps to show time.

The time shown by a verb is called its *tense*.

In this chapter, we'll look at two types of verbs: regular verbs, which change tense according to a standard pattern, and irregular verbs, which change in other ways. Study the material carefully to learn how to form each verb tense correctly and, more important, *when* to use each tense.

Verbs change form in order to show tense, but they also change form depending on their subjects. You'll learn how to make sure that your subjects and verbs match each other in this chapter.

Verb Tense

Simple Tenses

How does the verb *wait* change in the following sentences to show the simple past, simple present, and simple future tenses?

> Frank **waited** all evening for his girlfriend to call.
> Frank **waits** by the phone every evening.
> Frank **will wait** by the phone tomorrow night, too.

Sometimes a single-word verb is used; at other times a verb phrase is needed, such as *will wait*, which shows future tense. In this example, *wait* is the base verb and *will* is a helping verb.

The main verb in a verb phrase is called the *base verb*. Other verbs in a verb phrase are called *helping verbs*. All verb tenses are formed by adding endings and helping verbs to the base verb.

Simple Present Tense

The simple present tense is used for things that are happening or are true now and for actions that are performed regularly. Also, the simple present tense is used when a statement is always true.

> I **need** a cup of coffee.
> The sun **rises** every morning.
> Most toddlers **love** candy.

The simple present tense is formed by using the base verb or the base verb plus *s*. Study the following chart showing the simple present tense of the verb *wait*.

I, you, we, they	wait
he, she, it	waits

The simple present tense of a regular verb is just the base form except when the subject is *he, she, it,* or a singular noun. When the subject is one of these, you must add *s* (or *es* if the verb ends in a hissing sound).

> My sister **plays** the piano.
> Herman **washes** his car on Saturdays.

You'll learn more about when to use the *s* and *es* endings in the "Subject-Verb Agreement" section of this chapter.

Write an example sentence of your own in the present tense:

_____

Simple Past Tense

The simple past tense shows action that occurred at a specific time in the past. The simple past for any subject is formed by adding *ed* to the base form of the verb.

> In 1988 Michael Dukakis **campaigned** for president.
> Last week I **started** an accounting course.

Write an example sentence of your own in the past tense:

_____

Simple Future Tense

The future tense shows an action that will occur in the future. Form the simple future for any subject by using *will* plus the base form of the verb.

> The plane **will leave** at 8:00 A.M.
> I **will help** you as soon as possible.

Write an example sentence of your own in the future tense:

_____

Time Clues

How can you decide which tense to use in a sentence? Often you'll find that the correct choice comes naturally. As you proofread a sentence or paragraph, be alert for time clues provided by other words. These clues have been circled in the examples below.

Simple Present
(Now) that I'm working, I **get** up at 6:30 every morning.
(Today) most people **buy** all their groceries at a supermarket.

Simple Past
(Last year) Sarah **entered** a poetry contest.
We **tried** to call you (yesterday.)

Future
(Next year) Andrea **will graduate** from college.
Will you please **write** (soon?)

Sometimes the clue words will be other verbs. Underline the correct verb tense in the sentence below.

> Nick picked up his saxophone and *(wails, wailed)* a mournful tune.

The verb *picked* is the clue to past tense. You can tell that both actions happened in the past, so the correct choice is *wailed*.

Exercise 4: Simple Tenses ───────────────────

Directions: For each sentence, underline the correct verb tense from the choices in parentheses. Circle any words that provide time clues to verb tense.

Example: I *(mail, mailed, will mail)* this letter (tomorrow.)

1. Tim *(satisfies, satisfied, will satisfy)* his hunger last night with a Reuben sandwich.

2. My daughter toddled up and *(asks, asked, will ask)* for a box of raisins.

3. Every day Jim leaves home at six o'clock and *(arrives, arrived, will arrive)* at work an hour later.

4. Tomorrow the truck drivers *(picket, picketed, will picket)* all P&Q grocery stores.

5. Light always *(travels, traveled, will travel)* at 186,000 miles per second.

6. Several times last year a lone gunman *(robs, robbed, will rob)* the convenience store on the corner.

7. Next week a new rhythm and blues group *(performs, performed, will perform)* at the club.

8. June usually *(skips, skipped, will skip)* breakfast and makes up for it at lunch.

9. Only an hour ago you *(want, wanted, will want)* to marry me.

10. Now you *(despise, despised, will despise)* the sight of me!

ANSWERS ARE ON PAGE 312.

Continuing Tenses

The continuing tenses are used to show continuing action in the past, present, or future. The present continuing tense shows action happening now:

John **is staring** at me.

The past continuing tense shows past action that continued for some time:

We **were watching** television that evening.

The future continuing tense shows ongoing action in the future:

Ann **will be staying** with her niece for a week.

As you can see from the example sentences above, the continuing tenses are formed by using helping verbs and the base form of the verb plus *ing*. The chart below shows how to form each of the continuing tenses.

Continuing Tenses			
Present continuing	I	am	looking
	he, she, it	is	
	we, you, they	are	
Past continuing	I, he, she, it	was	
	we, you, they	were	
Future continuing	I, he, she, it, we, you, they	will be	

Now write example sentences of your own using the continuing tenses:

Present continuing: _____

Past continuing: _____

Future continuing: _____

    Phrases like *right now*, *today*, and *at the moment* are clues to present continuing tense. For all three continuing tenses, keep in mind the idea of an action going on for some time.

Exercise 5: Continuing Tenses

Directions: For each sentence, underline the correct verb tense from the choices in parentheses. Circle any words that provide time clues to verb tense.

Example: (Right now) you (*are working*, *were working*, *will be working*) on Exercise 5.

1. Tomorrow at this time you (*are flying*, *were flying*, *will be flying*) to Puerto Rico.

2. At present, I (*think*, *am thinking*, *was thinking*) about moving to Canada.

3. At this time last year we (*are shivering*, *were shivering*) in subzero temperatures.

4. We (*are visiting*, *were visiting*, *will be visiting*) our cousins in Arizona again next winter.

5. I still (*am steaming*, *was steaming*) over that last remark!

6. At 3:45 yesterday afternoon, I (*am returning*, *was returning*, *will be returning*) to the office from a meeting.

7. Last night Ron (*is feeling*, *was feeling*, *will be feeling*) ill.

8. At the present the rich (*are continuing*, *were continuing*, *will be continuing*) to get richer.

9. At dawn yesterday the birds (*are chirping*, *were chirping*, *will be chirping*) mercilessly.

10. Next fall Greg (*is going*, *was going*, *will be going*) through basic training.

ANSWERS ARE ON PAGES 312–13.

Perfect Tenses

The perfect tenses are used to show action completed before or continuing to a specific time. Two of the three perfect tenses are actually special forms of the past tense, and the other perfect tense is a special form of the future.

Three Types of Past Tense

You have already studied the simple past and the past continuing tenses. These tenses show actions that have been completed in the past:

> She **tripped** over the cord.
> Paul **was napping** in the other room.

The other two types of past tense are perfect tenses: the present perfect and the past perfect. These special past tenses show more specific time relationships.

The Present Perfect Tense

The present perfect tense shows an action that started in the past and continues into the present or has just been completed.

> Sam **has worked** here since 1983.
> I **have finished** my book.

As you can see from the examples above, the present perfect tense is formed by combining either *has* or *have* with the base form of the verb plus *ed*.

Present Perfect		
he, she, it	has	looked
I, you, we, they	have	

The Past Perfect Tense

The third type of past tense is the past perfect tense, which shows that something took place before a specific time in the past.

> By 8:00 the guests **had finished** all the beer.

The past perfect tense is formed by combining *had* with the base form of the verb plus *ed*.

Past Perfect	
I, you, he, she, it, we, they	had looked

Now write example sentences of your own using the present perfect and past perfect tenses:

Present perfect: _____

Past perfect: _____

The Future Perfect Tense

You have already studied the simple future tense, which shows an action that will take place in the future:

You **will take** the GED Tests next week.

A different type of future tense, the future perfect tense, shows an action that will be completed by a specific time in the future.

By next year I **will have finished** this project.

The future perfect tense is formed by combining the helping verbs *will have* with the base form of the verb plus *ed*.

Future Perfect	
I, you, he, she, it, we, they	will have looked

Now write an example sentence of your own using the future perfect tense:

_____

Time Clues to Perfect Tenses

Time clues to perfect tenses include phrases beginning with *by*. These phrases indicate a time by which something was or will be completed.

By 7:30 yesterday morning I **had finished** the book.
By next spring, I **will have driven** my new car 5,000 miles.

Phrases beginning with *since* and *for* often signal present perfect tense because they show an action beginning in the past and continuing in the present.

Since yesterday afternoon, I **have worked** without stopping.
For the last five years he **has ordered** the same sandwich every day.

The words *just* and *already* may also be clues to present perfect tense. They signal an action that has recently been completed.

We **have** just **received** word about an earthquake in Mexico City.
Has Diane **finished** that book already?

Exercise 6: Perfect Tenses

Directions: For each sentence, underline the correct verb tense from the choices in parentheses. Circle any words that provide time clues to verb tense.

Example: (Fifteen minutes from now,) you *(have finished, had finished, will have finished)* this exercise.

1. By six o'clock last night, we *(cleaned, have cleaned, had cleaned)* out the refrigerator.

2. Raoul *(worked, has worked, will have worked)* for me since 1986.

3. Before retiring last year, Mrs. Tonini *(supervised, has supervised, had supervised)* the parts department.

4. By this time next year, you *(are passing, pass, will have passed)* all your GED tests.

5. I *(missed, have missed, am missing)* the first bus every morning for the past week.

6. By next fall, the construction company *(will have started, is starting, starts)* on the multimillion-dollar project.

7. Long before Columbus's voyage in 1492, Viking ships *(traveled, have traveled, had traveled)* to the New World.

8. Before last week's race, I *(have, had, will have)* been running ten miles a day.

9. In the past five years, Floyd *(has failed, had failed, will have failed)* to appear on time only once.

10. In less than five minutes last night, our calm discussion *(has degenerated, had degenerated, is degenerating)* into name-calling.

ANSWERS ARE ON PAGE 313.

Passive Verbs

Passive verbs show action performed on the subject by somone or something else. Passive verbs can be in past, present, or future tenses. The present passive tense shows a present condition created by someone or something else. In the following example, using the passive form shows that "someone" has programmed the computer.

The computer **is programmed** to self-destruct.

The past passive tense shows an action performed on the subject in the past:

The gang members **were watched** closely by the police.

The future passive tense shows a future action that will be performed on the subject:

>The patient **will be wheeled** into surgery at 6:45.

As you can see from the examples above, the passive tenses are formed by combining helping verbs with the base verb plus *ed*. The following chart shows all the forms of the passive tenses.

Passive Tenses			
Present passive	I	am	
	he, she, it	is	
	you, we, they	are	
Past passive	I, he, she, it	was	watched
	we, you, they	were	
Future passive	I, you, he, she, it, we, they	will be	

Now write example sentences of your own using the passive tenses:

Present passive: _____

Past passive: _____

Future passive: _____

By Phrases

In many sentences requiring a passive verb, you will find a phrase beginning with *by* and ending with a noun. This phrase identifies the performer of the action in the sentence.

>Jack's car **was demolished** by a garbage truck.

(The garbage truck did the demolishing.) Even when the *by* phrase is not included, you can mentally add one to see whether a passive verb is required. Can you add a *by* phrase to the sentence below?

>Walter was picked for the volleyball team.

It's easy to include a *by* phrase at the end of the sentence; just use your imagination!

>Walter was picked for the volleyball team by Caren.

Exercise 7: Passive Verbs

Directions: For each sentence, underline the correct verb tense from the choices in parentheses. Circle any words that provide time clues to verb tense and any *by* phrases that signal the need for a passive verb.

Example: Twenty protesters *(are carried, were carried, carried)* to the paddy wagon by the riot squad last night.

1. Tomorrow morning the time capsule *(is opened, will be open, will be opened)* by the governor.

2. Yesterday evening a homemade bomb *(was tossed, was toss, tossed)* through my window by a passing motorist.

3. This masterpiece *(is painted, was painted, has painted)* in 1564.

4. The next song *(recorded, is recorded, was recorded)* by Chicago in 1983.

5. Beginning next month, an improved health insurance package *(is offered, will be offered, will offer)* to all employees.

6. All hospital staff *(are required, are requiring, are require)* to have a complete physical examination every year.

7. Smoking *(is prohibit, is prohibited, is prohibiting)* in this section of the plane.

8. For the next several hours, the patient's condition *(will monitor, will be monitor, will be monitored)* closely by nurses in the intensive care unit.

9. Because of his bravery under fire, the Marine *(is awarded, was awarded, will be awarded)* a Bronze Medal in 1971.

10. Until further notice, this plant *(is close, is closed, closed)*.

ANSWERS ARE ON PAGES 313–14.

Spelling Regular Verb Forms

In the Subject-Verb Agreement section of this chapter, you will review rules for adding *s* and *es* to present-tense verbs. The following rules for adding *ed* and *ing* are also useful to know, not just because they will certainly be tested on Part 2 of the GED Writing Skills Test, but also because they're used so often and have so few exceptions.

1. When adding *ed* and *ing* to most verbs, keep the normal spelling of the simple present form.

   look⟶looked, looking
   stagger⟶staggered, staggering

   model ⟶ _____ _____

   allow ⟶ _____ _____

   radio ⟶ _____ _____

   delay ⟶ _____

2. When the simple present form of the verb ends in *y* preceded by a consonant, change the *y* to *i* before adding *ed*, and keep the *y* before *ing*.

    marry——→married, marrying
    study——→studied, studying

    bury——→_____   _____

    bully——→_____   _____

    worry——→_____   _____

3. When the simple present form of the verb ends in a silent *e*, drop the *e* before adding *ed* or *ing*.

    glare——→glared, glaring
    fire——→fired, firing
    cope——→_____   _____

    complete——→_____   _____

    smile——→_____   _____

4. When the simple present form of the verb ends in *ie*, drop the silent *e* before adding *ed*, and change the *ie* to *y* before adding *ing*.

    die——→died, dying

    tie——→_____   _____

    lie——→_____   _____

5. When the simple present form of the verb ends in a single vowel and a single consonant other than *h*, *w*, and *x* and when the accent falls on the last (or only) syllable of the verb, double the final consonant before *ed* or *ing*. Otherwise, keep the normal spelling.

    snap——→snapped, snapping
    plot——→plotted, plotting

    mug——→_____   _____

    prefer——→_____   _____

    commit——→_____   _____

    But
    pinch——→pinched, pinching

    Why? _____

    sail——→sailed, sailing

    Why? _____

    label——→labeled, labeling

    Why? _____

Exercise 8: Regular Verb Review

This exercise tests your understanding of when to use simple, continuing, perfect, and passive tenses.

Part A

Directions: Write the correct forms of the main verbs in the following sentences. Look for helping verbs that might be clues to form. Be careful to spell the verbs correctly.

Example: (type) Last night Sue *typed* _____ the first chapter of her book.

1. *(play)* Last summer we _____ tennis twice a week.

2. *(hate)* Tom has always _____ to go to the dentist.

3. *(earn)* That kid is _____ extra money by selling earplugs to the parents of hard rock fans.

4. *(carry)* In the past, most hardware stores _____ plumbing supplies.

5. *(stop)* Fran and Bob often _____ for a pizza after work.

6. *(hope)* Only last month, Theresa _____ to become a professional mud wrestler.

7. *(permit)* For New Year's Eve, they are _____ their children to stay up until midnight.

8. *(study)* At the moment, the class is _____ verb forms.

9. *(compare)* The two girls were _____ notes on their dates.

10. *(refer)* My family doctor finally _____ me to a specialist.

Part B

Directions: For each sentence, underline the correct verb tense from the choices in parentheses. Circle any words or phrases that provide clues to the correct tense. Refer to the rules and explanations on pages 71–80 as much as you need to in order to answer correctly.

1. At this moment someone in Hollywood *(films, is filmed, is filming)* a sequel to *Rocky XXIII.*

2. At ten o'clock tomorrow morning, the senator *(will announce, has announced, will be announced)* her candidacy for reelection.

3. Apparently the thieves *(are gaining, have gained, had gained)* entry by breaking a basement window sometime before 6:20.

4. Since 1980 Don *(is purchasing, purchases, has purchased)* a new car every year.

5. With a little luck and a lot of hard work, I *(will be earning, am earning, have earned)* two hundred dollars a week within six months.

6. In a fit of foul temper, William snarled at his goldfish and *(was drop-kicking, drop-kicked, drop-kicks)* the flower pot.

7. Two-year-olds typically *(are overusing, overused, overuse)* the word *no.*

8. The package *(will ship, is shipping, will be shipped)* to you COD within two weeks.

9. Several suspicious-looking characters *(were loitering, are loitering, loiter)* outside the apartment house last night.

10. In our neighborhood the garbage *(had picked, is pick, is picked)* up every Wednesday.

11. By next week Ramona *(will complete, will have completed, is completing)* plans for the addition to her house.

12. Passersby often *(remark, are remarking, will remark)* on the eerie lavender glow around the Munsons' garage.

ANSWERS ARE ON PAGES 314–15.

Irregular Verb Forms

A thief **breaks** into a basement apartment and **steals** a stereo. A passing police officer **sees** him, **goes** after him, and **catches** him. At the trial two weeks later, the jury **finds** him guilty of burglary. He **gets** a five-year sentence.

Let's use the rules you just learned to change the paragraph above from present to past tense. Here's our result:

A thief **breaked** into a basement apartment and **stealed** a stereo. A passing police officer **seed** him, **goed** after him, and **catched** him. At the trial two weeks later, the jury **finded** him guilty of burglary. He **getted** a five-year sentence.

We've created a perfectly logical but incorrect paragraph. The source of our errors is the fact that not all English verbs shift to different tenses according to the rules for regular verbs.

Because many irregular verbs are so commonly used, you know most of these forms already. Check your skills right now by correcting the sample paragraph about the break-in. Cross out each incorrect verb and write the correct one above it.

This is how it ought to read. How well did you do?

A thief **broke** into a basement apartment and **stole** a stereo. A passing police officer **saw** him, **went** after him, and **caught** him. At the trial two weeks later, the jury **found** him guilty of burglary. He **got** a five-year sentence.

You can be sure that some questions about irregular verbs will appear on Part 1 of the GED Writing Skills Test.

Principal Parts of Verbs

When you are studying irregular verbs, the three parts of each verb that you must learn are the base form, the simple past tense, and the past participle, which is used in all perfect and passive tenses. Regular verbs all simply add *ed* or *d* to form the past tense and past participle. Irregular verbs do not follow this pattern for the past tense and the past participle. Study the following comparison of the principal parts of a regular and an irregular verb.

	Base Form	Simple Past	Past Participle
Regular verb	look	looked	looked
Irregular verb	see	saw	seen

As you may have guessed, you will need to memorize the past and past participle forms of irregular verbs you don't already know. In the following exercises, you'll practice using the most common irregular verbs.

Must-Learn Verbs

Some irregular verbs are used so frequently that learning them is essential to smooth writing. If your study time is limited, concentrate on these. The usual error with these verbs is confusing the simple past and past participle forms. Remember that the simple past is used alone; the past participle is used in a verb phrase with *has, have,* or *had.*

> INCORRECT: I **seen** you at the pool hall.
> CORRECT: I **saw** you at the pool hall.
> CORRECT: I **have seen** you at the pool hall.

Present	Past	Past Participle
am, is, are	was, were	(have) been
do, does	did	(have) done
has, have	had	(have) had
go, goes	went	(have) gone
come	came	(have) come
run	ran	(have) run
see	saw	(have) seen
bring	brought	(have) brought

Exercise 9: Must-Learn Verbs

Directions: Underline the correct verb form to complete each sentence. If you choose the past participle, circle its helping verb. Some helping verbs may be in contractions, such as *I've* or *she's*.

Examples: I don't know where they(ve) *(went, gone)*.
She *(was, been)* a real pest on this trip.

1. I certainly hope that the werewolves have *(went, gone)*.

2. Last night we *(saw, seen)* a television program on humpback whales.

3. Have we *(ran, run)* out of brown sugar?

4. Jim *(brung, brought)* his new girlfriend over last night.

5. I've never *(did, done)* an exercise quite like this.

6. The dog just *(came, come)* in with burrs matted in his coat.

7. We *(were, been)* expecting your call sooner.

8. Lisa has *(ran, run)* in the Boston Marathon before.

9. I've *(saw, seen)* that man somewhere before.

10. Summer has *(came, come)*.

11. Jane and Ron *(did, done)* all the housecleaning before noon last Saturday.

12. Last year we *(went, gone)* to Wyoming on vacation.

13. Has the mail carrier *(brung, brought)* the mail in yet?

14. The surgeon *(did, done)* an excellent job on the bypass.

15. Suddenly Shelby *(saw, seen)* a rhinoceros looming in the distance.

ANSWERS ARE ON PAGE 315.

I-A-U Pattern

Some irregular verbs follow similar patterns. One common pattern is a vowel shift from *i* in present to *a* in past to *u* in past participle form.

Present	Past	Past Participle
drink	drank	(have) drunk
ring	rang	(have) rung
begin	began	(have) begun
shrink	shrank	(have) shrunk
sing	sang	(have) sung
sink	sank	(have) sunk
swim	swam	(have) swum

Exercise 10: I-A-U Verbs

Directions: Underline the correct verb form to complete each sentence. If you choose the past participle, circle its helping verb.

Example: So far this morning, Janet (has) (drank, <u>drunk</u>) four cups of coffee.

1. We *(began, begun)* to doubt the truth of his story.

2. Has anyone ever *(swam, swum)* across the Gulf of Mexico?

3. Darrin *(sang, sung)* with a rock group for three years.

4. Gene's army uniform must have *(shrank, shrunk)* in the last ten years.

5. The oven timer just *(rang, rung)*.

6. Denise jumped into the swimming pool and *(sank, sunk)* like a rock.

7. In the last few days, the baby has *(began, begun)* smiling and cooing.

8. I've never *(swam, swum)* in the ocean.

9. The telephone has *(rang, rung)* off the wall today.

ANSWERS ARE ON PAGES 315–16.

En and *N* Verbs

Many verbs shift to their past participle form by adding an *-en* or *-n* ending. Here are some of the most common:

Present	Past	Past Participle
arise	arose	(have) arisen
break	broke	(have) broken
speak	spoke	(have) spoken
freeze	froze	(have) frozen
steal	stole	(have) stolen
choose	chose	(have) chosen
ride	rode	(have) ridden
write	wrote	(have) written
eat	ate	(have) eaten
take	took	(have) taken
grow	grew	(have) grown
know	knew	(have) known
throw	threw	(have) thrown
tear	tore	(have) torn
wear	wore	(have) worn

Exercise 11: En *and* N *Verbs*—————————

Directions: Underline the correct verb to complete each sentence. If you choose the past participle, circle its helping verb.

1. The police have *(took, taken)* Tim into custody.

2. We *(choose, chose, chosen)* a new union steward at our last meeting.

3. Jack has *(stole, stolen)* everything from rubber bands to car stereos.

4. Somehow I *(knowed, knew)* the answer to that question.

5. The kid has *(grew, grown)* five inches in three months!

6. We've already *(ate, eaten)* supper.

7. I *(wrote, written)* him a letter instead of a birthday card.

8. Negotiations with management have *(broke, broken)* down completely.

9. We got up late and *(eat, ate)* a big breakfast.

10. Sue has just *(wrote, written)* her first letter to the editor.

ANSWERS ARE ON PAGE 316.

Exercise 12: Other Common Irregular Verbs—————

Directions: The chart on pages 88 to 89 lists the simple present, simple past, and past participle forms of other common irregular verbs in alphabetical order. You'll already know many of them. To find the ones you need to practice, use this procedure:

☐ Cover the second and third columns with a sheet of paper.

☐ Make a short sentence using the present-tense verb in column 1 by using *I* as the subject.

I draw.

☐ Test for the past-tense form by saying, "Yesterday I _____ ."

Yesterday I drew.

☐ Test for the past participle form by saying, "I have _____ ."

I have drawn.

☐ Check your answers against the verbs printed in columns 2 and 3.

☐ Mark for study any that differ from your answers.

☐ Study the verbs you missed by repeating their correct forms over and over in sentence form ("Yesterday I _____ ; I have _____ ") until they start to sound right to you.

ANSWERS WILL VARY.

Present	Past	Past Participle
awake	awoke, awaked	(have) awaked, awoken
become	became	(have) become
bend	bent	(have) bent
bet	bet	(have) bet
bid (to offer)	bid	(have) bid
bind	bound	(have) bound
bite	bit	(have) bitten
blow	blew	(have) blown
build	built	(have) built
burst	burst	(have) burst
buy	bought	(have) bought
cast	cast	(have) cast
catch	caught	(have) caught
cling	clung	(have) clung
cost	cost	(have) cost
creep	crept	(have) crept
cut	cut	(have) cut
deal	dealt	(have) dealt
dig	dug	(have) dug
drag	dragged	(have) dragged
draw	drew	(have) drawn
dream	dreamed, dreamt	(have) dreamed, dreamt
drive	drove	(have) driven
fall	fell	(have) fallen
feed	fed	(have) fed
feel	felt	(have) felt
fight	fought	(have) fought
find	found	(have) found
flee	fled	(have) fled
fly	flew	(have) flown
forget	forgot	(have) forgotten
get	got	(have) gotten
give	gave	(have) given
hear	heard	(have) heard
hide	hid	(have) hidden
hold	held	(have) held
hurt	hurt	(have) hurt
keep	kept	(have) kept
lay (put or place)	laid	(have) laid
lead	led	(have) led
leave	left	(have) left
lend	lent	(have) lent
lose	lost	(have) lost
make	made	(have) made
mean	meant	(have) meant
meet	met	(have) met
pay	paid	(have) paid
put	put	(have) put

read	read	(have) read
rid	rid	(have) rid
rise	rose	(have) risen
say	said	(have) said
seek	sought	(have) sought
sell	sold	(have) sold
send	sent	(have) sent
set	set	(have) set
shake	shook	(have) shaken
shine	shone	(have) shone
shine (polish)	shined	(have) shined
shoot	shot	(have) shot
sit	sat	(have) sat
sleep	slept	(have) slept
spend	spent	(have) spent
spin	spun	(have) spun
stand	stood	(have) stood
strike	struck	(have) struck
swear	swore	(have) sworn
teach	taught	(have) taught
tell	told	(have) told
think	thought	(have) thought
understand	understood	(have) understood

Three Troublesome Verb Pairs

Because they sound so much alike, yet have slightly different meanings, three verb pairs are particularly tricky to use correctly: *lie-lay, sit-set,* and *rise-raise.*

The first verb *(lie, sit,* and *rise)* is used when the subject of the sentence is moving (or resting). It might help you to remember that the second letter of each of these verbs is *i.*

> Our cat **lies** on the windowsill to catch the afternoon sun.
> We sometimes **sit** on the porch swing and swat mosquitoes.
> I **rise** reluctantly from bed every morning.

The second verb *(lay, set,* and *raise)* is used when the subject of the sentence moves an object.

> I frequently **lay** my car keys down and forget where I put them.
> The students usually **set** their books under their desks.
> Dick **raises** his hand hesitantly for fear of giving a wrong answer.

The charts on page 90 summarize the forms of these three pairs of verbs.

Subject Is Moving

Simple Present	Present Participle	Simple Past	Past Participle
lie	lying	lay	lain
sit	sitting	sat	sat
rise	rising	rose	risen

Subject Moves an Object

Simple Present	Present Participle	Simple Past	Past Participle
lay	laying	laid	laid
set	setting	set	set
raise	raising	raised	raised

Notice that the same spelling is used for the simple past form of *lie* and the simple present form of *lay*. Can you see how the context of the sentence reveals the difference in meaning in the examples below? One of these sentences shows a subject moving an object. Circle the object being moved.

> William **lay** in bed moaning for three days with the flu.
> The Wilsons sometimes **lay** a log on the fire and eat popcorn all evening.

In the first sentence, the simple past of *lie* is used. The subject, *William*, acted alone. In the second sentence, the simple present of *lay* is used. The subject, *The Wilsons*, move *a log*. You should have circled *log*.

Exercise 13: Lie-Lay, Sit-Set, Raise-Rise————

Directions: Underline the correct form of the verb to complete each sentence. Circle the object that is moved, if there is one.

1. The dog has been *(lying, laying)* on my bed again.

2. Don't *(sit, set)* on that chair with the broken leg.

3. A cadet *(rises, raises)* the flag at exactly 7:00 A.M.

4. She *(sat, set)* the coffee cup carefully on the table.

5. Who *(lay, laid)* this money on my desk?

6. Abe *(rose, raised)* from his seat and strode to the platform.

7. The jewelry has *(lain, laid)* in the bank vault for years.

8. Are you *(sitting, setting)* in the front row?

9. We've *(lain, laid)* our plans carefully.

10. I'd love to be *(lying, laying)* on a beach in Jamaica right now.

ANSWERS ARE ON PAGE 316.

Verb Tense in a Passage

Time clues don't appear in every sentence. In fact, in a whole paragraph there may be only one or two sentences that contain such signals. In this situation it's particularly important to be consistent in verb tense. Don't slip unnecessarily from present to past or from past to present. Such slips are confusing; they leave the reader wondering when the action actually occurred.

Two slips in tense appear in the following paragraph, which should be written entirely in past tense. Locate and circle these errors.

A loud growl silenced the crowd around the bar. They looked apprehensively at the entrance. Suddenly a hulking figure throws open the door and lumbered into the room. The other patrons sidled out of his path, trying to make themselves inconspicuous. Head lowered, the monstrous creature charged up to the quivering bartender and says threateningly, "One Shirley Temple on the rocks."

Did you find the two out-of-place present tense verbs? They were *throws* and *says*. Their past tense forms, *threw* and *said*, should have been used to make the paragraph consistent in tense.

Some of the questions on Part 1 of the GED Writing Skills Test will ask you to make sure that verb tense is consistent within a passage.

Editing hint: You can check for consistent verb tense within a passage by reading the passage twice. The first time through, get a general sense of the tense of the passage as a whole. The second time, carefully check each sentence to make sure the verbs fit into the passage as a whole.

Exercise 14: Verb Tense Review

Directions: Proofread the following paragraph for eleven errors in verb form or verb tense. Cross out the incorrect form and write the correct form above it.

Example: Joe ~~done~~ *did* a great job on the car yesterday.

Before last night, neither the Mad Dogs nor the Spartans played a good game all season. However, last night's football game begun as a defensive battle and ended as a scoring free-for-all. During the first half, both teams ran the ball. The defensive lines on both sides are strong. At the end of the first half, the score was tyed at 0–0.

In the second half, both teams openned with a new strategy. They passed the ball whenever they seen an opening. The quarterbacks done a superb job of setting up plays. The defensive lines, on the other hand, were tireing. They aren't blocking nearly as well. As a result, the final score will be 47–39. By the end of that game, the Spartans winned their first victory of the season.

ANSWERS ARE ON PAGE 316.

Subject-Verb Agreement

Basic Subject-Verb Agreement

By learning how to choose and write the correct verb tense, you've gone halfway toward achieving proper verb form. Your final step is to learn when and how to make verbs agree with their subjects. Look at the two pairs of sentences below.

> The employees **think** the manager is an idiot.
> The employees **thinks** the manager is an idiot.
>
> The manager **wants** to open the office at 6:00 A.M.
> The manager **want** to open the office at 6:00 A.M.

Why is the first sentence in each pair correct, but not the second? The answer to this question lies in the link between present-tense subjects and verbs. In the first pair, is the subject singular or plural? *Employees* is plural, and the verb that fits with a plural subject is the plural verb *think*. Is the subject in the second pair also plural? No. *Manager* is singular. The verb *wants* fits with this singular subject.

Choosing present-tense verbs to match singular or plural subjects is called *subject-verb agreement.*

You can most easily learn the matching pattern for subject-verb agreement by using personal pronouns as subjects at first. Look at the pattern shown in the following example. Which pronouns require a verb with an *s* ending?

> I
> You
> We } **hate** to get up in the morning.
> They
>
> He
> She } **hates** to get up in the morning.
> It

Which verbs end in *s*? Only those that follow the singular subjects *he, she, it.*

Some verbs require an *es* ending instead of the basic *s* ending. Study the example that follows.

> I
> You
> We } **lurch** into the kitchen.
> They

$$\left.\begin{array}{l} \text{He} \\ \text{She} \\ \text{It} \end{array}\right\}$$ **lurches** into the kitchen.

You may recall that verbs ending in a hissing sound (*s, sh, ch, x,* and *z*) take an *es* ending. This rule is very similar to the rule about noun plurals that you studied on page 46.

When personal pronouns are used as subjects, only the singular subjects *he, she,* and *it* are followed by verbs ending in *s* or *es.*

Does a similar subject-verb agreement rule apply in sentences using nouns as subjects? What pattern do you find in the pairs of sentences below?

The worker **belongs** to a union.
The workers **belong** to a union.

An artichoke **cooks** slowly.
Artichokes **cook** slowly.

In each pair, the subject of the first sentence is singular. The verb in each first sentence ends in *s*. The subject of the second sentence is plural in each pair. No *s* is added to the verb in the second sentence of each pair. Now you can see that nouns as subjects follow the same rule as personal pronouns.

Basic Rules for Subject-Verb Agreement
1. The present-tense verbs of singular subjects (except *I* and *you*) end in *s* or *es*.

2. The present-tense verbs of plural subjects (and *I* and *you*) do not end in *s*.

Irregular Verbs

Do the basic rules apply for irregular verbs, too? Look at the pair of sentences below.

Jeremy **is** a member of the softball team.
The players **are** ready for the game.

The first sentence has a singular subject, and the verb ends in *s*. The second sentence has a plural subject, and the verb does not end in *s*. In fact, the rules hold for irregular verbs as well.

Carefully study the following very common irregular verbs with different subjects. These verbs are very important because they are common helping verbs. If you learn to match these subjects and verbs correctly, you may clear up many verb problems. You'll see that although the spellings are irregular, the correct forms for *he, she,* and *it* all end in *s*.

Am/Is/Are	
I	am
he, she, it	is
you, we, they	are

Have/Has	
I, you, we, they	have
he, she, it	has

With only one exception, past-tense verbs do not change form when the subject changes, as in the following example.

I, you, he, she, it, we, they	loved

That exception is *was* and *were*, which follow the same pattern as *is* and *are* unless the subject is *I*.

Was/Were	
I, he, she, it	was
you, we, they	were

Editing hint: Don't forget subject-verb agreement when you use the words *doesn't* and *don't*.

doesn't = does not   don't = do not

The verb *does* matches singular subjects, and the verb *do* matches plural subjects.

He **does** the dishes.   They **do** the dishes.
Joan **does** enjoy jazz.   The Johnsons **do** enjoy jazz.

The same pattern works with the contractions.

He **doesn't** dry the dishes.   They **don't** dry the dishes.
Joan **doesn't** enjoy rock.   The Johnsons **don't** enjoy rock.

If you're not sure whether to use *don't* or *doesn't*, take the contractions apart to test them.

It *(doesn't, don't)* matter to me.

Test: *It does not matter. . . . It do not matter. . . . It* is singular, so *does* agrees with it. Since *it does not* is correct, choose *doesn't.*

It **doesn't** matter to me.

Exercise 15: Basic Subject-Verb Agreement━━━━━

Part A
Directions: Underline the form of the verb that agrees with the subject of each sentence. First decide whether the subject is singular or plural. Then choose the verb that agrees with the subject.

Example: Al Capone *(was*, were) a famous gangland figure in the 1920s.

1. Alice *(doesn't, don't)* work here anymore.

2. We *(was, were)* just getting ready to leave.

3. The Browns' daughters *(moves, move)* to a different apartment every three months.

4. They *(lives, live)* on less than one hundred dollars a week.

5. It *(doesn't, don't)* make any sense.

6. They *(was, were)* here a few minutes ago.

    7. Every other morning Jim *(jogs, jog)* to work. **8.** He *(runs, run)* in good weather and bad. **9.** Even thunderstorms *(doesn't, don't)* stop him. **10.** I *(thinks, think)* that's remarkable.

Part B
Directions: Write a paragraph of at least five sentences describing a daily routine of yours. For subject-verb agreement practice, make *I* the subject of each sentence. Underline every verb, making sure that it agrees with the subject.

Example: Every weekday morning I <u>get</u> up at 5:30.

Part C
Directions: Rewrite the paragraph you wrote in Part B by changing the subjects from *I* to *he* or *she* and making the verbs match. Again, underline every verb.

Example: Every weekday morning he <u>gets</u> up at 5:30.

ANSWERS ARE ON PAGES 316–17.

Special Problems in Subject-Verb Agreement

Some Tricky Patterns

Except for a couple of troublesome speech habits like "we was" and "it don't," you'll probably find that matching verbs to subjects isn't difficult. However, a few sentence patterns can cause problems, either because the subject is hard to find or because it's hard to decide whether the subject is singular or plural. In this section you'll have a chance to practice subject-verb agreement with four tricky patterns: compound subjects, inverted word order, interrupters between subject and verb, and indefinite pronouns as subjects.

Compound Subjects

The subjects of the following sentences are identical, but the verbs are not. Why? Circle the words that differ in the two sentences.

Samantha and Luigi eat out every night.
Samantha or Luigi eats out every night.

When compound subjects are used in a sentence, subject-verb agreement depends on the conjunction used to connect the two subjects. The word *and* joins two things together.

Samantha + Luigi = two people

You could logically substitute the plural pronoun *they* for the two names.

~~Samantha and Luigi~~ *They* eat out every night.

When a compound subject is connected by *and*, the subject is always plural. Therefore the present-tense verb does not end in *s*.

CORRECT: George and his wife **bowl** every Tuesday night.
INCORRECT: George and his wife **bowls** every Tuesday night.

CORRECT: A pen, a ruler, and an eraser **are** in the top desk drawer.
INCORRECT: A pen, a ruler, and an eraser **is** in the top desk drawer.

What happens if the two subjects are linked by *or* instead of *and*? Look at the new sentence.

Samantha or Luigi **eats** out every night.

Now only one person eats out, not two. In this case, the verb agrees with the subject closer to it: *Luigi eats.* The same reasoning applies to the conjunction *nor.* It makes the reader concentrate on one subject at a time.

Neither Samantha nor Luigi **eats** out every night.

The words *or* and *nor* split a compound subject into two choices that are considered one at a time. The verb agrees with the subject closer to it.

This rule is easy to use. If you're checking subject-verb agreement when the subjects are joined by *or* or *nor,* just cover the subject farther from the verb and work with the sentence that's left.

Either John or the twins *(walks, walk)* the dog hourly.

Cover the subject farther from the verb. Is the subject that's left singular or plural? *Twins* is plural. Pick the verb that agrees with the subject: Twins *walk.*

Either John or the twins **walk** the dog hourly.

Now it's your turn:

Either the twins or John *(walks, walk)* the dog hourly.

Cover the subject farther from the verb. Is the subject that's left singular or plural?

_____

Pick the verb that agrees with the subject.

_____

Either the twins or John **walks** the dog hourly.

Notice that reversing the order of the singular and plural subjects requires a different verb choice.

Exercise 16: Compound Subjects

Directions: Underline the correct verb in each sentence below. Refer to the two rules and their explanations on pages 96–97 as much as necessary to answer correctly.

Example: James and Elizabeth *(finds, find)* raw celery disgusting.

1. Neither Melissa nor Saundra *(wants, want)* to be a hockey player forever.

2. Both the subway and the bus *(stops, stop)* near the main post office.

3. Either George or Dorothy *(checks, check)* on their elderly neighbor every evening.

4. A deadbolt lock and a burglar alarm *(provides, provide)* some security against break-ins.

5. Both sweet potatoes and carrots *(contains, contain)* large amounts of vitamin A.

6. Neither North Dakota nor Montana *(is, are)* known for mild winters.

7. Both San Francisco and Boston *(offers, offer)* many opportunities for walking tours.

8. Either a nurse or the parents *(stays, stay)* with the infant at all times.

9. Poor spelling and sloppy handwriting *(interferes, interfere)* with a writer's message.

10. Neither mountainclimbing nor downhill skiing *(appeals, appeal)* to people with a fear of heights.

ANSWERS ARE ON PAGE 317.

Inverted Word Order

You learned in Chapter 2 that subjects sometimes follow verbs in questions and in sentences beginning with *here* or *there*. Here is a common mistake you can learn to avoid:

INCORRECT: Do Jim have an extra pair of shorts?

What is the subject of this sentence? The subject is *Jim*. Does the verb in the sentence agree with the subject? Check: *Jim do have.*
You know now that a singular subject takes a verb that ends in *s*. Would you say *Jim do have* or *Jim does have*?

_____

CORRECT: **Does** Jim have an extra pair of shorts?

Circle the subjects in the sentences below.

Why are disaster films so popular?
Does the audience enjoy violence on a grand scale?
There are several explanations.

Did you circle *films, audience,* and *explanations*? If you had trouble finding the subjects, put the sentences back in normal word order. Rephrase questions as statements, and reverse the order of sentences beginning with *here* or *there*.

Disaster **films are** so popular.
The **audience does enjoy** violence on a grand scale.
Several **explanations are** there.

With the sentences in normal word order, you can easily make the verbs agree with their subjects.

Exercise 17: Verbs Before Subjects

Directions: Circle the subject and underline the verb that agrees with it in each of the following sentences.

Example: Where *(is, <u>are</u>)* my ⟨glasses?⟩

1. There *(is, are)* three sponges playing tag in the kitchen sink.

2. There *(is, are)* a cartoon special on television tonight.

3. Here *(is, are)* the black sock you lost in the wash last week.

4. *(Is, Are)* the car keys in your coat pocket?

5. Where *(is, are)* the morning paper?

6. There *(is, are)* an apple and a ham sandwich in the refrigerator for you.

7. Here *(is, are)* your hat and coat.

8. What *(is, are)* you planning to do on New Year's Eve?

9. Why *(is, are)* the Bulls and the Pistons bitter rivals?

10. When *(does, do)* this country expect to achieve full employment?

11. *(Does, Do)* anyone over six really believe in the Tooth Fairy?

12. *(Has, Have)* this planet entered another ice age?

13. There *(doesn't, don't)* seem to be a doctor in the house.

14. Why *(doesn't, don't)* the government devise a fair tax system?

15. What *(has, have)* the two of you done with my gerbil?

ANSWERS ARE ON PAGE 317.

Interrupters

Prepositional Phrases

Some simple subjects are hard to locate because they're separated from the verb by describing phrases. If you can recognize these phrases, you'll simplify your task of making subject and verb agree. What is the simple subject of the following sentence?

> The price of electricity never goes down.

If you're not sure whether the subject is *price* or *electricity*, find the verb, *goes*, and ask "*Who* or *what* never goes down?" The answer is the simple subject: *price*. The words *of electricity* are an interrupting phrase, called a *prepositional phrase*, that describes *price*.

A *prepositional phrase* is a word group that starts with a preposition and ends with a noun or pronoun. It describes some other word in the sentence.

Here are some common prepositions to look for, with sample prepositional phrases that they might introduce. These phrases are important to recognize because they *never* contain the simple subject of a sentence.

Prepositions	Prepositional Phrases
of	of the three women, of December
in	in the entire universe, in a long line
for	for the little girl, for a new car
to	to the cab company, to them
from	from the president, from Mars
with	with the Doberman, with the beady eyes
on	on the third floor, on television

Other common prepositions include *above, across, at, before, between, down, into, near, through, under,* and *up.*

Use this three-step process to make subjects and verbs agree in sentences with prepositional phrase interrupters. Try the sample sentence below.

The cars on the showroom floor *(is, are)* next year's models.

1. Cross out the prepositional phrase.

   The cars ~~on the showroom floor~~ *(is, are)* next year's models.

2. Circle the simple subject of the sentence. With the phrase blocked off, it's easy to see that *cars* is the subject.

3. Choose the verb that agrees with the subject.

   The (cars) ~~on the showroom floor~~ **are** next year's models.

Try this three-step process with another practice sentence. First, cross out the interrupting phrase. Second, circle the simple subject. Third, underline the correct verb.

A vase of assorted wildflowers *(stands, stand)* on the kitchen table.

The correct sentence would read like this:

A (vase) ~~of assorted wildflowers~~ **stands** on the kitchen table.

Other Interrupters

Watch out for the words in the box at the top of page 101. Sometimes they seem to make the subject plural, but they actually introduce interrupting phrases.

as well as	along with	besides
in addition to	together with	

These phrases are usually easy to spot because they're set off by commas.

> Joan Perez, **along with her three sons**, runs the photocopy shop on Clark Street.

The verb *runs* agrees with the singular subject *Joan Perez*. Subject-verb agreement isn't influenced by the interrupting phrase. Contrast this pattern to a sentence using a compound subject.

> **Joan Perez and her three sons run** the photocopy shop on Clark Street.

In this case, the verb *run* agrees with the compound subject *Joan Perez and sons*. Although the two sentences have essentially the same meaning, the subject-verb agreement patterns are different.

Exercise 18: Interrupters

Directions: Circle the subject, cross out the interrupter, and underline the verb that agrees with the subject in each of the following sentences.

Example: The (dishes) in the sink (is, *are*) clean.

1. A box of butter cookies *(is, are)* sitting on the dining room table.

2. Santa Claus, with the aid of a multitude of spies, *(knows, know)* whether you've been naughty or nice.

3. Five members of the commission *(has, have)* agreed to issue a minority report.

4. Several television specials about John Kennedy *(was, were)* broadcast on the anniversary of his assassination.

5. Several members of the Central City Chamber of Commerce *(has, have)* been suspended for drug abuse.

6. The eggs in this carton *(is, are)* rotten.

7. Snow on open farmlands *(blows, blow)* mercilessly across roads and highways.

8. A charming smile, together with a healthy bank account, *(makes, make)* a bachelor eligible.

9. Ice cubes in an insulated glass *(melts, melt)* slowly even on hot summer days.

10. An unopened package of potato chips *(crunches, crunch)* like dry leaves underfoot.

11. A car loaded with five passengers *(takes, take)* longer to stop than a car with only a driver.

12. The football coach, as well as the team members, *(does, do)* calisthenics every morning.

ANSWERS ARE ON PAGES 317–18.

Indefinite Pronouns

Some subjects are easy to spot but difficult to label as singular or plural. What about the word *everyone*, for instance? Which is correct: *Everyone knows that you're right* or *Everyone know that you're right*? Although we could logically argue that *everyone* clearly means more than one person, the word is always considered singular. *Everyone knows that you're right* is correct.

A whole group of words, called **indefinite pronouns**, are always considered singular in standard written English. You'll learn them easily if you concentrate on the word *one*, *thing*, or *body* at the end of each. These word parts all make you think of *one* or *single*.

Singular Indefinite Pronouns	
each (one)	no one
either (one)	nothing
neither (one)	nobody
one	anyone
someone	anything
something	anybody
somebody	everyone
	everything
	everybody

Note the singular verbs in each of the sample sentences below.

> Nobody **understands** him.
> **Does** anyone **agree** with me?
> Neither of the radios **works**.
> Each of the survivors **gets** an equal share.

Editing hint: Remember to block out any interrupting phrases as you check for subject-verb agreement with indefinite pronouns. Add the word *one* after *each*, *either*, or *neither* to remind yourself that these words are singular.

> Neither of the companies *(employs, employ)* part-time workers.

> Neither *(one)* of the companies **employs** part-time workers.

Not all indefinite pronouns are singular. In fact, the indefinite pronouns in the box below are always plural.

Plural Indefinite Pronouns

both   few   many   several

Many are called. Few are chosen.
Both write extremely well.

Some indefinite pronouns may be either singular or plural depending on their antecedents. (Remember, the noun that a pronoun refers to is called its *antecedent.*)

Singular or Plural Indefinite Pronouns
some   any   none   most   all

Study the examples below. In one sentence, *all* is plural. In the other, *all* is singular. Notice that the verb forms are different.

All of the **snow has** melted.
All of the **candy bars have** disappeared.

In the first sentence, *all* is singular because it refers to *snow,* which is singular. In the second sentence, *all* is plural because it refers to the plural noun *bars.* Is *all* singular or plural in the following example?

All of my money has been stolen.

Because it refers to the singular noun *money, all* is singular in this sentence.

Sometimes you may have to look in an earlier sentence for the pronoun's antecedent. Is *all* singular or plural in the pair of sentences below?

Three other girls used to live on my block. All have moved away.

Because its antecedent is *girls, all* is plural.

Exercise 19: Indefinite Pronouns

Directions: Circle the subject, underline any interrupters, and underline the verb that agrees with the subject in each sentence.

Example. (Each) of the children (*receives*, receive) a prize at the end of the party.

1. Everyone in the club (*wants*, want) to have a party next week.

2. None of the marbles (*belongs*, belong) to Geraldine.

3. Some of the ice from the polar caps *(melts, melt)* each summer.

4. Most of the listeners *(understands, understand)* the speaker's purpose.

5. Few of our neighbors *(likes, like)* our boa constrictor.

6. Someone in the audience *(has, have)* a question.

7. Nobody *(wishes, wish)* to argue with a rattlesnake.

8. All of the cake *(is, are)* gone.

9. All of the pieces of cake *(is, are)* gone.

10. Only one of these dogs *(bites, bite)* without provocation.

11. Anyone with an ounce of brains *(knows, know)* that the earth is round.

12. Many of my friends *(attends, attend)* night classes.

ANSWERS ARE ON PAGE 318.

Exercise 20: Subject-Verb Agreement Review

The purpose of this exercise is to test your understanding of all different patterns of subject-verb agreement. Do the exercise carefully and refer to the rules and explanations on pages 92–103 as much as necessary to answer correctly.

Part A
Directions: Underline the correct verb in each sentence below.

1. One of my pet peeves *(is, are)* people refusing to say hello when they *(enters, enter)* a room.

2. Even nonprescription drugs like aspirin *(causes, cause)* dangerous side effects in some patients.

3. Either credit cards or a personal check *(is, are)* acceptable at that store.

4. Cotton and wool *(provides, provide)* better insulation than most synthetic fibers.

5. Everybody with a lottery ticket *(hopes, hope)* to win the jackpot.

6. Why *(does, do)* the bride and groom exchange rings?

7. Some of the cookie crumbs *(has, have)* fallen onto your shirt.

8. There *(is, are)* several cars stuck on the icy streets.

9. The clown wearing the huge plastic sunglasses *(makes, make)* my daughter giggle.

10. Neither a killer tornado nor flooded streets after the storm *(was, were)* enough to stop the mail delivery.

Part B

Directions: Proofread the passage below for **five errors** in subject-verb agreement and correct them.

Example: Most Americans ~~wants~~ *want* to look trim and youthful.

Is Americans becoming more interested in physical fitness? Evidence from a variety of sources indicate that they are. Jogging, swimming, or even brisk walking are becoming part of the daily routine of millions. In many offices, employees participate in exercise sessions offered by company wellness programs. Buying patterns also indicate an interest in fitness. Some of the most popular books on the market deal with dieting and nutrition. In grocery stores there is large displays of low-calorie meals. Apparently, both men and women in this country hopes to live longer, healthier lives.

ANSWERS ARE ON PAGES 318–19.

Exercise 21: Verb Review

Directions: Read each question carefully, then choose the best answer.

1. **Stan slammed the door shut, <u>throw</u> the car into reverse, and shot down the driveway.**

   Which of the following is the best way to write the underlined portion of this sentence? If you think the original is the best way to write the sentence, choose option (1).

   (1) throw
   (2) throws
   (3) throwed
   (4) threw
   (5) thrown

2. **One of the hottest rock groups in the country <u>was performing</u> at the Metro Stadium last night.**

   Which of the following is the best way to write the underlined portion of this sentence? If you think the original is the best way to write the sentence, choose option (1).

   (1) was performing
   (2) were performing
   (3) is performing
   (4) are performing
   (5) performing

3. **Jim is exhausted. He <u>have just ran</u> in a marathon.**

   Which of the following is the best way to write the underlined portion of this sentence? If you think the original is the best way to write the sentence, choose option (1).

   (1) have just ran
   (2) has just ran
   (3) had just ran
   (4) have just run
   (5) has just run

4. **Rounding the corner, Chuck stopped short and gasped at the sight. Tenants were running from the flaming building, screaming in terror, chokeing on the smoke.**

   What correction should be made to these sentences?

   (1) change *gasped* to *gasps*
   (2) change *running* to *runing*
   (3) change *screaming* to *screamming*
   (4) change *chokeing* to *choking*
   (5) no correction is necessary

5. **Neither Martha nor her seven younger brothers <u>sings</u>, "Hi-ho, hi-ho," on the way to work.**

   Which of the following is the best way to write the underlined portion of this sentence? If you think the original is the best way to write the sentence, choose option (1).

   (1) sings
   (2) sing
   (3) is singing
   (4) has sung
   (5) was singing

6. **Later this year, the company <u>was adding</u> a second shift to boost production.**

   Which of the following is the best way to write the underlined portion of this sentence? If you think the original is the best way to write the sentence, choose option (1).

   (1) was adding
   (2) has added
   (3) will add
   (4) have added
   (5) were adding

7. **Two small boys crept up to the house, rung the doorbell, then ran to the side of the house and hid behind a huge lilac bush.**

   What correction should be made to this sentence?

   (1) change *crept* to *creeped*
   (2) change *rung* to *rang*
   (3) change *ran* to *run*
   (4) change *hid* to *hidden*
   (5) no correction is necessary

8. **The little canary sat on its perch and sang its heart out. Meanwhile, a huge gray cat was laying below the cage, planning its attack.**

   What correction should be made to these sentences?

   (1) change *sat* to *set*
   (2) change *sang* to *sung*
   (3) change *laying* to *lying*
   (4) change *planning* to *planing*
   (5) no correction is necessary

9. **"Do every town in this state have a statue of a colonel on horseback?" she asked, grinning.**

   What correction should be made to this sentence?

   (1) change *Do* to *Does*
   (2) change *have* to *has*
   (3) change *asked* to *ask*
   (4) change *grinning* to *grining*
   (5) no correction is necessary

10. **"Would you rather lie on the beach or sit on the veranda?"**
    "It don't matter to me. I've done all my work today."

    What correction should be made to these sentences?

    (1) change *lie* to *lay*
    (2) change *sit* to *set*
    (3) change *don't* to *doesn't*
    (4) change *done* to *did*
    (5) no correction is necessary

11. **Last night at 8:00, my friend and I were listening to the radio, making lasagna, and sipping his home-brewed mulberry wine.**

    What correction should be made to this sentence?

    (1) change *were* to *was*
    (2) change *listening* to *listenning*
    (3) change *making* to *makeing*
    (4) change *sipping* to *siping*
    (5) no correction is necessary

12. **By 9:00 we had drunk two liters of wine, broken three plates, tiped over the radio, and forgotten about the lasagna.**

    What correction should be made to this sentence?

    (1) change *drunk* to *drank*
    (2) change *broken* to *broke*
    (3) change *tiped* to *tipped*
    (4) change *forgotten* to *forgot*
    (5) no correction is necessary

13. **According to police reports, neither of the suspects <u>were carrying</u> a gun at the time.**

    Which of the following is the best way to write the underlined portion of this sentence? If you think the original is the best way to write the sentence, choose option (1).

    (1) were carrying
    (2) was carrying
    (3) were carring
    (4) was carring
    (5) was carrieing

14. **At the moment, Shirley <u>was raking</u> leaves. She should be finished soon.**

    Which of the following is the best way to write the underlined portion of this sentence? If you think the original is the best way to write the sentence, choose option (1).

    (1) was raking
    (2) raked
    (3) has raked
    (4) will rake
    (5) is raking

15. **Frank brung his car over yesterday. We spent four hours on it last night and took two more this morning to wash and wax it. Now it looks brand-new.**

    What correction should be made to these sentences?

    (1) change *brung* to *brought*
    (2) change *spent* to *spend*
    (3) change *took* to *take*
    (4) change *looks* to *look*
    (5) no correction is necessary

ANSWERS ARE ON PAGE 319.

Chapter 3 Review Evaluation Chart

Question Type	Review Pages	Question Number	Number of Questions	Number Correct
Choosing correct tense	71–80	6, 14	2	/2
Spelling of verb forms	80–83	4, 12	2	/2
Irregular verb form	83–91	1, 3, 7, 8, 15	5	/5
Subject-verb agreement	92–105	2, 5, 9, 10, 13	5	/5
No error		11	1	/1

Passing score: 11 right out of 15 questions

Your score: _____ right out of 15 questions

If you missed more than one question in any of the categories listed above, review the pages indicated in the chart.

Cumulative Review

Editing Practice

Part A

Directions: Find and correct the eleven errors contained in the following passage. Four of these errors are related to skills that you learned in Chapter 2: sentence structure, nouns, and pronouns. You may want to review the checklist on page 57 to refresh your memory on what to look for. The other seven errors are related to verbs. To locate them, use this checklist as your proofreading guide.

☐ Do present-tense verbs agree in number with their subjects?

☐ Is the correct verb tense used for each sentence and for the passage as a whole?

☐ Are irregular verb forms used correctly?

☐ Are regular verb forms spelled correctly?

As a child I loved having a yard full of trees. I climbed the smaller ones and set for hours on the lower branchs. Munching apples and reading. Often my friends and me used the trees for Wild West games. The outlaw laid in wait behind their broad trunks, and prepared to spring out at unsuspecting settlers. During the long summer days, our laughter mingles with bird songs and the chatterring of squirrels.

Now I stare out of my apartment onto a barren parking lot and remembered those days with a sigh. Is some other children haveing the time of their lives in my old trees today?

ANSWERS ARE ON PAGE 319.

Part B

Directions: Using the checklist from Part A, proofread and correct the two paragraphs that you wrote for Exercise 3 on page 70.

ANSWERS WILL VARY.

★ **GED PRACTICE** ★

Multiple-Choice Practice

Directions: Read each passage completely, looking for possible errors. Then answer the questions that follow concerning individual sentences in the passage.

(1) Why is dogs such popular pets worldwide? (2) They are messier then cats and less intelligent than pigs. (3) They can't be kept in cages. (4) Like hamsters and parakeets. (5) Yet not one of these other animals has been refered to as "man's best friend." (6) One reason for the popularity of dogs are their loyalty. (7) By nature following the leader of the pack just like wolves and coyotes. (8) In a dog's case, the leader of the pack had been a human being. (9) A properly trained dog obeys it's master's commands enthusiastically.

1. Sentence 1: **Why is dogs such popular pets worldwide?**

   Which of the following is the best way to write the underlined portion of this sentence? If you think the original is the best way to write the sentence, choose option (1).

   (1) is dogs
   (2) was dogs
   (3) are dogs
   (4) is dogs being
   (5) has dogs been

2. Sentence 2: **They are messier than cats and less intelligent than pigs.**

   What correction should be made to this sentence?

   (1) change *are* to *is*
   (2) insert a comma after *cats*
   (3) replace *cats and* with *cats. And*
   (4) insert a comma after *and*
   (5) no correction is necessary

3. Sentences 3 and 4: **They can't be <u>kept in cages. Like</u> hamsters and parakeets.**

   Which of the following is the best way to write the underlined portion of these sentences? If you think the original is the best way to write the sentences, choose option (1).

   (1) kept in cages. Like
   (2) kept in cages like
   (3) kept in cage's like
   (4) keeped in cages. Like
   (5) keeped in cages like

4. Sentence 5: **Yet not one of these other animals has been refered to as "man's best friend."**

   What correction should be made to this sentence?

   (1) insert a comma after *animals*
   (2) change *has* to *have*
   (3) change *refered* to *referred*
   (4) change *man's* to *mans*
   (5) no correction is necessary

5. Sentence 6: **One reason for the popularity of dogs are their loyalty.**

   What correction should be made to this sentence?

   (1) change *dogs* to *dog's*
   (2) insert a comma after *dogs*
   (3) change *are* to *is*
   (4) insert a comma after *are*
   (5) no correction is necessary

6. Sentence 7: **By nature following the leader of the pack just like wolves and coyotes.**

   What correction should be made to this sentence?

   (1) replace *following* with *they follow*
   (2) replace *pack just* with *pack. Just*
   (3) change *wolves* to *wolfs*
   (4) insert a comma after *wolves*
   (5) change *coyotes* to *coyote's*

7. Sentence 8: **In a dog's case, the leader of the pack had been a human being.**

   Which of the following is the best way to write the underlined portion of this sentence? If you think the original is the best way to write the sentence, choose option (1).

   (1) had been
   (2) have been
   (3) was
   (4) is
   (5) are

8. Sentence 9: **A properly trained dog obeys it's master's commands enthusiastically.**

   What correction should be made to this sentence?

   (1) change *obeys* to *obeying*
   (2) change *it's* to *its*
   (3) change *master's* to *masters*
   (4) change *commands* to *command's*
   (5) no correction is necessary

(1) Today some of the world's richest farmland was located in the American Midwest. (2) Thousands of acres of corn soybeans, and wheat cover flat plains and gently rolling hills. (3) Occasionally a grove of trees or a grain silo raises above the landscape. (4) Dairy and beef cattle graze in green fields under cottony skys. (5) Our ancestors seen a much different picture. (6) Two hundred years ago the Midwest was coverred with prairie grass and forests. (7) There were no neat farmsteads or parallel rows of grain. (8) Herds of shaggy bison roam the plains. (9) Only the clouds were the same.

9. Sentence 1: **Today some of the world's richest farmland was located in the American Midwest.**

   Which of the following is the best way to write the underlined portion of this sentence? If you think the original is the best way to write the sentence, choose option (1).

   (1) was located
   (2) is located
   (3) is locate
   (4) will locate
   (5) had located

10. Sentence 2: **Thousands of acres of corn soybeans, and wheat cover flat plains and gently rolling hills.**

    What correction should be made to this sentence?

    (1) insert a comma after *corn*
    (2) insert a comma after *wheat*
    (3) change *cover* to *covers*
    (4) change *plains* to *plaines*
    (5) insert a comma after *plains*

11. Sentence 3: **Occasionally a grove of trees or a grain silo raises above the landscape.**

    Which of the following is the best way to write the underlined portion of this sentence? If you think the original is the best way to write the sentence, choose option (1).

    (1) raises
    (2) raise
    (3) is raising
    (4) rises
    (5) rise

12. Sentence 4: **Dairy and beef cattle graze in green fields under cottony skys.**

What correction should be made to this sentence?

(1) insert a comma after *dairy*
(2) change *graze* to *grazing*
(3) replace *fields under* with *fields. Under*
(4) change *skys* to *skies*
(5) no correction is necessary

13. Sentence 5: **Our ancestors <u>seen</u> a much different picture.**

Which of the following is the best way to write the underlined portion of this sentence? If you think the original is the best way to write the sentence, choose option (1).

(1) seen
(2) saw
(3) seed
(4) had saw
(5) have saw

14. Sentence 6: **Two hundred years ago the Midwest <u>was covered</u> with prairie grass and forests.**

Which of the following is the best way to write the underlined portion of this sentence? If you think the original is the best way to write the sentence, choose option (1).

(1) was coverred
(2) was covered
(3) was cover
(4) were coverred
(5) were covered

15. Sentence 7: **There were no neat farmsteads or parallel rows of grain.**

What correction should be made to this sentence?

(1) change *were* to *was*
(2) change *farmsteads* to *farmstead's*
(3) insert a comma after *farmsteads*
(4) change *rows* to *rowes*
(5) no correction is necessary

16. Sentence 8: **Herds of shaggy bison <u>roam</u> the plains.**

Which of the following is the best way to write the underlined portion of this sentence? If you think the original is the best way to write the sentence, choose option (1).

(1) roam
(2) roaming
(3) are roaming
(4) have roamed
(5) roamed

ANSWERS ARE ON PAGES 319–20.

Cumulative Review Evaluation Chart

Questions From	Question Number	Number of Questions	Number Correct
Chapter 2 Fragments, Nouns, and Pronouns	3, 6, 8, 10, 12	5	/5
Chapter 3 Verbs	1, 4, 5, 7, 9, 11, 13, 14, 16	9	/9
No error	2, 15	2	/2

Passing score: 12 right out of 16 questions

Your score: _____ out of 16 questions

4

◪PATTERNS OF ORGANIZATION

In Chapter 3 you learned that a good paragraph should have a topic sentence backed by specific, relevant supporting sentences. The paragraph below meets these standards. Do you rate it a good paragraph?

> If you drive a car, you should become familiar with this simple procedure to change a flat tire. Remove the flat and replace it with a spare tire. Place a jack under the car near the flat tire and raise the car far enough to lift the tire off the ground. Lower the car, remove the blocks, and be sure to put the tools back in the trunk. Use a lug wrench to loosen the nuts holding the tire on the axle. Block the wheels opposite the flat with bricks or large stones to keep the car from rolling. Tighten the lug nuts as much as possible.

The answer to the question is clear: this paragraph is a disaster! Although it has a main idea supported by specific details, the explanation is too disorganized to follow. To change a flat, what should you do first? second? third? After reading this paragraph, who could tell? To our definition of a good paragraph, we must add one final rule:

A good paragraph must be well organized.

The best way to organize a paragraph will vary depending on the topic and purpose of the paragraph. In this chapter you'll study four useful patterns of organization: time order, cause and effect, comparison and contrast, and simple listing. These patterns are not just ways to organize sentences. They are also ways to organize your thinking, as you will see in the following pages.

Time Order

When to Use Time Order

You want to tell a beginning cook how to make great spaghetti sauce. You have to file an accident report on a fender-bender you were involved in yesterday. In a letter to a friend, you decide to describe a typical day at your new job as a salesclerk. How could you organize your information in each case?

The most logical choice is to use time order. You would place your supporting sentences in the order in which events occur.

When To Use a Time Order Pattern

1. To list steps in a process

2. To explain how something works

3. To describe a routine

4. To tell about an event

Organizing Details in Time Order

Paragraphs requiring time order practically organize themselves. After brainstorming a list of details, you simply need to ask yourself which happens first, second, third, and so on. Number your list accordingly. An organized list for the scrambled paragraph at the beginning of this chapter appears below as a sample.

How to Change a Flat

⑤ Remove flat and replace with spare

② Put jack under car

③ Jack car up

⑦ Lower car

⑧ Remove blocks and replace tools

④ Use lug wrench to loosen nuts

① Block wheels with bricks

⑥ Tighten lug nuts

The paragraph from page 113 was rewritten using this list as a guide. Note how much easier the directions are to follow now that they're sequenced in time order. Circle the words like *first* that alert the reader that the writer is moving from one step to another.

> If you drive a car, you should become familiar with this simple procedure to change a flat tire. First block the wheels opposite the flat with bricks or large stones to keep the car from rolling. Then place a jack under the car near the flat tire and jack the car up enough to lift the tire off the ground. Use a lug wrench to loosen the nuts holding the tire on the axle. Remove the flat and replace it with a spare tire. Using the wrench again, tighten the lug nuts as much as possible. Finally, lower the car, remove the blocks, and put the tools back in the trunk so you'll have them for your next emergency.

You should have circled the words *first, then,* and *finally.* These are called **transition words**. Writers often use transition words to give readers clues to how ideas fit together. You'll study more about transition words in Chapter 6.

Exercise 1: Using Time Order

Directions: Number each brainstorm list below in time order. The first few items in List 1 have been marked as an example.

1. Recent Presidents of the United States

   (a) __2__ Ford

   (b) _____ Reagan

   (c) __3__ Carter

   (d) __1__ Nixon

   (e) _____ Bush

2. How to make a cake using a mix

   (a) _____ Bake at 350 degrees about 30 minutes

   (b) _____ Blend ingredients until moist

   (c) _____ Place mix, ⅓ cup oil, and 3 eggs in mixing bowl

   (d) _____ Beat blended mixture for 2 minutes

   (e) _____ Pour into greased cake pan

   (f) _____ Cool completely before frosting

3. Steps for planning a piece of writing

   (a) _____ Brainstorm a list of details

   (b) _____ Analyze what you're writing about and why

   (c) _____ Organize the list logically

4. My disastrous morning

    (a) _____ Argument with boss

    (b) _____ Burned toast for breakfast

    (c) _____ Alarm didn't go off at 6:00

    (d) _____ Missed bus

    (e) _____ Woke up at 7:30

ANSWERS ARE ON PAGE 320.

Exercise 2: Writing in Time Order

Directions: A friend from out of state is coming to visit you for the first time. Using some logical starting point like the edge of town or the nearest airport, railroad station, or bus depot, write a paragraph describing how to reach your home from that spot.

Writing Steps

    ☐ Brainstorm a list of the steps your friend would need to take.

    ☐ Cross out irrelevant details.

    ☐ Add helpful reference points like traffic lights or store names.

    ☐ Number the list in time order.

    ☐ Write a paragraph based on your list.

Revising Your Paragraph

You may find you want to make some changes in your paragraph now that you have written it. First make any changes you now know you want to make. Then check your paragraph against this checklist and make any further revisions that would improve your writing.

    ☐ Is there a topic sentence?

    ☐ Does the topic sentence state the central point of the paragraph?

    ☐ Are the supporting sentences arranged in time order?

ANSWERS WILL VARY.

Cause and Effect

When to Use Cause and Effect

You've missed work more than three days, and you're required to submit a written explanation of the reason for your absence. An accident on the assembly line has placed two workers in the hospital; as safety inspector, you must investigate and report on the causes. Your local school board will vote next week on closing the elementary school in your neighborhood; you decide to write the board a letter explaining how the closing would harm the community. How could you organize your writing for these projects?

Although time order might be involved in your organization, your purpose will not just be to relate a series of events in the sequence they occurred. In these cases you must tell *why* something has happened or *what will result* if a certain action is taken. That is, you'll need to trace **causes** and **effects**.

You use the cause-effect thought pattern often in everyday life. How many times have you asked questions like "Why didn't I get a raise this year? Why has Steve been so moody lately? How would my family react if I decided to take some college courses? Why didn't I get that job?"

This pattern is also used more formally by historians, scientists, and public policy makers: What were the causes of our involvement in the Vietnam War? What effect does cigarette smoking have on our lungs? What would happen if we raised federal income taxes to improve welfare programs? How has the use of computers affected our society?

When to Use a Cause-Effect Pattern

1. To trace the reasons why an event occurred

2. To trace the results of an event

3. To predict the results of an event

What to Include

Suppose you've been asked to contribute a short article on cigarette smoking by teens to your PTA newsletter. You would like to explain why teens smoke regardless of the publicity about the dangers of smoking. What details might you use in your article?

The word *why* is the clue to the kinds of details to include. You are looking for causes of teens' smoking. On the next page is a sample brainstorming list for your article. Place a check next to the items that would *not* belong in your article.

Why Teens Smoke

_____ 1. think they look like adults

_____ 2. rebellion against authority

_____ 3. increased chance of lung cancer

_____ 4. desire to do what their friends do

_____ 5. more girls smoking now than twenty years ago

Did you mark items 3 and 5? These are not possible causes for cigarette smoking by teens. Item 3 is an effect, not a cause, of cigarette smoking, so it doesn't belong in the paragraph. Item 5 provides information about how many girls are smoking, but it doesn't explain *why* they smoke. So now you have three good supporting ideas for your paragraph.

From these three causes, you can write a solid paragraph for your article. Here's a sample of what you might say. Underline the topic sentence and number each cause from the brainstorming list as you locate it below.

> Young teens experiment with cigarette smoking for a variety of reasons. Some kids get started because they associate smoking with adulthood. If Mom and Dad finish two packs of Marlboros a day, why shouldn't they? At the same time, smoking gives kids a chance to rebel against authority. The more their teachers and parents warn them not to smoke, the more eager they are to try it. But probably the most powerful influence on young teens is their peers. They don't want to be called "square" or "goody-goody" by their friends.

Let's look at a second example of cause-effect thinking. Suppose that you're writing a letter to a friend in which you describe how your decision to go back to school for your GED has affected the rest of your family. What kinds of details would you write about in your letter?

The key word in your topic is *affected*. You want to describe the **effects** of your decision on your family. Here's a sample brainstorming list one writer made for this topic. Place a check next to the items that would *not* belong in her letter.

_____ **1.** friends tease me, but I know they're proud of me

_____ **2.** kids take more responsibility for housework—do some of the cooking and cleaning to give me time to study

_____ **3.** kids more serious about doing their own schoolwork

_____ **4.** husband a little anxious; wonders whether I'll still look up to him if I have a diploma and he doesn't

_____ **5.** need a diploma to get a better job

You should have checked items 1 and 5. Item 1 is irrelevant since it describes the reactions of friends, not family. Item 5 deals with a reason for going back to school, not an effect. But she still has plenty of good material left for her letter.

Her finished letter might look something like the paragraph below. Underline the topic sentence. Number each of the items you just saw in the brainstorming list as you come to them in the paragraph.

> When I decided to go back to school for my GED, I had no idea how much the decision would affect Steve and the kids. Steve doesn't say too much, but he seems a little anxious when he sees me studying. Last night he asked me whether I would still respect him if I had a diploma and he didn't. The kids, on the other hand, are really proud of me. Both Jason and Rick have been taking more responsibility for the housework. They're sharing some of the cooking and cleaning jobs to give me more time to study. Best of all, they're getting more serious about their own schoolwork. Often, all three of us sit down and hit the books together.

Exercise 3: Practicing Cause and Effect

Directions: Each of the following topics asks you to identify either causes or effects. For each topic, brainstorm a list of ideas you could include in a paragraph about that topic. Then read over your list carefully and cross out any ideas that don't really fit. For now, you don't need to write the paragraph—just brainstorm.

Example: What are some of the causes of people's overeating?

> *portions too big in restaurants*
> ~~*lots of people are overweight*~~
> *people eat too fast*
> *we're taught to clean our plates*
> *sometimes you just feel like munching*

1. What are some of the effects of smoking?

2. What causes people to want to live in suburbs instead of in cities?

3. Why do people want to own cars?

4. For one reason or another, you stopped your traditional education before completing high school. What effects has leaving school had on your life?

A SAMPLE BRAINSTORM LIST IS ON PAGE 320.

Exercise 4: Writing Cause-and-Effect Paragraphs

Directions: Choose **two** of the topics from Exercise 3. Write paragraphs based on your brainstorm lists for the two topics you choose.

You may find you want to make some changes in your paragraphs after you have written them. First make any changes you now know you want to make. Then check your paragraphs against the checklist on page 120 and make any further revisions that would improve your writing.

Revision Checklist

☐ Is there a topic sentence?

☐ Does the topic sentence state the cause-effect relationship you discuss in the paragraph?

☐ Do all the other sentences further develop the cause-effect relationship?

A SAMPLE PARAGRAPH IS ON PAGE 320.

Comparison and Contrast

When to Use Comparison-Contrast

You're writing a letter to the editor explaining why you favor Candidate A over Candidate B for mayor. Your company is buying a microwave for the coffee room, and your boss has asked you to investigate and report on the merits of three leading brands. You've just moved from Detroit to Denver, and you want to write a Michigan friend about your impression of the similarities and differences between the two cities. How could you organize your thinking and writing in each instance? Your task in these cases is to show how things are alike or different—in other words, to **compare** and **contrast** them.

Like the cause-and-effect pattern, comparison-contrast thinking is often used in both everyday and formal situations. Have you ever had to decide which of two apartments to rent? which job to apply for? which person to date? If so, you've probably compared and contrasted your choices before deciding. It's the same process that an economist uses to compare communism to capitalism or that an astronomer uses to see how Mercury and Jupiter differ.

When to Use a Comparison-Contrast Pattern

1. To describe similarities or differences

2. To explain advantages and disadvantages

Planning a Comparison-Contrast Paragraph

Writing a comparison-contrast paragraph requires careful planning to help your reader understand exactly how your subjects are alike or different. Using a chart in the planning step will help you organize your thinking.

To construct your chart, make three columns. Label the middle and right-hand columns with the names of the subjects you're comparing. Label the column on the left "Items to Discuss."

Items to Discuss	Subject A	Subject B

Let's take an example to see how the chart works. Suppose you're buying a new car. You are seriously considering two cars. You want to compare and contrast the two cars to see which would be the better car for you. What aspects of the cars will you discuss?

The price is very important, but you want to know you're getting a good car for your money. You want to get good gas mileage, and you want to buy a model with a good repair record. You decide that interior room is important because you have a family of four. These qualities are the "items to discuss." List them in the left-hand column of the chart.

Items to Discuss	Ford Aristo	Dodge Lido
Price		
Gas mileage		
Repair record		
Interior room		

Now you're ready to fill in the information you've gathered about the two cars.

Items to Discuss	Ford Aristo	Dodge Lido
Price	$7,125	$7,775
Gas mileage	25 city 32 highway	28 city 36 highway
Repair record	better than average	average
Interior room	fits 2 adults comfortably in backseat	2 kids comfortable in backseat but not two adults

Now the chart is filled in with supporting details that you can use in the paragraph. At this point you have a choice on how to organize it. You may decide to choose a **whole-to-whole pattern**; that is, write everything you have to say about one car and then go on to the other car, as in the sample paragraph below.

On the whole, I think a new Ford Aristo is a better value than a new Dodge Lido. The Aristo costs $7,125. It gets 25 city miles per gallon and 32 highway miles per gallon. Furthermore, the repair record on this model is better than average. Another advantage of the Aristo is its roomy rear seat, which is big enough for two adults to ride in comfortably. On the other hand, the Dodge Lido is also a nice car. At $7,775, it costs more than the Aristo. It gets better gas mileage too, with 28 city and 36 highway miles per gallon. However, it has only an average repair record. In addition, the Lido has a smaller rear seat. In a few years, my kids might not fit back there! It looks like the Aristo is a better value for me.

Often, you'll find that your reader will understand your comparisons more easily if you compare your subjects **point by point**; that is, take up one discussion item at a time, as in the paragraph below.

On the whole, I think a new Ford Aristo is a better value than a new Dodge Lido. At $7,125, the Aristo costs less to purchase than the $7,775 Lido. The main advantage of the Lido is gas mileage. The Lido gets 28 city miles per gallon and 36 on the highway, while the Aristo gets 25 in the city and 32 on the highway. However, the Lido could cost more to operate in the long run because its repair record is not as good as the Aristo's. In addition, the Aristo has a very roomy rear seat. I'm afraid my kids would outgrow the backseat of the Lido in a couple of years. It looks like the Aristo is a better value for me.

Exercise 5: Writing Comparison-Contrast Paragraphs

Directions: There are two comparison-contrast topics below. For each,

- Make a chart like the one in the example and fill it in with the details you would like to write about in your paragraph.
- Decide whether you want to write your paragraph whole to whole, like the first example on pages 121–22, or point by point, like the second example on page 122.
- Write your paragraph.

Part of the first chart is shown to help you get started.

1. Compare and contrast eating a meal in a restaurant with eating at home.

Items to Discuss	Eating in a Restaurant	Eating at Home
1. cost	paying someone else to do the work costs more	cooking and cleaning up yourself is cheap
2. convenience		

2. People become close friends because they have something in common: background, attitudes, or interests. Yet no two people are exactly alike. How are you and your best friend alike? How are you different? Write a paragraph comparing the two of you.

Revising Your Paragraphs

When you have finished writing your paragraphs, you may find you want to make some changes in them. First make any changes you know now you want to make. Then check your paragraphs against this checklist and make any further revisions that would improve your writing.

☐ Is there a topic sentence?

☐ Does the topic sentence state what you are comparing and contrasting?

☐ Do all the other sentences support the point that it makes?

☐ Are the sentences arranged in a logical order that will assist the reader in understanding the paragraph?

A SAMPLE CHART AND PARAGRAPH ARE ON PAGE 321.

Simple Listing

When to Use Simple Listing

You're writing a letter to an out-of-state friend describing the tourist attractions in your area. You've been asked to write a brief summary of the fringe benefits offered by your company. In a job reference letter for a friend, you want to include a paragraph giving examples of your friend's problem-solving skills. How could you organize your writing in these situations?

For this kind of topic, no particular thought pattern imposes itself on your writing. Your supporting details can be presented in almost any order without causing confusion because they are related to one another only as specific examples of the main idea. The organization you need is simple listing.

You use simple listing to answer ordinary questions like "What things do you dislike about your job? What entrees are on the menu at the Royal Rib? What do you like about living near the ocean?" In more formal situations, simple listing might be used to answer such questions as "What are the arguments against the latest tax reform plan?" or "What are the different classes of mammals?"

When to Use a Simple Listing Pattern

1. To give examples to support a main point

2. To list characteristics of an item

3. To break a large group into smaller categories

Putting the List in Order

Although no particular order is required for details when the simple listing pattern is used, you may want to establish your own order: smallest to largest, least to most unusual, least to most important. In the following sample paragraph, least to most important order has been used.

> During the five years that Jacob Van Keulen worked for me, he was my most valuable employee. Mr. Van Keulen never called in sick, nor did he leave work early for any reason. On the job he produced 20 percent more parts than anyone else on the line. In fact, his time-saving suggestions resulted in a 10 percent increase in productivity for the plant as a whole.

Exercise 6: Using the Simple Listing Pattern

Directions: As part of a job application letter, you want to include a paragraph listing your qualifications for the job. Pick a job for which you feel qualified and write that paragraph. Take at least ten minutes to plan your paragraph before you write.

After you write your paragraph, take a few minutes to revise it. Make sure you have written a clear topic sentence and that your reader will be able to understand what you have written.

ANSWERS WILL VARY.

Reading Essay Questions

Part of your task on Part 2 of the GED Writing Skills Test will be to choose an appropriate pattern of organization for your essay. Often a clue word or phrase in the test question will help you pick the right pattern. For instance, in an earlier exercise, the following directions were given: *How are you and your best friend alike? How are you different? Write a paragraph comparing the two of you.* Circle the words that provided clues to the pattern of organization.

Did you find *alike*, *different*, and *comparing*?

Some common terms associated with each pattern of organization are listed on the next page.

Time Order	Comparison and Contrast	Simple Listing
how to	compare	list
an incident or event	contrast	kinds of
the process	similarities	types of
the procedure	alike	examples
	different	
Cause and Effect	favor	
reasons for	prefer	
causes of	better	
effects of		
results of		
why		

Exercise 7: Reading Essay Questions

Directions: Label the pattern of organization (time order, cause and effect, comparison/contrast, or simple listing) that each question requires and circle the terms in the question that provide a clue to the pattern.

Example: *time order* (Explain how) to change the oil in a car.

_____ 1. Is baseball or football a more typically American game?

_____ 2. Why are guns so common in the United States?

_____ 3. Explain how to calm an angry toddler.

_____ 4. What effect has the use of antibiotics had on society?

_____ 5. Compare the advantages of living at home with your parents to living alone in an apartment.

_____ 6. List ways that young teens might earn extra money.

_____ 7. Give examples of some tourist attractions in your state.

_____ 8. Trace the causes of unemployment in your city.

_____ 9. Describe an embarrassing incident in your life.

_____ 10. Discuss the reasons for or against a national lottery.

ANSWERS ARE ON PAGE 321.

Chapter Highlights: Patterns of Organization

1. A good paragraph must be well organized.

2. A time order pattern is used to describe processes, routines, and events.

3. A cause-effect pattern is used to trace reasons for an event and to trace or predict results.

4. A comparison-contrast pattern is used to describe similarities or differences and to explain advantages or disadvantages.

5. A simple listing pattern is used to give examples, list characteristics, and categorize.

6. Check for clues to patterns of organization in essay test questions.

★ GED PRACTICE ★

Exercise 8: GED Writing Topic

Directions: To help you prepare for Part 2 of the GED Writing Skills Test, a sample writing topic is included with Chapter 4 and each of the following chapters in this book. Try writing on this topic within the forty-five-minute limit that you will have on the actual test. Put all the writing skills to use that you have learned so far in paragraph construction, sentence structure, word choice, punctuation, and spelling.

Be sure to take ten minutes or so for planning. Read the question carefully to determine topic, purpose, audience, and probable pattern of organization. Circle any words that give clues to a particular pattern. Brainstorm a list of details. Finally, after you write your paragraph, save the last five minutes to edit it.

> During the past thirty years, television has become a core part of American life. Nearly every household has at least one television set. Some people say that television has benefited our society, while others see it as a cause of many problems. Explain how television has affected you. Support your explanation with specific examples.

A SAMPLE PARAGRAPH IS ON PAGE 321.

 Journal Writing

Are you writing in your journal regularly? If so, you are getting valuable writing practice. Try writing on one or more of the following topics in your journal. Or think of your own topics. Remember, you're just writing for yourself. No one else needs to read your journal.

- What have you learned about yourself since you have been learning to write? Do you think you will continue to write even after you have completed the GED Writing Skills Test? Why or why not?

- Describe a favorite place of yours in detail. Try to cover all five senses in your description—sight, sound, smell, touch, and taste.

- Write about a trip you have been on. How did you get where you were going? What was traveling like? What did you do? Whom did you meet?

23 COMBINING IDEAS IN SENTENCES

Two versions of the same paragraph appear below. Which version sounds better to you?

> America has often been called the land of opportunity. My mother first came to this country at age eighteen. Her opportunities were limited indeed. She had no money for a place of her own. She boarded with her uncle and aunt. Her first year in America was spent working in a restaurant for her uncle. He was the head chef there. Mom's job was to carry heavy tubs of dirty forks, knives, and spoons into the kitchen. She was too proud to tell her parents about her real work. She wrote home, "I'm in charge of silverware!"

> America has often been called the land of opportunity, but when my mother first came to this country at age eighteen, her opportunities were limited indeed. Because she had no money for a place of her own, she boarded with her uncle and aunt. Her first year in America was spent working in a restaurant for her uncle, who was the head chef there. Mom's job was to carry heavy tubs of dirty forks, knives, and spoons into the kitchen. She was too proud to tell her parents about her real work, so she wrote home, "I'm in charge of silverware!"

Although the first version is grammatically correct, its sentences are all short and choppy, and the connections between them are not always clear. The second version is a definite improvement. The writer has combined sentences by using connecting words and punctuation, creating logical, smooth links among ideas.

Circle the connecting words that have been added in the second version. These words—*but, when, because, who,* and *so*—and others like them convert simple sentences into more complicated structures. Many of these structures are already part of your spoken English. In this section you'll learn to choose the correct wording and punctuation when you write them. As you study the next few pages, notice how often the connecting words help to reveal time order, cause-effect, comparison-contrast, and simple listing relationships.

Throughout this section, we'll be using a term you should become familiar with: *clause.*

A *clause* is a group of words containing a subject and a verb.

We'll look at two kinds of clauses on the following pages: independent clauses and dependent clauses.

Linking Independent Clauses

Compound Sentences

How might you combine each pair of sentences?

> My mother hauled tubs of silverware at the restaurant. Her cousin poured coffee.
> Their uncle hired them. He didn't pay them well.
> The girls had borrowed money for their tickets to America. They had to work to repay their loans.

Although you have several possibilities, the simplest way to combine related ideas is to make a **compound sentence**. Here are the combined sentences:

> My mother hauled tubs of silverware, **and** her cousin poured coffee.
> Their uncle hired them, **but** he didn't pay them well.
> The girls had borrowed money for their tickets to America, **so** they had to work to repay their loans.

A *compound sentence* contains two or more connected independent clauses. Each clause is independent in that it could stand alone as a sentence. An **independent clause** makes a complete statement by itself.

Conjunctions

The examples above show the most common method of connecting independent clauses in a compound sentence: using a comma followed by a conjunction. You learned a few conjunctions when you studied compound elements in Chapter 2. Here's a complete list of conjunctions that link independent clauses.

Conjunctions	Use
and	adds related information
but yet	shows an opposite or unexpected situation
or	presents a choice
nor	shows a rejection of both choices

for	links effect to cause
so	links cause to effect

Dan mowed the lawn, **and** Sue raked it.

Dan enjoyed the work, **but** Sue hated it.

Sue hated the work, **yet** she completed it.

Please be quiet, **or** I'll ask you to leave.

I won't be quiet, **nor** will I leave.

She left the dinner table, **for** she hated artichokes.

They served artichokes, **so** she left the table.

When clauses are combined with these conjunctions, the wording of both clauses is unchanged except when *nor* is used. Then the subject and verb in the second clause are reversed.

He doesn't like anchovies. He doesn't like pizza.
He doesn't like anchovies, nor **does he** like pizza.

He hasn't called. He hasn't sent a letter.
He hasn't called, **nor has he** sent a letter.

Compound Sentences

INDEPENDENT CLAUSE   CONJUNCTION   INDEPENDENT CLAUSE
My son jumped off the garage roof,   but   he wasn't hurt.

Editing hint: Check to be sure the second part of any compound sentence is really an independent clause by using the tests for a complete sentence. Remember, an independent clause can stand on its own as a sentence. Here are the tests for a complete sentence or an independent clause: (1) The sentence must have a subject. (2) The sentence must have a predicate. Remember that the predicate contains the verb. (3) The sentence must express a complete thought.

The following sentence contains a very common compound sentence error. Can you find it?

Jacob went to the refrigerator, and pulled out a fish.

Test the second part of the sentence (everything that follows the conjunction) to make sure the independent clause can stand as a complete sentence: *pulled out a fish.* What is the problem? There is no subject. You could correct this problem like this:

Jacob went to the refrigerator, and **he** pulled out a fish.

Now test the second part of the sentence: *he pulled out a fish*. The clause now passes the tests for a complete sentence.

Not all clauses work well together in a compound sentence. What's wrong with the examples below?

Our house needs to be repainted, and our dog loves to eat tennis shoes.

Our house needs to be repainted, for we want it to sell more quickly, and the chimney needs to be repaired, but we don't have much money, so we'll have to do the work ourselves.

In the first sentence, the two clauses aren't logically related at all. They belong in separate sentences. A better version, with related clauses, might read like this:

Our house needs to be repainted, and the chimney needs to be repaired.

The second sentence got carried away. There are so many independent clauses strung together with conjunctions that the sentence reads as a breathless six-year-old would speak. In general, two independent clauses in a sentence are fine. Three are shaky, and four or more are bad style. Correct the problem by breaking the sentence into shorter ones:

Our house needs to be repainted, for we want it to sell more quickly. The chimney needs to be repaired, too. We don't have much money, so we'll have to do the work ourselves.

Cautions on Compound Sentences
1. Make sure the second part of the sentence is really an independent clause.

2. Don't connect unrelated clauses.

3. Don't connect too many clauses.

Exercise 9: Compound Sentences with Conjunctions▪

Part A
Directions: If the sentences below will combine well in a compound sentence, re-write them by placing a comma and one of the following conjunctions between them: *and, but, or, nor, for, so, yet.* (Often more than one conjunction will make sense.) Then make any necessary wording changes. If the sentences should not be combined, place an X in the space provided.

Examples: _____ **a.** Bob never jogs. He doesn't swim.

Bob never jogs, and he doesn't swim.

___X___ **b.** Dick despises egg salad sandwiches. He plays the banjo.

_____ 1. Color photographs are bright at first. They begin to fade in a few years.

_____ 2. Do you want spaghetti for supper tonight? Would you prefer pizza?

_____ 3. Some comic strips aren't intended to be funny. Comics are printed in color for the Sunday edition.

_____ 4. The crowd roared its approval. The cheerleaders jumped for joy.

_____ 5. The walls of the living room are magenta. The carpet is daffodil yellow.

_____ 6. Andrea was afraid to dive off the high board. She knew she would do a belly flop.

_____ 7. Neither Sam nor Barbara had finished high school. They managed to put their three children through college.

_____ 8. It was the first warm spring day. Kelly begged to go outside.

_____ 9. Television quiz shows are exciting. Ron Matthews is the host of a local radio talk show.

_____ 10. We might look for work in the Minneapolis area. We might move to Phoenix.

Part B

Directions: Complete each compound sentence below by using the conjunction indicated for each and adding a logical independent clause. Remember to place a comma before the conjunction.

1. *(but)* The Amadeos wanted a new car

2. *(or)* I may decide to move to Texas

3. *(yet)* He wanted to be respected

4. *(nor)* Dr. Brady didn't make house calls

5. *(for)* Tua is studying computer science

6. *(and)* Mrs. Perez painted her bathroom

7. *(so)* Frank Cataldo wants his son to do well in school

SAMPLE ANSWERS ARE ON PAGE 322.

FOCUS ON PUNCTUATION

Commas with *And*

Many beginning writers want an answer to one simple question: "Do you use a comma before *and,* or don't you?" After studying compound elements in Chapter 2 and compound sentences in this chapter, you know that there are three answers to that question.

1. Use a comma before *and* if it connects two complete thoughts (independent clauses).

   John washed the dinner dishes, **and** Gina photographed the event.
   The night was dark, **and** the wind whistled ominously through the trees.

2. Use a comma before *and* in a series of three or more compound elements.

   Mashed potatoes, black pepper, **and** sherry are ingredients in this bread.
   Stanley turned, sneered, **and** strode out of the room.

3. Don't use a comma before *and* when it connects only two compound elements.

   Dimley Wedgewood **and** his sister Heloise have lived in this mansion for years.
   Every afternoon Dimley drinks a cup of tea **and** retires to the den to harass the canary.

How does the above example differ from this one?

   Every afternoon Dimley drinks a cup of tea, **and he** retires to the den to harass the canary.

By adding the subject *he* after the conjunction *and,* we've made a compound sentence requiring a comma.

Exercise 10: Commas with And

Directions: Some of the sentences below need a comma inserted before *and.* Using the three rules given above, punctuate the sentences correctly.

Examples: **a.** Jennifer checked the oil and put some air in the tires.

   b. Jennifer checked the oil, and after that she put some air in the tires.

1. A cup of coffee and a piece of toast were all she ate that day.

2. A cup of coffee, a piece of toast and an orange were all she ate that day.

3. Tom politely requested an application form and sat down to fill it out.

4. Tom politely requested an application form and after that he sat down to fill it out.

5. Julio plans to become a diesel mechanic and Michael wants to play drums in a rock band.

6. Anita puts a big pot of soup on the stove every morning and dips in whenever she's hungry.

7. Automatic transmission, power steering and power brakes are standard on most models.

8. Job openings are available in restaurants, clothing stores and lawn care.

9. Maria was watching her favorite soap and Toni was studying a racing form.

10. The squirrel glanced up, froze momentarily and darted for the tree.

ANSWERS ARE ON PAGE 322.

Connectors

In formal writing, a second method of connecting clauses in compound sentences is sometimes used. You might be able to spot the joining word or phrase and the punctuation used with it in the following examples.

> America has often been called the land of opportunity; however, my mother's opportunities were limited indeed.
> She was too proud to tell her parents about her real work; therefore, she wrote home, "I'm in charge of silverware!"

This second pattern uses a semicolon before connectors such as *however* and *therefore* and a comma after them. Here's a list of the most common connectors used in this pattern.

Connector	Use
moreover furthermore in addition	adds related information (like *and*)
however nevertheless	shows a contrasting or unexpected situation (like *but*)
therefore consequently	links cause to effect (like *so*)
otherwise	shows an alternative (like *or*)

for instance for example	gives specifics to illustrate a general idea
then	shows time order

Dan excels at tennis; **moreover,** he's the fastest sprinter on the track team.

The doctors had given Stacy only six months to live; **nevertheless,** she returned to work full time.

Samuel was angry with his boss; **therefore,** he refused to work overtime.

Sit down and stop causing trouble; **otherwise,** I'll rearrange your face.

Inflation is more obvious to older people; **for instance,** I can remember buying gasoline for a quarter per gallon.

First we soaped the dog thoroughly; **then** we poured a bucket of water over her. *(Notice that no comma is needed after* then.*)*

The meaning of a connector is very important because it shows the relationship between the two ideas in a sentence. Why is the connector *moreover* used in the following example?

Tomas is a handsome man; moreover, he's very intelligent.

Moreover signals that the second clause will add related information to the first: both make positive comments about Tomas.

What relationship is signaled by the connector in the next example?

Tomas is a handsome man; consequently, women are attracted to him.

This sentence shows a cause-effect relationship. Tomas is handsome, so the women like him.

Could *consequently* also be used to link the two sentences below?

Tomas is a handsome man. Elsa thinks he's ugly.

The two sentences are linked by contrast, not by cause-effect. The word *consequently* won't link them logically. What connector would logically link these two sentences? If you're not sure, look back for contrast connectors in the chart on pages 133–34. One connector that will work is *nevertheless:*

Tomas is a handsome man; nevertheless, Elsa thinks he's ugly.

Exercise 11: Compound Sentences with Connectors-

Part A

Directions: Combine each pair of sentences below by choosing the most logical connector and rewriting them as one sentence. If you're unsure of which connector to use, check the chart on pages 133–34 for meaning. Be sure to punctuate the sentence correctly.

Example: Tina was an independent baby. At ten months she insisted on holding her own bottle.
   a. however
   b. in addition
   c. for example
   d. then

Tina was an independent baby; for example, at ten months she insisted on holding her own bottle.

1. The bus driver was frequently late to work. She lost her job.
   a. however
   b. therefore
   c. in addition
   d. for example

2. I can't stand your cooking. I despise your taste in music.
   a. moreover
   b. however
   c. therefore
   d. otherwise

3. The rear license plate was missing. The police officer didn't give Leon a ticket.
   a. furthermore
   b. however
   c. consequently
   d. for instance

4. Catch up on your child support payments by next month. We'll garnishee your wages.
   a. in addition
   b. however
   c. otherwise
   d. for example

5. Cynthia is sometimes forgetful. Once she bought three bags of groceries at the supermarket and drove home without them.
   a. furthermore
   b. otherwise
   c. therefore
   d. for instance

6. Popcorn is a tasty snack. It's more nutritious than candy.
   a. moreover
   b. nevertheless
   c. consequently
   d. for instance

7. Our ambassador spoke only English. He needed an interpreter with him at all times.
   a. furthermore
   b. however
   c. consequently
   d. otherwise

8. Eric was placed on probation for two years. He was ordered to pay back the money he stole.
   a. in addition
   b. consequently
   c. for instance
   d. however

9. She deeply distrusted his motives. She gave him her address.
   a. moreover
   b. therefore
   c. otherwise
   d. nevertheless

10. We hate hot, humid weather. We plan to stay in tropical Florida.
    a. in addition
    b. therefore
    c. however
    d. for example

Part B

Directions: Complete each compound sentence below by using the connector indicated for each and adding a logical independent clause. Remember to place a semicolon before and a comma after the connector.

1. *(however)* Shan loves to stay up late

2. *(therefore)* I want to earn $50,000 a year

3. *(moreover)* Kelly bakes the best pies in town

4. *(otherwise)* You should cut down on your drinking

5. *(for example)* Theodore is the meanest kid on the block

ANSWERS AND SAMPLE SENTENCES ARE ON PAGES 322–23.

FOCUS ON PUNCTUATION

Run-ons and Comma Splices

Now that you know two legal ways to connect clauses in compound sentences, you'll find it easier to avoid the illegal connections. In standard written English, it is illegal to

- commit a run-on sentence (jam two independent clauses together with no connecting words or punctuation)

  ILLEGAL: Jim says he's not feeling well he's coming to work anyway.
  LEGAL: Jim says he's not feeling well, but he's coming to work anyway.

- commit a comma splice (sneak two independent clauses together with just a comma)

  ILLEGAL: Ron is a real slob, he hasn't washed his socks in two years.
  LEGAL: Ron is a real slob. He hasn't washed his socks in two years.

Writers often commit run-ons and comma splices when they have two related ideas in mind but the relationship doesn't come through in writing. What is the relationship link between the ideas in the comma splice below?

ILLEGAL: The car wouldn't start again today, I must need a new battery.

The link is cause to effect. If you find a run-on or comma splice like the one above while proofreading, how can you correct it?

There are three ways to correct run-ons and comma splices:

- Connect the clauses with a comma and one of the following conjunctions: *and, but, or, nor, for, so, yet.*

  The car wouldn't start again today, so I must need a new battery.

- Connect the clauses with a semicolon, connector, and comma. (Remember, connectors are words like *however, therefore,* and *furthermore.*)

  The car wouldn't start again today; therefore, I must need a new battery.

- Place a period after the first clause to make two sentences.

  The car wouldn't start again today. I must need a new battery.

Editing hint: Comma splices and run-ons are most likely to occur when one of the words in the list below begins the second clause. Except for *then* and *there,* the words are subject pronouns. If a word from this list starts the second clause of a compound sentence, be sure that the ideas in the sentence are connected properly.

> I you he she it we they then there
>
> INCORRECT: Sandy didn't want her case to go to trial, she
> knew she would be found guilty.
> CORRECT: Sandy didn't want her case to go to trial, **for** she
> knew she would be found guilty.
>
> INCORRECT: We slept late, there was no reason to get up early.
> CORRECT: We slept late. **There** was no reason to get up early.

Exercise 12: Run-ons and Comma Splices

Part A

Directions: Correct each run-on or comma splice below by using one of the three methods listed above. Be sure you have used each method at least once by the time you have finished the exercise.

Example: Many teenagers don't mind lying to their parents, they can't stand having their parents lie to them.

Many teenagers don't mind lying to their parents, but they can't stand having their parents lie to them.

1. Harvey couldn't believe his eyes there was an iguana in the bathtub.

2. He tried to trap the iguana in his old guitar case, it had other ideas.

3. Harvey stared thoughtfully at the iguana, the creature stared back.

4. Suddenly Harvey slapped his forehead then he jumped up and ran out of the bathroom.

5. The iguana waited patiently for round two it was in no hurry to leave its porcelain palace.

6. Falling in love can be delightful, it can also be total hell. 7. Women think they have to be gorgeous men spend all their time trying to be tough. 8. Some couples manage to give up the pretenses and just love each other, those are the best relationships. 9. People need to learn to be themselves first then they are ready to handle being in love. 10. Ready or not, people will probably always fall in love it's just human nature.

Part B

Directions: There are six run-ons and comma splices in the paragraph below. Cross out and correct them using any of the three methods you've learned. The first error has been corrected as an example.

Used cars are fairly cheap to ~~buy, they're~~ *buy, but they're* not always cheap to run. We bought a car with seventy thousand miles on the odometer it ran just fine for three months then our troubles began. The car began to gulp two quarts of oil a week, there was always a cloud of black smoke following us. Then the transmission started to go we had to swear at it to get it out of reverse. The electrical system was the last straw. We would turn the heater on, and the lights would go off. We'd had enough, we sold our bargain to a junk collector for ten dollars.

SAMPLE ANSWERS ARE ON PAGE 323.

Linking Dependent Clauses

Complex Sentences

You've already seen this type of sentence structure:

> My mother had no money for a place of her own, so she boarded with her uncle and aunt.

As you know, the above example is a compound sentence: two independent clauses joined by a conjunction. If we removed the conjunction *so*, each clause could stand alone as a sentence. In the sentence below, you'll find the same meaning but a different pattern used. Read each half of the sentence aloud. Could each clause stand alone?

> Because my mother had no money for a place of her own, she boarded with her uncle and aunt.

This time the first clause does not make sense by itself. It raises a question for the second clause to answer: What happened because my mother had no money? Since this first clause depends on the second to complete the thought of the sentence, it is called a *dependent clause*. Together the clauses make a **complex sentence**.

A *complex sentence* contains a **dependent clause** connected to an independent clause.

Circle the word *because* in the sample sentence on page 139. Now read the first clause without that word:

My mother had no money for a place of her own.

The clause can stand alone again, can't it? It's the word *because* that changes the clause from independent to dependent. A **subordinating conjunction** like *because*, *after*, or *if* makes its clause dependent and shows the logical link to the independent clause. Either clause can be placed first in the sentence:

Lola was not at the wedding **although** the bride was her best friend.
Although the bride was her best friend, Lola was not at the wedding.

To see more clearly how the conjunction provides a logical link between clauses, compare the three sentences below. Each is a complex sentence with identical clauses except for the conjunction. Circle the conjunctions. How do they change the meaning of the sentences?

After Ann lost her job, she spent a week cleaning her apartment.
Because Ann lost her job, she spent a week cleaning her apartment.
Whenever Ann lost her job, she spent a week cleaning her apartment.

The word *after* in the first example shows a time relationship between two events: first she lost her job; then she cleaned. *Because* shows a cause-effect relationship: the reason Ann cleaned was that she had lost her job. *Whenever* shows a habitual relationship: apparently Ann regularly cleaned her apartment after losing a job. In each case just one word, the conjunction, can change the meaning of the sentence.

The following list of subordinating conjunctions is grouped by the relationships that they show. Note how many of these words are useful in expressing the thought patterns (time order, cause-effect, and comparison-contrast) that you studied earlier in the chapter.

Time
before
after
while
when
whenever
until
as soon as
as long as

Georgia becomes surly **whenever** Stan watches a football game

As soon as the water boils, we'll make the poison.

Reasons (Cause and Effect)
because
since
so that
in order that

We began saving our money **so that** we could make a down payment on a house.

Conditions
if
unless
whether

Unless the snow stops soon, we'll have to spend the night here.

Contrast
though
although
even though
in spite of the fact that
despite the fact that
whereas

Although Julio faints at the sight of blood, he wants to become a surgeon.

I'm leaving you **despite the fact that** I care for you very much.

Similarity
as though
as if

This leftover stew looks **as if** it should be thrown away

Place
where
wherever

Wherever she went, the hamster went, too.

Editing hint: Pay particular attention to the conjunctions listed under "Contrast." These words have approximately the same meaning as *but*. If you're unsure whether one of them is correct to use when combining two sentences, try substituting *but*.

> EXAMPLE: Lisa felt terrible. She smiled cheerfully.
> TRY *BUT*: Lisa felt terrible, but she smiled cheerfully.

It works; the sentences do show a contrast between how Lisa felt and what she did. Therefore, we can use *despite the fact that* to combine them:

> Despite the fact that Lisa felt terrible, she smiled cheerfully.

Whether you're writing on your own or taking Part 1 of the GED Writing Skills Test, it's important to choose a conjunction that clearly shows the relationship between clauses. Which subordinating conjunctions from the list might logically fit into the sentence below?

> Horace became very quiet _____ he learned his fiancee was now a professional wrestler.

The words *after* and *when* make perfect sense in this sentence since the two clauses have a time relationship. Test some other choices, like *so that* and *wherever*. They make no sense at all. Be sure to read a complex sentence carefully to make sure your conjunction is logical.

What is the relationship between the two sentences below?

> Lucille preferred her grasshoppers boiled. She occasionally ate them raw.

These sentences contrast with each other. Using a conjunction from the contrast category above, combine them into one sentence.

_____   _____

_____

You could have combined them like this:

> **Although** Lucille preferred her grasshoppers boiled, she occasionally ate them raw.

Let's try one more example. What conjunction might fit into the sentence below?

> Vincent's mother made him stay in the house on Saturday _____ he refused to brush his teeth.

The relationship between the clauses is cause-effect. Either *because* or *since* will link them clearly.

Exercise 13: Choosing Subordinating Conjunctions—

Directions: Choose the best conjunction for the underlined part of the sentence. If the sentence is correct as written, mark choice (a). If you have trouble choosing the conjunction, check the meaning of each choice in the list on pages 140–41.

Example: Tim was shattered <u>as if</u> his team lost by thirty points.
    a. as if
    b. unless
    c. although
    d. in order that
    (**e.**) when

1. <u>Whereas</u> we looked in Veronica's room, there were clothes.
    a. Whereas
    b. Wherever
    c. As long as
    d. Since
    e. While

2. You look as pale <u>as if</u> you'd seen a ghost.
    a. as if
    b. as soon as
    c. after
    d. if
    e. because

3. <u>Because</u> you eliminate your tardiness, we'll have to fire you.
    a. Because
    b. If
    c. After
    d. In order that
    e. Unless

4. Kristin sobbed loudly <u>if</u> everyone else in the room would feel properly sympathetic.
   a. if
   b. as long as
   c. so that
   d. whenever
   e. despite the fact that

5. <u>Even though</u> Harriet's car broke down on the way to work, she still arrived ten minutes early.
   a. Even though
   b. Because
   c. Since
   d. As though
   e. Before

6. <u>Unless</u> you crack your knuckles one more time, I'll be forced to chop your fingers off.
   a. When
   b. Because
   c. Where
   d. If
   e. Although

7. <u>When</u> the hour was late, the party showed no signs of winding down.
   a. When
   b. Before
   c. Though
   d. If
   e. As though

8. Clementine was never very popular <u>in order that</u> she had great clothes and piles of money.
   a. in order that
   b. as if
   c. as soon as
   d. despite the fact that
   e. wherever

9. <u>After</u> she had been in the wreck, Karen never again asked to borrow the car.
   a. After
   b. Before
   c. Whenever
   d. Whereas
   e. Although

10. <u>Until</u> she could answer his question, he fell fast asleep.
    a. Until
    b. Before
    c. After
    d. In order that
    e. As though

ANSWERS ARE ON PAGE 323.

Punctuating Complex Sentences

You have seen that a conjunction and the dependent clause that follows it may appear at the beginning or at the end of a complex sentence. The punctuation of the sentence is controlled by the location of the dependent clause. After studying the two pairs of sentences below, can you explain when to use a comma and when not to?

After we scolded him, the dog retreated into his house.
The dog retreated into his house after we scolded him.

Because he hated to get drunk, Jeff stayed home from the
New Year's Eve party.
Jeff stayed home from the New Year's Eve party because he
hated to get drunk.

In the first sentence of each pair, the dependent clause comes first and is followed by a comma. In the second sentence of each pair, the independent clause comes first, and no comma is needed before the dependent clause. Notice, too, that no comma is used *after* the conjunction in a complex sentence.

INCORRECT: Jeff stayed home because, he hated to get drunk.
CORRECT: Jeff stayed home because he hated to get drunk.

Rules for Punctuating Complex Sentences

1. When the dependent clause comes first, separate it from the independent clause with a comma.

2. When the independent clause comes first, don't use a comma.

Exercise 14: Punctuating Complex Sentences

Directions: Place a comma where needed in the sentences below. If no comma is needed, place a *C* in the space provided.

Examples: _____ **a.** If I hear that song once more, I'll break the radio.

_____*C*____ **b.** I'll break the radio if I hear that song once more.

_____ **1.** The senator was met with hostility wherever he traveled that

day. _____ **2.** When he tried to speak he was pelted with rotten eggs. _____ **3.** After his constituents had booed him for the tenth time in fifteen minutes he wadded up his speech and left the platform. _____ **4.** He felt as if his political career was over. _____ **5.** Although he had done his best there was no chance for reelection.

_____ **6.** Harriet arrived at the department store before the doors were unlocked. _____ **7.** While she waited for the store to open she planned her shopping strategy. _____ **8.** Although she was the only customer waiting outside she stayed close to the door. _____ **9.** All the best buys could be snatched up if anyone got into the store before her. _____ **10.** Since this clearance sale happened only once a year she was determined to take advantage of it.

ANSWERS ARE ON PAGES 323–24.

FOCUS ON PUNCTUATION

Eliminating Dependent Clause Fragments

Remember, a written sentence should not raise unanswered questions for the reader. Does the word group below make sense by itself?

When John called last night.

The word group does have a subject, *John*, and a verb, *called*; however, it leaves you with the question "What happened when John called last night?" Therefore, it's a fragment.

> Don't mistake a dependent clause for a sentence.

Writers often overlook dependent clause fragments because within the paragraph as a whole these word groups often make sense. To find them more easily, try reading the paragraph backward, sentence by sentence. Each time you find a subordinating conjunction such as *if*, *because*, or *unless*, check to be sure that the clause following it is part of a complex sentence rather than a fragment set off by itself.

Try this technique on the passage below. Find and underline two dependent clause fragments.

Although they used to be just science fiction toys. Robots are now a reality in the business world. These computerized creatures have revolutionized the manufacturing industry. Because they can perform repetitive precision tasks with absolute accuracy, robots are replacing people on assembly lines. You can expect to see more and more in use. As companies retool for the twenty-first century.

The two fragments are *Although they used to be just science fiction toys* and *As companies retool for the twenty-first century.* Once you've found dependent clause fragments, correcting them is easy. In our sample paragraph, the first fragment can be attached to the sentence that follows it, and the second fragment can be attached to the sentence that precedes it:

Although they used to be just science fiction toys, robots are now a reality in the business world.

You can expect to see more and more in use as companies retool for the twenty-first century.

Exercise 15: Dependent Clause Fragments

Part A
Directions: Label each group of words in the following paragraph as a sentence *(S)* or a dependent clause fragment *(F)* in the space provided.

Examples: ___F___ **a.** When you read this. ___S___ **b.** Look at each word group by itself.

_____ **1.** Riding the bus to work is an adventure in people watching. _____ **2.** Each morning after I get on at 7:30. _____ **3.** The same motley cast assembles. _____ **4.** At the first stop after mine, a teenaged couple gets on. _____ **5.** They hurry to the back of the bus. _____ **6.** So that they can hug and kiss undisturbed. _____ **7.** Then the sports enthusiast appears. _____ **8.** He sits across from the driver and talks nonstop about the latest game. _____ **9.** If the driver tries to change the subject. _____ **10.** He simply interrupts. _____ **11.** My favorite character is the tiny old lady with the shopping bags. _____ **12.** Although she never says anything. _____ **13.** She observes the other passengers with as much interest as I do.

Part B
Directions: Rewrite the paragraph in Part A to eliminate the fragments you found. As you attach these dependent clauses to independent clauses, be sure to insert commas where necessary.

ANSWERS AND THE CORRECTED PARAGRAPH ARE ON PAGE 324.

Wording in Complex Sentences

Which of these sentences is incorrect?

Although Sam had hoped for a son, he was delighted with his twin daughters.

Although Sam had hoped for a son, but he was delighted with his twin daughters.

Sam had hoped for a son, but he was delighted with his twin daughters.

The first is a complex sentence linked by the subordinating conjunction *although*. The third is a compound sentence linked by the coordinating conjunction *but*. The second is an incorrect sentence because it uses double signals: both *although* and *but*. Some linking words used in compound and complex sentences have similar meanings. Don't use both in the same sentence.

Use one connecting word from each of the following groups in a single sentence, but not more than one.

GROUP 1: although, but, yet, however

GROUP 2: because, so, therefore

GROUP 3: after, then

GROUP 4: when, then

Exercise 16: Avoiding Double Signals————

Directions: Each sentence below contains a double signal. Correct each sentence in two ways by using each of the signals in the original sentence correctly. Be sure to punctuate each new sentence properly.

Example: Because Jim was tired, so he fell asleep after dinner.
Because Jim was tired, he fell asleep after dinner.
Jim was tired, so he fell asleep after dinner.

1. After the last guest left, then we cleaned the apartment.
   a.
   b.

2. When the wind blows hard, then the windows rattle.
   a.
   b.

3. Although Sue wants to lose weight; however, she can't resist buttered popcorn.
   a.
   b.

4. Because I'd left the headlights on all day, so the car wouldn't start.
   a.
   b.

5. Dick wanted a new coat, but however his budget wouldn't stretch any further.
   a.
   b.

ANSWERS ARE ON PAGE 324.

Rewriting Sentences

Combining Ideas in Different Ways

Writers often try to combine two short sentences that each contain one idea into one longer sentence that carries all the information. Combining sentences makes writing smoother, and, as you have seen, connecting words also help make the relationship between ideas clearer. In this section, you'll work on finding several different ways to combine sentences without changing meaning. This work will help you prepare for a special type of question on Part 1 of the GED Writing Skills Test.

When you are trying to combine two ideas into one sentence, usually more than one choice of sentence pattern will work to connect the ideas logically. You have learned several sentence structures and many connectors and conjunctions in this chapter. How many ways can you think of to combine the ideas in the following two sentences? It's fine to change a word or two or rearrange the order of ideas. Just make sure the meaning stays the same.

> Pat had had a long hard week at work.
> She was ready for a Friday night on the town.

On a piece of scratch paper, jot down three different ways you could correctly and logically combine these two sentences into one sentence.

You probably realized that the two sentences have a cause-effect relationship. Any of the following combined sentences would be correct. You might have thought of other combinations as well.

> Pat had had a long hard week at work, so she was ready for a Friday night on the town.

> Pat was ready for a Friday night on the town because she had had a long hard week at work.

> Since Pat had had a long hard week at work, she was ready for a Friday night on the town.

> Pat had had a long hard week at work; as a result, she was ready for a Friday night on the town.

In the following exercise, you'll practice combining sentences in different ways. Be sure to retain the meaning of the original sentences in all the combined sentences. Stretch your imagination and your knowledge of sentence structure to think of different ways to combine the same ideas.

Exercise 17: Sentence Combining

Directions: Combine each of the following pairs of sentences three different ways.

1. Leroy had had difficulty with math as a child.
   At fifty-six he mastered fractions, decimals, and percents.

2. An iguana climbed out of Harvey's bathtub.
   Harvey called the dogcatcher.

3. Bridget has lost twenty-five pounds.
   She is determined to lose fifteen pounds more.

4. I put the brownies on the highest shelf.
   My children used a stepladder to get them down.

SOME POSSIBLE SENTENCES ARE ON PAGE 324.

Rewriting Sentences in Different Ways

Now you have worked on finding different ways of rewriting two separate sentences to make one combined sentence. What if you wanted to rewrite a single sentence that already contained two ideas, but you didn't want to change the meaning? Sometimes you might decide that a sentence does not show the relationship between ideas as clearly as it could. Or you might decide that you had used the same sentence structure too many times, making your writing dull.

How many different ways can you think of to rewrite the following sentence? Look at the two parts of the sentence. How are the parts related? You will want to show the relationship in any new sentence you write. Try to rearrange the ideas and fit them together in new ways. You will probably have to change a few words as well as the punctuation.

Ellen sat down at the desk, and a painting fell on her head.

On a piece of scratch paper, jot down at least three ways you could correctly rewrite this sentence without changing the meaning.

You probably noticed that the two parts of the sentence are related by time order. Any of the following sentences would correctly express the same meaning as the old sentence, and other correct sentences are possible.

Ellen sat down at the desk; then a painting fell on her head.

A painting fell on Ellen's head after she sat down at the desk.

When Ellen sat down at the desk, a painting fell on her head.

In the following exercise, you'll practice rewriting sentences in different ways. Be sure to retain the meaning of the original sentence in all the rewritten sentences. Stretch your imagination and your knowledge of sentence structure to think of different ways to restate the same ideas.

Exercise 18: Rewriting Sentences

Directions: Rewrite each of the following sentences three different ways.

1. Tom did not tell Jill about losing the airline tickets, so she was angry with him.

2. Gigi was anxious to get home because she needed to feed her cats.

3. Sarah ordered lunch for the department; then she made us all watch a soap opera.

4. When Ann dialed a wrong number, she got the city morgue.

SOME POSSIBLE SENTENCES ARE ON PAGE 325.

Sentence Combining in GED Test Questions

One kind of question on Part 1 of the GED Writing Skills Test will require you to change the pattern of a sentence or combine two sentences without changing the meaning. The original sentence or sentences will contain no error at all. Your job will be to figure out what the writer is trying to say and then to choose a pattern that expresses the same idea clearly. If you can recognize which linking words in compound and complex sentences have similar meanings, you'll be able to answer many of these questions correctly. There are two types of these questions, so study the following examples carefully to get an idea of each type.

Example 1: **Although the fire was extinguished immediately, there was considerable smoke damage.**

If you rewrote the sentence beginning with

The fire was extinguished immediately,

the next word should be

    a. so
    b. then
    c. but
    d. and
    e. if

Check: **The fire was extinguished immediately, but there was considerable smoke damage**. If you do this check with the other answer choices, the sentence will not make sense. The relationship between the two ideas is a contrast.

Example 2: **Terry ran out of the house in tears. He had heard a ghost in the attic.**

The most effective combination of these sentences would include which of the following groups of words?

a. Then he had heard a ghost in the attic, so Terry
b. Because he had heard a ghost in the attic, Terry
c. Terry had heard a ghost in the attic; nonetheless, he
d. Terry had heard a ghost in the attic, but he
e. Unless he had heard a ghost in the attic, Terry

Check: **Because he had heard a ghost in the attic, Terry ran out of the house in tears.** If you test the other answer choices this way, the combination sentence will not make sense. The relationship between the two sentences is cause and effect.

Exercise 19: GED Practice

Directions: Read each question carefully and mark the answer in the space provided. Check your answer by reading the entire revised sentence aloud.

1. **Joan put the baby to bed. Then she poured herself a cup of coffee.**

   The most effective combination of these sentences would include which of the following groups of words?

   a. After Joan put the baby to bed, she
   b. After Joan put the baby to bed when
   c. Because Joan put the baby to bed when
   d. Joan put the baby to bed when
   e. Because Joan put the baby to bed; then

2. **Because the grocery store was closed, we couldn't buy more milk.**

   If you rewrote the sentence beginning with

   The grocery store was closed,

   the next word should be

   a. because
   b. for
   c. although
   d. and
   e. so

3. **The vandals kicked in the door. They didn't steal anything.**

   The most effective combination of these sentences would include which of the following groups of words?

   a. Although the vandals kicked in the door, they
   b. Because the vandals kicked in the door, but
   c. Although the vandals kicked in the door, and
   d. Because the vandals kicked in the door, they
   e. Although the vandals kicked in the door, and

4. **When the clock struck twelve, the guests decided to leave.**

   If you rewrote this sentence beginning with

   The clock struck twelve;

   the next word should be

   a. after
   b. for
   c. then
   d. until
   e. when

5. **Although the patient is in critical condition, the doctors expect him to recover.**

   If you rewrote the sentence beginning with

   The patient is in critical condition;

   the next word should be

   a. therefore
   b. however
   c. moreover
   d. then
   e. otherwise

ANSWERS ARE ON PAGE 325.

Sequence of Tenses

Showing Time Relationships

You'll remember from Chapter 3 that a verb shows time by its tense. For instance, *will walk, walk, walked, have walked, had walked, are walking*, and *were walking* each indicate a different aspect of present, past, and future. To review these tenses, you may want to go back and look at pages 71–79 right now.

As you learned in the last section, a complex sentence has a dependent clause and an independent clause joined by a conjunction like *if* or *since*. A complex sentence always has two verbs, one in each clause. The tenses of these verbs must be related logically in order for the sentence to make sense.

Which of the following sentences is correct?

When George passes the last test, he received his GED.

When George passes the last test, he will receive his GED.

In the first sentence, the verb tenses are not related logically. The present tense *passes* in the dependent clause doesn't make sense with the past tense *re-*

ceived in the independent clause. Has George finished, or hasn't he? In the second sentence, the verb tenses make sense. The present tense *passes* connects logically with the future tense *will receive* to show that George has not yet finished his GED tests.

The following examples show the usual sequence of tense patterns in complex sentences. Check to make sure you understand each one by writing your own example in the space provided.

A dependent clause in the present tense and an independent clause in the future tense show a look into the future, with the action in the dependent clause occurring first.

PRESENT   FUTURE

If George passes his last test, he will celebrate for a week.

Your example: _____

_____

A dependent clause in the present tense and an independent clause also in the present tense show that the statement is always true.

PRESENT   PRESENT

When a student passes the last test, he is relieved.

Your example: _____

_____

A dependent clause in the past continuing tense and an independent clause in the past or past continuing tense shows two continuing actions happening at the same time.

PAST CONTINUING   PAST

While George was taking the test, his wife kept her fingers crossed.

PAST CONTINUING   PAST CONTINUING

While George was taking the test, his wife was keeping her fingers crossed.

Your example: _____

_____

A dependent clause in the past continuing tense and an independent clause in the past tense show a continuing action in the past during which something occurred.

PAST CONTINUING   PAST

While George was taking the test, someone pulled the fire alarm.

Your example: _____

_____

A dependent clause in the past perfect tense and an independent clause in the past tense show that both actions occurred in the past. The action in the past perfect tense occurred first.

PAST PERFECT   PAST
After he had studied for a month, George took the last test.

Your example: _____

_____

You've already learned how to use helping verbs like *is, was, have,* and *had* to form various tenses. There are a few other helpers that you should be familiar with for proper sequence of tenses. Some are used as present or future tense verbs, others as past tense. The following chart will show you how each is used.

Present or Future	Past
can	could
shall	should
will	would
may	might
must	had to

If the other clause is in the present tense, use a helping verb from the "present or future" column. If the other clause is in the past tense, use a verb from the "past" column.

PRESENT   FUTURE
When he **can walk** again, he **will leave** the rehabilitation center.

PAST   PAST
When he **could walk** again, he **left** the rehabilitation center.

Editing hint: When you're trying to figure out what verb tenses to use in different clauses, you may find it helpful to isolate the subject and verb in each clause. First, read the entire sentence to understand its meaning. Then mentally read just the conjunction and the subjects and verbs from each clause:

Before we go to the movie, we will eat dinner at Maud's.

PRESENT   FUTURE
Before we go . . . , we will eat . . . .

Isolating the conjunction and the subjects and verbs may help you identify errors in sequence of tense. What is the sequence of events in the next sentence?

INCORRECT: Because Amy already read the funnies, she gave Ellen the newspaper.
Because Amy read . . . , she gave . . .

You know that when two events occurred in the past and one happened before the other, the earlier event should be in the past perfect tense. The corrected sentence should read like this:

PAST PERFECT   PAST
Because Amy already had read the funnies, she gave Ellen the newspaper.

Exercise 20: Sequence of Tenses

Directions: Pick the correct tense for the underlined verb in each sentence. If you think the original form is correct, mark choice (a). Isolate the subject and verb in each clause to help you choose the correct tense.

Example: Jack <u>moved</u> into his own apartment when he turns nineteen.
    a. moved
    b. was moving
    c. has moved
    (d.) will move
    e. had moved

1. When Sandra saw her husband's face, she <u>knows</u> something was wrong.
    a. knows
    b. will know
    c. knew
    d. had known
    e. has known

2. Tracy will visit her brother in Canada if she <u>can</u> get a week off.
    a. can
    b. could
    c. will
    d. would
    e. might

3. When the president holds a press conference, all the networks <u>are carrying</u> it live.
    a. are carrying
    b. carry
    c. carried
    d. have carried
    e. had carried

4. After my dog <u>had finished</u> its supper, it stretched out on my bed.
    a. had finished
    b. was finishing
    c. finishes
    d. will finish
    e. has finished

5. Make hay while the sun <u>will shine</u>.
    a. will shine
    b. shined
    c. shines
    d. has shined
    e. had shined

6. After Sam <u>leaves</u> town, he missed his girlfriend.
    a. leaves
    b. had left
    c. is leaving
    d. was leaving
    e. will leave

7. I <u>sleep</u> while you were talking.
    a. sleep
    b. had slept
    c. have slept
    d. am sleeping
    e. was sleeping

8. Because Tom <u>ate</u> already, Cindy dined alone.
    a. ate
    b. had eaten
    c. will eat
    d. has eaten
    e. is eating

9. If you win the lottery, <u>would</u> you head for Hawaii?
    a. would
    b. could
    c. might
    d. did
    e. will

10. Wherever Weird Harold <u>walked</u>, people stare.
    a. walked
    b. had walked
    c. has walked
    d. walks
    e. will walk

ANSWERS ARE ON PAGE 325.

Exercise 21: Writing Complex Sentences

Part A
Directions: Using the conjunction provided, complete each sentence logically. Write several sentences with the dependent clause at the beginning of the sentence and several with the dependent clause at the end. Be careful to punctuate each sentence correctly and to use the correct verb tense.

Example: (despite the fact that) I passed the GED Tests

Answer: *I passed the GED Tests despite the fact that my hands were trembling during the Writing Skills Test.*

or

Despite the fact that my hands were trembling during the Writing Skills Test, I passed the GED Tests.

1. *(if)* We move next year

2. *(because)* His parents were divorced

3. *(although)* The lake is shallow

4. *(whenever)* Hortense coughed

5. *(after)* The alien spacecraft had landed

6. *(if)* The nation will be in trouble

7. *(when)* David became furious

Part B
Directions: Write eight complex sentences of your own using the subordinating conjunctions indicated. Half of your sentences should begin with a dependent clause. Pay attention to logic and punctuation, and be sure to use verb tenses correctly.

1. although
2. because
3. whenever
4. if
5. as though
6. despite the fact that
7. before
8. until

SAMPLE ANSWERS ARE ON PAGES 325-26.

Chapter Highlights: Combining Ideas in Sentences

1. Simple sentences can be combined in a variety of ways to show the logical connections between them and to make a paragraph sound smoother.

2. A clause is a group of words containing a subject and a verb.

3. Two independent clauses can be combined in a compound sentence connected by
   a. a comma and a conjunction like *and, but,* or *so*
   b. a semicolon, a connector like *however* or *therefore,* and a comma

4. Run-ons and comma splices occur when two independent clauses are connected improperly.

5. A dependent clause beginning with a conjunction like *when, because,* or *if* can be combined with an independent clause to form a complex sentence.

6. A dependent clause cannot stand alone as a sentence.

7. The words used to connect clauses should show the logical link between them.

Exercise 22: Sentence Combining Review

Directions: The following items are based on paragraphs which contain numbered sentences. Some of the sentences may contain errors in sentence structure, usage, and mechanics related to combining ideas in sentences. Read the paragraph and then answer the items based on it. For each item, choose the answer that would result in the most effective writing of the sentence or sentences.

(1) I'll never forget the day where my purse was stolen. (2) Because I had heard there were file clerk positions open at an insurance company, I went to put in my application. (3) When I first walked in a secretary took me to the waiting room outside the personnel office. (4) In a few minutes my name was called, and I went in for an interview. (5) Without thinking, I left my purse in the waiting room. (6) After the interview was over, then I returned to the waiting room. (7) My purse was gone. (8) At first, I kept checking the same chair in order that the purse was just temporarily invisible. (9) Then I asked the secretary if she had seen anyone take it, she said she hadn't. (10) Finally, I realized that I would have to replace everything from my lipstick to my pictures of family members. (11) Although I got the job as a file clerk, it was not my lucky day.

1. Sentence 1: **I'll never forget the day <u>where</u> my purse was stolen.**

   Which of the following is the best way to write the underlined portion of this sentence? If you think the original is the best way to write the sentence, choose option (1).

   (1) where
   (2) when
   (3) whenever
   (4) because
   (5) as though

2. Sentence 2: **Because I had heard there were file clerk positions open at an insurance company, I went to put in my application.**

   If you rewrote the sentence beginning with

   I had heard there were file clerk positions open at an insurance company,

   the next word should be

   (1) and
   (2) but
   (3) for
   (4) yet
   (5) so

3. Sentence 3: **When I first walked in a secretary took me to the waiting room outside the personnel office.**

   Which of the following is the best way to write the underlined portion of this sentence? If you think the original is the best way to write the sentence, choose option 1.

   (1) walked in a
   (2) walked in. A
   (3) walked in, a
   (4) walk in; a
   (5) walk in, a

4. Sentence 4: **In a few minutes my name was called, and I went in for an interview.**

   Which of the following is the best way to write the underlined portion of this sentence? If you think the original is the best way to write the sentence, choose option 1.

   (1) called, and
   (2) called and
   (3) called, for
   (4) called for
   (5) called. For

5. Sentence 6: **After the interview was over, then I returned to the waiting room.**

   What correction should be made to this sentence?

   (1) replace *After* with *While*
   (2) insert a comma following *After*
   (3) remove the comma after *over*
   (4) remove *then*
   (5) no correction is necessary

6. Sentence 8: **At first, I kept checking the same chair <u>in order that</u> the purse was just temporarily invisible.**

   Which of the following is the best way to write the underlined portion of this sentence? If you think the original is the best way to write the sentence, choose option 1.

   (1) in order that
   (2) despite the fact that
   (3) as if
   (4) as
   (5) if

7. Sentence 9: **Then I asked the secretary if she had seen anyone take it, she said she hadn't.**

   What correction should be made to this sentence?

   (1) insert a comma after *secretary*
   (2) remove the comma after *it*
   (3) replace *it, she* with *it. She*
   (4) change *hadn't* to *hasn't*
   (5) no correction is necessary.

8. Sentence 11: **Although I got the job as a file clerk, it was not my lucky day.**

   What correction should be made to this sentence?

   (1) replace *Although* with *Because*
   (2) remove the comma after *clerk*
   (3) replace *clerk, it* with *clerk, but it*
   (4) change *was* to *is*
   (5) no correction is necessary

(1) Do you have an inherited tendency toward a specific disease? (2) There may be good news for you. (3) Medical researchers have found that many people can reduce their risk of developing the disease. (4) If they take proper care of themselves. (5) Men who have a history of heart disease in their families should exercise regularly; however, they should keep their cholesterol level down by eating foods that are low in animal fats. (6) People with a tendency toward diabetes should watch their diets, too, they should be especially careful not to consume too much sugar. (7) Although, these protective measures won't guarantee freedom from disease, they will dramatically increase the chances for a long and healthy life. (8) Unfortunately, there are still some diseases for which heredity is everything. (9) People who are born with a certain genetic blueprint will inevitably develop sickle-cell anemia. (10) Until a breakthrough in genetic engineering is made, their suffering continued.

9. Sentences 1 and 2: **Do you have an inherited tendency toward a specific disease? There may be good news for you.**

   The most effective combination of sentences 1 and 2 would include which of the following groups of words?

   (1) If you have
   (2) As if you have
   (3) Unless you have
   (4) Where you have
   (5) Whereas you have

10. Sentences 3 and 4: **Medical researchers have found that many people can reduce their risk of developing the <u>disease. If they take</u> proper care of themselves.**

    Which of the following is the best way to write the underlined portion of these sentences? If you think the original is the best way to write the sentences, choose option 1.

    (1) disease. If they take
    (2) disease. If they took
    (3) disease; if they took
    (4) disease, if they take
    (5) disease if they take

11. Sentence 5: **Men who have a history of heart disease in their families should exercise regularly; however, they should keep their cholesterol level down by eating foods that are low in animal fats.**

    What correction should be made to this sentence?

    (1) replace *Men* with *If men*
    (2) replace *regularly; however* with *regularly, however*
    (3) replace *however* with *in addition*
    (4) remove the comma after *however*
    (5) no correction is necessary

12. Sentence 6: **People with a tendency toward diabetes should watch their diets, <u>too, they</u> should be especially careful not to consume too much sugar.**

    Which of the following is the best way to write the underlined portion of this sentence? If you think the original is the best way to write the sentence, choose option (1).

    (1) too, they
    (2) too. They
    (3) too, then they
    (4) too, although they
    (5) too, nor should they

13. Sentence 7: **Although, these protective measures won't guarantee freedom from disease, they will dramatically increase the chances for a long and healthy life.**

    What correction should be made to this sentence?

    (1) change *Although* to *As though*
    (2) remove the comma after *Although*
    (3) remove the comma after *disease*
    (4) change *will* to *would*
    (5) no correction is necessary

14. Sentences 8 and 9: **Unfortunately, there are still some diseases for which heredity is everything. People who are born with a certain genetic blueprint will inevitably develop sickle cell anemia.**

    The most effective combination of sentences 8 and 9 would include which of the following groups of words?

    (1) everything, but people
    (2) everything; for instance, people
    (3) everything, however, people
    (4) everything; however, people
    (5) everything; in addition, people

15. Sentence 10: **Until a breakthrough in genetic engineering is made, their suffering continued.**

    What correction should be made to this sentence?

    (1) replace *Until* with *If*
    (2) insert a comma after *Until*
    (3) remove the comma after *made*
    (4) change *continued* to *will continue*
    (5) no correction is necessary

ANSWERS ARE ON PAGE 326.

Chapter 4 Review Evaluation Chart

Question Type	Review Pages	Question Number	Number of Questions	Number Correct
Wording independent clauses	128–36	2, 11, 14	3	/3
Punctuating independent clauses	128–39	4, 7, 12	3	/3
Wording dependent clauses	139–49	1, 5, 6, 9	4	/4

Punctuating dependent clauses	144–45	3, 10, 13	3	/3
Sequence of tenses	152–57	15	1	/1
No error		8	1	/1

Passing score: 12 out of 15 correct

Your score: _____ out of 15 correct

If you missed more than one question in any of the categories listed above, review the pages indicated in the chart.

CUMULATIVE REVIEW

Editing Practice

Part A

Directions: Find and correct the nine errors in the passage to the right. Four of these errors are related to skills that you learned in earlier chapters: complete sentences, compound elements, pronouns, subject-verb agreement, and verb forms. You may want to review the checklists on pages 57 and 109 to refresh your memory on what to look for. The other five errors are related to combining ideas in sentences. For these errors, use the checklist below as your proofreading guide.

☐ Are clauses linked logically by conjunctions or connectors?

☐ Are compound and complex sentences punctuated correctly?

☐ Have comma splices and run-ons been avoided?

☐ Have dependent clause fragments been avoided?

☐ Do verbs follow a logical sequence of tenses?

Do you remember when being a child meant having, red measles, German measles, mumps, and whooping cough? If you do you're probably at least thirty, for in the last few decades scientists has developed vaccines that immunize children against all of these diseases. Although many people thought they were harmless, however, they could actually be quite dangerous. If a pregnant woman catched German measles. Her child might have severe birth defects. Another serious disease was mumps it could cause sterility in adult males. Today even though the medical community has worked so hard to eliminate them, these diseases are not likely to bother you or you're children.

THE CORRECTED PARAGRAPH IS ON PAGE 326.

Part B

Directions: Revise one of the paragraphs you wrote in Exercises 4, 5, and 6 in this chapter. Combine sentences where appropriate to add variety and to link ideas logically. Then apply the proofreading checklist that you used in Part A to check for errors.

★ GED PRACTICE ★

Multiple-Choice Practice

Directions: The following items are based on paragraphs which contain numbered sentences. Some of the sentences may contain errors in sentence structure, usage, and mechanics. Read the paragraph and then answer the items based on it. For each item, choose the answer that would result in the most effective writing of the sentence or sentences.

(1) As I sat down in the jury box, I realized that a person's reputation and freedom was in my hands. (2) I seen the defendant sitting next to the defense attorney with his arms folded. (3) He was staring at the other jurors and I as if he wanted to read our minds. (4) He whispered something to the defense attorney, then he glanced at us again. (5) We all rose when the judge entered the courtroom. (6) Officially beginning the trial at that moment. (7) Witness after witness was sworn in questioned, and cross-examined. (8) I listened carefully to the police officer who had made the arrest, the owner of the car that had been stolen, and the defendant's girlfriend. (9) The defendant was expressionless throughout the proceedings. (10) The constant drumming of his fingertips on the table in front of him revealed his nervousness. (11) The case was going badly, and he will have to testify next.

1. Sentence 1: **As I sat down in the jury box, I realized that a person's reputation and freedom was in my hands.**

   What correction should be made to this sentence?

   (1) replace *As* with *If*
   (2) replace *sat* with *set*
   (3) remove the comma after *box*
   (4) change *person's* to *persons*
   (5) change *was* to *were*

2. Sentence 2: **I seen the defendant sitting next to the defense attorney with his arms folded.**

   What correction should be made to this sentence?

   (1) change *seen* to *saw*
   (2) replace *defendant sitting* with *defendant. Sitting*
   (3) replace *attorney with* with *attorney. With*
   (4) change *arms* to *arms'*
   (5) no correction is necessary

3. Sentence 3: **He was staring at the other jurors and I as if he wanted to read our minds.**

   Which of the following is the best way to write the underlined portion of this sentence? If you think the original is the best way to write the sentence, choose option (1).

   (1) I as
   (2) I, as
   (3) I; as
   (4) me as
   (5) me, as

4. Sentence 4: **He whispered something to the defense attorney, then he glanced at us again.**

   Which of the following is the best way to write the underlined portion of this sentence? If you think the original is the best way to write the sentence, choose option (1).

   (1) attorney, then he glanced
   (2) attorney then he glanced
   (3) attorney; then he glanced
   (4) attorney. Then glanced
   (5) attorney. Then glancing

5. Sentence 5: **We all rose when the judge entered the courtroom.**

    What correction should be made to this sentence?

    (1) replace *rose* with *raised*
    (2) insert a comma after *rose*
    (3) change *entered* to *enters*
    (4) insert a comma after *entered*
    (5) no correction is necessary

6. Sentence 6: **Officially beginning the trial at that moment.**

    Which of the following is the best way to write the underlined portion of this sentence? If you think the original is the best way to write the sentence, choose option (1).

    (1) Officially beginning the trial at that moment.
    (2) The trial beginning officially at that moment.
    (3) At that moment when the trial officially began.
    (4) At that moment the trial officially began.
    (5) At that moment the trial officially begun.

7. Sentence 7: **Witness after witness was sworn in questioned, and cross-examined.**

    What correction should be made to this sentence?

    (1) change *sworn* to *swore*
    (2) insert a comma after *in*
    (3) change *questioned* to *question*
    (4) remove the comma after *questioned*
    (5) no correction is necessary

8. Sentence 8: **I listened carefully to the police officer who had made the arrest, the owner of the car that had been stolen, and the defendant's girlfriend.**

    What correction should be made to this sentence?

    (1) change *had made* to *made*
    (2) change *had been* to *have been*
    (3) change *stolen* to *stole*
    (4) change *defendant's* to *defendants*
    (5) no correction is necessary

9. Sentences 9 and 10: **The defendant was expressionless throughout the proceedings. The constant drumming of his fingertips on the table in front of him revealed his nervousness.**

    The most effective combination of sentences 9 and 10 would include which of the following groups of words?

    (1) proceedings; however, the constant
    (2) proceedings, and the constant
    (3) proceedings because the constant
    (4) proceedings; furthermore, the constant
    (5) proceedings if the constant

10. Sentence 11: **The case was going badly, and he will have to testify next.**

    Which of the following is the best way to write the underlined portion of this sentence? If you think the original is the best way to write the sentence, choose option (1).

    (1) will have to
    (2) will
    (3) would have to
    (4) has to
    (5) must

(1) Space travel, which once was just a subject of science fiction storys, became an amazing reality in the early 1960s. (2) A whole nation pauses in 1961 as Americans gathered around their television sets to watch Alan Shepard become the first American astronaut to rocket into space. (3) When John Glenn orbited the earth a year later we looked on in awe again. (4) These astronauts became instant national heroes. (5) They received banner headlines and ticker tape parades for being pioneers in space. (6) In the following months, reporters kept their names alive by writting countless feature stories. (7) Space travel became big news again in 1986. (8) Schoolteacher Christa MacAuliffe was chosen to be the first civilian in space. (9) Then the crew, MacAuliffe, and the shuttle was destroyed in the most tragic accident in the history of space flight. (10) This accident had a profound effect on space programs for years to come.

11. Sentence 1: **Space travel, which once was just a subject of science fiction storys, became an amazing reality in the early 1960s.**

    What correction should be made to this sentence?

    (1) change *was* to *is*
    (2) change the spelling of *storys* to *stories*
    (3) change *became* to *become*
    (4) change the spelling of *amazing* to *amazeing*
    (5) no correction is necessary

12. Sentence 2: **A whole nation pauses in 1961 as Americans gathered around their television sets to watch Alan Shepard become the first American astronaut to rocket into space.**

    What correction should be made to this sentence?

    (1) change *pauses* to *paused*
    (2) replace *as* with *whenever*
    (3) change *Americans* to *American's*
    (4) change the spelling of *gathered* to *gatherred*
    (5) replace *astronaut to* with *astronaut. To*

13. Sentence 3: **When John Glenn orbited the earth a year later we looked on in awe again.**

    What correction should be made to this sentence?

    (1) replace *When* with *Even though*
    (2) change the spelling of *orbited* to *orbitted*
    (3) insert a comma after *later*
    (4) change *looked* to *look*
    (5) no correction is necessary

14. Sentences 4 and 5: **These astronauts became instant national heroes. They received banner headlines and ticker tape parades for being pioneers in space.**

    Which of the following is the best way to write the underlined portions of these sentences? If you think the original is the best way to write the sentences, choose option (1).

    (1) heroes. They
    (2) heroes, they
    (3) heroes they
    (4) heroes because they
    (5) heroes, because they

15. Sentence 6: **In the following months, reporters kept their names alive by writing countless feature stories.**

    What correction should be made to this sentence?

    (1) change the spelling of *months* to *monthes*
    (2) replace *months reporters* with *months. Reporters*
    (3) replace *alive by* with *alive. By*
    (4) change the spelling of *writting* to *writing*
    (5) no correction is necessary

16. Sentences 7 and 8: **Space travel became big news again in 1986. Schoolteacher Christa MacAuliffe was chosen to be the second civilian in space.**

    The most effective combination of sentences 7 and 8 would contain which of the following groups of words?

    (1) When schoolteacher Christa MacAuliffe
    (2) If schoolteacher Christa MacAuliffe
    (3) In spite of the fact that schoolteacher Christa MacAuliffe
    (4) Although schoolteacher Christa MacAuliffe
    (5) As if schoolteacher Christa MacAuliffe

17. Sentence 9: **Then the crew, MacAuliffe, and the shuttle was destroyed in the most tragic accident in the history of space flight.**

What correction should be made to this sentence?

(1) insert a comma after *shuttle*
(2) change *was* to *were*
(3) remove the comma after *crew*
(4) change *was* to *has been*
(5) no correction is necessary

18. Sentence 10: **This accident had a profound effect on space programs for years to come.**

Which of the following is the best way to write the underlined portion of this sentence? If you think the original is the best way to write the sentence, choose option (1).

(1) had
(2) was having
(3) will have
(4) had been
(5) has

ANSWERS ARE ON PAGES 326–27.

Cumulative Review Evaluation Chart

Questions From	Question Number	Number of Questions	Number Correct
Chapter 2 Fragments, Nouns, and Pronouns	3, 6, 7, 11	4	/4
Chapter 3 Verbs	1, 2, 12, 15, 17, 18	6	/6
Chapter 4 Combining Ideas in Sentences	4, 9, 10, 13, 14, 16	6	/6
No error	5, 8	2	/2

Passing score: 13 right out of 18 questions
Your score: _____ right out of 18 questions

5

![icon] WRITING AN ESSAY

In Chapter 4, you wrote a paragraph describing how television has affected you. You might have had a lot to say about this topic—maybe even more ideas than you could fit easily into one paragraph. Here is the topic again:

> During the past thirty years, television has become a core part of American life. Nearly every household has at least one television set. Some people say that television has benefited our society, while others see it as a cause of many problems. Explain how television has affected you. Support your explanation with specific examples.

With this topic, you might want more room to answer the question than one paragraph would give you. To respond really thoroughly, with enough details to satisfy both you and your reader, you could write an essay.

An **essay** is a group of related paragraphs about one topic.

Like a paragraph, an essay has a main idea that is usually stated at the beginning and followed by support. In an essay, however, the main idea usually appears in a separate **introductory paragraph**.

The supporting ideas in an essay are organized in separate paragraphs. This section, the main **body**, is what makes the essay roomy enough to accommodate several related ideas.

Finally, because of its length, an essay needs a **concluding paragraph** to give the writing a sense of completeness. Study the pictures below to see how the parts of a paragraph and the parts of an essay compare.

Paragraph

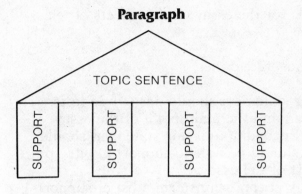

Essay

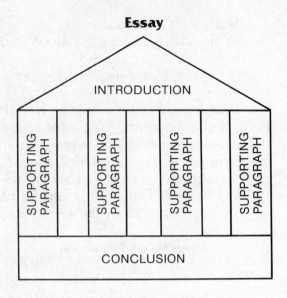

Writing a good essay requires planning, writing, revising, and editing. This is the same process you've been using to write paragraphs. In this chapter, you'll follow along as one writer composes an essay on the effects of television, and you'll also compose an essay of your own.

This chapter demonstrates a careful, thorough approach to writing an essay so that you will become familiar with the structure of an essay. In Chapter 7, you'll learn strategies for approaching the GED Test essay.

Planning

The Unifying Statement

The planning phase is even more important in essay writing than in paragraph writing because of the greater length of the essay. You need to make sure that you have a clear main point with plenty of supporting details organized logically.

To give some direction to your planning, try to state the main point of an essay in one simple statement.

A *unifying statement* is a sentence that summarizes the main point of the essay. (You may have heard it called a *thesis statement*.)

The same unifying statement you use to help focus your brainstorming may not actually be used in your essay. Later, you'll consider how you might expand or revise a unifying statement into an introduction for the essay.

Many unifying statements are possible for the essay on the effects of television. This writer chose the following one:

Television has provided several benefits to me.

Like a good topic sentence, a unifying statement should pass three tests. First, it should identify the topic (television) and the main point of the essay (television has provided several benefits). Second, a unifying statement should be a complete sentence. Third, the writer should be able to support it with specific examples, reasons, or ideas in the rest of the essay.

With the unifying statement in mind, you can brainstorm a list of supporting details. Here's what the writer jotted down:

Benefits of Television
Sports—basketball, wrestling, gymnastics
Movies—old, last year, made for TV
News—wars, arms race, Congress, presidential press conference, city
      council
Way to relax—tired, sit down in comfortable chair, doze off
Documentaries—science, history, other cultures
Singer, musical groups—specials

Grouping and Outlining

Now, how can the list be organized? Since you'll be writing several paragraphs, you need to group the details for each paragraph. An **outline** is a convenient way to accomplish this task. Its main headings will become topic sentences for your paragraphs, and its subpoints will become the supporting sentences.

Looking over the brainstorm list on benefits of television, the writer found one clear statement of benefit: it's a good way to relax. The rest of the items were types of programs he watched. How could those be grouped? Sports, movies, and musical groups are all forms of entertainment. News and documentaries are both informative. He decided to try a three-part grouping: relaxation, entertainment, and information.

Benefits of Television
Sports—basketball, wrestling, gymnastics *> entertainment*
Movies—old, last year, made for TV
information News—wars, arms race, Congress, presidential press conference, city
      council
Way to relax—tired, sit down in comfortable chair, doze off *-relaxation*
Documentaries—science, history, other cultures
Singer, musical groups—specials

If you had been writing this essay, your grouping might have been entirely different from his. There is no one correct way to sort items from a brainstorm list; just make sure to group details in a way that makes sense to you and that will seem logical to your reader.

After the items have been grouped informally, you can make an outline. Each label for a group will become a heading in the outline, showing how the items under it are related to one another. When you outline, you decide on the order in which you will present the ideas in your essay. Think about how you might want to order your paragraphs. You could put ideas in order of importance, for example. Or your ideas might suggest a time sequence.

The writer made three headings for his outline and listed them in order of least to most important:

      I. Provides an easy way to relax
     II. Provides variety of entertainment
    III. Provides information about world

His complete outline appears below:

Effects of Television
Unifying statement: Television has provided several benefits to me.

I.   Provides an easy way to relax
    A.   When I'm tired, makes no demands on me
    B.   Sit down in comfortable chair
    C.   Doze off if I want to

II.   Provides variety of entertainment
    A.   Sports
        1.   Basketball
        2.   Wrestling
        3.   Gymnastics

    B.   Movies
        1.   Classics—*High Noon*
        2.   More recent movies—*Fatal Attraction*

    C.   Music
        1.   Rock groups
        2.   Country
        3.   Jazz, classical

III.   Provides information about world
    A.   News
        1.   Local—city council
        2.   National—presidential press conference
        3.   International—war, arms race

    B.   Documentaries
        1.   Science
        2.   History
        3.   Other countries

As you can see from this example, this writer used indenting and numbering to show the parts of his outline. Indenting in an outline separates major parts from supporting details and groups details under those points. Numbering separates items from one another.

Notice that the writer gave the most important headings in the outline Roman numerals (such as *II*). Subpoints under these headings are marked with capital letters, and supporting details under the subpoints get Arabic numerals (such as *2*). This alternating of numbers and letters, like indenting, helps to separate main points from support. Some people find a formal outlining system like this helpful in organizing their thinking. You may want to experiment with it yourself.

Once you have made an outline, check it against your unifying statement. Is everything relevant to that statement? Should the statement be reworded to cover the outline, or should the outline be changed? This is the time to cross out irrelevant material and to add missing details.

How to Make an Outline

1. Brainstorm a list of details.

2. Group related details.

3. Make a heading for each group.

4. Choose an order for the headings.

5. List the related details under each heading.

6. Check the outline against the unifying statement.

Exercise 1: Outlining

Directions: Sort details from the following lists into logical groups, create headings to label the groups, and arrange headings and details in outline form. Use the outline skeletons provided, if you wish, or construct an outline of your own. The first one has been started for you.

1. waterskiing, hockey, baseball, golf, tennis, ice skating, cross-country skiing

Outdoor Sports

I. *Summer sports*

  A. *Waterskiing*

  B.

  C.

  D.

II.

  A.

  B.

  C.

2. buses, helicopters, motorcycles, planes, cars, bicycles, trains

Transportation

    I.

        A.

        B.

        C.

    II.

        A.

        B.

   III.

        A.

        B.

3. argue with boss, steal office supplies, get in fights with coworkers, regularly arrive late for work, take long breaks, steal store merchandise, treat customers rudely, leave work early

How to Lose Your Job

    I.

        A.

        B.

        C.

    II.

        A.

        B.

        C.

   III.

        A.

        B.

SOME POSSIBLE OUTLINES ARE ON PAGE 327.

Exercise 2: Planning for an Essay

Directions: Choose *one* of the topics below and work through the entire planning phase *only*, using the following steps:

- Write a preliminary unifying statement. Make sure that it is a complete sentence that states the main point of the essay. Be sure that you can support it with specific examples. (If you're not certain what your main point will be, you can brainstorm first and then decide what unifying statement your details will support.)

- Brainstorm items to include.

- Sort the items into logical groups.

- Organize an outline.

You'll be using this material throughout the rest of the chapter to create a complete essay, so be sure to keep it.

1. Growing up on a farm or in a small town is a much different experience from growing up in a metropolitan area of several million people. What were the advantages or disadvantages of growing up in a community the size of yours? (If you lived in many places as a child, choose one that you remember especially well.) Give specific, concrete details in your answer.

2. All over the world, people have pets even though these animals cost money and take time to care for. Why do you think people keep pets? Support your opinion with specific examples.

3. From time to time it has been suggested that all young Americans should be required to perform a period of public service similar to the military draft. Between the ages of eighteen or nineteen and twenty-one, they would spend a year working in places like nursing homes, hospitals, or community centers. Do you favor or oppose a policy of required public service? State your opinion and back it with reasons and examples.

ANSWERS WILL VARY.

Writing a Draft

What Is a Rough Draft?

After you have completed an outline, the next step in writing an essay is to write a draft. At this point, you expand the words and phrases in the outline into sentences and paragraphs. The draft won't be a finished product, but it will give you some material to examine and polish by revising and editing.

Write carefully when you're writing the first draft of a piece of writing, but don't labor over a spelling problem or tricky grammar question. You'll have plenty of time to come back and fix up your work later. When you're writing a rough draft, your goal should be simply to get your ideas down on paper.

Editing hint: To make later changes with ease, write your first draft on every other line and leave plenty of space in the right and left margins.

Writing an Introduction

A good introductory paragraph will accomplish four purposes. First, it will identify the topic of the essay. It will also indicate the writer's main point. An introductory paragraph will help the reader predict the content and organization of the body of the essay. Finally, it will arouse the reader's interest.

Some version of the unifying statement will meet the first three objectives. Continuing with the essay on television, the writer could create a short introduction like this:

> Television has benefited my life in many ways. It offers relaxation after a hard day's work. It provides me with a variety of inexpensive entertainment, and it gives me information about the world around me.

This paragraph accomplishes three things. It identifies the topic: *television*. It presents the main point: *has benefited my life*. Third, it previews content and organization: *relaxation, entertainment, and information.* (As you know from the outline on page 171, these are exactly the points that will be covered.)

When you are writing an introduction, keep these points in mind:

1. **State your main point clearly.** If your readers know what point you are trying to make, they will find it easier to understand everything in the essay. In addition, stating your main point clearly is a good check for yourself to make sure you really know where your essay is going. As you write your essay, you can keep referring to your introduction to make sure everything you write supports your main point.

2. **Give your readers an idea of the content and organization of your essay.** If you have three major supporting arguments for your main point, you may want to list them in the introduction, just as the writer did in the example above. Previewing content and organization in this way makes the essay easier for readers to understand. And, like stating your main point, it is a good check for you. If you can't describe the content and organization of your essay, maybe you're not quite ready to write yet.

3. **Arouse your readers' interest in your essay.** There are lots of ways to do this. Following are two examples of ways the writer of the essay on the benefits of television could modify his introductory paragraph to make it more interesting. This first example shows how he uses questions to get his readers interested in answers that he will include in his essay.

> What do you do when you come home from work exhausted? What do you do when you want to see a good movie but don't have the money for a ticket? What do you do when you wonder whether Congress has voted to raise taxes today? If you're like me, you turn on

your television set. Television is an important part of my life that provides relaxation, entertainment, and information about the world around me.

In this second example, he gives some background to show why his topic is important—showing that he has a sense of history or of social trends.

> When television was introduced in the 1940s, few people guessed how quickly this invention would spread around the world. Today, nearly every American household has at least one television set, and satellites bounce programs from one continent to another. Some people may argue about whether this invention is worthwhile, but for me the answer is a definite yes. Television provides many benefits to me, including relaxation, entertainment, and information about the world around me.

Which introduction is the best? There is no one correct answer to this question. Your own preferences and the audience you're writing for (such as your family, a friend, or the general public) will help you decide what kind of introduction to write.

Problems to Avoid

There are some standard traps to avoid when writing an introduction:

1. Don't announce your plans. Your ideas and organization should speak for themselves. Avoid sentences like these:

I am going to discuss the benefits of television in this essay.
My first paragraph will show how television relaxes me.

2. Don't apologize for your essay. You want to convince your reader that you have something to say. Never make an excuse like this one:

This is a hard essay to write because I really don't watch much television, so here goes nothing.

3. Don't use empty words just to sound important and don't repeat yourself just to make the introduction longer. Can you see the problem below?

Television has had many important effects on me. Its impact on my life has been tremendous. In fact, I've been influenced a great deal by television.

4. Don't assume that your reader has read the essay question or the title of your essay. Always restate the subject of the essay or summarize the essay question in your introduction. After the question "How has television affected your life?" or the title "Benefits of Television," don't begin your introduction like this:

For one thing, it helps me relax.

Exercise 3: Writing Introductions

Directions: Using the unifying statement and outline that you prepared in Exercise 2 on page 174, write two possible introductory paragraphs for your essay. Write on every other line so you will have room to revise later.

Check each paragraph to make sure that it identifies the topic, indicates your main point about the topic, predicts the content and organization of the essay, and arouses your reader's interest.

ANSWERS WILL VARY.

Writing the Body

With the outline in front of you, you can draft the body of the essay fairly quickly. Each main heading in the outline will become the topic sentence of a paragraph. The details under the heading will become supporting sentences. Here's what the writer produced for the body of his television essay:

I. Provides an easy way to relax
    A. When I'm tired, makes no demands on me
    B. Sit down in comfortable chair
    C. Doze off if I want to

II. Provides variety of entertainment
    A. Sports
        1. Basketball
        2. Wrestling
        3. Gymnastics
    B. Movies
        1. Classics—*High Noon*
        2. More recent movies—*Fatal Attraction*
    C. Music
        1. Rock groups
        2. Country
        3. Jazz, classical

III. Provides information about world
    A. News
        1. Local—city council
        2. National—presidential press conference
        3. International—war, arms race
    B. Documentaries
        1. Science
        2. History
        3. Other countries

Watching television is an easy way for me to relax at the end of a long, hard day. I don't have to stay alert as I would at a game of cards or use any physical energy as I would in football. I can just sit back in a comfortable chair and watch. If I doze off in the middle of a program, no one will be annoyed.

When I want to be entertained, television provides a variety of choices. All kinds of sports programs are available, from pro wrestling to gymnastics, and I can get a better view of the athletes on television than I could if I were sitting in the bleachers. Movies are another option, whether they are classics like *High Noon* or more recent films like *Fatal Attraction*. Television also offers plenty of musical programs by rock, country, and jazz musicians. All this entertainment comes directly to my home at no cost.

Thanks to television, I know much more about the world around me. Each evening I can watch news about local, national, and international events. I can find out what the city council did at its last meeting, watch a presidential press conference live, or even find out about wars and famines in other parts of the world. Documentaries about science, history, and other countries further broaden my understanding.

Notice that the outline has been used as a guide, not a straitjacket. The writer added a few details that weren't in the outline. Compare the paragraphs to the outline in the margin. These ideas occurred during the actual drafting; since they're all relevant to the unifying statement, the writer decided to include them. If new ideas occur to you at any stage, it's fine to put them in. Just be sure to make sure they are relevant to the unifying statement.

Exercise 4: Writing the Body

Directions: Choose the introduction you like best from Exercise 3, page 177. Using the outline you developed in Exercise 2 on page 174, write the body of your essay. Turn the main headings of your outline into topic sentences and the details under the headings into supporting sentences. Add more details as they occur to you. Don't worry too much about spelling or grammar. Write on every other line so you will have room to revise later.

ANSWERS WILL VARY.

Writing the Conclusion

Now that the introduction and body of the essay are written, it's time to draw your writing to a close with a concluding paragraph. But you've already made your main point and you've used up the entire outline. What is there left to write?

Don't worry. The last paragraph of an essay isn't intended to cover new material. In most cases, the concluding paragraph has two main purposes. Its first purpose is to give the essay a sense of completeness, like the top slice of bread on a sandwich. The beginning and the middle need an end to keep your reader from wondering if the last page of your essay is missing! The second purpose of the concluding paragraph is to help the reader remember your main point.

To accomplish these purposes, you can use as your conclusion a reworded version of the unifying statement. If the writer of the television essay had chosen this approach, he might have ended this way:

> By helping me unwind, entertaining me, and educating me, television has made my life more pleasant and more interesting. This is one appliance that I would hate to do without.

Note that this summarizing conclusion touches on the main idea—"television has provided several benefits to me"—and the three groups of benefits discussed in the body: relaxation, entertainment, and information. Only the wording has been changed to keep from sounding monotonous.

A second kind of conclusion goes one step beyond summarizing and opens out to discuss the broader importance of the subject.

> Clearly, my reaction to television is positive. My favorable opinion isn't unique. Millions, perhaps billions, of people have had their lives

enriched by this magic box. By watching it, we can relax, we can laugh and cheer, and, most important, we can better understand one another and the world we live in.

This time the unifying statement has been expanded to apply to television viewers in general rather than just the writer.

Problems to Avoid

Conclusions are like introductions in that there are many possibilities for good paragraphs. The traps to avoid in writing conclusions are also similar to those involved in creating introductions:

1. Don't announce your plans. Avoid concluding like this:

   I would like to end this essay by saying that my television set is one of my most important possessions.

2. Don't apologize for your essay like this:

   I'm sorry this wasn't very good, but at least I tried. Of course, if I watched television more, I would have better examples.

3. Don't bring up new topics like this writer did:

   My television set is my second most important possession. Only my car is more important because it gets me to work, takes me wherever I want to go on vacations, and lets me get together with my friends.

Exercise 5: Writing a Conclusion ━━━━

Directions: Complete the draft that you worked on in Exercises 2, 3, and 4 by writing a conclusion. To get a running start, reread the introduction and the body. Remember, it's fine if you reword your unifying statement for the conclusion. Write on every other line so you will have room to revise later.

ANSWERS WILL VARY.

The Completed Rough Draft

Now the writer has a working draft, with an introduction, body, and conclusion tied to a unifying statement. He's accomplished a great deal!

However, this probably won't be his final version of the essay. He may need to revise it to link the paragraphs more smoothly to one another and to provide more specific examples. (What would be some good examples of musical programs and documentaries, for instance?) He may want to change the wording in a few places. And what about editing considerations: spelling, punctuating, capitalizing? We'll look in detail at the revising and editing stages of the writing process in Chapter 6.

Exercise 6: Your Completed Rough Draft

Directions: When you complete your entire draft, use the following checklist to evaluate it. Make some notes about any changes you would like to make in your essay. Don't make the changes now; you'll revise the essay in Chapter 6.

- Does the introduction contain a unifying statement? Put an asterisk (✱) in the margin next to it.

- Does the introduction help arouse the reader's interest? Does it avoid common traps?

- Does each paragraph in the body support the unifying statement with specific details?

- Does each paragraph in the body contain a topic sentence?

- Are the paragraphs in the body arranged logically?

- Does the conclusion restate the main idea of the essay? Does it avoid common traps?

ANSWERS WILL VARY.

Chapter Highlights

1. An essay is a group of related paragraphs about one topic. It consists of an introduction, supporting paragraphs, and a conclusion.

2. Begin planning your essay by writing a unifying statement and brainstorming a list of details.

3. Group brainstormed details in an outline from which you will write a working draft.

4. Use the unifying statement as the basis for the introduction to your essay. The introduction might begin with a question, an incident, a contrast, a general statement, or background information.

5. In the body of the essay, expand the outline in sentence and paragraph form. Turn each main heading in the outline into the topic sentence of a paragraph.

6. Restate your main point in the conclusion. You may also show the broader importance of the subject.

7. Expect to revise and edit the working draft.

As they gain writing experience, writers develop their own versions of this writing process. Often the steps aren't nearly as clear-cut as they have been presented here. Writing a rough draft can turn into revising as a writer notices how the wording of a sentence can be clarified. Drafting may even give way to more planning when the writer temporarily gets stuck on a paragraph and decides to brainstorm more details. Don't hesitate to modify this process to suit your own writing style.

★ GED PRACTICE ★

Exercise 7: GED Writing Topic

Here is your second sample writing topic to help you practice for Part 2 of the GED Writing Skills Test. Try writing on this topic within the forty-five-minute time limit that you will have on the actual test. Put all the writing skills to use that you have learned so far in essay and paragraph construction, sentence structure, word choice, punctuation, and spelling.

Be sure to take ten minutes or so to plan your essay. Look for clue words in the question to help you identify topic, purpose, and the kinds of details to include. Make a unifying statement and brainstorm a list of details. Although you may not have time to make a formal outline, do try to group your details logically. Check for relevance, completeness, and organization.

When you begin drafting, don't worry if you can't think of a catchy introduction. Just use your unifying statement and fill out the paragraph with another sentence or two.

Save the last five to ten minutes for revising and editing your essay. Apply the checklist on page 180 as a revising guide.

> Playing the "if only" game seems to be a natural human activity. We often imagine what our lives would be like if only one circumstance were changed. Even young children play the game: "If only I had a little brother, there would be someone to play with around here," or "If only I didn't have a little brother, I wouldn't have to share my toys."
>
> Pick one circumstance in your life—past, present, or future—that you would like to change and describe the effects that change would have on your life.

A SAMPLE ESSAY IS ON PAGES 327–28.

Journal Writing

Have you written in your journal recently?
Here are some suggestions of things you could write about in your journal. Choose one or more of them to write about, or think of some topics on your own.

- Write about something wonderful about yourself that you wish everyone knew.

- Write about something that is very important to you.

- What are your biggest complaints about life?

⚈ KEEPING YOUR STORY STRAIGHT

Read each pair of sentences below and place a check beside the one that you think is written correctly.

_____ Hurrying to leave for work on time, the toast burned and coffee spilled on Michelle's white blouse.

_____ Hurrying to leave for work on time, Michelle burned the toast and spilled coffee on her white blouse.

_____ She hated starting her day with an empty stomach and food stains on her clothes.

_____ She hated starting her day with an empty stomach and staining her clothes.

_____ Michelle was so disgruntled that she hardly spoke to Maria, which rode to work with her.

_____ Michelle was so disgruntled that she hardly spoke to Maria, who rode to work with her.

Did you find the choice difficult? If so, don't worry. The errors weren't nearly as obvious as a sentence fragment or misused verb. Instead, they involved questions of logic in word order and word choice. By studying the material in this chapter, you'll learn to recognize and write clear sentences with wording that doesn't confuse your readers or distract them from the point you want to make.

You'll be working with three problem areas in sentence structure: use of modifiers, parallel structure, and pronoun reference. This work in sentence structure will be helpful in both Parts 1 and 2 of the GED Writing Skills Test.

Modifiers

How Are Modifiers Used?

Prepositional Phrases

In Chapter 4 you learned how to combine ideas in sentences by connecting *clauses*, which you learned are groups of words that contain subjects and verbs. Sometimes ideas can be combined without using entire clauses. How might you combine the following pair of sentences?

Governor Morrison won reelection yesterday. He won by a margin of seventy thousand votes.

Here are two possibilities:

Governor Morrison won reelection yesterday **by a margin of seventy thousand votes.**
By a margin of seventy thousand votes, Governor Morrison won re-election yesterday.

In both cases, the prepositional phrase from the second sentence *(by a margin of seventy thousand votes)* was inserted into the first sentence. (If you need to refresh your memory about prepositional phrases, review pages 99–100.) The phrase answers the question "By how much did the governor win?" In other words, it modifies, or describes, the word *win*.

A *modifier* is a word or phrase that describes another word in the sentence. A modifier answers a question: *when? where? why? how? how much? which one?* or *how many?*

Try combining a second pair of sentences in the same way: insert the modifying phrase from the second sentence into the first sentence.

The city's recreation department will hold a summer festival. The festival will be at Oak Park on June 24 and 25.

_____

_____

Again you have two choices:

The city's recreation department will hold a summer festival **at Oak Park on June 24 and 25**.
At Oak Park on June 24 and 25, the city's recreation department will hold a summer festival.

Verb Phrases

A prepositional phrase is only one kind of modifier. Other modifying phrases begin with verbs. Watch how the following pairs of sentences can be combined.

Sid swerved to avoid a squirrel. The squirrel was scampering across the street.
Sid swerved to avoid a squirrel **scampering across the street.**

Teresa wanted to learn how to protect herself. She enrolled in a karate class.
To learn how to protect herself, Teresa enrolled in a karate class.

Jim was angered by my sarcastic comments. He turned and left.
Angered by my sarcastic comments, Jim turned and left.

In each combined sentence above, the phrase in bold type is a modifier. *Scampering across the street* tells you which squirrel Sid swerved to avoid. *To learn to protect herself* explains why Teresa enrolled in a karate class. *Angered by my sarcastic comments* explains why Jim turned and left.

FOCUS ON PUNCTUATION

Introductory Phrases

When a modifying phrase begins a sentence, separate it from the rest of the sentence with a comma. Usually, no comma is needed when the phrase appears at the end of a sentence.

> **At 12:01 a.m. on June 28,** her first grandchild was born.
> Her first grandchild was born **at 12:01 a.m. on June 28**.

> **In order to annoy her parents,** Christine popped her knuckles and swore.
> Christine popped her knuckles and swore **in order to annoy her parents**.

Exercise 8: Writing Sentences with Modifying Phrases

Directions: Combine the following pairs of sentences by turning one sentence into a modifying phrase. Be sure to insert commas after introductory phrases.

Example: Something happened in the middle of the night. The bed collapsed.

In the middle of the night, the bed collapsed.

1. Samantha was smiling seductively. Samantha sauntered toward Steve.

2. Something happened in the middle of the president's speech. A reporter shouted a question.

3. The governor wanted to prevent looting after the shopping mall fire. The governor called out the National Guard.

4. The campers were awakened by a bear. It was rummaging through the food supplies.

5. Vandals smashed the windshields of twelve cars. The cars were in the vicinity of West High School last night.

6. The crowd were shouting and whistling their approval. The crowd gave Slime Green a standing ovation.

7. The trucker drove an alternate route. The trucker wanted to avoid the weigh station.

8. Dick's Get 'n' Go was robbed. The incident occurred for the third time in less than a year.

9. Some people want to reduce the chances of catching a cold. Some people take large doses of vitamin C.

10. Smitty and Josh stared in fascinated horror at the tarantula. It was crawling across their sleeping friend's face.

SAMPLE ANSWERS ARE ON PAGE 328.

Placement of Modifiers

In the following sentence, who was dangling from a window: Mavis or her husband? How can you tell?

> Dangling from a seventh-story window, Mavis dimly heard her husband yelling.

The answer to the question is based on word order. Since the modifying phrase *dangling from a seventh-story window* appears directly before *Mavis*, you can assume that she is the person it describes.

To avoid confusing or unintentionally amusing your reader, place a modifying phrase as close as possible to the word it describes.

Here's an example of what may happen if this rule is violated:

> Wearing nothing but a diaper, Mrs. Craig worried that the baby would catch cold.

Who was wearing the diaper? Although common sense tells you that it was the baby, the sentence structure implies that it was Mrs. Craig.

A **misplaced modifier** can be corrected in two ways:

- Move the modifier closer to the word it describes.

  Mrs. Craig worried that the baby wearing nothing but a diaper would catch cold.

- Turn the modifying phrase into a dependent clause.

  Because the baby was wearing nothing but a diaper, Mrs. Craig worried that he would catch cold.

Underline the misplaced modifier in the following sentence.

> Teetering up the driveway in a pair of high-heeled shoes, we smiled at the little girl.

Who was wearing the shoes: *we* or *the little girl?* The misplaced modifier is the introductory phrase.

Try correcting the sentence both ways. First, place the modifier directly after the word it describes.

_____

_____

Second, leave the modifier in its original position but turn it into a dependent clause by adding the words *As she was* at the beginning.

_____

_____

> We smiled at the little girl teetering up the driveway in a pair of high-heeled shoes.
> As she was teetering up the driveway in a pair of high-heeled shoes, we smiled at the little girl.

Exercise 9: Correcting Misplaced Modifiers

Directions: Underline the misplaced modifying phrase in each sentence below. Then rewrite the sentence to correct it either by moving the modifier or by changing it to a dependent clause. Be sure to punctuate the new sentence correctly. If a dependent clause begins the sentence, follow it with a comma.

1. Stuck under his chair, Morris felt a large, moist blob of bubble gum.

2. Destroyed by hail, Larry Gunderson stared gloomily at his wheat field.

3. Swinging effortlessly from branch to branch, the children watched the chimpanzee.

4. The prisoner was escorted to Death Row by four guards screaming for mercy.

5. Gasping for air, the fans encouraged the marathon runner to complete the last hundred yards.

6. Hidden behind a layer of dense brown smog, we could barely see the outlines of the mountains.

7. A suave gentleman strolled through the park with a neatly trimmed moustache and beard.

8. Sonja draped her boa constrictor around the trunk of the apple tree with a slight smile.

9. Eager to recruit top athletes, promising high school seniors are offered full scholarships by some colleges.

10.   Fuzzy and shriveled, we finally found the decaying orange in Will's top file drawer.

THE MISPLACED MODIFIERS AND REWRITTEN SENTENCES ARE ON PAGE 328.

Dangling Modifiers

Read the sentence below and answer this question: Who was working on the car?

> After flushing the radiator and installing a new thermostat, the car still overheated.

You couldn't answer the question, could you? Sentence structure tells you that the modifying phrase *After flushing the radiator and installing a new thermostat* describes the word *car*, but common sense argues that the car couldn't work on itself. The modifier just dangles by itself at the beginning of the sentence.

Dangling modifiers are describing phrases that have no word to describe in a sentence. They can be corrected in two ways:

- Add a word in the main sentence for the modifier to describe. (Be sure to place it near the modifier.)

    After flushing the radiator and installing a new thermostat, **Annette found that** the car still overheated.

- Turn the modifying phrase into a dependent clause.

    After Annette flushed the radiator and installed a new thermostat, the car still overheated.

Underline the dangling modifier in the following sentence.

> Exhausted after a twelve-hour shift, a hot meal and a hot bath sounded good.

Did you mark the introductory phrase as the dangling modifier?

Now correct the sentence in two ways. First, revise the main sentence to include a word for the phrase to modify.

_____

_____

Second, turn the modifying phrase into a dependent clause. (Hint: You could start the dependent clause with *Because*.)

_____

_____

You might have corrected the sentence like this:

> Exhausted after a twelve-hour shift, **Kelly thought** a hot meal and hot bath sounded good.
> **Because Kelly was exhausted after a twelve-hour shift**, a hot meal and a hot bath sounded good.

Not all dangling modifiers appear at the beginning of a sentence. Find and underline the dangling modifier in the sentence below.

> Seat belts should be fastened to avoid serious injuries during a crash.

Did you mark *to avoid serious injuries during a crash*?
Again, the sentence can be revised in two ways. First, change the main sentence to give the phrase a word to modify. (Hint: start the sentence with *You.*)

_____

_____

Second, turn the modifying phrase into a dependent clause.

_____

_____

You might have corrected the sentences like this:

> **You should fasten your seat belts** to avoid serious injuries during a crash.
> Seat belts should be fastened **if you want to avoid serious injuries during a crash.**

Exercise 10: Correcting Dangling Modifiers

Directions: Underline the dangling modifier in each sentence below. Then correct the sentence by adding a word for the modifier to describe or by turning the modifier into a dependent clause. Be sure to punctuate the new sentence correctly.

1. Being the only guy she'd ever dated, she was desperate to get married right away.
2. Garlic necklaces were worn at all times to keep from getting the flu.
3. Returning my library books two weeks late, the fine was $1.20.
4. The getaway car sped down Highway 37 unaware of the road block.
5. Eager to break for cocktails and dinner, the meeting was adjourned until eight o'clock the following morning.
6. Stumbling over a fallen log, the rifle discharged.
7. Despondent about losing his job and filing for bankruptcy, suicide was a tempting prospect.

8. Cleaning fluids and medicines should be locked away from small children to prevent accidental poisoning.

9. Curious about the strange visitors and eerie music night after night, the house was placed under surveillance.

10. Giggling uncontrollably, the room seemed to spin around me after my fourth glass of champagne.

SAMPLE ANSWERS ARE ON PAGES 328–29.

Renaming Phrases as Modifiers

So far you've looked at sentence combining using prepositional phrases and phrases formed from verbs. A third kind of modifying phrase is a **renaming phrase** (sometimes called an *appositive*). Here are some examples of how the renaming phrase can be used.

> "The Edge of Disaster" features plots about divorce, disease, and drug addiction. "The Edge of Disaster" is my favorite soap opera.
> **becomes**
> "The Edge of Disaster," my favorite soap opera, features plots about divorce, disease, and drug addiction.

Circle the phrase *my favorite soap opera* in the new, combined sentence and draw an arrow to the word or phrase it describes.

Did you extend the arrow to "The Edge of Disaster"?

Try a second example:

> One successful halfway house for juvenile offenders is run by Dave Jackson. Dave is a former reform school resident.
> **becomes**
> One successful halfway house for juvenile offenders is run by Dave Jackson, **a former reform school resident.**

Circle the phrase *a former reform school resident* in the combined sentence and draw an arrow to the word or phrase it describes.

Notice that, once again, the modifying noun phrase describes another noun: *Dave Jackson.*

Just like the other modifying phrases you've been studying in this chapter, renaming phrases must be placed carefully in a sentence. Renaming phrases always come right after the noun they refer to.

A *renaming phrase* supplies additional information about another noun (person, place, thing, or idea) in the sentence. A renaming phrase appears directly after the noun it describes.

FOCUS ON PUNCTUATION

Renaming Phrases

Renaming phrases are separated by commas from the rest of the sentence. If a renaming phrase comes in the middle of a sentence, put commas before and after it.

Tim Baysinger, **my sister's ex-husband**, simply quit his job and disappeared.
My vote goes to Pennington, **a person with experience and integrity**.

Exercise 11: Using Renaming Phrases

Part A
Directions: Punctuate the renaming phrases in the following sentences.

1. The Statue of Liberty a gift from France stands at the entrance to New York Harbor.

2. Bone strength depends on an adequate supply of calcium a mineral found in dairy products and some vegetables.

3. This week's lottery winner a mother of ten from the Bronx will receive twenty thousand dollars a year for the next twenty years.

4. Use Dazzle a revolutionary new detergent to get your clothes sunshine clean.

5. Our store detective is Farley Finck a man who can spot a shoplifter at fifty paces.

Part B
Directions: Combine the following pairs of sentences by using renaming phrases as modifiers. Be careful to punctuate the phrases correctly.

Example: For dinner we're having your favorite meal. Your favorite meal is spaghetti and meatballs.

For dinner we're having your favorite meal, spaghetti and meatballs.

1. The movie being shown tonight is *Rocky. Rocky* is a film about a common man who makes his dream come true.

2. Unfortunately, my fiancé's favorite vegetable is cauliflower. Cauliflower is the one food I'm allergic to.

3. Stephen King's novels are popular with young adults. Stephen King's novels are fast-paced horror stories.

4. Paula Hansen owns the hardware store on Second Street. Paula is my next-door neighbor.

5. The plane crashed while attempting to make an emergency landing. The plane was a B-17.

6. I've always wanted to visit New Orleans. New Orleans is a city with a reputation for fine food and great jazz.

7. Dr. Sidney Boldt had never developed a smooth bedside manner. Dr. Boldt was a sour man with a persistent frown on his face.

8. The band was playing "You Ain't Nothin' But a Hound Dog" when Angelo realized he'd forgotten to feed his poodle. The song was an old Elvis Presley hit.

9. Our next speaker is Sharon Moser. She is a woman with a keen sense of justice and a determination to protect the rights of all our citizens.

10. Maggie may have been a Scot, but she refused to eat haggis. Haggis is a disgusting concoction of oatmeal and the vital organs of sheep.

SAMPLE ANSWERS ARE ON PAGE 329.

Parallel Structure

What Is Parallel Structure?

In Chapter 2, you learned that a sentence may contain compound elements connected by a conjunction such as *and* or *or*.

>   Pam likes water skiing, swimming, and sailing.

In this sentence there are three compound elements connected by the conjunction *and: water skiing, swimming,* and *sailing.* Notice that the three elements are consistent in form: each one ends in *ing.*

> Compound elements that are all in the same form have **parallel structure.** Using parallel structure makes a sentence easier and smoother to read.

Compare the sample sentence on page 191 with a sentence lacking parallel structure.

NONPARALLEL: Pam likes water skiing, to swim, and sails.

This time each element has a different form. The first contains an *ing* verb, the second *to* plus a verb, the third a simple present-tense verb. The sentence could be corrected in either of two ways. The writer could use all *ing* verbs, as in the original example. Or she could use *to* plus a verb for each element.

PARALLEL: Pam likes **to water ski, to swim,** and **to sail**.

Always use parallel structure with compound elements, whether they are single words, phrases, or clauses. Here are some examples of sentences that lack parallel structure, followed by their corrected parallel form. In each pair, circle the element that is changed to make the sentence correct.

Single Words

NONPARALLEL: Morris was so surprised by the question that he **paused** and **was stammering**.
PARALLEL: Morris was so surprised by the question that he **paused** and **stammered**.

In the incorrect sentence above, one verb is in simple past tense *(paused)* and the other is past continuing *(was stammering)*. In the corrected sentence, both verbs are in simple past tense.

NONPARALLEL: The qualities I admire most in a man are **honesty, courageous,** and **compassion**.
PARALLEL: The qualities I admire most in a man are **honesty, courage,** and **compassion**.

In the incorrect sentence above, there are two nouns and one describing word among the elements that should be parallel. In the corrected sentence, all the elements are nouns.

Phrases

NONPARALLEL: The goal of American democracy is a government **of the people, by the people,** and **that is run for the people**.
PARALLEL: The goal of American democracy is a government **of the people, by the people,** and **for the people**.

In the incorrect sentence above, there are two prepositional phrases and one clause among the elements that should be parallel. In the corrected sentence, they are all prepositional phrases.

NONPARALLEL: He's returning to school to **retrain for a higher-paying job** and **as an example for his sons**.
PARALLEL: He's returning to school to **retrain for a higher-paying job** and **to set an example for his sons**.

In the incorrect sentence, one phrase begins with *to* plus a verb and the other is a prepositional phrase. In the corrected sentence, both phrases begin with *to* + verb.

Making Elements Parallel

To check for parallel structure, you must first identify the compound elements. Look for the conjunction *and, but, or,* or *nor*; then decide which words the conjunction joins. After you've located the compound elements, check to be sure that the word forms are alike.

Remember, you're looking for similarity in form, not meaning. *Journalist, lawyer,* and *engineering* are related in meaning: all deal with occupations. However, the first two nouns refer to people, while the third refers to a career. A parallel list would be *journalist, lawyer,* and *engineer* (all people) or *journalism, law,* and *engineering* (all careers).

Underline the compound elements in the following sentence. Then circle the element that is not parallel to the others.

> Elizabeth draws attention to herself by dyeing her hair lavender, wearing green fingernail polish, and she speaks with a fake French accent.

The first two elements are phrases beginning with *ing* verbs, while the third is a clause. There is no need to repeat the subject in the third compound element.

Now rewrite the sentence using parallel structure.

_____

_____

> Elizabeth draws attention to herself by dyeing her hair lavender, wearing green fingernail polish, and **speaking with a fake French accent**.

Exercise 12: Revising for Parallel Structure

Part A

Directions: Underline the compound elements in each sentence below and circle the element that is not parallel in structure to the others. Then rewrite the sentence to create parallel structure.

Example: That man is arrogant, (a snob,) and selfish.
    That man is arrogant, snobbish, and selfish.

1. A gymnast must be well coordinated, agile, and have strength.

2. Knitting nose warmers and to play Wahoo were Albert's hobbies.

3. Mr. Bubany was brave, honest, and a compassionate man.

4. We can solve arithmetic problems by adding, subtracting, multiplication, and dividing.

5. Why does Elizabeth love to cook but she hates to do dishes?

6. When Sue had the flu, she took aspirin, drank plenty of liquids, and she slept a lot.

7. Long ago I discovered that I could relax by sipping a cup of hot tea or if I listened to soft music.

8. The kids tracked mud in the hallway, through the kitchen, and they got it on the living room carpet.

9. John stopped, was scratching his head, and wondered what to do next.

10. One of life's greatest sorrows is to have a child, to care for him lovingly as he grows, and then when you lose him to drugs.

Part B

Directions: Use parallel structure to complete the following sentences.

1. Three character traits that I admire in a person are

   _____ , _____ , and

   _____ .

2. _____ , _____ ,

   _____ , and _____ are

   all careers that interest me.

3. In my spare time I like to _____ or

   _____ .

4. I would like to find out _____ ,

   _____ , and _____ .

5. Yesterday morning I _____ ,

   _____ , and _____ .

6. This country will be a better place to live when our citizens

   _____ and _____ .

7. An effective speaker talks _____ and

   _____ .

8. _____ , _____ ,

   _____ , and _____ are good

   ways to pass the time on a rainy Saturday.

9. Whenever I lose something, I look _____ ,

_____ , and _____ .

10. An ideal spouse should be _____ ,

_____ , and _____ .

ANSWERS AND SAMPLE SENTENCES ARE ON PAGES 329–30.

Pronoun Reference

Noticing Confusing Pronouns

How would you react to a friend who walked up to you and began a conversation like this?

"It was incredible! I've never seen anything like it! You could see them coming, but we couldn't tell how fast. And then it happened! You can't begin to describe it! They said I would be in shock for a while, and they're right!"

Probably you would respond by firing questions back as fast as you could: "What was incredible? What haven't you seen anything like? Who was coming? Was I really there? What happened? Who said you would be in shock?"

The problem with your friend's speech is the confusing use of pronouns. You'll remember from Chapter 2 that pronouns (words like *I, him, this,* and *it*) replace and refer to nouns. Used properly, they're certainly helpful little words. However, if they aren't used clearly and logically, communication can clank to a halt.

To avoid confusing and frustrating your reader, follow two basic rules when using pronouns:

1. Pronouns must refer clearly to their antecedents.

2. Pronouns must agree with their antecedents.

Avoid Confusing Pronouns

As you learned in Chapter 2, an antecedent is the word a pronoun refers to. If there is any possible confusion about the antecedent of a pronoun, don't make your reader guess. Sometimes you can use a noun instead of one of the pronouns to make the sentence's meaning clear.

CONFUSING: Fumiko refused to share an apartment with Liyuh because **she** despised **her** taste in music.

CLEAR: Fumiko refused to share an apartment with Liyuh because **Liyuh** despised her taste in music.

CLEAR: Fumiko refused to share an apartment with Liyuh because she despised **Liyuh's** taste in music.

In the confusing sentence, you don't know whether Fumiko despised Liyuh's taste or Liyuh despised Fumiko's. You can't tell what the antecedents for *she* and *her* are. Notice that the meaning of the sentence changes depending on how you correct it.

A second way to eliminate confusion is to rephrase the sentence.

CONFUSING: Your wife is picking up your daughter at school, so **she** won't meet you at the office.

CLEAR: Your daughter won't meet you at the office because your wife is picking her up at school.

CLEAR: Your wife won't meet you at the office because she is picking up your daughter at school.

In the confusing sentence, you don't know who won't be at the office, the wife or the daughter.

Circle the confusing pronoun in the sentence below.

Jason will ride home with Dave if he gets off work early.

The problem pronoun is *he*. Will Dave or Jason get off work early? Rewrite the sentence, substituting one of the names for the confusing pronoun.

Exercise 13: Eliminating Confusing Pronouns

Directions: Rewrite each sentence containing a confusing pronoun to make the meaning clear. Either replace the confusing pronoun with a noun or rephrase the sentence. Mark any correct sentences with a *C*.

Example: _____ Susan never saw Anne again after she moved to Los Angeles.

After Anne moved to Los Angeles, Susan never saw her again.

_____ 1. Sam and Ted got into a bitter argument after he called him a liar.

_____ 2. As the dog approached the wounded bear, it was snarling menacingly.

_____ 3. I like November much better than February; it's such a dreary month.

_____ 4. Steven will probably never speak to James again now that he's a millionaire.

_____ 5. I can't decide whether to buy the brown shoes or the black ones; they're more expensive, but they'll probably last longer.

_____ 6. Sonja never spoke to Maria again although she wanted to maintain their friendship.

_____ 7. Mrs. Perez smiled fondly as she watched her toddler playing in the wading pool.

_____ 8. Just as he was about to step from the curb, Sean glanced up and shouted, "Tim, watch out!"

_____ 9. Because fish is high in protein but low in cholesterol, it's better for most people than beef.

_____ 10. The country music fans and the rock fans never got along because they thought the others were stupid and crude.

SAMPLE ANSWERS ARE ON PAGE 330.

Avoid Vague Pronouns

In the last section, you looked at pronouns that were confusing because they could logically refer to two antecedents. Pronouns can also be confusing if they have no antecedent at all.

CONFUSING: Doyle Garrison insists that the welfare system is run poorly because **they** just don't understand what it means to be poor.

CLEAR: Doyle Garrison insists that the welfare system is poorly run because **politicians** just don't understand what it means to be poor.

In the confusing sentence, who are _they_: members of Congress? state legislators? social workers? There is no antecedent for _they_ in this sentence. To avoid such vagueness, replace the pronoun with an appropriate noun, as the writer did in the clear sentence.

Editing hint: Always be sure to read the entire sentence or paragraph when you correct a confusing pronoun. Be sure you match the intended meaning of the sentence.

It, they, and _this_ are the pronouns most likely to lack an antecedent. Whenever you see one of these words as you're proofreading, make sure that it clearly refers to a specific noun. If it doesn't, add the necessary noun.

Circle the vague pronoun in the following sample passage.

Tom told Stephanie that he was going bowling with his buddies every Monday night. She found out later that he was spending the evening with an exotic dancer. This made Stephanie so angry that she promptly sued for divorce.

Did you circle _This_? The word has no clear antecedent. What made Stephanie angry: Tom's lie? his affair? his preference for exotic dancing over ballet? Rewrite the last sentence of the passage in whatever way you think is logical to make the meaning clear.

_____

_____

You might have answered like this:

> **Tom's lying and cheating** made Stephanie so angry that she promptly sued for divorce.

Try one more example. Circle the vague pronoun in the sentence below.

> Everyone in the hall, including the bride and groom, was drunk; it almost turned into a riot.

The word _it_ is the vague pronoun this time. Replace it with a noun that summarizes the action.

_____

_____

You might have answered like this:

> Everyone in the hall, including the bride and groom, was drunk; the reception almost turned into a riot.

Exercise 14: Eliminating Vague Pronouns

Directions: In each of the following sentences, cross out the vague pronoun and replace it with a word or phrase that makes the meaning clear. Mark any correctly worded sentences with a _C._

Example: As the sergeant entered the barracks, ~~they~~ _the soldiers_ snapped to attention.

_____ 1. You should have seen the children chasing each other around the playground; it was hilarious.

_____ 2. With the growing importance of computers, they need more qualified instructors at all levels.

_____ 3. Although the doctor lectured the teenagers on the dangers of smoking, it didn't stop them from experimenting.

_____ 4. They say that animals grow thicker fur before an unusually harsh winter.

_____ 5. When the father rocked and sang to his baby, it seemed to quiet the child.

_____ 6. We asked Laura to get some counseling, but she insisted that they do more harm than good.

_____ 7. Mr. Cutforth was notified last night that he'd won. This excited him so much that he nearly passed out.

_____ 8. In the article they say that acid rain is endangering wildlife and forests in the Northeast.

_____ 9. When Smith and Torriello wrote the book, they didn't expect it to sell fifty thousand copies.

_____ 10. Marian wanted to go into engineering because they have an excellent income.

SAMPLE ANSWERS ARE ON PAGE 330.

Humans and Nonhumans

A small group of pronouns called *relative pronouns* link two ideas within a sentence. You must make sure that relative pronouns agree with their antecedents. Look at a sample sentence:

> Sandra Martin, **who** is a successful local realtor, will present a workshop for prospective homebuyers next Tuesday.

In this sentence the pronoun *who* is used to link two ideas:

> Sandra Martin is a successful local realtor.
> Sandra will present a workshop next Tuesday.

Let's look at another example:

> The Sears Tower, **which** is located in Chicago, is one of the tallest buildings in the world.

Here the pronoun *which* combines two ideas:

> The Sears Tower is in Chicago.
> The Sears Tower is one of the tallest buildings in the world.

Now study one final sentence:

> The speaker **that** we heard last night works for an insurance company **that** might relocate in San Diego.

The pronoun *that* links ideas in this third sentence:

> The speaker works for an insurance company.
> We heard the speaker last night.
> The insurance company might relocate in San Diego.

Why did the first sample sentence use *who*, the second one *which*, and the third one *that*? The answer lies in the antecedents. In the first example, the antecedent for *who* is a person, Sandra Martin. In the second sentence, the antecedent for *which* is an object, the Sears Tower. In the third sentence, *that* referred once to a person (the speaker) and once to a thing (the insurance company).

Relative pronouns (*who*, *which*, and *that*) must agree with their antecedents.

Relative Pronoun	Refers to
who (whom, whose)	humans
which	nonhumans (animals and objects)
that	humans or nonhumans

Exercise 15: Choosing the Correct Relative Pronoun—

Directions: In each sentence, circle the antecedent for the relative pronoun. Then underline the relative pronoun that agrees with it.

Example: My (Uncle Ben) *(who, which)* is a retired carpenter, gave me some excellent advice on remodeling the kitchen.

1. The horror movie *(who, that)* we saw last night was too gruesome for me.

2. The shortstop fired the ball to the catcher, *(who, which)* tagged the runner out at home plate.

3. Soccer, *(which, who)* involves more running and less body contact than football, is becoming popular throughout the United States.

4. Zebra finches are small gray birds *(who, that)* sound like a child's squeeze toy.

5. Much outdoor furniture is made of redwood, *(who, which)* is highly resistant to variations in moisture and temperature.

6. Lyndon Johnson, *(who, which)* became president after John Kennedy's assassination, was elected to a full term in 1964.

7. I've always preferred cats to dogs, *(which, who)* seem totally lacking in self-respect and dignity.

8. A shift in Pacific Ocean currents, *(which, who)* occurs every few years, may dramatically change weather patterns in the United States.

9. The teller *(who, which)* was robbed at gunpoint yesterday is my sister.

10. A fire destroyed the house *(who, that)* the Bensons had been renting for years.

ANSWERS ARE ON PAGES 330–31.

Agreement in Number

In Chapter 3, you learned that subjects and present-tense verbs must agree in number: singular subjects take verbs ending in -s, and plural subjects take verbs with no -s. A similar rule applies to pronouns.

Pronouns must agree in number with their antecedents.

The hawk dipped **its** wings into the water as **it** skimmed across the surface of the lake.

The hawks dipped **their** wings into the water as **they** skimmed across the surface of the lake.

In the first sentence above, *its* and *it* are singular because their antecedent, *hawk*, is singular. In the second sentence, the pronouns *their* and *they* are plural because their antecedent, *hawks*, is plural.

Study the following chart to remind yourself which pronouns are singular and which are plural.

Singular Pronouns
I, me, my, mine
you, your, yours
he, she, it, him
her, his, hers, its

Plural Pronouns
we, us, our, ours
you, your, yours
they, them, their, theirs

To check for agreement in number, follow these three steps:

1. Find the antecedent of the pronoun.

2. Decide whether the antecedent is singular or plural.

3. Make sure that the pronoun agrees in number with the antecedent.

Use the three steps to decide whether the pronoun *they* is used correctly in the sentence below.

The government became so huge that **they** didn't listen to the people anymore.

1. What is the antecedent of *they*?
   The antecedent is *government*.

2. Is *government* singular or plural?
   Government is singular.

3. Does the pronoun *they* match a singular noun?
   No. *They* is a plural pronoun.

Here's how the sentence should be written:

> The government became so big that **it** didn't listen to the people anymore.

Be careful to maintain agreement in number with antecedents throughout a passage. As you check for errors in Part 1 and Part 2 of the GED Writing Skills Test, correct any incorrect shifts between singular and plural words.

Circle the pronoun that does not agree in number with the rest of the passage in the example below.

> A taxicab driver is an independent person. He owns his own cab and sets his own work hours. The city usually licenses them to operate within the metropolitan area.

The first sentence refers to a singular subject: *a driver*. The pronouns *he* and *his* in the second sentence refer to *driver*; they are also singular. However, the pronoun *them* in the third sentence is plural. To agree with the antecedent *driver*, the pronoun should be *him*.

As you learned in Chapter 3, some words like *either, neither,* and *both* control whether a compound subject is singular or plural. Study the following examples:

> Both Jeremy and his brother **enjoy** cooking.
> Neither Jeremy nor his brother **enjoys** doing dishes.

In the first example sentence above, *Both* joins the subjects together to make a plural subject. In the second sentence, *Neither* separates the subjects. The subject closest to the verb, *brother*, is singular. The verb forms agree with the subjects accordingly.

Words like *both* and *neither* also control pronoun-antecedent agreement. Study the following examples:

> Both Jeremy and his brother clean **their** rooms annually.
> Neither Jeremy nor his brother cleans **his** room weekly.
> Neither Jeremy nor his brothers clean **their** rooms weekly.

In the first example sentence above, the plural subject requires a plural pronoun. In the second sentence, the part of the subject closest to the pronoun, *brother*, is singular, so the pronoun is singular. In the third sentence, the part of the subject that is closest to the pronoun, *brothers*, is plural, requiring the plural pronoun *their*.

For further review on these special words, you may want to restudy pages 96-97.

Exercise 16: Making Pronouns Agree in Number——

Part A

Directions: For each sentence, underline the pronoun that matches its antecedent in number. Circle the antecedent.

Example: Every (recruit) must make (*his*, their) bed by 6:15.

1. After World War II, Germany received millions of dollars in foreign aid to help rebuild *(their, its)* cities.

2. Neither woman wanted to spend *(her, their)* day off cooking and cleaning house.

3. Both Carter and Reagan spent much of *(his, their)* leisure time at Camp David.

4. Either the cat or the dogs have left *(its, their)* footprints on my clean kitchen floor.

5. The dog and the cat have left *(its, their)* footprints on my clean kitchen floor.

6. When learning about metric measurements, think of an ordinary paper clip. *(They weigh, It weighs)* exactly one gram, and *(their, its)* wire is one millimeter thick.

7. The insurance company sent *(its, their)* agent to discuss a new policy.

8. Although finches are attractive little birds to keep as pets, *(it, they)* can't be taught to talk.

9. All of the staff members signed the petition to have *(their, his)* supervisor removed for incompetence.

10. When a man nears forty, *(they begin, he begins)* to think about growing old.

Part B

Directions: Proofread the following paragraph for errors in agreement in number. Make corrections by crossing out the error and writing in the correct word or words in the space above. Make sure that the paragraph maintains agreement in number from sentence to sentence. You may occasionally need to change a verb to agree with the new pronoun. The first error has been corrected as an example.

Children are much less upset by hospital stays if ~~he has~~ *they have* been prepared properly for the experience. If possible, he should be taken on a tour of the hospital before he is admitted. Becoming familiar with these new surroundings will reduce his anxiety and help them adjust more quickly to being away from home.

ANSWERS ARE ON PAGE 331.

Agreement in Person

Personal pronouns can be grouped in three categories: first person, which refers to the speaker or writer (I); second person, which refers to the audience (you); and third person, which refers to the individual or group spoken about (he, she, they). Study the box on page 204.

Personal Pronouns

First person: I, me my, mine, we, us, our, ours

> When I applied for the job, I stated my qualifications clearly.

Second person: you, your, yours

> When you applied for the job, Joan, you stated your qualifications clearly.

Third person: he, she, it, him, her, his, hers, its, they, them, their, theirs

> When Carol applied for the job, she stated her qualifications clearly.

Within a sentence or longer passage, don't shift from one category of pronouns to another. Maintain agreement in person.

> DOES NOT AGREE: When **we** finally reached the summit, **you** could see for miles in every direction.
> AGREES: When **we** finally reached the summit, **we** could see for miles in every direction.

In the first example sentence above, the pronoun shifts from first to second person. The second sentence correctly shows that the writer, not the reader, saw the view.

> DOES NOT AGREE: If **a worker** is injured on the job, **you** will receive worker's compensation.
> AGREES: If **a worker** is injured on the job, **he** will receive worker's compensation.

In the first example sentence above, the pronoun shifts from third to second person. The second sentence correctly shows that the worker, not the reader, should receive benefits.

Circle the pronouns in the following sentence. Do they agree in person?

> When we walked into the kitchen, you could smell the aroma of freshly baked bread.

The pronouns *we* and *you* do not agree, since *we* is a first-person pronoun and *you* is second person. Write the sentence correctly in the space below.

_____

_____

You might have written the following answer, or you might have used *you* instead of *we*:

> As **we** walked into the kitchen, **we** could smell the aroma of freshly baked bread.

Just as you should check a passage for agreement in number, you should proofread for agreement in person. It's especially easy to slip from first or third to second person. Don't use *you* unless you're speaking directly to your reader.

Circle the pronoun that does not agree in person with the rest of the passage below.

When we heard a rumble of thunder, we looked out the window apprehensively. By the erratic flicker of lightning, you could see tree branches whipping back and forth. We scurried around the house, closing windows and hunting for flashlights in case of a power outage.

Did you circle the pronoun *you* in the second sentence? Cross it out and replace it with *we* to write the passage consistently in first person.

Exercise 17: Making Sentences Agree in Person———

Part A

Directions: Underline the pronoun that agrees in person with its antecedent. Circle the antecedent.

1. As our plane was crossing the Atlantic, *(we, you)* saw a magnificent sunrise.

2. If *(you're not, one isn't)* careful around farm machinery, you can be seriously injured.

3. Jim's favorite actor was John Wayne because *(you, he)* always knew that in the end Wayne would overpower the forces of evil.

4. Most farmers and construction workers agree that plain water satisfies *(your, their)* thirst far better than any carbonated soft drink.

Part B

Directions: Proofread the passage below for agreement in person. Cross out and replace any underlined pronouns that do not agree with the rest of the paragraph. Some of the underlined pronouns are correct as written.

As we neared the seacoast, the fog enveloped us so thickly that you couldn't see two feet in front of our car. One felt as if you were moving in outer space, with no signposts, no trees, not even a roadway to orient you. Even the sounds were muffled. An occasional car droned past us, its driver slowly feeling his way in the opposite direction. Most of the time, though, all you could hear was the dull throb of the waves on the beach and the mournful foghorns warning ships away from hidden rocks.

ANSWERS ARE ON PAGE 331.

Chapter Highlights: Keeping Your Story Straight

1. You can use a modifying phrase to combine ideas in a single sentence. To make sure that the sentence is clear, place the modifying phrase as close as possible to the word it describes.

    WRONG: The motorcycle gang intimidated the neighborhood roaring down the street in formation.

    RIGHT: Roaring down the street in formation, the motorcycle gang intimidated the neighborhood.

2. Set off renaming phrases and introductory modifying phrases with commas.

    Mortimer, my pet toad, just zapped a fly.
    Having finished his lunch, Mortimer dozed on a rock.

3. Use parallel structure whenever you include compound elements in a sentence. That is, use a similar word form for all items in a list.

    WRONG: Timothy was dishonest, crude, and he was a coward.

    RIGHT: Timothy was dishonest, crude, and cowardly.

4. Make pronouns refer clearly to their antecedents. Avoid confusing pronouns that could logically refer to either of two antecedents, and avoid vague pronouns that have no antecedent at all.

    WRONG: The couple was playing cards, but Todd thought it looked boring.

    RIGHT: The couple was playing cards, but Todd thought the game looked boring.

5. Make pronouns agree with their antecedents.

    a. Use the relative pronoun *(who, which,* or *that)* that matches its human or nonhuman antecedent.

        The man who used to live here played the drums.
        His pet cat, which still wanders by, is deaf.

    b. Make pronouns agree with their antecedents in number and person.

        WRONG: When we visited New York City, you couldn't go up in the Statue of Liberty.

        RIGHT: When we visited New York City, we couldn't go up in the Statue of Liberty.

6. When correcting confusing pronouns, be sure to read the passage as a whole to make sure the correction fits in with the rest of the pronouns in the passage.

★ GED PRACTICE★

Exercise 18: Sentence Structure Review

Directions: The following items are based on paragraphs which contain numbered sentences. Some of the sentences may contain errors in sentence structure, usage and punctuation related to modifiers, parallel structure, and pronoun reference. Read the paragraph and then answer the items based on it. For each item, choose the answer that would result in the most effective writing of the sentence or sentences.

(1) Calculators, once bulky and expensive machines have become much smaller and cheaper in the past twenty years; as a result, they are revolutionizing the way math is taught. (2) Because pocket calculators are now widely available at low prices, they say that elementary school students should spend less time drilling their addition and multiplication facts. (3) Instead, the children should be taught to analyze a word problem, they should select the information needed to solve it, and decide whether to add, subtract, multiply, or divide. (4) The calculators will perform the mechanical operations. (5) The children will be able to concentrate on the real thinking skills. (6) The danger in this shift from drill is that you may not recognize a simple error caused by hitting the wrong key on the calculator. (7) The best math students will continue to be the children which have good problem-solving skills and a strong command of arithmetic facts.

1. Sentence 1: **Calculators, once bulky and expensive machines have become much smaller and cheaper in the past twenty years; as a result, they are revolutionizing the way math is taught.**

    What correction should be made to this sentence?

    (1) remove the comma after *calculators*
    (2) insert a comma after *machines*
    (3) replace *cheaper* with *cheaply*
    (4) replace *they are* with *it is*
    (5) no correction is necessary

2. Sentence 2: **Because pocket calculators are now widely available at low prices, they say that elementary school students should spend less time drilling their addition and multiplication facts.**

    What correction should be made to this sentence?

    (1) remove *Because pocket calculators are*
    (2) replace *they* with *some educators*
    (3) replace *elementary school students* with *they*
    (4) replace *addition* with *adding*
    (5) no correction is necessary

3. Sentence 3: **Instead, the children should be taught to analyze a word problem, they should select the information needed to solve it, and decide whether to add, subtract, multiply, or divide.**

   Which of the following is the best way to write the underlined portion of this sentence? If you think the original is the best way to write the sentence, choose option (1).

   (1) they should select
   (2) selecting
   (3) to select
   (4) select
   (5) that they select

4. Sentences 4 and 5: **The calculators will perform the mechanical operations. The children will be able to concentrate on the real thinking skills.**

   The most effective combination of sentences 4 and 5 would include which of the following groups of words?

   (1) While the calculators perform the mechanical operations, the children
   (2) By performing the mechanical operations, the children
   (3) Concentrating on the real thinking skills, the calculators
   (4) The mechanical operations performed by the children
   (5) When the calculators concentrate on the real thinking skills,

5. Sentence 6: **The danger in this shift from drill is that you may not recognize a simple error caused by hitting the wrong key on the calculator.**

   Which of the following is the best way to write the underlined portion of this sentence? If you think the original is the best way to write the sentence, choose option (1).

   (1) you
   (2) we
   (3) he
   (4) they
   (5) one

6. Sentence 7: **The best math students will continue to be the children which have good problem-solving skills and a strong command of arithmetic facts.**

   What correction should be made to this sentence?

   (1) change *which* to *who*
   (2) replace *have good problem-solving skills* with *are skillful at solving problems*
   (3) insert *possessing* after *and*
   (4) replace *strong command* with *commanding strongly*
   (5) no correction is necessary

(1) Frank's parents warned him not to overuse his first credit card, which he cheerfully ignored and bought a new stereo system. (2) An expensive car, buying a large television set, and a trip to Las Vegas were next on Frank's list of plastic purchases. (3) By the middle of the following month, financial reality began to catch up with him; as a result, his spending spree screeched to a halt. (4) Frank always a carefree person, became depressed, withdrawn, and irritable. (5) After being confronted with a bill for twenty thousand dollars, the credit card was cut into tiny pieces.

7. Sentence 1: **Frank's parents warned him not to overuse his first credit card, which he cheerfully ignored and bought a new stereo system.**

   What correction should be made to this sentence?

   (1) replace *his* with *your*
   (2) replace *his* with *a person's*
   (3) replace *card, which he cheerfully ignored* with *card. He cheerfully ignored it*
   (4) replace *card, which he cheerfully ignored* with *card. He cheerfully ignored their advice*
   (5) no correction is necessary

8. Sentence 2: **An expensive car, buying a large television set, and a trip to Las Vegas were next on Frank's list of plastic purchases.**

   Which of the following is the best way to write the underlined portion of this sentence? If you think the original is the best way to write the sentence, choose option (1).

   (1) buying a
   (2) to buy a
   (3) bought a
   (4) he also bought a
   (5) a

9. Sentence 3: **By the middle of the following month, financial reality began to catch up with him; as a result, his spending spree screeched to a halt.**

   What correction should be made to this sentence?

   (1) insert a comma after *middle*
   (2) remove the comma after *month*
   (3) replace *him* with *them*
   (4) replace *his* with *your*
   (5) no correction is necessary

10. Sentence 4: **Frank always a carefree person, became depressed, withdrawn, and irritable.**

    What correction should be made to this sentence?

    (1) insert a comma after *Frank*
    (2) remove the comma after *person*
    (3) change *withdrawn* to *withdrew*
    (4) insert *he was* after *and*
    (5) no correction is necessary

11. Sentence 5: **After being confronted with a bill for twenty thousand dollars, the credit card was cut into tiny pieces.**

    What correction should be made to this sentence?

    (1) remove the comma after *dollars*
    (2) replace *the credit card was cut* with *Frank cut the credit card*
    (3) insert a comma after *cut*
    (4) insert *by Frank* after *pieces*
    (5) no correction is necessary

    (1) As Dave was pulling on his hiking boots and Jack was filling his backpack, Dave asked me if I was prepared for pain. (2) Within the first few hundred feet of our climb I discovered what he meant. (3) With every step up the steep mountain trail, I felt my pack grow heavier, my legs grow more tired, and my lungs become more desperate for oxygen. (4) We climbed higher and higher. (5) My heart was beating faster. (6) We finally reached the peak, and the view from the peak made our struggle worthwhile. (7) You could see range after range of mountains marching to the horizon.

12. Sentence 1: **As Dave was pulling on his hiking boots and Jack was filling his backpack, Dave asked me if I was prepared for pain.**

    What correction should be made to this sentence?

    (1) replace *As Dave was* with *With Dave*
    (2) replace *was filling* with *filled*
    (3) replace *Dave asked* with *he asked*
    (4) insert a comma after *prepared*
    (5) no correction is necessary

13. Sentences 2 and 3: **Within the first few hundred feet of our climb I discovered what he meant. With every step up the steep mountain trail, I felt my pack grow heavier, my legs grow more tired, and my lungs become more desperate for oxygen.**

    What correction should be made to these sentences?

    (1) insert a comma after *climb*
    (2) insert a comma after *step*
    (3) omit the comma after *trail*
    (4) change *become* to *became*
    (5) no correction is necessary

14. Sentences 4 and 5: **We climbed higher and higher. My heart was beating faster.**

    The most effective combination of sentences 4 and 5 would contain which of the following groups of words?

    (1) As we climbed higher, the faster
    (2) Climbing higher and higher, my heart
    (3) Although we climbed higher and higher, my heart
    (4) The higher we climbed, the faster
    (5) The higher we climbed, and my heart

15. Sentence 6: **We finally reached the peak, and the view from the peak made our struggle worthwhile.**

    If you rewrote sentence 6 beginning with

    Upon finally reaching the peak,

    the next words should be

    (1) the view
    (2) it made
    (3) our struggle
    (4) we decided
    (5) the peak's view

16. Sentence 7: <u>**You could see range after range of mountains marching to the horizon.**</u>

    Which of the following is the best way to write the underlined portion of this sentence? If you think the original is the best way to write the sentence, choose option (1).

    (1) You could see range after range of mountains marching to the horizon.
    (2) Marching to the horizon, you could see range after range of mountains.
    (3) We could see range after range of mountains marching to the horizon.
    (4) We could see range after range of mountains, marching to the horizon.
    (5) Marching to the horizon, range after range of mountains.

    ANSWERS ARE ON PAGES 331–32.

Chapter 5 Review Evaluation Chart

Question Type	Review Pages	Question Number	Number of Questions	Number Correct
Dangling/ misplaced modifiers	182–91	4, 11, 15	3	/3
Punctuation of modifiers	184, 190–91	1, 10, 13	3	/3
Parallel structure	191–95	3, 8, 14	3	/3
Pronoun reference	195–205	2, 5, 6, 7, 16	5	/5
No error		9, 12	2	/2

Passing score: 12 correct out of 16 items.

Your score: _____ correct out of 16 items.

If you have more than one item wrong in any category, you should review the explanations for the particular items you missed.

Cumulative Review

Editing Practice

Part A

Directions: Find and correct the twelve errors in the following passage. Five of these errors are related to skills that you learned in earlier chapters: subject-verb agreement, verb forms, fragments, and run-ons. You may want to review the checklists on pages 57, 109, and 163 to refresh your memory on what to look for. The other seven errors are related to problems you studied in this chapter. For these errors, use the checklist to the right as your proofreading guide.

☐ Are modifying phrases placed close to the words they describe?

☐ Are commas used to set off renaming phrases and introductory modifying phrases?

☐ Do pronouns refer clearly to their antecedents?

☐ Are pronouns consistent with their antecedents?

☐ Is parallel structure used for compound elements?

Break-ins, muggings, and rapes has increased dramatically in our community since 1960. With this increase in street crime we citizens have lost much of our freedom. Growing up, our front door was never locked. You simply didn't worry about someone walking in and stealing our property. At eight years old, my parents let me ride the bus downtown by myself. My mother always a protective person, had no qualms about my safety. A few years later when I was in high school, my friends and I would often meet at five o'clock in the morning and walk six blocks to the park, to play tennis. No reason to fear being robbed or raped.

My daughter, which is now ten, doesn't enjoy the same freedom I had. Our house is equiped with plenty of locks for the doors and a burglar alarm as well. We don't allow Cindy to take the bus alone or walking around the neighborhood after dark, there are too many reports of robberies and rapes for us to feel safe. For her and for most other children, the fear of crime has taken some of the fun out of childhood.

ANSWERS ARE ON PAGE 332.

Part B

Directions: Revise the essay you wrote on pages 177, 178, and 179. Use modifying phrases where appropriate to add variety and to link ideas logically. Then apply the proofreading checklist dealing with modifiers, pronouns, and parallel structure that you used in Part A to check for errors.

★ GED PRACTICE ★

Multiple-Choice Practice

Directions: The following items are based on paragraphs which contain numbered sentences. Some of the sentences may contain errors in sentence structure, usage, and mechanics. Read the paragraph and then answer the items based on it. For each item, choose the answer that would result in the most effective writing of the sentence or sentences.

(1) Although it may be less popular than softball or football. (2) Competitive swimming is an ideal summer sport for most children. (3) Certainly swimming provides healthful exercise. (4) Done regularly, it builds muscular strength in the upper body and the legs, increases flexibility, and will improve heart and lung capacity. (5) It provides this with minimal danger of injury. (6) Of course, a swimmer, like participants in other sports, risks an occasional pulled muscle. (7) However, there's no knee injuries from tackling and no concussions from unexpected contact with a line drive. (8) In addition to its physical pluses, swimming provides psychological benefits for children by promoting cooperation among team members as they cheered one another on, particularly in the relay events. 9) Equally important is the chance for each swimmer to chart their own progress. (10) Not everyone can earn a blue ribbon in an individual event. (11) Even swimmers who come in last can be satisfied if they have swum a second faster than they did in the previous meet.

1. Sentences 1 and 2: **Although it may be less popular than softball or football. Competitive swimming is an ideal summer sport for most children.**

   Which is the best way to rewrite the underlined portion of these sentences? If you think the original is the best way to write the sentences, choose option (1).

   (1) football. Competitive
   (2) football; competitive
   (3) football, competitive
   (4) football competitive
   (5) football, but competitive

2. Sentence 4: **Done regularly, it builds muscular strength in the upper body and the legs, increases flexibility, and will improve heart and lung capacity.**

   What correction should be made to this sentence?

   (1) change *builds* to *built*
   (2) change *builds* to *is building*
   (3) insert *your* after *increases*
   (4) replace *will improve* with *improves*
   (5) no correction is necessary

3. Sentence 5: **It provides this with minimal danger of injury.**

   What correction should be made to this sentence?

   (1) replace *it provides* with *By providing*
   (2) replace *It* with *And*
   (3) change *provides* to *provided*
   (4) replace *this* with *these benefits*
   (5) replace *this* with *that*

4. Sentence 6: **Of course, a swimmer, like participants in other sports, risks an occasional pulled muscle.**

   What correction should be made to this sentence?

   (1) replace *a swimmer* with *swimmers*
   (2) change *risks* to *risk*
   (3) change *risks* to *has risked*
   (4) insert a comma after *risks*
   (5) no correction is necessary

5. Sentence 7: **However, there's no knee injuries from tackling and no concussions from unexpected contact with a line drive.**

   What correction should be made to this sentence?

   (1) replace *there's* with *there is*
   (2) replace *there's* with *there are*
   (3) change the spelling of *tackling* to *tackleing*
   (4) replace *tackling and* with *tackling. And*
   (5) no correction is necessary

6. Sentence 8: **In addition to its physical pluses, swimming provides psychological benefits for children by promoting cooperation among team members as they cheered one another on, particularly in the relay events.**

   Which of the following is the best way to write the underlined portion of the sentence? If you think the original is the best way to write the sentence, choose option (1).

   (1) cheered
   (2) cheer
   (3) cheers
   (4) will be cheering
   (5) were cheering

7. Sentence 9: **Equally important is the chance for each swimmer to chart their own progress.**

   What correction should be made to this sentence?

   (1) change *is* to *was*
   (2) change *is* to *will be*
   (3) replace *each swimmer* with *swimmers*
   (4) replace *their* with *your*
   (5) no correction is necessary

8. Sentences 10 and 11: **Not everyone can earn a blue ribbon in an individual event. Even swimmers who come in last can be satisfied if they have swum a second faster than they did in the previous meet.**

The most effective combination of sentences 10 and 11 would include which of the following groups of words?

(1) because even
(2) but even
(3) if even
(4) when even
(5) in addition, even

(1) When automobiles and airplanes might symbolize the changes in American technology in the first half of this century, computers certainly symbolize the second half. (2) These electronic marvels once room-sized monstrosities full of wires and vacuum tubes, have been reduced in size and introduced into countless household and business settings. (3) In the home, computers control appliances as varied as microwave ovens, cameras, and television sets. (4) Automobiles and trucks also contain computers. (5) The computers regulate their fuel and electrical systems. (6) Wherever financial transactions take place, computers is likely to appear. (7) They have replaced cash registers in supermarkets and department stores. (8) Not only do they print receipts listing the items sold, but they also maintain an inventory of merchandise on hand. (9) Automatic tellers allowed banks' customers to make deposits, withdrawals, and transfers by pressing a few buttons. (10) Even gas stations have became computerized as customers paying by credit card wait while a central computer thousands of miles away checks card numbers and records transactions.

9. Sentence 1: **When automobiles and airplanes might symbolize the changes in American technology in the first half of this century, computers certainly symbolize the second half.**

Which of the following is the best way to write the underlined portion of this sentence? If you think the original is the best way to write the sentence, choose option (1).

(1) When
(2) Because
(3) As though
(4) Wherever
(5) Whereas

10. Sentence 2: **These electronic marvels once room-sized monstrosities full of wires and vacuum tubes, have been reduced in size and introduced into countless household and business settings.**

What correction should be made to this sentence?

(1) insert a comma after *marvels*
(2) remove the comma after *tubes*
(3) replace *size and* with *size. And*
(4) insert a comma after *household*
(5) no correction is necessary

11. Sentence 3: **In the home, computers control appliances as varied as microwave ovens, cameras, and television sets.**

What correction should be made to this sentence?

(1) change the spelling of *varyed* to *varied*
(2) change the spelling of *ovens* to *ovenes*
(3) remove the comma after *ovens*
(4) insert *have computers* after *cameras*
(5) no correction is necessary

12. Sentences 4 and 5: **Automobiles and trucks also contain computers. The computers regulate their fuel and electrical systems.**

    The most effective combination of sentences 4 and 5 would include which of the following groups of words?

    (1) computers, and the computers regulate
    (2) computers that regulate
    (3) computers, they regulate
    (4) computers although they regulate
    (5) computers who regulate

13. Sentence 6: **Wherever financial transactions take place, computers is likely to appear.**

    What correction should be made to this sentence?

    (1) replace *Wherever* with *Even though*
    (2) insert a comma after *Wherever*
    (3) remove the comma after *place*
    (4) change *is* to *are*
    (5) no correction is necessary

14. Sentence 8: **Not only do they print receipts listing the items sold, but they also maintain an inventory of merchandise on hand.**

    Which of the following is the best way to write the underlined portion of this sentence? If you think the original is the best way to write the sentence, choose option (1).

    (1) they also maintain
    (2) also maintaining
    (3) to be maintaining
    (4) also to maintain
    (5) also maintains

15. Sentence 9: **Automatic tellers allowed banks' customers to make deposits, withdrawals, and transfers by pressing a few buttons.**

    Which of the following is the best way to write the underlined portion of this sentence? If you think the original is the best way to write the sentence, choose option (1).

    (1) allowed
    (2) allowing
    (3) allows
    (4) allow
    (5) are allowed

16. Sentence 10: **Even gas stations have became computerized as customers paying by credit card wait while a central computer thousands of miles away checks card numbers and records transactions.**

    What correction should be made to this sentence?

    (1) change *became* to *become*
    (2) replace *computerized as customers* with *computerized, customers*
    (3) insert a comma after *wait*
    (4) change *wait* to *waits*
    (5) change *checks* to *check*

    ANSWERS ARE ON PAGE 332.

Cumulative Review Evaluation Chart

Questions From	Question Number	Number of Questions	Number Correct
Chapter 3 Verbs	2, 5, 6, 11, 13, 15, 16	7	/7
Chapter 4 Combining Ideas in Sentences	1, 8, 9	3	/3
Chapter 5 Keeping Your Story Straight	3, 7, 10 12, 14	5	/5
No error	4	1	/1

Passing score: 12 out of 16 correct.

Your score: _____ out of 16 correct.

6

 POLISHING YOUR WRITING

When you complete a rough draft of an essay, does an enormous sense of relief sweep over you—a "Whew! That's done!" sort of feeling? Finishing a draft should give you a sense of accomplishment. Planning and drafting an essay require a great deal of mental effort.

But before you set your essay aside as a finished product, remember the final stages in the writing process: **revising** and **editing**. Like the difference between a rough-cut gem and a diamond gleaming in a jewelry store window, the difference between a promising piece of writing and a fine essay lies in the polishing.

You've been editing throughout this book. You've learned to check for complete sentences, clearly combined ideas, consistent verbs and pronouns, and correct punctuation and spelling. By correcting these surface features of your writing, you'll make sure that your reader can concentrate on your ideas.

Revising, however, is different. Revising is the process of strengthening the content, organization, and wording of a piece of writing. In this step, you'll be putting yourself in the reader's place in order to decide what changes will sharpen meaning and make your writing more convincing.

It isn't easy to shift from viewing your paper as the writer to viewing it as a reader. After all, *you* know exactly what you mean! If possible, let your first draft rest a few days before you revise it. This breather will help give you a new perspective on the paper—fresh eyes to use in the task ahead.

By now, at least a few days will have passed since you finished your essay on page 179 of Chapter 5. Take the draft out and reread it, imagining that you are seeing it for the first time. Can you find the unifying statement? Is the meaning clear throughout? Does the paper move logically from one point to another? Is the material convincing? Take a few minutes right now to jot down ideas for any changes that would make your paper clearer to your reader.

There is no one correct way to revise an essay. You'll find yourself adding, removing, replacing, and moving material in order to strengthen meaning. In this chapter you'll study three possible ways to improve an essay through revision: using specifics, using sentence and paragraph links, and tightening the wording.

As you study each section, you'll see how one writer revised parts of an essay written in response to a question in Chapter 5: "Should young adults be required to perform a year of public service?" Then you'll revise your own Chapter 5 essay.

The original draft of the sample essay is printed below. As you read through the essay for the first time, notice how you respond to it. Are you convinced by the writer's arguments? Do you notice errors? How could this essay be improved?

America needs the help and assistance of its young adults during times of peace as well as during times of war. The drafting of young people shouldn't be limited to military purposes. At least one year of public service should be required. This requirement would be beneficial and helpful in many ways.

Public service jobs would provide automatic employment for young adults. They would no longer be causing trouble because they were bored. Young adults would be learning skills that they needed them to be good workers.

If the public service program were set up like the military service program, young adults could earn educational benefits by completing their year of duty. The money could be used for further training toward the career of their choice.

Required public service it would emphasize the importance our society places on helping others. Young people would learn how important it is to provide care for various groups who need help.

Required public service is an idea that its time has come. It will help the youth who work in the program, and it will help American society as a whole.

Using Specific Reasons

When someone is trying to persuade you, what makes his argument convincing? Usually you'll be willing to consider his point of view if he offers good reasons to back up his opinions.

Use specific reasons to explain your opinions.

Many writers make the mistake of circular reasoning when they attempt to persuade their readers. That is, rather than providing a specific reason to support their opinion, they restate the opinion in other words.

> PROBLEM: Teenagers are too young to drink alcoholic beverages because they aren't mature enough to handle alcohol.
>
> BETTER: Teenagers are too young to drink alcoholic beverages because they tend to be daredevils. They're willing to drink to excess because they're still testing their limits.

The problem sentence is saying "Teenagers are too young to drink because they're too young to drink." Can you see that *aren't mature enough* means the same thing as *too young*? In the revised version, the writer added two specific reasons why teenagers are too young to drink. Now look at another example.

> PROBLEM: *Sacred Ruby of the Ganges* is the most exciting film I've ever seen. Every other film was boring in comparison.
>
> BETTER: *Sacred Ruby of the Ganges* is the most exciting film I've ever seen because of the suspenseful chases, the romantic tension between the lead characters, and the constant danger from jungle animals.

The problem sentences are saying "The film was the most exciting because it was the most exciting." Can you see that *the most exciting film I've ever seen* says the same thing as *Every other film was boring in comparison*? The revised version gives specific reasons why the film was exciting.

Test the reasons you provide for each of your opinions in an essay. If you discover that you've restated something in other words, revise that section to make your support more convincing.

One of the three sentences below displays circular reasoning. Find it and correct it in the space provided.

> Japanese cars are better than American cars because Japanese cars are more sturdily made and use less gas.
>
> That book is boring because it simply doesn't interest me.
>
> A tax increase is needed because the county needs to raise wages to keep up with inflation.

_____

_____

Did you revise the second sentence? *Boring* and *doesn't interest me* are two ways of saying the same thing.

Exercise 1: Using Specific Reasons

Directions: Read each of the following sentences. If it provides a specific reason to support an opinion, write *OK*. If it uses circular reasoning, revise to add specific reasons.

Example: The mandatory retirement age should be raised because sixty-five is too low.

The mandatory retirement age should be raised because most sixty-five-year-old people are in better physical and mental health than older people were thirty-five years ago.

1. City life is more stressful than farm life because city life has more tension.

2. In my opinion, the federal government wastes taxpayers' money by spending it on overpriced goods like two-hundred-dollar hammers.

3. Cigarette smoking is a harmful habit because cigarettes are dangerous.

4. The automobile is one of the most useful inventions of this century; it has provided many benefits.

5. The telephone has brought the world closer together by allowing people thousands of miles apart to communicate instantly.

6. I believe that water pollution is a serious environmental problem in this country because it is a threat to our surroundings.

7. America needs tougher gun control legislation because too many people are killed each year in accidental shootings and shootings related to domestic arguments.

8. Elementary school children should be required to learn a foreign language because learning a foreign language should be part of every child's education.

9. College athletes should be paid for playing because they deserve money for their services.

10. The minimum wage should be increased by at least one dollar per hour because the current wage is too low.

POSSIBLE ANSWERS ARE ON PAGE 333.

Using Specific Examples

Which of the following passages creates a clearer image in your mind?

> Old people in nursing homes are often neglected. Their relatives ignore them, and the staff is too busy to attend to anything but their basic survival needs.

> Old people in nursing homes are often neglected. Their relatives ignore them, and the staff is too busy to attend to anything but their basic survival needs. Imagine an eighty-six-year-old man strapped into his chair for hours, staring vacantly at the nurses hurrying past without a glance in his direction. In the eight years since he entered the nursing home, his son has visited twice.

Without a doubt, the second passage is more vivid. Notice that the writer has not just added more words that say the same thing. What makes the difference is the use of specific examples. Note the specific illustrations for the general statements summarized in the chart below.

General	Specific
old people	an eighty-six-year-old man
neglected	strapped in his chair for hours
relatives ignore them	son has visited twice in eight years
staff too busy	nurses hurry by without a glance

Using examples like these can make your writing interesting and convincing to your reader. You can draw examples from your own personal experience and that of your family and friends. You can also draw examples from the newspaper, what you have seen on television or in movies, or just your imagination.

How could you add a specific example to the general statement below?

People are obsessed with money.

You can probably think of a lot of examples of how people are obsessed with money. You could write about yourself or someone you know, like this:

People are obsessed with money. My friend Carl walks three miles to work and back every day just to save $1.20 in bus fare.

Or you could use less personal examples, like this:

People are obsessed with money. Every day you hear stories of families feuding over who's going to get Grandpa's money.

People are obsessed with money. I've read that most marital problems are caused by couples arguing about money.

Exercise 2: Adding Specific Examples

Directions: Add a specific example to each of the following general statements. You can draw on personal experience, your general knowledge, or your imagination.

1. High school students drop out of school for a variety of reasons.

2. We could learn a lot from older people if only we spent more time with them.

3. Many workers are dissatisfied with their jobs.

4. Having a lot of money does not always make people happy.

5. Big cities can be dangerous.

SAMPLE ANSWERS ARE ON PAGE 333.

Using Specific Details

Use Specific Words and Phrases

You can add detail and color to your writing in several ways. One easy way to dress up your writing is to use specific nouns and verbs to create a sharper picture for your reader. For example, a general sentence such as *A man walked into the building* might become *A trucker strode into Todd's Diner*, or *A drunk staggered into the hotel bar*, or even *General Patton marched into the Pentagon*. By giving specific people, places, and actions, these new sentences create very different events for the reader.

On the lines below, make up two more revisions of your own of the sentence *A man walked into the building.*

_____

_____

You can also add describing words and phrases to help your readers see what you want them to. Include details that answer the questions *what kind? which one? how many? where? when? how?* and *why?* about the nouns and verbs in the sentence. You could rewrite the sentence *A trucker strode into Todd's Diner* like this:

> At eight o'clock last night, a two-hundred-fifty-pound trucker with a tattoo of a snake on his left forearm strode menacingly into Todd's Diner to confront his ex-girlfriend, Sadie, who's a waitress there.

How about the sentence *A drunk staggered into the hotel bar?* You could rewrite it like this:

> Nearly tripping over the doorsill, a disheveled drunk in a rumpled business suit staggered into the Starlight Hotel's bar at midnight for one last shot of whiskey.

Don't you get a better picture when the writer uses more describing words and phrases? Revise the two sentences that you wrote above. Add at least three describing words or phrases to each—more if you can.

_____

_____

_____

Show, Don't Tell

Another way to add specifics to your writing is to show your reader what you mean. Don't just tell him what you think. Provide the specific details that allow your readers to reach the same conclusions you've made.

TELLING: My daughter was delighted.
SHOWING: My three-year-old daughter danced around the room, clapping her hands and giggling.

TELLING: The garden was beautiful.
SHOWING: The garden contained banks of golden and copper chrysanthemums flanked by dark green juniper hedges.

TELLING: The proposed freeway will destroy the neighborhood.
SHOWING: The proposed freeway will slice through King Memorial Park and require the demolition of St. Mary's Church, a one-hundred-year-old structure.

As you can see, specific observations will make your writing much more interesting and convincing. Try revising the following sentence by changing from telling to showing.

The dog was incredibly ugly.

(Imagine an ugly dog. Describe it so the reader can picture it, too.)

_____

_____

_____

Exercise 3: Adding Specific Details

Part A
Directions: Revise the sentences below by using specific nouns and verbs, adding describing words and phrases, or replacing telling statements with showing statements to make the reader see what you see. Use your imagination!

Example: Two vehicles collided in an intersection.
A dump truck smashed into a motorcycle at the intersection of State Street and Tenth Avenue last Friday night.

1. The victim was upset.

2. A dog attacked the woman.

3. This neighborhood is run-down.

4. The new father was obviously nervous.

5. Vandalism is a problem in this community.

6. The musician played an instrument.

7. The teenager spoke to his parent.

8. The shopping mall was crowded.

9. Grocery prices have increased.

10. The federal government is wasteful.

Part B

Directions: Revise the paragraph below by adding "showing statements" to support the writer's conclusions. You may decide to replace some sentences with specific sentences of your own, or you may choose to add sentences that provide supporting examples.

> Joe's Cafe is the worst place to eat in town. The building is filthy inside and out. Whether there is only one other customer or ten, the service is poor. Worst of all, the food tastes terrible. Even so, it's expensive.

POSSIBLE ANSWERS ARE ON PAGE 333.

Strengthening an Essay with Specifics

To see how specifics can strengthen an essay, study some changes made by the writer of the essay on required public service for young people. Notice how the use of specifics has made this part of the essay clearer, more interesting, and more convincing.

Editing hint: Note that the writer hasn't recopied the essay in the following example. He has made changes by using carets (∧) to show where new material has been inserted. You'll find this revising technique especially useful when you're working under timed conditions, such as when you take Part 2 of the GED Writing Skills Test.

> If the public service program were set up like the military service program, young adults could earn educational benefits by completing ~~their year of duty.~~ *One year's worth of tuition at a public community college or university could be earned for one year of public service.* ∧ ~~The money could be used for further training toward the career of their choice.~~ ∧ *Americans would be investing their money to produce well-trained engineers, auto mechanics, police officers, nurses, and teachers.*

Exercise 4: Revising For Specifics

Directions: Revise the essay you wrote in Chapter 5 by making your writing more specific. You may want to use more specific nouns and verbs, add describing words and phrases, use showing statements, and include specific reasons.

Rather than rewriting the essay at this point, cross out material you want to delete and use carets (∧) to show where insertions belong.

ANSWERS WILL VARY.

Sentence and Paragraph Links

Organization and Paragraphing

When you are revising an essay, you should look carefully at the overall organization of the piece. In what order are your main points presented? Does that order make sense? Each of your main points should be developed in a separate paragraph. Have you sorted details, examples, or reasons that support each main point into the right paragraph?

Take a few minutes now to look at your essay from Chapter 5 again. Are there places where a new paragraph should start? If so, use the symbol ¶ to show the start of a new paragraph. Should the paragraphs be rearranged in a more logical order? If so, use arrows or numbering to show the new order.

Transition Words

Making the relationships among your ideas clear to the reader is the key to making it more readable. You've already worked with patterns of organization for paragraphs in Chapter 4 and the overall structure of an essay (introduction, body, and conclusion) in Chapter 5. In this section, you'll look closely at how to help your reader follow the organization of your essay by using transition words and phrases.

Transition words and phrases help your reader follow your thoughts from sentence to sentence and from paragraph to paragraph. In the chart below, you'll find a few of the most common transition words and phrases and their uses.

Transitions	Use
first, second, next, then, later, finally	to show time order
one, another, also, in addition, the most important	to separate and rank items in a list
also, both, similar, like, on the other hand, different, disadvantage, advantage	to compare and contrast

You may also want to use the connectors you studied in Chapter 4 as transition words. To refresh your memory, some connectors are listed on page 227. You will probably think of others to use in your writing.

Connectors	Use
moreover furthermore in addition	adds related information
however nevertheless	shows a contrasting or unexpected situation
therefore consequently	links cause to effect
otherwise	shows an alternative
for instance for example	gives specifics to illustrate a general idea

Transitions Between Sentences

Now let's take a look at how to choose transitions when you're revising your writing. This writer wants to explain why, with all its problems, she prefers living in a large city. She has written the two sentences below, and she wants to use a transition between them that will help her readers see the point she's making. Think of a transition she could use.

> Small towns may be quiet and peaceful. I prefer the excitement and variety of a big city.

She should choose a transition that shows contrast, such as *however* or *on the other hand*. Read the sentences again with the transition word *however* inserted. Can you see how much easier it is to understand the writer's point?

> Small towns may be quiet and peaceful. However, I prefer the excitement and variety of a big city.

FOCUS ON PUNCTUATION

Transition Words

When connectors are used as transitions between sentences, they should be separated by commas from the rest of the sentence.

> Candy and carbonated soft drinks provide nothing but empty calories to the consumer. **However,** fruits and vegetables provide important vitamins and minerals with fewer calories.

The transition word doesn't always appear at the beginning of the sentence. Here is the same example with the transition word embedded in the second sentence. Notice that commas come before and after *however*.

Candy and carbonated soft drinks provide nothing but empty calories to the consumer. Fruits and vegetables, **however,** provide important vitamins and minerals with fewer calories.

Many other common transitional words and phrases are probably familiar to you. They are all set off by commas. Circle the transitional phrases in the following example.

In my opinion, Congress should pass a tax reform bill. The Senate, as a matter of fact, is debating the issue this week. Of course, the chances for passage are slim in an election year.

Did you circle *In my opinion, as a matter of fact,* and *of course*?

Exercise 5: Using Transition Words

Directions: Insert transition words in the sentences below to show the logical links between ideas. Punctuate the sentences correctly.

Example: Sylvester insisted that his friends call him Rocky.

His parents *, however,* continued to use his given name.

1. One hundred years ago settlers needed guns to protect themselves from wild animals. _____ those frontier days are long past.

2. The migration of people to the Southwest has created some serious problems. States like Arizona and New Mexico _____ may run short of water for their new residents.

3. _____ shake the can vigorously. _____ point it at your target before pulling the tab to open it.

_____ laugh your head off and run away.

4. Many immigrants face a language barrier when they try to find jobs here. _____ they must adapt to unfamiliar interviewing practices.

5. The scenery in *The Secret of Machu Pichu* is breathtaking. The acting _____ is terrible.

POSSIBLE ANSWERS ARE ON PAGE 334.

Transitions Between Paragraphs

Below are two paragraphs from the essay on living in a big city. How could the writer use a transition word or phrase to link the two paragraphs? Think of at least one good transition.

Small towns may be quiet and peaceful. However, I prefer the excitement and variety of a big city. Big city entertainment ranges from live blues bars to ethnic street festivals. I can go see old movies for $2 or go to a fancy nightclub. No matter how much or how little money I have in my pocket, there's always something to do.

Job opportunities are better in a big city. New businesses are opening all the time here, and the "help wanted" ads on Sundays fill two whole sections of the paper. No matter what part of the nation's economy is growing, the growth is likely to happen in a big city.

What relationship do these two paragraphs have? They both give information about the advantages of living in a big city. The writer could revise the topic sentence of the second paragraph in any number of ways to make a smoother transition. Here are a few examples:

Furthermore, job opportunities are better in a big city.
In addition, job opportunities are better in a big city.
More important, job opportunities are better in a big city.
Another advantage is that job opportunities are better in a big city.

Two paragraphs of the sample essay on public service appear below, revised to include transitional words and phrases to emphasize overall organization and to link ideas clearly.

One benefit of a public service program would be ~~Public service jobs would provide~~ automatic employment for young

adults. They would no longer be hanging around street corners, getting

drunk, and vandalizing property because they were bored. *Instead, young* ~~Young~~

adults would be learning skills that they needed them to be good

workers such as being prompt, following directions, and serving clients

courteously.

In addition to gaining employment,
~~If the public service program were set up like the military service~~

~~program,~~ young adults could earn educational benefits by completing
If the public service program were set up like the
military service program, a
their year of duty. ~~A~~ year's worth of tuition at a public community col-

lege or university could be earned for one year of public service. Amer-

icans would be investing their money to produce well-trained engi-

neers, auto mechanics, police officers, nurses, and teachers.

Exercise 6: More Transition Words

Part A
Directions: Rewrite the following passages, adding transition words and phrases wherever possible to make the relationships between ideas clearer to the reader.

1. You can make Tante Hanne's Apple Macaroons for dessert in forty-five min-
    utes if you follow these simple directions. Butter a pie tin and slice four or
    five medium apples into it. Cover the apples with half a cup of sugar and as
    much cinnamon as desired. Cream together four tablespoons of margarine
    and half a cup of sugar. Beat in one egg. Mix in half a cup of flour and a
    dash of salt. Spoon the batter over the apples and bake for half an hour at
    350 degrees.

2. High school students should not be allowed to drive for several reasons.
    They're not mature enough to handle the responsibility. Every Friday night
    one seventeen-year-old I know downs a six-pack of beer and then challenges
    his classmates to drag race down Main Street.
        Cars detract from schoolwork. Most students who own cars work to pay
    for gas and insurance. They spend less time on the schoolwork that should
    be their primary concern.
        Cars give them too much freedom. Instead of cruising the streets look-
    ing for parties to crash or girls to pick up, they should be with their fami-
    lies, where more adult supervision is provided.

POSSIBLE ANSWERS ARE ON PAGE 334.

Part B
Directions: Continue revising the rough draft of the essay you wrote in Chapter
5. This time revise for smooth links among sentences and paragraphs.

ANSWERS WILL VARY.

Revising for Smooth Wording

Repetition

Does your writing seem to repeat itself? Perhaps you've overused a word or phrase, as in the following paragraph. Read the passage and circle the repetitive words and phrases.

> Dick is one of the most versatile people I know. Dick teaches math, chemistry, and electronics for a living. Dick plays the banjo and sings in a bluegrass band on the side. Dick writes his own computer programs as a hobby. Dick also paints as a hobby.

Each sentence in the paragraph uses the standard subject-verb pattern; in fact, each begins with the same subject: Dick. In addition, the phrase *as a hobby* is used twice.

If repetition is a problem, look for ways to rephrase the writing. You'll remember from Chapter 2 that pronouns like *he, they, our,* and *it* can take the place of nouns. Another way to avoid repetition is to use words or phrases that have similar meanings.

Substituting **synonyms** (words and phrases that have the same meaning) and pronouns can eliminate repetition.

Here's a revised version of the repetitive paragraph, with synonyms, pronouns, and varied sentence structure making the passage much more pleasant to read.

> Dick is one of the most versatile people I know. **He** teaches math, chemistry, and electronics for a living, **and he plays** the banjo and sings in a bluegrass band on the side. **As a hobby,** Dick writes his own computer programs. **Another of his pastimes is painting.**

Editing hint: Read your draft aloud to hunt for repetitive wording. Your ear is likely to detect what your eye might miss.

Exercise 7: Eliminating Repetitive Wording ──────

Directions: Rewrite the following paragraph to eliminate repetition. Delete words, substitute synonyms or pronouns, and revise sentence structure as necessary to improve the sound of the paragraph. The first change has been made as an example.

Frank was annoyed with Lisa because ~~Lisa~~ *she* never became angry with ~~Frank~~ *him*. Whenever Frank complained to Lisa about anything, Lisa apologized to Frank instead of becoming angry in return. Frank found it impossible to have a good argument with Lisa because Lisa refused to argue. Lisa's refusal to argue simply made Frank even angrier than Frank was to begin with.

POSSIBLE ANSWERS ARE ON PAGE 334.

Wordiness

Even if no words are repeated unnecessarily in a passage, it still may suffer from wordiness. What idea is repeated unnecessarily in the following sentence? *A great big huge dog attacked the mail carrier.* Three words are used to describe the size of the dog when one is enough. You could revise the sentence like this: *A huge dog attacked the mail carrier.*

Wordiness is the unnecessary repetition of ideas in a passage or the use of more words than necessary to express a thought.

As you revise, look for ways to reduce the number of words in your essay without losing important ideas. This process, called *tightening*, will make your writing clearer and more forceful. When you cut words, don't cut interesting details or reasons or examples that support your argument. Just look for ways to make your points in fewer words.

Note the changes made to tighten each of the following sentences.

WORDY: Ricardo is a man who has great strength.
TIGHT: Ricardo is very strong.

WORDY: The doctor took a look at the patient's leg.
TIGHT: The doctor looked at the patient's leg.

WORDY: It is a fact that our bodies need vitamin A to prevent night blindness.
TIGHT: Our bodies need vitamin A to prevent night blindness.

How can the sentence below be tightened? Rewrite it in the space provided.

Substances that are hazardous or dangerous shouldn't be dumped near locations that are residential areas.

_____

_____

You might have rewritten the sentence like this:

Hazardous substances shouldn't be dumped near residential areas.

Editing hint: As you check your essay for wordiness, be especially careful to look for unnecessary pronouns.

INCORRECT: My father **he** was born in the Netherlands.
CORRECT: My father was born in the Netherlands.

Sentences using *who, which,* or *that* are especially likely to contain these errors.

INCORRECT: The milk that we bought **it** at the store yesterday is sour.
CORRECT: The milk that we bought at the store yesterday is sour.

Cross out the unnecessary pronoun in the following sentence.

The silver dollars that she gave him they were worth fifty dollars each.

You should have crossed out *they.*

Exercise 8: Tightening

Part A
Directions: Revise the sentences below to eliminate wordiness. Change the wording as necessary. Be sure that as you revise you don't cut out important details. If a sentence does not contain any wordiness, write *OK.*

Example: The house that was old and rickety was on the market for sale.
The old, rickety house was for sale.

1. The dress is blue in color and cotton in fabric.
2. Acid rain is a serious problem in the Great Lakes region.
3. The chicken wings in the refrigerator they can be warmed up for supper.
4. The sign that the vandals destroyed it last night will cost a thousand dollars to replace.
5. At last we finally found an apartment that is large in size but inexpensive in cost.

Part B

Directions: Revise the paragraph below to eliminate wordiness. Change the wording as necessary.

At this particular point in time, heating costs are dangerously high for people living near or below the poverty level. Retired people who aren't working anymore must rely on a fixed income that doesn't change from month to month. As a rule, their social security checks they just aren't large enough in amount to cover higher utility bills when the weather is cold in the wintertime. Congress should pass a bill or law that it would offer some relief and assistance for such people who are in this type of situation.

POSSIBLE ANSWERS ARE ON PAGE 334.

Tightening in an Essay

Here, one last time, is a part of the sample essay with which we began this chapter. Note the changes made by the writer to eliminate unnecessary repetition and wordiness.

One benefit of the public service program would be automatic employment for young adults. They would no longer be hanging around street corners, getting drunk, and vandalizing property because they were bored. Instead, ~~young adults~~ *they* would be learning skills that they needed ~~them~~ to be good workers, such as ~~being prompt, following di~~ *promptness,* ~~rections, and serving clients courteously.~~ *accuracy, and courtesy.*

Exercise 9: Tightening the Wording of an Essay

Directions: Complete your revision of the draft of your essay from Chapter 5 by checking for unnecessary repetition and wordiness.

☐ Delete unnecessary words (check especially carefully for excess pronouns).

☐ Replace repetitive phrases with synonyms and pronouns to improve the sound of the writing.

☐ Simplify the phrasing of bulky sentences.

You may be able to make these changes neatly by crossing out the words you want to remove and using carets (∧) to signal insertions.

ANSWERS WILL VARY.

Editing

Editing is the final step in the process of completing a piece of writing. You have practiced editing throughout this book. As you already know, editing is proofreading your writing for mistakes in grammar, punctuation, capitalization, and spelling. In the second half of this chapter, you'll be learning important rules that will help you edit for capitalization and spelling errors.

Following are some editing strategies that experienced writers use to find mistakes in their writing. Take a few minutes now to test each one. Pick a paragraph or essay of your own and try to find errors using each of the strategies listed.

1. Read your writing out loud. Listen carefully to how it sounds. Does anything jar your ear or sound awkward or incorrect? Mark problems to come back to after you have finished reading the whole piece.

2. Read your writing backward, sentence by sentence. Look at each sentence carefully, isolated from the rest of the writing. This technique is especially helpful in locating fragments.

3. Read your writing several times, each time looking for a different type of error. Choose two to four errors that you most commonly have trouble with to search for. For example, if you have trouble with subject-verb agreement, you might look at the subject and verb of each sentence in turn to make sure they agree.

Chapter Highlights

1. Revising is the process of strengthening the content, organization, and wording of a piece of writing.

2. Use specifics to help your reader get the picture. Use specific nouns and verbs. Add describing words and phrases. Show your reader what you mean; don't just tell him what you think. Add examples and reasons that reinforce your points.

3. Use transitional words and phrases to show the logical links between paragraphs and sentences.

4. Eliminate unpleasant repetition by substituting synonyms and pronouns.

5. Eliminate wordiness by deleting unnecessary words and revising sentence structure to simplify phrasing.

6. Edit your writing for errors in grammar, punctuation, spelling, and capitalization.

★ GED PRACTICE ★

Exercise 10: GED Writing Topic

Directions: Here is your third sample writing topic to help you practice for Part 2 of the GED Writing Skills Test. Try writing on this topic within the forty-five-minute time limit that you will have on the actual test. Put all the writing skills to use that you have learned so far in essay and paragraph construction, sentence structure, word choice, punctuation, and spelling.

Be sure to take ten minutes or so to plan your essay. Look for clue words in the question to help you identify the topic and the kinds of details and examples to include. Write a unifying statement and brainstorm a list of details. Although you may not have time to make a formal outline, do try to group your details logically. Check for relevance, completeness, and organization.

Be sure to save the last five to ten minutes for revising and editing. This time, emphasize the revising skills that you've learned in this chapter. Use the following checklist as a revising guide.

☐ Does the essay contain an introduction, body, and conclusion?

☐ Does the introduction contain a clear unifying statement?

☐ Does the body develop the unifying statement with reasons and specific supporting details?

☐ Do transitional words show the logical links between sentences and paragraphs?

☐ Has unnecessary repetition of words and ideas been eliminated?

Make any changes you want by neatly crossing out words and by using carets (⌃) or asterisks (✳) to show insertions.

> Drunken driving is a serious problem in the United States. To help solve the problem, some people have proposed that anyone convicted of drunken driving be given an automatic thirty-day jail sentence, with no possibility of probation or parole. Write a statement supporting or opposing the proposal. Explain your reasons.

A SAMPLE ESSAY APPEARS ON PAGES 334–35.

Journal Writing

Have you been writing in your journal a few times each week? If you have, you have been getting valuable practice in putting your thoughts down on paper. Here are some topics you might want to write about in your journal. Or you might want to come up with more ideas of your own.

● Everyone has a "job," although not everyone brings home a paycheck. What is your job? What do you do? Do you like your job? Why or why not?

● Whom do you think of when you think of your family? You may think of a lot of people or just a few. What is your family like?

28 CAPITALIZATION AND SPELLING

Based on the revision techniques you learned in the first section of this chapter, the following paragraph is well written. It contains plenty of specific details, clear transition words, and no unnecessary repetition. Yet it needs further polishing; in fact, it contains twenty-five errors! As you read it, circle any mistakes you notice.

> The two-hour special episode of "The Edge of Disaster" wensday nite was excelant. Frist, doctor Rasmussen discovered that his cancer was to advanced to be treated. Then his freind Joshua returned form a trip to thailand with a rare form of asian flu, barley able to breath. The hole emergancy room staff at Blackhawk county hospital got food posioning from the Eggnog served at the new year's Eve Party. Finaly, a suprise blizzard left Tina and Rick stranded on highway 34.

If you had trouble locating all twenty-five errors, read on! They're all connected to capitalization and spelling. Although errors like these are unrelated to the meaning of a piece of writing (they would go undetected by a listener if the paragraph were read aloud), they distract readers from the writer's message. Instead of concentrating on Joshua's rare disease, for instance, they'll be thinking about the correct spelling of *friend* or wondering why the writer didn't capitalize *Thailand.*

Editing for standard capitalization and spelling won't make a bad piece of writing good, but it will make good writing better. You can use these final polishing skills to good advantage on your essay for Part 2 of the GED Writing Skills Test. In addition, you'll find capitalizing and spelling tested in Part 1.

Capitalization

You already know two important capitalization rules: the first word of every sentence and the pronoun *I* are always capitalized. In addition, when you practiced making sentences more specific in the first section of this chapter, you may have used some nouns beginning with capital letters. How can you be sure what to capitalize and what not to? Try to decide what rules explain the use of capital letters in the passage at the top of page 238.

Early yesterday morning a house at the northwest corner of Walnut Street and Fifth Avenue burned to the ground. Its owners, Doctor and Mrs. James H. Turner, were out of the state vacationing in Texas. According to Captain Thomas, the cause of the fire has not yet been determined. Neighbors reported seeing a car with an Indiana license plate stopped in the street right in front of the house moments before the fire broke out. Fire inspectors will issue a full report late next week.

You may have noticed that the capital letters were used for special names and titles. In fact, capitalization rules can be summarized in one broad principle.

Capitalize names of specific people and places.	
Specific	**General**
Doctor James H. Turner	owner
Captain Thomas	inspector
Texas	state
Fifth Avenue	street
Walnut Street	

Fill in the blanks in the following sentences, being sure to capitalize specific names.

My name is _____.

I live in the state of _____.

The name of the street I live on is _____.

Now that you know the basic rule for capitalizing, this second one will make sense.

Words derived from the names of specific people and places are also capitalized.

Natives of Italy speak **Italian.**
A family born in China has opened a **Chinese** restaurant here in town.
Do people in Denmark enjoy **Danish** pastries as much as I do?
Many **American** business representatives wish they spoke **Japanese** as well as people in Japan speak **English.**

Answer the following questions, being sure to capitalize properly.

What language(s) do you speak? _____

What nationalities were your ancestors? _____

What kinds of ethnic food do you enjoy? _____

Exercise 11: Capitalizing Specific Names————

Directions: Proofread the following sentences for words that should be capitalized. Cross out each incorrect lowercase (small) letter and place a capital letter above it.

Example: The first people in this part of the ~~u~~nited ~~s~~tates were ~~i~~ndians, followed by ~~s~~panish and ~~f~~rench explorers.

1. Although margaret was born in london, her parents were german citizens.
2. The largest continent in both geography and population is asia, but the highest standards of living are enjoyed by europeans and north americans.
3. What a different world this would be without the inventions of thomas a. edison and alexander graham bell!
4. Thanks to vaccines, potentially dangerous childhood diseases like mumps and german measles have been almost eliminated in the united states.
5. The relations between this country and our latin american neighbors have not always been friendly.

ANSWERS ARE ON PAGE 335.

Problems in Capitalization
Stick to the Basic Rule

Now that you are familiar with the most basic rule of capitalization, look more closely at a few potentially troublesome capitalization rules. As you study these rules, notice that each one still follows the basic rule: capitalize names of specific people and places. If you're ever in doubt about whether to capitalize something, apply that rule.

Titles

Words used as titles should be capitalized.

> My physician's name is **Doctor** Bone.
> As I was growing up, **Uncle** David was my favorite relative.
> In my opinion, **Mayor** Sly should be soundly defeated in the next election.

In each of the preceding examples, the title was used as part of a person's name. Sometimes when you are speaking directly to a person, you use the title as the whole name.

> You're just in time, **Doctor**.
> I'm sorry, **Mayor**, but I can't support you for reelection.

Doctor and *Mayor* are used like first names in the examples you just saw, so they are capitalized. You could say, "You're just in time, Anne," or "I'm sorry, Alfonso" instead.

Don't capitalize words like *doctor* and *mayor* when they're simply used as occupational labels.

The **doctor** is running an hour late on appointments.

In the example above, *doctor* is not used as a first name. Try substituting your own name, and you'll see that it doesn't make sense. You wouldn't say, "The Anne is running an hour late."

Places

Capitalize geographical labels when they are part of a specific name.

GENERAL: I love to hike in the **mountains**.
SPECIFIC: I love to hike in the Rocky **Mountains**.

GENERAL: We took the ferry across the **lake**.
SPECIFIC: We took the ferry across **Lake** Michigan.

GENERAL: We saw a deer lying beside the **highway**.
SPECIFIC: We saw a deer lying beside **Highway** 415.

GENERAL: The **avenue** will be widened to four lanes.
SPECIFIC: University **Avenue** will be widened to four lanes.

This rule also applies to *north, south, east,* and *west*. Don't capitalize them when they refer to a direction, but do capitalize them when they are part of the name of a specific place.

GENERAL: We were hiking **north** on the trail, but when we got in the car, we drove **south**.
SPECIFIC: The high school in **South** Bend will hold its senior prom in the **North** Star Dance Hall.

Dates

Capitalize days of the week and months, but not seasons.

Last **Thursday** I missed my dentist's appointment.
Workers can expect a two-week layoff in **August**.

but

Early **spring** is one of the dreariest seasons.
My favorite season is **autumn**, with its bright colors and crisp weather.

Capitalize names of holidays.

The **New Year's Eve** party got out of hand when someone began shooting off fireworks in the kitchen.
Some Americans use **Thanksgiving Day** as an excuse for overeating.

Editing hint: When you are looking for capitalization errors in your own writing or in Part 1 of the GED Writing Skills Test, look for capital letters that should be small letters as well as small letters that should be capitalized.

Exercise 12: More Capitalizing Specific Names——

Directions: Four words are in bold type in each of the following sentences. Cross out the error in capitalization (either a missing capital letter or an unnecessary one) and write it correctly in the space above.

Example: Later this <del>M</del>onth or early in **July**, we're planning a trip to **Niagara Falls**.

1. Last week a **Laotian** couple moved into the red brick **house** on **Oakdale road**.

2. Our **Independence Day** is not an official **Holiday** in **England**.

3. On **Monday** morning **governor O'Reilly** will begin a campaign swing around the **state**.

4. An **indonesian restaurant** offers **diners** rice dishes, peanut sauce, chicken and pork, and baked bananas for **dessert**.

5. When it's time for **Spring** cleaning, **Aunt Gladys** and her **neighbor** roll up their sleeves and scour from attic to basement.

6. Two **senators** and a **Judge** were indicted on **April** 26 for accepting **bribes**.

7. The **Mississippi** is the longest **River** in the **United States**, but not the longest in the world.

8. Both **Hannukah** and **Christmas** are **Winter holidays**.

9. The **Smoky mountains** of **Tennessee** are named aptly because of the **haze** that often covers them.

10. Turn right off the **county road** when you reach **highway** 75 and drive five miles until you see the sign for Spring Lake **Park**.

ANSWERS ARE ON PAGE 335.

Spelling

Spelling Well

Of all the tasks that beginning writers face, spelling seems to be the most dismaying. In fact, some people are convinced that they can't be good writers because they're not good spellers.

You know now that there is much more to writing than correct spelling. Stating your ideas clearly and supporting them thoroughly are the essential skills for good writing. The best spelling skills in the world won't compensate for lack of thought in an essay.

On the other hand, a well-planned, well-supported essay deserves the final polishing that correct spelling provides. If you care about the piece you've written, you'll want to present it to your reader in the smoothest possible form.

What, then, can you do to improve your spelling skills? First, maintain a positive attitude. You've already learned how to spell many words correctly. (In addition to the words you knew before you opened this book, you've learned how to spell plurals and how to add *s, ed*, and *ing* endings to verbs.) You can learn more. Second, follow a logical plan for spelling improvement.

General Hints for Better Spelling

1. **Analyze your spelling problems.** With the help of your instructor or a friend who spells well, make a list of the words you've misspelled in your writings so far. In one column place your original spelling of the word, and in a second column, place the correct spelling. Save a third column for a note on the kind of error you've made. For instance, did the problem occur when you added a suffix (word ending)? Did you substitute one word for another that sounds like it? Did you use the wrong vowel? reverse letters? leave some letters out? Just put down an explanation that makes sense to you.

Sample Spelling List

My Spelling	Correct Spelling	Type of Error
to	too	soundalike word
prefered	preferred	adding suffix
goverment	government	omitted letter
diffrence	difference	omitted letter
telavision	television	wrong vowel

This list has several uses. For one thing, it will help you concentrate on learning words that *you* use. For another, by identifying words with similar spelling errors, you'll be able to work on spelling patterns that apply to a whole group of words, not just one at a time. Finally, you'll be more sensitive to the kinds of words that give you trouble, so you'll know when to reach for a dictionary to check your work.

2. **Learn the rules that apply to the greatest number of words first.** Some of the most important rules apply to words to which prefixes (beginnings) and suffixes (endings) have been added; they're presented on pages 245–48. Learning them may immediately solve many of your spelling problems. Another very important rule is the Ie-Ei rule on page 249.

3. **Learn to distinguish the meanings of soundalike words.** Find out what the difference is between words like *too* and *to*, *course* and *coarse*, *advice* and *advise*. Soundalike words are presented on pages 251–253. Practice using them correctly in your own sample sentences.

4. **Learn to use pronunciation as an aid to spelling.** For practice, you may even want to mispronounce a word to make it sound more like the way it's spelled. For instance, make *attendance* rhyme with *dance* to help you remember the *ance* ending.

5. **Practice, practice, practice.** How do basketball players learn to make free throws consistently? How do typists learn to key eighty words per minute with no errors? How do cooks learn to get the vegetables, potatoes, and meat done at the same time? How do writers improve their spelling? They practice.

Word Parts

When you want to learn to spell a long word, you'll find it helpful to divide the word into parts. Which of the following ways to separate a word makes its spelling easier to remember?

c-h-a-r-a-c-t-e-r-i-s-t-i-c
char-ac-ter-is-tic

Like most people, you probably find the second kind of division more useful. It reduces the number of separate items to remember. Instead of memorizing fourteen separate letters in *characteristic*, you learn five chunks. In addition, you can connect the sound of each part of the word with its spelling. This method is called dividing words into syllables.

A *syllable* is a word part containing a single vowel sound.

Say the word *delicious* aloud. How many syllables do you hear? There are three: *de-li-cious*. Even though there are three vowels in the last syllable, it has only one vowel sound: *uh*.

Notice that in the word *delicious*, the second syllable receives more punch than the others: *de-LI-cious*. This stress is called the *accent* in the word. Identifying accented syllables is sometimes useful in deciding whether to double a letter or not, as you'll see in a later section.

Write the number of syllables you hear in the following words. Then rewrite the words in syllables, capitalizing the letters in the accented syllable.

apparatus
cafeteria
scientific
exhilaration
temperament

You might have written the words like this:

        4   ap-pa-RAT-us
        5   ca-fe-TER-i-a
        4   sci-en-TIF-ic
        5   ex-hil-a-RA-tion
        4   TEM-per-a-ment

You may sometimes have divided the words in slightly different places (such as *ap-pa-RA-tus* instead of *ap-pa-RAT-us*). That's all right, as long as you have only one vowel sound per syllable.

Many students have found this five-step process useful in memorizing words of more than one syllable.

1. Say the word aloud and count the number of syllables you hear.

2. Write the word in syllables.

3. Trace over each syllable, pronouncing it as you write. Repeat this step until you feel you know the word.

4. Fold your paper over so that you can't see the word, and quiz yourself by writing it syllable by syllable.

5. Check your work. If you misspelled it, go back to the tracing step. If you spelled it correctly, fold the paper over once more and try it again.

Writing the word correctly twice without looking means that you're well on your way to mastering it. You'll want to review it periodically to set the correct spelling permanently in your mind.

The method works well because it lets you use so many of the ways to learn to spell—seeing, saying, and writing—a triple whammy for your brain!

Exercise 13: Memorizing Long Words

Directions: From the following list, choose at least seven words that you can't spell. Use the five-step process described above to learn to spell the words. If you can't find seven words on this list that you can't spell, turn to the list on pages 268–71 and find words that you don't know on that list.

approximate	exhilaration
association	fundamental
auxiliary	guarantee
calculator	intelligence
congratulate	kindergarten
communicate	miscellaneous
concentration	monotonous
conscientious	perpendicular
consequently	prescription
efficient	significant
eligibility	symmetrical
emphasize	tremendous
exaggeration	versatile

ANSWERS WILL VARY.

Compound Words

You'll find it more useful to learn the spelling of some words by dividing them into their meaningful parts than by dividing them into syllables. ***Compound*** words are combinations of two words. Don't change the spelling of either when you combine them.

room + mate = roommate

him + self = himself

news + stand = _____

over + coat = _____

police + man = _____

news + paper = _____

Prefixes and Suffixes

Not all meaningful word parts can be used as separate words. Instead, prefixes (beginning word parts) and suffixes (ending word parts) may be added to a base word.

	PREFIX	BASE	SUFFIX
independence =	in +	depend +	ence
unusual =	un +	usual	
changeable =		change +	able

Here are a few of the most commonly used prefixes and suffixes in the English language and their meanings.

Prefix	Meaning	Example
anti	against	antifreeze
dis	apart, not	disappear
im, in	in	ingrained
im, in, ir, il, un	not	irrelevant independent
inter	between	interstate
mis	wrongly	misspelled
pre	before	presoak
re	again	rewrite
trans	across	transatlantic

Suffix	Meaning	Example
able, ible	able to	irresistible, acceptable
ability, ibility	ability to	eligibility, respectability
al	relating to	personal
ance, ence	state of	maintenance, permanence
er, or, ar, ist	someone or something that performs an action	visitor, propeller, scientist
er, est	more, most	heavier, heaviest
ful, ous	full of, having	beautiful, ridiculous
ic	nature of	scientific
ity	state or quality	electricity
ive	tending toward	persuasive
ly	in a certain manner	mournfully
ment	result of, act of	government
tion, sion	act, process	repetition, persuasion

Learning the following rules for combining these prefixes and suffixes with base words will take care of many spelling problems.

Adding Prefixes

When you add a prefix to a base word, don't change the spelling of the prefix or the base.

dis + appoint = disappoint

ir + relevant = irrelevant

im + migrant = _____

mis + spelled = _____

As you can see, this rule explains why some words have double consonants. If the prefix ends with the same letter that the base word begins with, the word will have a double consonant *(unnatural, dissatisfied)*.

Adding Suffixes

In Chapters 2 and 3, you learned how to add the *s, ed,* and *ing* endings to nouns and verbs. You may want to review these sections right now; they're located on pages 46 and 80–81. You'll find that the rules you studied in those earlier chapters apply to more than noun and verb endings.

> In general, when you add a suffix to a base word, don't change the spelling of the suffix or the base.

care + ful = careful

affection + ate = affectionate

counsel + or = _____

real + ist + ic = _____

However, unlike the prefix rule, the suffix rule doesn't always hold. Here are some common exceptions:

1. When the base word ends in *y* preceded by a consonant, keep the *y* before a suffix beginning with *i (ism, ist, ing)*, but change the *y* to *i* before adding any other suffix.

   study + ing = studying

   happy + ness = happiness

   carry + ing = _____

   carry + age = _____

   marry + age = _____

2. When the base word ends in a silent *e*, keep the *e* before adding a suffix beginning with a consonant.

   care + less = careless

   immediate + ly = immediately

   require + ment = _____

   sincere + ly = _____

   Exceptions:
   true + ly = truly

   judge + ment = judgment

3. When the base word ends in a silent *e*, drop the *e* before adding a suffix beginning with a vowel.

> adventure + ous = adventurous
>
> please + ure = pleasure
>
> write + er = _____
>
> like + able = _____
>
> fascinate + ing = _____

Exceptions:
> peace + able = peaceable
>
> notice + able = noticeable
>
> courage + ous = courageous
>
> change + able = changeable

Notice that, in these exceptions, the base word ends in *ce* or *ge* and the suffix begins with an *a*. The *e* is needed to protect the "soft" sound of the *c* ("s" sound) or *g* ("j" sound) ahead of it.

4. The final consonant of a root word must be doubled if all of the following are true:

- the base word ends in a single vowel and a single consonant other than *h*, *w*, or *x*

- the accented syllable of the root word is on the last (or only) syllable

- the suffix begins with a vowel

> occur + ence = occurrence
>
> commit + ed = committed
>
> prefer + ed = _____
>
> refer + ed = _____
>
> propel + er = _____

> **but**

> quarrel + ing = quarreling *(accent not on last syllable)*
>
> accustom + ed = accustomed
>
> prefer + ence = _____
>
> interpret + ed = _____
>
> equip + ment = equipment *(suffix begins with a consonant)*
>
> develop + ment = _____
>
> embarrass + ment = _____

Ie-Ei Words

The following rhyme won't win a lyrics-of-the-year award, but it will help you remember the correct spelling of a large group of troublesome words.

> I before E
> Except after C
> Or when sounding like A
> As in *neighbor* and *weigh*.

Let's look at the rules presented in each part of the rhyme.

1. In most words using an *i* + *e* combination, *i* comes before *e*.

   niece   field   believe   friend

2. If the combination appears immediately after the letter *c*, *e* comes before *i*. (This rule does not apply when the *ci* together make a *sh* sound as in *ancient* or *conscience*.)

   receive   ceiling   conceit

3. When the combination sounds like an *A*, *e* comes before *i*.

   weight   eight   neighbor   reign

There are only a few common exceptions to these rules. You'll find most of them in this nonsense sentence: *Neither weird foreign financier seized their height at leisure.*

Exercise 14: Using Spelling Rules

Directions: Proofread each group of phrases below. Circle the misspelled word in each group and then write the correct spelling of the word in the space provided. If all the words are spelled correctly, place a *C* in the space.

Example: reference books
preferred to be alone
strange (occurence)
quarreled constantly

occurrence

1. interrupt the discussion
   interference with a police officer
   dissection of a grasshopper
   disappear into the sunset

   _____

2. newspaper delivery
   newstand robbery
   tomorrow afternoon
   kindergarten classrooms

   _____

3. immediatly left
   sincerely yours
   truly sorry
   severely burned

   _____

4. manageable problem
   valuable jewelry
   peaceable nature
   noticable difference

   _____

5. in the beginning
    equipped to serve
    committed to a mental ward
    preference for chocolate

    _____

6. second marrage
    carriage is waiting
    carrying on like a baby
    buried the bone

    _____

7. propellers whirled
    commitment to finish
    occasionnal showers
    performance of duties

    _____

8. mournfull sound
    hopeless situation
    careful study
    successful completion

    _____

9. customer is dissatisfied
    dissapprove of the decision
    diseased parakeet
    severe disappointment

    _____

10. in my judgment
    courageous act
    flower arrangment
    advantageous position

    _____

11. either man
    deceived his fiancée
    everybody's freind
    height of six feet

    _____

12. beleive in yourself
    file a grievance
    ten-year reign
    shriek of terror

    _____

13. receive a call
    seize the opportunity
    foriegn currency
    mischievous child

    _____

14. wrecked her bycicle
    boundary line
    artificial sweeteners
    ridiculous analysis

    _____

15. voted for the governor
    a carless mistake
    the dictator died
    conceal her prejudice

    _____

ANSWERS ARE ON PAGES 335–36.

Soundalike Words

The Most Commonly Confused Words

One of the most frustrating experiences in learning to spell in English is to have someone cheerfully tell you, "It's easy to spell. Just sound the words out." That well-intentioned advice might lead to a paragraph like this:

> I've **waisted** a **hole** year of my life on you, and now you say **your board**. **Write** now I don't **no weather** to laugh or cry. **Its plane** to me you haven't learned to **except** responsibility for your **personnel** life. I've **weighted** in **vein** for you to grow up. We're **threw**!

Every one of the words in bold type is "spelled the way it sounds." Every one is wrong.

The problem is that the English language has many ways to spell the same sound. This problem leaves us with many words that sound alike or almost alike but have different spellings and different meanings. To improve your spelling, you need to master these confusing word pairs. Learn how to spell and when to use each word.

In Chapter 2 you studied one group of soundalikes: possessive pronouns and contractions like *its-it's* and *theirs-there's*. You may want to review that list on page 55 again. Here are some other commonly confused words:

affect (act upon)	The new plan will affect everyone.
effect (result)	The effect of the plan will be disaster.
a lot (many, much)	You have a lot of nerve.
allot (set aside)	Please allot ten minutes to plan your paper.
all ready (completely ready)	I'm all ready to leave for vacation.
already (previously)	We've already eaten.
all right (there is no such spelling as *alright*)	Do you feel all right?
brake (stopping device)	Step on the brake fast!
break (fall to pieces; take a rest)	Don't break the vase.
	Take a coffee break.
coarse (rough; not fine)	Use coarse sandpaper first.
course (classroom subject; path; of course = naturally)	She's taking a computer course.
	The course is too wet for the race.
	Of course I'm right.
knew (was aware of)	He knew how to drive.
new (fresh, not old)	I want a new car.
know (be aware of)	I know my limits.
no (none, opposite of yes)	No sane person would do that.
loose (not tight)*	These trousers are too loose.
lose (misplace; fail to win)	Don't lose your money.
	They'll lose the game.

*Note the differences in pronunciation in this set.

passed (went by; succeeded)	Their car passed ours.
past (before the present; by)	He passed the test.
	The past was forgotten.
	We drove past the cemetery.
personal (belonging to an individual)*	She has personal problems.
personnel (referring to a group of workers)	The personnel department is taking applications.
principal (main; head of school)	Is smoking the principal cause of lung cancer?
principle (theory; belief)	The principal spoke to her students.
	Our government is based on democratic principles.
quiet (silent)*	Please be quiet.
quite (very)	This house is quite old.
right (opposite of left; correct)	Turn right.
write (put words on paper)	This answer is right.
	Write an essay.
their (belonging to them)	Their dog's in our yard.
there (in that place)	The flashlight is over there.
they're (they are)	There are three peaches.
	They're five minutes late.
thorough (careful, complete)*	Do a thorough job.
through (finished; into at one place and out at another)	I'm through with this saw.
	The dog ran through the yard.
threw (did throw)	She threw the baseball.
to (word before a verb; in a direction)	He loves to play football.
too (more than enough; also)	Drive to the next corner.
two (number after one)	He's too tired to think.
	Let me go, too.
	I want two helpings.
weather (atmospheric conditions)	Hot, humid weather makes me sick.
whether (if)	Do you know whether I'm working tomorrow night?
which (a pronoun)	Which do you want?
witch (performer of black magic)	The witch cackled hideously.

*Note the differences in pronunciation in this set.

More Soundalikes

The above list barely scratches the surface of English soundalikes, but it does include some of the most commonly confused word pairs. Concentrate on them first. Once you've learned that list, you may want to master a second group presented on page 253. Look up the meanings of any word pairs that you're unsure of.

accept–except
advice–advise*
all together–altogether
angel–angle*
board–bored
breath–breathe*
capital–capitol
council–counsel
desert–dessert*
diner–dinner*
heroin–heroine
hoarse–horse
later–latter*
lessen–lesson

moral–morale*
pair–pear
plane–plain
precede–proceed*
role–roll
sight–site
sole–soul
stationary–stationery
sweat–sweet*
vain–vein–vane
weak–week
whole–hole
wholly–holy

*Note the differences in pronunciation in this set.

Exercise 15: Using Soundalike Words——————

Directions: Underline the word in parentheses that will correctly complete the sentence.

Example: Minneapolis is *(to, too, two)* far north for orange trees to grow outside.

1. I'm *(quiet, quite)* sure that the *(principle, principal)* ingredient in this pie crust is cardboard.

2. Please *(write, right)* a letter of application to the *(personal, personnel)* department.

3. Have you *(all ready, already)* *(accepted, excepted)* the nomination for treasurer?

4. A *(thorough, through)* inspection of the syringe revealed a trace of *(heroin, heroine)*.

5. I hope you'll learn your *(lesson, lessen)* before you *(break, brake)* *(your, you're)* poor mother's heart!

6. The *(whole, hole)* team was *(week, weak)* after a bout with the flu.

7. Don't be *(to, too)* quick to *(loose, lose)* your temper.

8. For *(desert, dessert)* we ate some *(sweet, sweat)* *(rolls, roles)*.

9. With one last *(horse, hoarse)* *(breath, breathe)*, *(their, they're, there)* gerbil died.

10. *(Its, It's)* *(passed, past)* time for *(diner, dinner)*.

11. Please give me some *(advice, advise)* on *(weather, whether)* or not to *(break, brake)* my contract.

12. *(They're, There, Their)* *(wasting, waisting)* *(they're there, their)* *(desert, dessert)* by feeding it to the parrot.

13. Is it *(all right, alright)* to leave the *(board, bored)* *(they're, their, there)* until *(latter, later)* tonight?

14. Did you *(no, know)* that this is the *(dessert, desert)* where a *(plane, plain)* crashed last *(week, weak)*?

15. The father was awarded *(sole, soul)* custody upon the *(advise, advice)* of a child psychologist.

After you check your answers, restudy the meanings of any words you missed. Then practice using them and their soundalikes in sentences of your own.

ANSWERS ARE ON PAGE 336.

Using Pronunciation as a Spelling Aid

Pronounce Carefully

Although "sound it out" is not always a very helpful suggestion in spelling, you will find it easier to spell some words if you pronounce them carefully. People do tend to spell words as they sound. If they mispronounce a word by omitting or adding sounds, they're likely to misspell the word, too.

Omitted Sounds

Some words are typically mispronounced and misspelled by leaving out parts: letters or syllables. For instance, people who say "libary" are likely to omit the *r* when they spell *library*. Practice pronouncing the following words carefully, paying special attention to the underlined letters.

Feb<u>r</u>uary	quan<u>t</u>ity	charac<u>t</u>eristic
leng<u>t</u>h	comf<u>or</u>table	consc<u>ie</u>ntious
enviro<u>n</u>ment	gover<u>n</u>ment	lab<u>o</u>ratory
pa<u>r</u>ticular	prob<u>ab</u>ly	sep<u>a</u>rate
soph<u>o</u>more	su<u>r</u>prise	Wed<u>nes</u>day
san<u>d</u>wich	represent<u>a</u>tive	streng<u>t</u>h
lit<u>er</u>ature	mathem<u>a</u>tics	min<u>i</u>ature
recognize	int<u>er</u>est	temper<u>a</u>ture

Added Sounds

Other words are mispronounced by adding sounds, and they're also misspelled as a result. The word *pronunciation*, for example, is often incorrectly spoken and spelled *pronounciation*. Can you see the difference? Study the following list, making sure you pronounce the underlined sections carefully—without adding anything extra.

equipment (not equiptment)

explanation (not explaination)

mischievous (not mischievious)

grievous (not grievious)

peculiar (not perculiar)

persevere (not perservere)

similar (not similiar)

Make Sound Match Spelling

If you do tend to spell words as they sound, make that strategy work for you by pronouncing words as they're spelled when you practice spelling. Pronounce the *table* in *acceptable*, for example, to help you remember that it ends in *able*, not *ible*. Say *conSCIENCE* (like the study of nature) when you're learning how to spell *conscience*.

Here are a few words that might be learned more easily by changing the pronunciation to mimic the spelling. You'll be able to find more of your own. (Remember to do this for spelling practice only! Be sure you pronounce the word correctly in ordinary conversation.)

a bun DANCE
ac CI DENT (make the second syllable rhyme with *my*)
ac KNOW LEDGE
ad E QUATE (make the third syllable rhyme with *date*)
a GAIN, a GAINST, bar GAIN (make the vowel sound in the second syllable like the *ai* in *rain*)
assist ANT (like the insect)
DE scribe (make the first syllable rhyme with *me*)
ca LEN DAR, dol LAR (make the last syllable rhyme with *car*)
per sis TENT
sig nif I CANT
shep HERD (pronounce the silent *h* in the second syllable)
ve GE TABLE
vis IT OR

Recognize Different Spelling Patterns

Have you ever had a conversation like this?

YOU: "How do you spell _____ ?"
FRIEND: "Look it up in the dictionary."
YOU: "How can I look it up if I don't know how to spell it?"
Friend shrugs his shoulders and walks away.

There is an answer for this dilemma. If you know the possible spelling patterns for a given sound, you can try one pattern at a time until you find the word you're looking for.

For instance, suppose you're unsure how to spell the word meaning "remove," or "get rid of." Is it *alimanate, illimanate, ilimanate, elimenate,* etc.? If you know that the first sound of the word ("uh") could be spelled with any vowel and that the second sound could be spelled with one *l* or two, you have enough information to begin a systematic dictionary search: start with *ali-*, then *alli-*, then *eli-*. You'll find *eliminate* on your third try.

Knowing spelling patterns has a second advantage: it allows you to group the words you're learning by their spelling. *Ache, stomach, school,* and *psychology* are all words in which the "k" sound is spelled with a *ch.* To further emphasize the spelling similarities among these words, you might make up a sentence using them all: *The psychologist says that school gives him a stomach ache.*

The following chart summarizes the different spelling patterns for English sounds. Use it to learn what the spelling options are when you look words up in a dictionary and to categorize the words you're learning to spell.

Sound	Spelling Pattern
s	syllable, aggressive, miscellaneous, cereal, psychology
z	analyze, arouse, possess
sh	sheriff, chef, surely, efficient, association, possession
zh	usual, revision
ch	choose, catch, natural
h	hideous, whose
j	general, journal, exaggerate, badge
k	comedy, panicky, ache, kitchen, quart
m	moral, autumn
n	knock, narrative, gnat
f	factory, telephone
a	mistake, available, portrayal, neighbor, steak
e	employee, repeat, niece, deceive, precede
i	guidance, sight, by, aisle, island
o	loaf, associate, know
u	university, few
uh	aggravate, dozen, medicine, renovate, prejudice
er	dollar, doctor, cylinder
ense	absence, resistance, suspense
able	profitable, possible
el	nickel, natural, bicycle
ize	recognize, analyze, exercise
shun	appreciation, physician, session

Commonly Misspelled Words

In the back of this chapter on pages 268–71, you'll find a list of commonly misspelled words, some of which follow specific spelling rules and some of which do not. A page number following a word indicates the page where the spelling rule that applies to it can be found. All misspelled words in GED Test questions will be drawn from this list.

You will see from the list that there are many words that simply must be memorized because no rule applies. To study these words, use the strategies you've learned in this chapter, such as dividing the words into syllables, altering the pronunciation, and grouping words with similar spelling patterns. Perhaps a patient friend will dictate fifty words at a time to you so that you can find out which ones you already know and which need further study.

Exercise 16: Spelling Review

Part A

Directions: The spelling words in this exercise will check your knowledge of plurals, basic spelling rules, sound-alikes, and commonly misspelled words from the list on pages 268–71. Be sure you study the list before trying this exercise. Circle the misspelled word in each group and write it correctly in the space provided. If all the words are correct, place a *C* in the space.

Example: a beautiful sunrise
in (plane) sight
amateur boxing
expense account

plain

1. everything's all right
ripe strawberries
advertize for jobs
awkward landing

2. wiegh the odds
against all odds
whether or not
studying for a test

3. truly sorry
asociated with
severely scolded
unusually cheerful

4. marriage counselor
military cemeterys
switch partners
three policemen

5. in late Febuary
Wednesday night
sometime next week
tomorrow morning

6. disastrous descent
unnecessary advice
irritable baby
dissappointed child

7. become a soldier
under seige
seized her arm
from arteries to veins

_____

8. proceed with caution
succede at last
precede her daughter
complicated procedure

_____

9. it's your problem
is their anything wrong
the man whose car was stolen
you're absolutely right

_____

10. which one was it
bologna sandwich
government official
the principle reason

_____

11. steak and salad for diner
apple pie for dessert
the capital of Idaho
gardener's daughter

_____

12. prepare the prescription
around her waste
variety of automobiles
author of considerable fame
enormous grocery store

_____

13. loaf of bread
mystereous personality
pleasant neighbor
possible explanation

_____

14. frightening instinct
sudden tragedy
played the roll of mother
synonym for secretary

_____

15. several telegrams
tenant has a visitor
another bottle
acceptible bargain

_____

Part B

Directions: Proofread the following paragraph for spelling errors. Cross out each misspelled word and write the correct spelling above it. The first correction has been made as an example.

Organizing

~~Organizeing~~ a suprise party for a freind requires alot of planing. You'll need to attend to usal matters like invatations and refreshments, but you'll have to keep your activitys a secret. To prevent the guest of honor from gessing that anything's up, you must deside on a logical reson for inviting her to the place where the party will be held. Anouther concern is how to hide the rest of the guests until the proper moment. For the party to be successfull, you're timeing must be perfect.

ANSWERS ARE ON PAGE 336.

Exercise 17: Capitalization and Spelling Review

Directions: The following items are based on paragraphs that contain numbered sentences. Some of the sentences may contain errors in capitalization and spelling. Read each paragraph and then answer the items based on it. For each item, choose the answer that would result in the most effective writing of the sentence or sentences.

(1) Its becoming increasingly difficult for American political leaders to make national policies without considering their international effects. (2) Approving price supports for wheat grown in Kansas may mean that African Nations will look elsewhere for cheaper grain. (3) Reducing pollution controls for industries in the Ohio river region may anger Canadians because of environmental damage from acid rain. (4) Although raiseing the minimum wage may please labor unions here, it will also affect the balance of trade. (5) Competition from companys in countries with lower wages will reduce the number of goods exported from the United States. (6) The time has come for our government leaders to realize that their is no neat distinction between foreign and domestic affairs. (7) Befor they choose a policy position, they should remember that they're citizens of the world.

1. Sentence 1: **Its becoming increasingly difficult for American political leaders to make national policies without considering their international effects.**

   What correction should be made to this sentence?

   (1) replace *Its* with *It's*
   (2) replace *American* with *american*
   (3) replace *leaders* with *Leaders*
   (4) replace *their* with *there*
   (5) replace *effects* with *affects*

2. Sentence 2: **Approving price supports for wheat grown in Kansas may mean that African Nations will look elsewhere for cheaper grain.**

   What correction should be made to this sentence?

   (1) change the spelling of *Approving* to *Approveing*
   (2) replace *Kansas* with *kansas*
   (3) replace *African* with *african*
   (4) replace *Nations* with *nations*
   (5) no correction is needed

3. Sentence 3: **Reducing pollution controls for industries in the Ohio river region may anger Canadians because of environmental damage from acid rain.**

   What correction should be made to this sentence?

   (1) change the spelling of *Reducing* to *Reduceing*
   (2) change the spelling of *industries* to *industrys*
   (3) replace *river* with *River*
   (4) change the spelling of *environmental* to *enviormental*
   (5) no correction is necessary

4. Sentence 4: **Although raiseing the minimum wage may please labor unions here, it will also affect the balance of trade.**

   What correction should be made to this sentence?

   (1) change the spelling of *Although* to *Altough*
   (2) change the spelling of *raiseing* to *raising*
   (3) change the spelling of *minimum* to *mininum*
   (4) change the spelling of *unions* to *unnions*
   (5) replace *affect* with *effect*

5. Sentence 5: **Competition from companys in countries with lower wages will reduce the number of goods exported from the United States.**

   What correction should be made to this sentence?

   (1) change the spelling of *Competition* to *Compitition*
   (2) change the spelling of *companys* to *companies*
   (3) change the spelling of *countries* to *countrys*
   (4) replace *States* with *states*
   (5) no correction is necessary

6. Sentence 6: **The time has come for our government leaders to realize that their is no neat distinction between foreign and domestic affairs.**

   What correction should be made to this sentence?

   (1) change the spelling of *government* to *goverment*
   (2) change the spelling of *realize* to *realyse*
   (3) replace *their* with *there*
   (4) change the spelling of *foreign* to *foriegn*
   (5) no correction is necessary

7. Sentence 7: **Befor they choose a policy position, they should remember that they're citizens of the world.**

   What correction should be made to this sentence?

   (1) change the spelling of *Befor* to *Before*
   (2) replace *choose* with *chose*
   (3) replace *they're* with *their*
   (4) replace *world* with *World*
   (5) no correction is necessary

(1) After the dreary darkness of January and February, I'm always relieved when March arrives with its first breath of Spring. (2) At last the season of snowstorms, overcoats, bare branchs, and cold remedies is over. (3) The robins return on schedule, hopping across our lawn in search of nesting material. (4) Children hurry home from kindergarten to balance awkwardly on their new bicycles. (5) Once again I awake with the sun shinning through my bedroom window. (6) With the flip of a calendar page to this new month, my hole existence takes an optimistic turn. (7) No longer am I bored, exausted, and depressed. (8) My appetite for living has suddenly returned.

8. Sentence 1: **After the dreary darkness of January and February, I'm always relieved when March arrives with its first breath of Spring.**

   What correction should be made to this sentence?

   (1) change the spelling of *February* to *Febuary*
   (2) change the spelling of *relieved* to *releived*
   (3) replace *breath* with *breathe*
   (4) replace *Spring* with *spring*
   (5) no correction is necessary

9. Sentence 2: **At last the season of snowstorms, overcoats, bare branchs, and cold remedies is over.**

   What correction should be made to this sentence?

   (1) replace *season* with *Season*
   (2) change the spelling of *overcoats* to *overcoates*
   (3) change the spelling of *branchs* to *branches*
   (4) change the spelling of *remedies* to *remedys*
   (5) no correction is necessary

10. Sentence 3: **The robins return on schedule, hopping accross our lawn in search of nesting material.**

    What correction should be made to this sentence?

    (1) change the spelling of *schedule* to *scedule*
    (2) change the spelling of *hopping* to *hoping*
    (3) change the spelling of *accross* to *across*
    (4) change the spelling of *nesting* to *nestting*
    (5) no correction is necessary

11. Sentence 4: **Children hurry home from kindergarten to balance awkwardly on their new bicycles.**

    What correction should be made to this sentence?

    (1) change the spelling of *kindergarten* to *kindergarden*
    (2) change the spelling of *balance* to *ballance*
    (3) change the spelling of *awkwardly* to *akwardly*
    (4) change the spelling of *bicycles* to *bycicles*
    (5) no correction is necessary

12. Sentence 5: **Once again I awake with the sun shinning through my bedroom window.**

    What correction should be made to this sentence?

    (1) change the spelling of *Once* to *Ones*
    (2) change the spelling of *again* to *agen*
    (3) change the spelling of *shinning* to *shining*
    (4) change the spelling of *through* to *throught*
    (5) no correction is necessary

13. Sentence 6: **With the flip of a calendar page to this new month, my hole existence takes an optimistic turn.**

What correction should be made to this sentence?

   (1) change the spelling of *calendar* to *calander*
   (2) replace *hole* with *whole*
   (3) change the spelling of *existence* to *existance*
   (4) change the spelling of *optimistic* to *optomistic*
   (5) no correction is necessary

14. Sentences 7 and 8: **No longer am I bored, exausted, and depressed. My appetite for living has suddenly returned.**

What correction should be made to these sentences?

   (1) replace *bored* with *board*
   (2) change the spelling of *exausted* to *exhausted*
   (3) change the spelling of *appetite* to *appatite*
   (4) change the spelling of *suddenly* to *sudenly*
   (5) no correction is necessary

ANSWERS ARE ON PAGES 336–37.

Chapter 6 Review Evaluation Chart

Question Type	Review Pages	Question Number	Number of Quetions	Number Correct
Capitalization	237–41	2, 3, 8	3	/3
Spelling rules	245–49	4, 5, 9, 12	4	/4
Spelling sound-alikes	251–53	1, 6, 13	3	/3
Spelling commonly misspelled words	254–57	7, 10, 14	3	/3
No error		11	1	/1

Passing score: 11 out of 14 correct

Your score: _____ out of 14 correct

If you missed more than one in any category, review the pages indicated.

CUMULATIVE REVIEW

Editing Practice

Part A

Directions: Find and correct the sixteen errors in the following passage. Six of these errors are related to skills that you learned in earlier chapters: verb and pronoun forms, fragments, and punctuation. You may want to review the checklists on pages 57, 109, 163, and 212 to refresh your memory on what to look for. The other ten errors are related to capitalization and spelling. For these errors, use the checklist below as your proofreading guide.

☐ Are specific names of people and places capitalized?

☐ Are general names not capitalized?

☐ Are all words spelled correctly? Look especially carefully at words with prefixes and suffixes and at sound-alike words.

Editing hint: You may find it easier to check for spelling errors if you read from the end to the beginning of the passage. This technique lets you temporarily ignore meaning in order to concentrate on spelling.

Some physcologists suggest that pepole can reduce tension by imagining themselves in a peaceful setting. Whenever I use this advice. I remembered Cave Point, a Park in Wisconsin on the shore of lake Michigan. I picture myself sitting on top of a cliff overlooking the water. Despite the cool lake breeze, the sun shinning on my back makes a sweater unecessary. Closeing my eyes I soak in the warmth and listen to the rythemical thumping of water in the limestone caves carved by centuries of waves. Once agen this oasis of calm, works its magic and you can return to the hassles of everyday life with renewed inner strenth.

ANSWERS ARE ON PAGE 337.

Part B

Directions: Edit for capitalization and spelling the essay that you revised in the first part of this chapter. Use the checklist above to help you locate errors.

If you want further practice, edit as many of your earlier writings as you have time to correct.

ANSWERS WILL VARY.

★ GED PRACTICE ★

Multiple-Choice Practice

Directions: The following items are based on paragraphs that contain numbered sentences. Some of the sentences may contain errors in sentence structure, usage, and mechanics. Read each paragraph and then answer the items based on it. For each item, choose the answer that would result in the most effective writing of the sentence or sentences. The best answer must be consistent with the meaning and tone of the rest of the paragraph.

(1) In no other country on earth does citizens have as great a variety of national backgrounds as in America. (2) In the five hundred years since Christopher Columbus set sail from Italy, the American indians have been joined by wave after wave of newcomers from Europe, Africa, Asia, and Latin America. (3) Each of these groups has enriched our culture with its unique customs, food, music, and language. (4) Jazz, for example, is part, of our African heritage. (5) The tradition of Santa Claus a contribution of Holland. (6) Going out for dinner in most cities, you can choose among Italian, Mexican, Chinese, and French restaurants. (7) Although this mixing of cultures has benefited us in numerous ways, it has also caused problems. (8) Each new group has had to face discrimination in housing, education, and jobs. (9) This problem is due to the prejudice of people who have forgotten their immigrant roots. (10) Unfortunately, the suspicion of anything or anyone diffrent sometimes overpowers appreciation of the advantages of a multicultural society.

1. Sentence 1: **In no other country on earth does citizens have as great a variety of national backgrounds as in America.**

   What correction should be made to this sentence?

   (1) change *does* to *do*
   (2) change the spelling of *citizens* to *citazens*
   (3) change the spelling of *variety* to *veriaty*
   (4) insert a comma after *variety*
   (5) no correction is necessary

2. Sentence 2: **In the five hundred years since Christopher Columbus set sail from Italy, the American indians have been joined by wave after wave of newcomers from Europe, Africa, Asia, and Latin America.**

   What correction should be made to this sentence?

   (1) replace *set* with *has set*
   (2) remove the comma after *Italy*
   (3) replace *indians* with *Indians*
   (4) replace *newcomers from* with *newcomers. From*
   (5) remove the comma after *Asia*

3. Sentence 3: **Each of these groups has enriched our culture with its unique customs, food, music, and language.**

   Which of the following is the best way to write the underlined portion of this sentence? If you think the original is the best way to write the sentence, choose option (1).

   (1) has enriched
   (2) have enriched
   (3) has been enriched
   (4) have been enriched
   (5) enriching

4. Sentence 4: **Jazz, for example, is part, of our African heritage.**

   What correction should be made to this sentence?

   (1) remove the comma after *jazz*
   (2) remove the comma after *example*
   (3) remove the comma after *part*
   (4) replace *African* with *african*
   (5) replace *heritage* with *Heritage*

5. Sentence 5: **The tradition of Santa Claus a contribution of Holland.**

   Which of the following is the best way to write the underlined portion of this sentence? If you think the original is the best way to write the sentence, choose option (1).

   (1) Claus a
   (2) Claus, a
   (3) Claus, which is a
   (4) Claus being a
   (5) Claus is a

6. Sentence 6: **Going out for dinner in most cities, you can choose among Italian, Mexican, Chinese, and French restaurants.**

   What correction should be made to this sentence?

   (1) remove the comma after *cities*
   (2) replace *you* with *we*
   (3) change *choose* to *chose*
   (4) change the spelling of *restaurants* to *restraunts*
   (5) no correction is necessary

7. Sentence 7: **Although this mixing of cultures has benefited us in numerous ways, it has also caused problems.**

   If you rewrote this sentence beginning with

   This mixing of cultures has benefited us in numerous

   the next words should be

   (1) ways, it
   (2) ways, so
   (3) ways; however,
   (4) ways; therefore,
   (5) ways; for instance,

8. Sentences 8 and 9: **Each new group has had to face discrimination in housing, education, and jobs. This problem is due to the prejudice of people who have forgotten their immigrant roots.**

   The most effective combination of these sentences would contain which group of words?

   (1) Because of the prejudice of people
   (2) Because each new group
   (3) Although each new group
   (4) Because they are prejudiced, each new group
   (5) Being prejudiced, each new group

9. Sentence 10: **Unfortunately, the suspicion of anything or anyone diffrent sometimes overpowers appreciation of the advantages of a multicultural society.**

   What correction should be made to this sentence?

   (1) change the spelling of *diffrent* to *different*
   (2) insert a comma after *diffrent*
   (3) change *overpowers* to *overpower*
   (4) change the spelling of *appreciation* to *apreciation*
   (5) no correction is necessary

   (1) Technical advances in medical care, have raised new ethical questions for our society. (2) In the past, there were few remedies for patients with severe brain injuries and they died within a few days at most. (3) Today however, doctors can sustain life indefinitely by using artificial respirators and intravenous feedings. (4) Some patients lie in comas for years. (5) They're unable to respond to their environment. (6) There physicians and families must decide whether to prolong life-sustaining procedures that carry no hope of cure. (7) Family members were torn between a desire to end a loved one's suffering and the dread of imposing a death sentence. (8) Doctors, too, are understandably reluctant to withdraw life support, they've been trained to save lives, not end them.

10. Sentence 1: **Technical advances in medical <u>care, have</u> raised new ethical questions for our society.**

    Which of the following is the best way to write the underlined portion of this sentence? If you think the original is the best way to write the sentence, choose option (1).

    (1) care, have
    (2) care have
    (3) care has
    (4) care, has
    (5) care, having

11. Sentence 2: **In the past, there were few remedies for patients with severe brain injuries and they died within a few days at most.**

    What correction should be made to this sentence?

    (1) replace *there* with *their*
    (2) change *were* to *was*
    (3) change the spelling of *remedies* to *remedys*
    (4) insert a comma after *injuries*
    (5) no correction is necessary

12. Sentence 3: **Today however, doctors can sustain life indefinitely by using artificial respirators and intravenous feedings.**

    What correction should be made to this sentence?

    (1) insert a comma after *Today*
    (2) remove the comma after *however*
    (3) replace *indefinitely by* with *indefinitely. By*
    (4) insert a comma after *respirators*
    (5) no correction is necessary

13. Sentences 4 and 5: **Some patients lie in comas for years. They're unable to respond to their environment.**

    The most effective combination of these sentences would contain which of the following groups of words?

    (1) years they're
    (2) years, they're
    (3) years, so they're
    (4) years, or they're
    (5) years, unable

14. Sentence 6: **There physicians and families must decide whether to prolong life-sustaining procedures that carry no hope of cure.**

    What correction should be made to this sentence?

    (1) replace *There* with *Their*
    (2) replace *families* with *family's*
    (3) replace *whether* with *weather*
    (4) change the spelling of *procedures* to *proceedures*
    (5) replace *procedures that* with *procedures. That*

15. Sentence 7: **Family members <u>were torn</u> between a desire to end a loved one's suffering and the dread of imposing a death sentence.**

    Which of the following is the best way to write the underlined portion of this sentence? If you think the original is the best way to write the sentence, choose option (1).

    (1) were torn
    (2) was torn
    (3) were tore
    (4) are tore
    (5) are torn

16. Sentence 8: **Doctors too are understandably reluctant to withdraw life support, they've been trained to save lives, not end them.**

    What correction should be made to this sentence?

    (1) replace *too* with *to*
    (2) insert a comma after *reluctant*
    (3) replace *support, they've* with *support. They've*
    (4) change *trained* to *train*
    (5) no correction is necessary

ANSWERS ARE ON PAGE 337.

Cumulative Review Evaluation Chart

Chapter	Question Number	Number of Questions	Number Correct
Chapter 2 Fragments, Nouns, and Pronouns	5, 10	2	/2
Chapter 3 Verbs	1, 3, 15	3	/3
Chapter 4 Combining Ideas in Sentences	7, 11, 16	3	/3
Chapter 5 Modifiers/ Pronoun Reference	4, 6, 8, 13	4	/4
Chapter 6 Capitalization and Spelling	2, 9, 12, 14	4	/4

Passing score: 12 out of 16 correct

Your score: _____ out of 16 correct

Master List of Frequently Misspelled Words

All misspelled words on the GED Test will be taken from the following master list. Other forms of most of these words, including plurals and forms requiring suffixes, also may be tested.

A page number in parentheses tells you where you can find a spelling rule or hint to help you with the spelling of that word.

a lot (251)	again (255)	approval (248)	before
ability	against (255)	approve	beginning (248)
absence (256)	aggravate (255)	approximate (244)	being
absent	aggressive	argue	believe (249)
across	agree	arguing (248)	benefit (255)
abundance (255)	aisle (255)	argument (248)	benefited (248)
accept (253)	all right (251)	arouse	between
acceptable (256)	almost	arrange	bicycle (246)
accident	already (251)	arrangement (248)	board (253)
accommodate (244)	although	article	bored (253)
accompanied (247)	altogether (253)	artificial (244)	borrow
accomplish	always	ascend (255)	bottle
accumulation (244)	amateur	assistance (247)	bottom
accuse	American	assistant	boundary (255)
accustomed	among	associate (244)	brake (251)
ache (255)	amount	association (244)	breadth
achieve (249)	analysis (244)	attempt	breath (253)
achievement (247)	analyze (255)	attendance (255)	breathe (253)
acknowledge (255)	angel (253)	attention	brilliant (254)
acquaintance (255)	angle (253)	audience	building
acquainted (255)	annual	August	bulletin
acquire	another	author	bureau (255)
across	answer	automobile (245)	burial (247)
address	antiseptic (246)	autumn (255)	buried (247)
addressed	anxious	auxiliary (254)	bury (255)
adequate (255)	apologize (255)	available	bushes
advantageous (248)	apparatus (244)	avenue	business (255)
advantage	apparent (255)	awful	cafeteria
advertise (255)	appear	awkward	calculator (255)
advertisement (255)	appearance (247)	bachelor (254)	calendar (255)
advice (253)	appetite	balance	campaign
advisable (255)	application (244)	balloon	capital (253)
advise (253)	apply	bargain (255)	capitol (253)
advisor (255)	appreciate (244)	basic	captain (255)
aerial	appreciation (244)	beautiful (255)	career
affect (251)	approach	because	careful (247)
affectionate (244)	appropriate (244)	become	careless (247)

carriage (247)
carrying (247)
category (244)
ceiling (249)
cemetery (255)
cereal
certain
changeable (248)
characteristic (244)
charity
chief (249)
choose
chose
cigarette
circumstance
congratulate (244)
citizen
clothes
clothing
coarse (251)
coffee
collect
college
column (255)
comedy
comfortable (247)
commitment (248)
committed (248)
committee
communicate (244)
company
comparative (255)
compel
competent (255)
competition (244)
compliment (255)
conceal
conceit (249)
conceivable (248)
conceive (249)
concentration (244)
conception
condition (255)
conference (254)
confident (255)
conquer
conscience (255)
conscientious (255)
conscious (255)
consequence (255)
consequently
considerable (244)
consistency (255)
consistent (255)
continual

continuous (254)
controlled (248)
controversy (244)
convenience (254)
convenient (254)
conversation
corporal (254)
corroborate (244)
council (253)
counsel (253)
counselor (255)
courage
courageous (248)
course (251)
courteous
courtesy
criticism
criticize
crystal
curiosity
cylinder
daily
daughter
daybreak (245)
death
deceive (249)
December
deception
decide
decision (255)
decisive (255)
deed
definite
delicious (254)
dependent (255)
deposit
derelict
descend (255)
descent (255)
describe (255)
description (244)
desert (253)
desirable (248)
despair
desperate (255)
dessert (253)
destruction
determine (255)
develop
development (247)
device
dictator (255)
died
difference (254)
different (254)

dilemma
dinner (253)
direction
disappear (246)
disappoint (246)
disappointment (246)
disapproval (246)
disapprove (246)
disastrous
discipline
discover
discriminate (244)
disease (255)
dissatisfied (246)
dissection (246)
dissipate
distance (255)
distinction
division
doctor (255)
dollar (255)
doubt
dozen (255)
earnest
easy
ecstasy
ecstatic
education (254)
effect (251)
efficiency (255)
efficient (255)
eight
either
eligibility (244)
eligible
eliminate (255)
embarrass
embarrassment (247)
emergency
emphasis
emphasize
enclosure
encouraging (248)
endeavor (255)
engineer
English
enormous
enough
entrance
envelope
environment (254)
equipment (254)
equipped (248)
especially (255)
essential

evening (254)
evident
exaggerate (244)
exaggeration (244)
examine
exceed
excellent (255)
except
exceptional (247)
exercise (255)
exhausted (254)
exhaustion (254)
exhilaration (254)
existence (255)
exorbitant (254)
expense
experience (254)
experiment (254)
explanation
extreme
facility
factory
familiar (254)
fascinate (255)
fascinating (248)
fatigue
February (254)
financial (255)
financier (249)
flourish
forcibly
forehead (245)
foreign (249)
formal
former
fortunate (255)
fourteen (245)
fourth
frequent
friend (249)
frightening (254)
fundamental (244)
further (254)
gallon
garden
gardener (254)
general (254)
genius
government (254)
governor (255)
grammar (255)
grateful (247)
great
grievance (249)
grievous (254)

grocery (254)
guarantee
guess
guidance
half
hammer
handkerchief (254)
happiness (247)
healthy
heard
heavy
height (249)
heroes
heroine (253)
hideous
himself
hoarse (253)
holiday
hopeless (247)
hospital (255)
humorous
hurried (247)
hurrying (247)
ignorance (255)
imaginary (248)
imbecile
imitation
immediately (247)
immigrant (255)
incidental
increase
independence (255)
independent (255)
indispensable (255)
inevitable (255)
influence
influential (244)
initiate (255)
innocence (255)
inoculate (244)
inquiry
insistent
instead
instinct
integrity
intellectual (244)
intelligence (244)
intercede
interest
interfere
interference
interpreted
interrupt
invitation
irrelevant (255)

irresistible (255)
irritable (255)
island (255)
its (55)
it's (55)
itself
January (254)
jealous
judgment (247)
journal (255)
kindergarten
kitchen (255)
knew (251)
knock (255)
know (251)
knowledge (255)
labor (255)
laboratory (254)
laid
language
later (253)
latter (253)
laugh
leisure (249)
length (254)
lesson (253)
library (254)
license (255)
light
lightning (254)
likelihood (247)
likely (247)
literal
literature (254)
livelihood (247)
loaf
loneliness (247)
loose (251)
lose (251)
losing (248)
loyal
loyalty
magazine
maintenance (254)
maneuver
marriage (247)
married (247)
marry
match
material (254)
mathematics (254)
measure (255)
medicine (255)
million
miniature (254)

minimum
miracle (255)
miscellaneous (244)
mischief (249)
mischievous (254)
misspelled (246)
mistake
momentous
monkey
monotonous (244)
moral (253)
morale (253)
mortgage (254)
mountain (255)
mournful (246)
muscle (255)
mysterious (247)
mystery
narrative
natural (255)
necessary (244)
needle
negligence
neighbor (249)
neither (249)
newspaper (245)
newsstand (245)
niece (249)
noticeable (248)
o'clock
obedient (254)
obstacle (255)
occasion
occasional
occur
occurred (248)
occurrence (248)
ocean
offer
often
omission
omit
once
operate
opinion
opportune
opportunity (248)
optimist
optimistic
origin
original
oscillate
ought
ounce

overcoat (245)
paid
pamphlet (254)
panicky
parallel
parallelism (248)
particular
partner
pastime
patience
peace
peaceable (248)
pear
peculiar (254)
pencil
people
perceive (249)
perception
perfect
perform
performance
perhaps (254)
period
permanence (255)
permanent (255)
perpendicular (244)
perseverance (248)
persevere (254)
persistent (255)
persuade
personality
personal (252)
personnel (252)
persuade
persuasion
pertain
picture
piece (249)
plain
playwright
pleasant
please
pleasure (248)
pocket
poison
policeman (245)
political (255)
population
portrayal
positive
possess
possession (247)
possessive (247)
possible
post office

potatoes (46)
practical (254)
prairie
precede
preceding
precise
predictable (254)
prefer
preference
preferential
preferred (248)
prejudice
preparation (248)
prepare
prescription (254)
presence
president
prevalent (255)
primitive
principal (252)
principle (252)
privilege (255)
probably (254)
procedure
proceed
produce
professional
professor (255)
profitable (255)
prominent
promise
pronounce
pronunciation (254)
propeller (248)
prophet
prospect
psychology (255)
pursue
pursuit
quality
quantity
quarreling (248)
quart
quarter
quiet (252)
quite (252)
raise
realistic
realize
reason
rebellion (248)
recede
receipt
receive (249)

recipe
recognize (254)
recommend
recuperate (244)
referred (248)
rehearsal
reign (249)
relevant (255)
relieve (249)
remedy
renovate
repeat
repetition
representative (254)
requirements (247)
resemblance (255)
resistance (255)
resource
respectability (244)
responsibility (244)
restaurant (254)
rhythm
rhythmical
ridiculous
right
role (253)
roll (253)
roommate (245)
sandwich (254)
Saturday
scarcely (247)
scene
schedule (255)
science (255)
scientific (255)
scissors (255)
season
secretary (254)
seize (249)
seminar
sense
separate (254)
service
several (254)
severely (247)
shepherd (254)
sheriff
shining (248)
shoulder
shriek (249)
siege (249)
sight (253)
signal
significance (244)
significant (244)

similar
similarity
sincerely (247)
site (253)
soldier (254)
solemn
sophomore (254)
soul (253)
source
souvenir
special
specified
specimen
speech
stationary (253)
stationery (253)
statue
stockings
stomach (255)
straight
strength (254)
strenuous (254)
stretch
striking (248)
studying (247)
substantial (255)
succeed
successful
sudden
superintendent (254)
suppress
surely (247)
surprise (254)
suspense
sweat (253)
sweet (253)
syllable
symmetrical (244)
sympathy
synonym
technical
telegram
telephone
temperament (254)
temperature (254)
tenant
tendency (255)
tenement (255)
therefore (247)
thorough (252)
through (252)
title
together
tomorrow
tongue

toward (254)
tragedy
transferred (248)
treasury
tremendous
tries (247)
truly (247)
twelfth (254)
twelve
tyranny
undoubtedly (254)
United States
university
unnecessary (246)
unusual (246)
vacuum
useful (247)
usual
valley
valuable (254)
variety (255)
vegetable (254)
vein (249)
vengeance (248)
versatile (255)
vicinity
vicious (254)
view (259)
village
villain (255)
visitor (255)
voice
volume
waist
weak (253)
wear
weather (252)
Wednesday (254)
week (253)
weigh (249)
weird (249)
whether (252)
which (252)
while
whole
wholly (253)
whose
wretched

7

TEST-TAKING STRATEGIES

If you are ready for this chapter, you should be nearly ready for the GED Writing Skills Test. Either you have focused on a few weaknesses indicated by the pretest, or you've worked carefully through this book, building your skills to improve your chances for success. Whichever category you're in, you should realize that you've already acquired the most important test-taking skills for this portion of the GED tests: you've learned how to write and how to edit both your own writing and the writing of others.

In this chapter, you'll focus on putting these skills to work as efficiently as possible in a testing situation. Knowing what the test will be like and how best to attack each part should hold any butterflies of uneasiness to a manageable flutter when test day arrives.

Part 1 of the GED Writing Skills Test is multiple choice. Part 2 is the essay.

Getting Ready for the Multiple-Choice Test

What Is the Test Like?

In Part 1 of the Writing Skills Test you'll have 75 minutes to answer 55 multiple-choice questions based on a series of six or seven short passages, each ten to twelve sentences long. These questions will check your knowledge of sentence structure, standard usage, punctuation, capitalization, and spelling. You're already familiar with this format; you've seen it in the pretest and almost every chapter review and cumulative review exercise in this book.

How Will It Be Scored?

The score you get is based on the number of correct answers. There is no penalty for guessing. The number of items you answer correctly will be converted to a standard score. The number of points in your standard score for Part 1 will be combined with your score on Part 2 of the Writing Skills Test (the essay). This combined score will apply to the 225 points you need to pass the entire GED test battery.

How Should I Approach the Test?

Read Each Passage Carefully

Before you start answering questions on the test, first read carefully the passage that the questions are based on. There are two good reasons for reading a passage in advance. First, it gives you a head start on locating errors. You may not identify a specific mistake, but you'll often be able to point out the part of a sentence where something seems wrong. Second, you'll see what the passage as a whole means and how the ideas fit together in it. Seeing overall meaning will help you answer questions about connecting words and identify sentences in which verbs or pronouns don't agree with the rest of the passage.

Each paragraph will contain a variety of errors. The following list will remind you of the main possibilities to keep in mind as you preview the passage.

Types of Errors

1. Sentence fragments

   TYPICAL ERROR: Because we left the party early.

2. Run-on sentences or comma splices

   TYPICAL ERROR: Many Americans are **thoughtless, they** litter the highways with wrappers and beer cans.

3. Illogical connecting words

   TYPICAL ERROR: Computers are easy to use; **therefore,** many people are afraid of them.

4. Misplaced or dangling modifiers

   TYPICAL ERROR: **Sitting in front of a computer for hours,** her eyes began to burn.

5. Lack of parallel structure

   TYPICAL ERROR: On his days off Rodney enjoys sleeping, watching game shows, and **to play pool.**

6. Missing or misplaced commas

   TYPICAL ERROR: Whenever Robert loses at **pool he** breaks his cue.

7. Verb tenses used incorrectly

   TYPICAL ERROR: After the players returned to the locker room, the coach **scolds** them.

8. Lack of subject-verb agreement

   TYPICAL ERROR: Jim and Mary **was** at our apartment yesterday.

9. Lack of pronoun agreement with antecedents

   TYPICAL ERROR: If a person drinks too much alcohol, **you** shouldn't drive.

10. Incorrectly spelled words (plurals, verb endings, soundalikes, and commonly misspelled words)

    TYPICAL ERROR: Who bought **there** old house?

11. Incorrectly capitalized words

    TYPICAL ERROR: The **united states** is a relatively young country.

The following passage is a sample of the paragraphs you'll encounter on the Writing Skills Test. Can you find any errors as you preview it? For practice, circle the errors you find.

(1) Far more than any European nation, our country has became a throwaway society. (2) Italians lovingly preserve structures that are hundreds of years old, some even date back to Roman times. (3) Americans, on the other hand, are more likely to bulldoze an old building down to make room for a skyscraper or even a parking lot. (4) In other countries you buy sturdy clothes and keep them until they wear out. (5) Restitching ripped seams and patching worn elbows. (6) In the United States, styles that were fashionable six months ago may well be outdated tommorow. (7) This throwaway mentality even extended to our political attitudes. (8) We have a short interest span. (9) Burning political issues have an average life expectancy of six months. (10) Physical fitness of young people, hunger in America, energy conservation, oil pollution of the oceans, and space exploration, have all come and gone as newsstand fads. (11) Our passion for whatever is new and exciting have too often led us to ignore enduring values and concerns.

Read Each Question Carefully

Before you try to answer a question, read it carefully. Test all possible answers. You'll find three types of questions used in Part 1 of the Writing Skills Test: sentence correction, sentence revision, and construction shift. You have practiced all three in the review tests at the end of each chapter and in the pretest.

Question Types

Sentence Correction

Four to five questions for each passage (about half of the questions) will have a *sentence correction* format. In this type, you'll see a sentence from the passage, followed by the question "What correction should be made to this sentence?" The five possible answers will focus on different parts of the sentence. One choice might deal with a spelling change, another with punctuation, a third with usage, and a fourth with sentence structure. Sometimes the fifth choice will be "no correction is necessary." That choice occasionally will be correct.

Example:

Sentence 1: **Far more than any European nation, our country has became a throwaway society.**

What correction should be made to this sentence?

(1) replace *European* with *european*
(2) replace *nation* with *Nation*
(3) change *has* to *have*
(4) change *became* to *become*
(5) insert a comma after *became*

You may realize what the error in the sentence is right away. In that case, you should look for the answer that corrects that error.

Otherwise, the key to answering this kind of question is flexibility. Look carefully at the change suggested in each choice and see how it will fit into the sentence. Sometimes you also need to check the paragraph as a whole for verb tense or pronoun choice. Can you tell what rule is being tested in each of the five choices above?

Both (1) and (2) are checking your knowledge of capitalization. Choice (3) gives two present-tense forms of the same verb, so it's testing subject-verb agreement. Is *our country has* or *our country have* correct? Choice (4) presents two verb forms, too: past tense and past participle of *become*. Should it be *has became* or *has become*? The last choice offers a punctuation change. Is there any rule to support placing a comma after *became (our country has became, a throwaway society)*?

Can you eliminate any of these choices as clearly wrong? If you can, you'll increase your chances of picking the correct answer. Circle the answer that you think is correct.

Answer:

The correct answer is choice (4). The helping verb *has* must be combined with the past participle *become*. The corrected sentence would read *Far more than any European nation, our country has become a throwaway society.*

Sentence Revision

Three or four of the questions for each passage will be in sentence revision form. This time a sentence from the passage will be presented with one section underlined, and you'll be asked to choose the best wording for the underlined portion. The first choice will repeat the original wording; the other four give you alternative revisions to choose from. You will choose choice (1) if the sentence is correct as written.

Example:
Sentence 2: **Italians lovingly preserve structures that are hundreds of years old, some even date back to Roman times.**

Which of the following is the best way to write the underlined portion of this sentence? If you think the original is the best way to write the sentence, choose option (1).

(1) old, some
(2) old some
(3) old. Some
(4) old, in fact some
(5) old, for example, some

Since only one part of the sentence is used, this kind of question will probably focus on one or two rules rather than several. In the above example, you can see that the question deals with the correct way to connect the two halves of the sentence. Is the original sentence correct, or is it a comma splice? Which of the alternatives are punctuated correctly? See if you can eliminate the wrong answers. Now circle the correct choice.

Answer:
Choice (3) is correct. One way to revise the sentence is to make two complete sentences. All other choices would create a run-on sentence or a comma splice. The revision would read like this: *Italians lovingly preserve structures that are hundreds of years old. Some even date back to Roman times.*

Construction Shifts

One or two of the questions for each passage will be *construction shifts.* This type of question will ask you to choose the best way to rewrite a sentence or to combine two sentences. There are two kinds of construction shift items.

Example 1:
Sentences 8 and 9: **We have a short interest span. Burning political issues have an average life expectancy of six months.**

The most effective combination of sentences 8 and 9 would include which of the following groups of words?

(1) Since we have
(2) Although we have
(3) span; however, burning
(4) span, yet burning
(5) span because burning

Notice that in this question format, the original sentences contain no error. Your job is to decide how the ideas in these sentences are related and combine them logically. The most likely topic to be tested by a construction shift question is sentence structure.

To answer this type of question, test each possible response by thinking of the complete sentence in which it would appear. Then decide whether the sentence makes sense. Eliminate any alternatives that don't preserve the meaning of the original sentences.

(1)   Since we have a short interest span, burning political issues have an average life expectancy of six months.

(2)   Although we have a short interest span, burning political issues have an average life expectancy of six months.

(3)   We have a short interest span; however, burning political issues have an average life expectancy of six months.

Write the complete sentence for choices (4) and (5) below.

(4)   span, yet burning

_____

(5)   span because burning

_____

Now circle the number of the correct answer.

Answer:
     Choice (1) is correct. The word _Since_ makes sense as a link. It shows that our short interest span is the reason why political issues have such a short life expectancy.

     Follow the same process—think of the whole new sentence—when you're asked to rewrite a sentence, as in the following example. Suppose Sentence 8 were written as follows.

Example 2:
Sentence 8: **We have a short interest span; therefore, burning political issues have an average life expectancy of six months.**

If you rewrote sentence 8 beginning with

Burning political issues have an average life expectancy of six months

the next word should be

(1)   which
(2)   consequently
(3)   because
(4)   and
(5)   but

     Here again the original sentence contains no error. You must understand the relationship between the ideas in the sentence, then recombine them in a new way. Just as you did in the previous example, test each choice. Decide which one preserves the meaning of the original sentence.

Look at the Whole Passage

     Consider the context of the entire passage before choosing the correct answer. One or two questions from each passage will require you to think about passage meaning as well as sentence meaning. These questions deal with consistent verb and pronoun choice.

Example:

Sentence 7: **This throwaway mentality even <u>extended</u> to our political attitudes.**

Which of the following is the best way to write the underlined portion of this sentence? If you think the original is the best way to write the sentence, choose option (1).

(1) extended
(2) had extended
(3) extend
(4) extends
(5) will be extended

Several of the choices would make a grammatically correct sentence. However, only one fits in with the rest of the paragraph. Is the passage as a whole written in past, present, or future tense? The answer to that question will determine the correct verb for sentence 7. Look back at the passage on page 274; then circle the correct answer.

Answer:

The rest of the passage is written in present tense; therefore, the correct answer is choice (4). Pages 91 and 201-205 will refresh your memory on consistent verb and pronoun choices within a passage.

Answer All Fifty-Five Questions

Be sure to answer all the questions. There's no penalty for guessing, so a wrong answer won't count against your score any more than a blank answer. Don't take too long on any one question. If you find a confusing question, you may want to mark it to return to after you've finished the rest of the test. Be sure, however, to choose an answer for each question before turning in your test paper.

When you skip a question, put a mark on your answer sheet next to the space for the question you skipped. Keep checking throughout the test to make sure that the number of the questions in the test booklet matches the number you fill in on the answer sheet.

Use Your Time Wisely

Since both parts of the Writing Skills Test are given together as one test, you *will* be allowed to go on to Part 2, the writing sample, as soon as you finish Part 1, the multiple choice section. However, *avoid the temptation to rush through Part 1 so that you will have a longer time to write the essay.* If you have worked carefully through this book, you now know that 45 minutes is *plenty* of time to plan, write, and revise your writing sample. The best test-taking strategy is to work carefully through Part 1 and, if you have time, go back and check your work in that section. Be sure you are satisfied with your work on Part 1 *before* you go on to Part 2.

Remember that your final writing skills score comes from *both* parts of the test; in fact, Part 1 counts for a little bit more of the total score than does Part 2. It's important that you do well on both parts of the test. Although you may be concerned about the writing sample time limit, don't rush through Part 1 and do less than your best.

Getting Ready for the Essay

What Is the Essay Test Like?

In Part 2 of the GED Writing Skills Test, you'll have forty-five minutes to plan, write, revise, and edit an essay on a topic given to you at that time. The assignment will be to explain some everyday problem or occurrence. This topic won't require any specific background knowledge on your part; just being an adult should give you enough knowledge to handle it.

The instructions for the essay will suggest that you write an essay of about two hundred words. However, don't worry about the length of your essay. As long as you have written a good essay, its length will not affect your score at all.

How Will the Essay Be Scored?

Your completed essay will be scored by two readers trained to use a process called *holistic scoring*. With this method, readers don't mark misspelled words and misplaced commas, nor do they write comments about the content and structure of your writing. They read your paper once; then they use a six-point scale to record their overall impression of the quality of your writing, 1 being the lowest score and 6 the highest. The two readers' scores are added to produce the final score for your essay. That means your final score is actually between two and twelve. This score is combined with your score from Part 1 to produce a single score for the Writing Skills Test.

What Do the Scores Mean?

Part 2 of the Writing Skills Test checks your ability to state a point clearly and support it convincingly in well-organized paragraphs. Although serious problems with capitalization, punctuation, and spelling will detract from the overall quality of your paper, you're not expected to produce a mechanically perfect piece of writing under testing conditions. The essay readers will realize that your essay was produced within a strict time limit and that you weren't able to use a dictionary or a grammar book for proofreading.

Briefly, here's what the numerical scores mean:

6 The essay shows evidence of mature thinking, with a clear, appropriate organizational plan. Support for the author's opinions is thorough, specific, and relevant. Although there may be an occasional error in mechanics, the writing is smooth and graceful.

5 The essay is clearly organized and well supported throughout. Ideas are meaningful, but they may not be expressed as gracefully as those in a 6 paper. Although the writer has generally good control of sentence structure and mechanics, there may be an occasional problem.

4 The essay has been organized, but not as clearly as a 5 or 6 paper, and the support is not as thorough or as convincing. More errors in standard written English appear, but they aren't serious enough to interfere greatly with the meaning of the essay.

3 Although the essay shows some evidence of development, it is often a listing of unsupported statements about the topic. Many weaknesses in sentence structure, usage, and mechanics reduce the effectiveness of the paper.

2 The essay is poorly developed and inadequately supported, with problems in unity and little evidence of mature thinking. Errors in standard written English are so numerous that they seriously damage the effectiveness of the paper.

1 The essay is rambling, lacking a main point and an organizational plan. The writer has little control over the sentence structure, usage, and mechanics of standard written English.

0 The paper is blank, illegible, or completely off the assigned topic.

In general, scores of 6, 5, or 4 mean that the essay is

- clearly organized

- well supported

- correctly written according to the rules of standard written English

Scores of 3, 2, or 1 mean that there are serious flaws in one or more of these areas.

How Should I Approach the Essay?

If you've studied the first six chapters of this book, you should have a good start on answering this question. The writing exercises you've done so far, particularly the timed writings, have given you practice in responding to assigned topics. Here is a summary of the test-taking tips you've learned so far.

Budget Your Time

Don't begin scribbling in a panic the second the testing official says, "You may begin." Remember that you have forty-five minutes to plan and write your essay; use this time effectively. Here's one possible plan:

- 10 minutes to plan your essay

- 30 minutes to write it

- 5 minutes to revise and edit it

You've already done several timed writings. What division of time felt comfortable to you?

Read the Question Carefully

You may remember from Chapter 2 that the first step in planning a piece of writing is analyzing. Ask yourself two questions: What is the topic? What kinds of ideas and details does the essay question suggest? You should be able to answer these two questions after studying the essay topic you've been given. The essay question will contain clues to the kinds of ideas and details to include in your essay. Suppose you were given the following essay question:

> A female secretary may make $15,000 per year, while a male administrative assistant with the same skills may make $25,000 per year. In general, men have higher average incomes than women. Discuss the causes of this income difference between the sexes.

What is the topic? The topic is *the income difference between the sexes*.

What kinds of ideas and details does the question suggest? Look for clues in the question. The most important clue in the question is the word *causes*. What **causes** the income difference between the sexes?

Different essay questions will give you different clues. Are you being asked to **describe** the **effects** of something, or to **compare** two items?

Carefully read the essay topics below. Underline clues that tell you the kinds of ideas and details to include in your essay.

> Debates about the effects of television on children have raged for years. In particular, some groups have suggested that commercials be banned from children's programs. Describe some effects that television commercials can have on children.

Did you underline the word *effects*?

> More and more mothers of preschoolers are entering the work force. As a result, their children spend large parts of the day in day care centers or with babysitters. How do you think this child care arrangement affects small children as compared to children whose mothers stay at home? Give specific examples to explain your opinion.

Did you underline *affects* and *compared*? You might also have underlined *specific examples, explain,* or *opinion*. All these words can suggest what to include in your essay.

> In every society in the world, ceremonies are used to mark major events in people's lives. Installations of government leaders, marriages, deaths, even sports events are all accompanied by certain rituals. Why do you think that ceremonies are so important to people? Use specific examples to support your reasons.

Did you underline *why* and *reasons*? You might also have underlined *specific examples* and *support*. All these words could suggest ways to answer the essay question.

Plan Your Essay

In the actual test, you'll have scratch paper provided for planning. Use it. You learned how to brainstorm ideas in Chapter 2 and how to write a unifying statement and organize your essay in Chapter 5. Putting those skills to good use may be the single most important step you can take to earn a high score on your essay.

1. **Use the clues in the essay to focus your brainstorming.** Keeping these clue words in mind will help you think of relevant ideas. Underline the clues in the following essay question.

    > Throughout the history of art and literature, romantic love has been an enduring theme. Today, people are still enchanted by lovers—stories about lovers, movies about lovers, songs about lovers, and pictures of lovers.
    > Write a composition of about two hundred words explaining why people are so fascinated by love. Use specific details and examples in your answer.

    Did you underline *explaining why*? You might have also underlined *specific details and examples*. How can you use these clues to help you brainstorm?

2. **Write a unifying statement.** Writing a preliminary unifying statement also helps focus your brainstorming. Here's an example of a unifying statement for this essay topic:

    > People are fascinated by romantic love because they can see their own dreams acted out by other people.

    Can you see that this unifying statement could begin an essay *explaining why* people are so fascinated by romantic love?

    How would you approach this essay topic? Write your own unifying statement for this topic.

Writing your unifying statement before you begin to brainstorm can help you get ideas down that are really relevant. However, you may not be sure right away what your main point will be. If so, brainstorm first and develop a unifying statement by figuring out how you could pull together ideas in your brainstorm list.

3. **Make a brainstorm list.** How many items are enough for your list? For a two-hundred-word essay, you can expect to write a brief introduction, two to three well-developed supporting paragraphs, and a brief conclusion. So your brainstorming list should contain at least two main points (one for each supporting paragraph) and as many related details as you can think of (even though you may decide not to use all of them later). In addition, if you think of an effective introduction for your essay, make a note of it.

4. **Organize your list.** You won't have time to make a formal outline, but do make an effort to group the details that you want in each paragraph. Use arrows or circles, if you want, as a visual aid to your grouping. Check to make sure that each main idea is clearly related to the unifying statement and that each detail is clearly related to its main idea. Cross out any irrelevant material.

Since your time limit won't allow you to make extensive revisions of organization and content, the planning stage is doubly important. Use a little of your planning time to decide on the overall structure of your essay. How will you group your details? What order will make your ideas clear to your readers? Look once again at your brainstormed list of details. Are they specific enough? Are there enough to be convincing?

You may want to review the example of organizing a brainstorm list on pages 170–71.

Exercise 1: Planning Your Essay

Directions: Plan your responses to the following essay questions. Taking ten minutes for each question, write a unifying statement, brainstorm a list of ideas, group the items in the list, and number your groups to indicate the order in which you plan to write your paragraphs.

1. Debates about the effects of television on children have raged for years. In particular, some groups have suggested that commercials be banned from children's programs. Describe some effects that television commercials can have on children.

2. More and more mothers of preschoolers are entering the work force. As a result, their children spend large parts of the day in day care centers or with babysitters. How do you think this child care arrangement affects small children as compared to children whose mothers stay at home? Give specific examples to explain your opinion.

3. In every society in the world, ceremonies are used to mark major events in people's lives. Installations of government leaders, marriages, deaths, even sports events are all accompanied by certain rituals. Why do you think that ceremonies are so important to people? Use specific examples to support your reasons.

A SAMPLE ANSWER APPEARS ON PAGE 337.

Write Quickly and Carefully

If you have done justice to the planning stage, the writing stage shouldn't be too rough. You already know what your purpose is and what your major supporting points will be. Just put the information into sentence and paragraph form.

Write an introduction. Be sure the introduction contains a unifying statement and previews the organization of your essay for the reader. Then move on to the first supporting paragraph.

Write the body. As you write your supporting paragraphs, keep your unifying statement and overall organizational plan in mind. Write two or three supporting paragraphs. Work in appropriate transition words (*first, in addition, however,* etc.—the list is on page 226) to link the supporting paragraphs to the introduction and to one another. And remember, the more specific your supporting details are, the better.

If you think of new ideas as you write, feel free to include them as long as they're relevant and they fit in logically.

Write a conclusion. Like the introduction, the conclusion can be just a sentence or two. If your time is nearly up, simply rephrase the unifying statement.

Write quickly. Use your budgeted writing time wisely. If you get stuck because you can't think of the word you want to use or you can't remember how to spell it, leave a space and move on. Be sure, though, to fill something in before you hand in your paper. Again, your readers understand that you don't have access to a dictionary during the test. It won't hurt to take a stab at the spelling of the precise word you want to use rather than rewording your entire sentence to avoid the problem. The readers who will score your paper will not expect a polished piece of writing.

Write carefully. The instructions for this part of the Writing Skills Test will say nothing about the format of your writing. However, you should be sure to indent at the beginning of each paragraph and to leave side margins wide enough for adding a sentence or two if you decide to revise. Printing rather than cursive writing is perfectly acceptable, but if you print, use both capital and lowercase letters.

Exercise 2: Writing Your Essay

Directions: Choose **one** of the topics in Exercise 1 and write an essay based on your unifying statement and brainstorming list. Set a thirty-minute time limit for yourself.

A SAMPLE ANSWER APPEARS ON PAGE 338.

Revise and Edit Your Essay

Revise for content and organization first. Forty-five minutes won't allow you much time for revising and editing, so you'll need to have your priorities clear when you reach the last few minutes of the testing period. Study the revising checklist below to see what to concentrate on.

Revising Checklist

☐ Is the introduction worded clearly? If not, make some changes to clarify it.

☐ Will it be clear to the readers that the supporting paragraphs help prove the unifying statement? If not, change the wording to make the supporting points clearer.

☐ Are the details in each paragraph clear, specific, and relevant? Cross out irrelevant details and add details to make vague or general statements clear.

☐ Does the conclusion tie the essay together? You may just want to restate the unifying statement in slightly different words.

☐ Are paragraphs and sentences organized logically and linked smoothly? Add transition words to show connections clearly. You can also move material that seems to fit better in a different place.

Make any revisions neatly. Cross out material that is irrelevant to the paper and use a caret (∧) or an asterisk (✳) to show where inserted words belong. If you decide to move a sentence, circle it and draw an arrow to its new location. If you've forgotten to indent a new paragraph, use the symbol ¶ to show where it should begin.

Edit for sentence structure, usage, and mechanics. Check for the most serious problems first. Since sentence structure and punctuation errors can sometimes interfere with meaning, attend to them before you hunt for spelling or capitalization errors. Study the following editing checklist to help you maintain your priorities as your testing time draws to a close.

Editing Checklist

☐ Are sentences complete—no fragments or run-ons?

☐ Is wording clear? Are any words missing?

☐ Are endmarks and commas used correctly?

☐ Are verbs and pronouns used correctly and consistently?

☐ Are words spelled correctly? Look especially at plurals, verb endings, and sound-alikes.

☐ Are words capitalized correctly?

Exercise 3: Revising and Editing

Directions: Take five minutes right now to revise and edit the essay you wrote for Exercise 2.

A SAMPLE ANSWER APPEARS ON PAGE 338.

Exercise 4: Further Practice

Directions: If you need more practice writing essays before you move on to take the posttest, use any of the following topics. Remember to work for only forty-five minutes on each essay. Put into practice all you have learned about planning, drafting, revising, and editing.

1. American society is a mixture of races, religions, languages, and customs. This mixture has brought many benefits to our country, and it has also caused problems not experienced in nations where the citizens have similar backgrounds.

   Write a composition of about two hundred words describing the effects that our mixture of backgrounds has had on American society. You may describe the positive effects, the negative effects, or both. Be specific and use examples to support your view.

2. Many people in the United States are having smaller families. Rather than having three or four children, many parents choose to have only one or two children.

   Do you think this trend toward smaller families is good or bad? In a composition of about two hundred words, state your opinion and support it with specific reasons and examples.

3. The invention of the airplane has brought about a number of changes in American life. Although air travel has improved our lives in many ways, it has also brought new problems.

   Write a composition of about two hundred words describing the effect of the airplane on modern life. You may describe the positive effects, the negative effects, or both. Be specific and use examples to support your view.

4. Most people seem to think they don't have enough money. No matter how much they have, they always want more.

   Write a composition of about two hundred words explaining why, no matter how much money they make, people usually want more money. Be sure to support your views with specific reasons, details, and examples.

5. Even though fear and anxiety are unpleasant emotions, people regularly spend money to watch horror movies. What makes these movies so appealing?

   Write a composition of about two hundred words explaining why people go to horror movies. Use specific reasons and examples in your answer.

6. Fifty years ago, computers were unknown. Today these machines, from tiny pocket calculators up through room-sized mainframes, are used in schools, businesses, government, and homes. They check our tax returns and print out our bank statements and utility bills. They even ring up the sales at many supermarkets. The widespread use of computers has brought many benefits to our society, but it has also caused some problems.

   Write a composition of about two hundred words describing the effects of computers on modern life. You may describe the positive effects, the negative effects, or both.

ANSWERS WILL VARY.

WRITING SKILLS POSTTEST, PART 1

Directions: The following items are based on paragraphs which contain numbered sentences. Some of the sentences may contain errors in sentence structure, usage, or mechanics. A few sentences, however, may be correct as written. Read the paragraph and then answer the items based on it. For each item, choose the answer that would result in the most effective writing of the sentence or sentences. The best answer must be consistent with the meaning and tone of the rest of the paragraph.

Posttest Answer Grid

1 ① ② ③ ④ ⑤	20 ① ② ③ ④ ⑤	38 ① ② ③ ④ ⑤
2 ① ② ③ ④ ⑤	21 ① ② ③ ④ ⑤	39 ① ② ③ ④ ⑤
3 ① ② ③ ④ ⑤	22 ① ② ③ ④ ⑤	40 ① ② ③ ④ ⑤
4 ① ② ③ ④ ⑤	23 ① ② ③ ④ ⑤	41 ① ② ③ ④ ⑤
5 ① ② ③ ④ ⑤	24 ① ② ③ ④ ⑤	42 ① ② ③ ④ ⑤
6 ① ② ③ ④ ⑤	25 ① ② ③ ④ ⑤	43 ① ② ③ ④ ⑤
7 ① ② ③ ④ ⑤	26 ① ② ③ ④ ⑤	44 ① ② ③ ④ ⑤
8 ① ② ③ ④ ⑤	27 ① ② ③ ④ ⑤	45 ① ② ③ ④ ⑤
9 ① ② ③ ④ ⑤	28 ① ② ③ ④ ⑤	46 ① ② ③ ④ ⑤
10 ① ② ③ ④ ⑤	29 ① ② ③ ④ ⑤	47 ① ② ③ ④ ⑤
11 ① ② ③ ④ ⑤	30 ① ② ③ ④ ⑤	48 ① ② ③ ④ ⑤
12 ① ② ③ ④ ⑤	31 ① ② ③ ④ ⑤	49 ① ② ③ ④ ⑤
13 ① ② ③ ④ ⑤	32 ① ② ③ ④ ⑤	50 ① ② ③ ④ ⑤
14 ① ② ③ ④ ⑤	33 ① ② ③ ④ ⑤	51 ① ② ③ ④ ⑤
15 ① ② ③ ④ ⑤	34 ① ② ③ ④ ⑤	52 ① ② ③ ④ ⑤
16 ① ② ③ ④ ⑤	35 ① ② ③ ④ ⑤	53 ① ② ③ ④ ⑤
17 ① ② ③ ④ ⑤	36 ① ② ③ ④ ⑤	54 ① ② ③ ④ ⑤
18 ① ② ③ ④ ⑤	37 ① ② ③ ④ ⑤	55 ① ② ③ ④ ⑤
19 ① ② ③ ④ ⑤		

(1) The invention of the X-ray machine in 1895 gave medical personnel a way to see inside a patients body without performing surgery. (2) This new tool enabled doctors to diagnose and treat ailments ranging from broken bones to tumors more efficiently. (3) In recent years, the X-ray machine and the computer has been combined to produce new data-gathering possibilities for doctors. (4) The new equipment produces three-dimensional images. (5) The images are produced when it takes a series of X-ray scans and reassembles them for viewing. (6) Some versions of this technology actually takes moving pictures of internal organs like a beating heart. (7) Surgeons particularly pleased with the computerized X-rays. (8) By discovering the exact size and shape of a tumor before surgery they can reduce the amount of time that a patient is on the operating table. (9) This saves lives. (10) Pediatricians too found the equipment useful. (11) Because it can produce exact images within a few seconds, the doctors can recieve the information they need even when their young patients squirm around.

1. Sentence 1: **The invention of the X-ray machine in 1895 gave medical personnel a way to see inside a patients body without performing surgery.**

   What correction should be made to this sentence?

   (1) change *gave* to *give*
   (2) change the spelling of *personnel* to *personal*
   (3) replace *patients* with *patient's*
   (4) change the spelling of *performing* to *preforming*
   (5) no correction is necessary

2. Sentence 3: **In recent years, the X-ray machine and the computer has been combined to produce new data-gathering possibilities for doctors.**

   What correction should be made to this sentence?

   (1) insert a comma after *computer*
   (2) change *has* to *have*
   (3) replace *combined to* with *combined. To*
   (4) change the spelling of *possibilities* to *possibilitys*
   (5) no correction is necessary

3. Sentences 4 and 5: **The new equipment produces three-dimensional images. The images are produced when it takes a series of X-ray scans and reassembles them for viewing.**

   The most effective combination of sentences 4 and 5 would include which of the following groups of words?

   (1) By producing three-dimensional images, so it
   (2) By taking a series of X-ray scans and reassembling them for viewing, three-dimensional
   (3) After three-dimensional images are produced, the new equipment takes
   (4) images by taking a series of X-ray scans and reassembling
   (5) images, but it takes

4. Sentence 6: **Some versions of this technology actually takes moving pictures of internal organs like a beating heart.**

   Which of the following is the best way to write the underlined portion of this sentence? If you think the original is the best way, choose option (1).

   (1) takes
   (2) take
   (3) takeing
   (4) taking
   (5) taken

5. Sentence 7: **Surgeons particularly pleased with the computerized X-rays.**

   What correction should be made to this sentence?

   (1) replace *Surgeons* with *Surgeon's*
   (2) insert *are* after *Surgeons*
   (3) change the spelling of *particularly* to *paticularly*
   (4) change *pleased* to *please*
   (5) insert a comma after *pleased*

6. Sentence 8: **By discovering the exact size and shape of a tumor before surgery they can reduce the amount of time that a patient is on the operating table.**

   What correction should be made to this sentence?

   (1) change the spelling of *discovering* to *discoverring*
   (2) insert a comma after *tumor*
   (3) insert a comma after *surgery*
   (4) change the spelling of *operating* to *operateing*
   (5) no correction is necessary

7. Sentence 9: **This saves lives.**

   Which of the following is the best way to write the underlined portion of this sentence? If you think the original is the best way, choose option (1).

   (1) This saves lives.
   (2) Thus saving lives.
   (3) This procedure saves lives.
   (4) A life-saving procedure.
   (5) As a result, lives being saved.

8. Sentence 10: **Pediatricians too found the equipment useful.**

   Which of the following is the best way to write the underlined portion of this sentence? If you think the original is the best way, choose option (1).

   (1) too found
   (2) to found
   (3) too find
   (4) to find
   (5) to finding

9. Sentence 11: **Because it can produce exact images within a few seconds, the doctors can recieve the information they need even when their young patients squirm around.**

   What correction should be made to this sentence?

   (1) replace *Because* with *Although*
   (2) remove the comma after *seconds*
   (3) change the spelling of *recieve* to *receive*
   (4) replace *need even* with *need. Even*
   (5) no correction is necessary

(1) Today half of the married women with children under two work outside the home. (2) With infants and toddlers, the presence of so many working women has caused new strains in the workplace. (3) For instance employers may be requested to grant maternity leaves that extend several months beyond the birth or adoption of a baby. (4) Although in many European countries businesses routinely grant such leaves, they are expensive to employers because of the costs of finding and retraining temporary replacement help. (5) In addition, some employers in the United States argue that the policy discriminates against men by granting benefits exclusively to women. (6) Their opponents insists that since only women become pregnant, a law requiring maternity leaves is not unfair to men. (7) One compromise may be to develop a law guaranteeing parental leaves. (8) The law would allow either mothers or fathers to spend time with their new babies. (9) While parental leaves after childbirth occupy much National attention, a related issue affects many more working parents. (10) Should mothers and fathers be permitted to stay at home with sick children, or should sick leaves be used only when the workers themselves become ill? (11) Both issues pitted the financial interests of employers, who want to save money on employee benefits, against the physical and psychological well-being of children and parents.

10. Sentence 2: **With infants and toddlers, the presence of so many working women has caused new strains in the workplace.**

Which of the following is the best way to write the underlined portion of this sentence? If you think the original is the best way, choose option (1).

(1) With infants and toddlers, the presence of so many working women has caused new strains in the workplace.
(2) With infants and toddlers in the workplace, the presence of so many working women has caused new strains.
(3) The presence with infants and toddlers of so many working women has caused new strains in the workplace.
(4) The presence of so many working women with infants and toddlers has caused new strains in the workplace.
(5) The presence of so many working women in the workplace with infants and toddlers has caused new strains.

11. Sentence 3: **For instance employers may be requested to grant maternity leaves that extend several months beyond the birth or adoption of a baby.**

What correction should be made to this sentence?

(1) insert a comma after *instance*
(2) change *requested* to *request*
(3) insert a comma after *extend*
(4) insert a comma after *birth*
(5) no correction is necessary

12. Sentence 4: **Although in many European countries businesses routinely grant such leaves, they are expensive to employers because of the costs of finding and retraining temporary replacement help.**

If you rewrote sentence 4 beginning with

In many European countries, businesses routinely grant such leaves;

the next word should be

(1) moreover
(2) therefore
(3) then
(4) otherwise
(5) however

13. Sentence 6: **Their opponents insists that since only women become pregnant, a law requiring maternity leaves is not unfair to men.**

    What correction should be made to this sentence?

    (1) replace *Their* with *There*
    (2) change *insists* to *insist*
    (3) remove the comma after *pregnant*
    (4) change the spelling of *requiring* to *requireing*
    (5) change *is* to *are*

14. Sentences 7 and 8: **One compromise may be to develop a law guaranteeing parental leaves. The law would allow either mothers or fathers to spend time with their new babies.**

    The most effective combination of sentences 7 and 8 would contain which of the following groups of words?

    (1) leaves, who would allow
    (2) leaves, which would allow
    (3) leaves which it would allow
    (4) leaves, and the law
    (5) leaves, but the law

15. Sentence 9: **While parental leaves after childbirth occupy much National attention, a related issue affects many more working parents.**

    What correction should be made to this sentence?

    (1) insert a comma after *childbirth*
    (2) change *occupy* to *occupies*
    (3) change *National* to *national*
    (4) remove the comma after *attention*
    (5) no correction is necessary

16. Sentence 10: **Should mothers and fathers be permitted to stay at home with sick children, or should sick leaves be used only when the workers themselves become ill?**

    What correction should be made to this sentence?

    (1) change the spelling of *permitted* to *permited*
    (2) remove the comma after *children*
    (3) insert a comma after *or*
    (4) insert a comma after *only*
    (5) no correction is necessary

17. Sentence 11: **Both issues pitted the financial interests of employers, who want to save money on employee benefits, against the physical and psychological well-being of children and parents.**

    What correction should be made to this sentence?

    (1) change *pitted* to *pit*
    (2) change the spelling of *interests* to *intrests*
    (3) replace *who* with *which*
    (4) insert a comma after *physical*
    (5) no correction is necessary

(1) Quality circle programs have been adopted in a number of American businesses and industries in the last ten years. (2) They were originally used in Japan. (3) These programs are design to improve production efficiency and working conditions. (4) They operate on the principal that many problems in the workplace can best be solved by the workers themselves. (5) The circles consisted of groups of six to ten employees from the same work area who meet on a regular basis. (6) They choose the problems that they want to attack, identify possible causes, test to discover whether their analysis was accurate, and they consider possible solutions. (7) When they've settled on a workable solution, they make a formal management presentation to their supervisors. (8) The success of quality circles can be measured in reduced production costs, fewer industrial accidents, and greater output, in addition, the programs result in more satisfied employees. (9) Gaining some control over his working environment leads to a greater interest in making the company a success.

18. Sentences 1 and 2: **Quality circle programs have been adopted in a number of American businesses and industries in the last ten years. They were originally used in Japan.**

    The most effective combination of sentences 1 and 2 would include which of the following groups of words?

    (1) Originally used in Japan, quality
    (2) years so they were originally
    (3) Originally used in Japan, but
    (4) When quality circle programs in Japan
    (5) By using them in Japan, quality

19. Sentence 3: **These programs are design to improve production efficiency and working conditions.**

    Which of the following is the best way to write the underlined portion of this sentence? If you think the original is the best way, choose option (1).

    (1) are design
    (2) are designed
    (3) design
    (4) designed
    (5) designing

20. Sentence 4: **They operate on the principal that many problems in the workplace can best be solved by the workers themselves.**

    What correction should be made to this sentence?

    (1) change *operate* to *operates*
    (2) change the spelling of *principal* to *principle*
    (3) insert a comma after *workplace*
    (4) replace *workers* with *worker's*
    (5) no correction is necessary

21. Sentence 5: **The circles consisted of groups of six to ten employees from the same work area who meet on a regular basis.**

    What correction should be made to this sentence?

    (1) change *consisted* to *consist*
    (2) insert a comma after *employees*
    (3) change *who* to *which*
    (4) insert a comma after *meet*
    (5) no correction is necessary

22. Sentence 6: **They choose the problems that they want to attack, identify possible causes, test to discover whether their analysis was accurate, and** <u>they consider</u> **possible solutions.**

    Which of the following is the best way to write the underlined portion of this sentence? If you think the original is the best way, choose option (1).

    (1) they consider
    (2) to consider
    (3) considering
    (4) consider
    (5) considers

23. Sentence 7: **When they've settled on a workable solution,** <u>they make</u> **a formal management presentation to their supervisors.**

    Which of the following is the best way to write the underlined portion of this sentence? If you think the original is the best way, choose option (1).

    (1) they make
    (2) then they make
    (3) and they make
    (4) so they make
    (5) making

24. Sentence 8: **The success of quality circles can be measured in reduced production costs, fewer industrial accidents, and greater output, in addition, the programs result in more satisfied employees.**

    What correction should be made to this sentence?

    (1) change the spelling of *measured* to *mesured*
    (2) change the spelling of *accidents* to *accedents*
    (3) replace *output, in* with *output; in*
    (4) remove the comma after *addition*
    (5) change *result* to *results*

25. Sentence 9: **Gaining some control over his working environment leads to a greater interest in making the company a success.**

    What correction should be made to this sentence?

    (1) change *his* to *their*
    (2) change the spelling of *environment* to *enviornment*
    (3) insert a comma after *environment*
    (4) change *leads* to *lead*
    (5) change the spelling of *interest* to *intrest*

(1) Are you looking, for a form of exercise that keeps your heart and lungs in good shape without endangering the rest of your body? (2) Do you need a sport that doesn't require any expensive equipment or a special place to play? (3) If so, consider walking. (4) This form of exercise is an equal opportunity sport. (5) If you stretch your muscles before you begin and cooled down slowly after you stop, you'll find that a brisk pace provides all the conditioning you want without the stress to bones and joints that jogging causes. (6) In fact, his swinging arm movement may actually provide more exercise than jogging does. (7) For maximum benefit, plan to walk at least two or three times a week. (8) Because you live near your place of work, you may decide to walk there instead of driving or using public transportation. (9) On the other hand, you may prefer to map a route around your neighborhood or down a quite country road for an early evening stroll. (10) Regardless of where you going, there will be a noticeable new spring in your step after only a few weeks of regular walking.

26. Sentence 1: **Are you looking, for a form of exercise that keeps your heart and lungs in good shape without endangering the rest of your body?**

    What correction should be made to this sentence?

    (1) remove the comma after *looking*
    (2) insert a comma after *heart*
    (3) replace *shape without* with *shape? Without*
    (4) insert a comma after *without*
    (5) no correction is necessary

27. Sentence 2: **Do you need a sport that doesn't require any expensive equipment or a special place to play?**

    What correction should be made to this sentence?

    (1) change *Do* to *Did*
    (2) change the spelling of *equipment* to *equitment*
    (3) insert a comma after *equipment*
    (4) change the spelling of *special* to *speshal*
    (5) no correction is necessary

28. Sentences 3 and 4: **If so, consider walking. This form of exercise is an equal opportunity sport.**

    The most effective combination of sentences 3 and 4 would contain which of the following groups of words?

    (1) If so, this form
    (2) being an equal opportunity sport, consider
    (3) walking, but this form
    (4) walking, which this form
    (5) walking, an equal

29. Sentence 5: **If you stretch your muscles before you begin and cooled down slowly after you stop, you'll find that a brisk pace provides all the conditioning you want without the stress to bones and joints that jogging causes.**

    Which of the following is the best way to write the underlined portion of this sentence? If you think the original is the best way, choose option (1).

    (1) cooled
    (2) cooling
    (3) cool
    (4) have cooled
    (5) will cool

30. Sentence 6: **In fact, <u>his</u> swinging arm movement while walking may actually provide more exercise than jogging does.**

    Which of the following is the best way to write the underlined portion of this sentence? If you think the original is the best way, choose option (1).

    (1) his
    (2) their
    (3) our
    (4) your
    (5) my

31. Sentence 8: **<u>Because</u> you live near your place of work, you may decide to walk there instead of driving or using public transportation.**

    Which of the following is the best way to write the underlined portion of this sentence? If you think the original is the best way, choose option (1).

    (1) Because
    (2) If
    (3) Although
    (4) Until
    (5) After

32. Sentence 9: **On the other hand, you may prefer to map a route around your neighborhood or down a quite country road for an early evening stroll.**

    What correction should be made to this sentence?

    (1) remove the comma after *hand*
    (2) change the spelling of *prefer* to *perfer*
    (3) insert a comma after *neighborhood*
    (4) change the spelling of *quite* to *quiet*
    (5) no correction is necessary

33. Sentence 10: **Regardless of where you going, there will be a noticeable new spring in your step after only a few weeks of regular walking.**

    What correction should be made to this sentence?

    (1) change *going* to *go*
    (2) change the spelling of *there* to *their*
    (3) change the spelling of *noticeable* to *noticable*
    (4) replace *step after* with *step; after*
    (5) no correction is necessary

(1) As oil and coal supplies dwindle and with the shrinkage of available farmland, people may increasingly turn to the ocean for fuel and food. (2) Scientists are already conducting encouraging experiments in the Pacific ocean off the coast of Hawaii. (3) In one project, the scientists are pumping warm ocean water around pipes containing ammonia, a substance that has a very low boiling point. (4) When the ammonia boiled, its evaporation into a gas turns a turbine. (5) As it cools, it returns to its liquid state and it is recycled through the system. (6) Another group of scientists working with aquaculture, or ocean farming. (7) They've found that the icy water two thousand feet below the surface is rich with nutrients; however, it's too far from sunlight to harbor harmful bacteria. (8) Abalone is a shellfish considered a seafood delicacy, and this environment is ideal for growing it. (9) In a third experiment, farmers are pumping the cold ocean water through pipes lain in strawberry fields. (10) Water vapor in the air condenses on the pipes, providing the cool moisture needed to produce exceptionally sweet berries is provided in this way. (11) These experiments are just the beginning of a variaty of ocean industries that will develop in the twenty-first century.

34. Sentence 1: **As oil and coal supplies dwindle and <u>with the shrinkage of available farmland</u>, people may increasingly turn to the ocean for fuel and food.**

    Which of the following is the best way to write the underlined portion of this sentence? If you think the original is the best way, choose option (1).

    (1) with the shrinkage of available farmland
    (2) with shrinking available farmland
    (3) with available farmland shrinking
    (4) available farmland shrinks
    (5) available farmland shrank

35. Sentence 2: **Scientists are already conducting encouraging experiments in the Pacific ocean off the coast of Hawaii.**

    What correction should be made to this sentence?

    (1) replace *already* with *all ready*
    (2) change the spelling of *encouraging* to *encourageing*
    (3) change *Pacific* to *pacific*
    (4) change *ocean* to *Ocean*
    (5) change *coast* to *Coast*

36. Sentence 4: **When the ammonia <u>boiled</u>, its evaporation into a gas turns a turbine.**

    Which of the following is the best way to write the underlined portion of this sentence? If you think the original is the best way, choose option (1).

    (1) boiled
    (2) was boiling
    (3) boiling
    (4) boils
    (5) boil

37. Sentence 5: **As it cools, it returns to its liquid state and it is recycled through the system.**

    What correction should be made to this sentence?

    (1) change *cools* to *cool*
    (2) remove the comma after *cools*
    (3) insert a comma after *state*
    (4) change the spelling of *through* to *threw*
    (5) no correction is necessary

38. Sentence 6: **Another group of <u>scientists working</u> with aquaculture, or ocean farming.**

    Which of the following is the best way to write the underlined portion of this sentence? If you think the original is the best way, choose option (1).

    (1) scientists working
    (2) scientists are working
    (3) scientist's working
    (4) scientists' working
    (5) scientists' are working

39. Sentence 8: **Abalone is a shellfish considered a seafood delicacy, and this environment is ideal for growing it.**

    If you rewrote sentence 8 beginning with

    This environment is ideal for growing abalone,

    the next word should be

    (1) a
    (2) who
    (3) being
    (4) they
    (5) it

40. Sentence 9: **In a third experiment, farmers are pumping the cold ocean water through pipes lain in strawberry fields.**

    What correction should be made to this sentence?

    (1) remove the comma after *experiment*
    (2) replace *farmers* with *farmers'*
    (3) change *are pumping* to *pumped*
    (4) insert a comma after *water*
    (5) replace *lain* with *laid*

41. Sentence 11: **These experiments are just the beginning of a variaty of ocean industries that will develop in the twenty-first century.**

    What correction should be made to this sentence?

    (1) remove *are*
    (2) change the spelling of *variaty* to *variety*
    (3) replace *industries that* with *industries. That*
    (4) replace *that* with *who*
    (5) change the spelling of *develop* to *develope*

(1) Few houses built before 1970 were designed to be energy efficient. (2) Because natural gas and other petroleum products were cheap and abundant, builders can easily reduce construction costs by using little or no insulation. (3) Furnaces also fuel wasters. (4) In fact, 30 percent or more of the heat produced went strait up the chimney. (5) During the 1970s, political and economic events in the Middle East raised the price of oil imported from Arab countries, and suddenly energy conservation became important. (6) Faced with skyrocketing costs for heating and cooling their homes, many homeowners began searching for ways to increase energy efficiency. (7) They discover that weatherstripping around windows and doors reduced both drafts and fuel bills. (8) Adding an extra layer of insulation in the attic kept homes warmer in Winter and cooler in summer. (9) Although the initial cost was high, blowing insulation behind the outside walls brought long-term energy savings. (10) Looking back, American homeowners realized that the energy crisis had made them wiser energy consumers.

42. Sentence 1: **Few houses built before 1970 were designed to be energy efficient.**

    What correction should be made to this sentence?

    (1) change *built* to *build*
    (2) change the spelling of *before* to *befor*
    (3) insert a comma after *1970*
    (4) change *were* to *was*
    (5) no correction is necessary

43. Sentence 2: **Because natural gas and other petroleum products were cheap and abundant, builders can easily reduce construction costs by using little or no insulation.**

    What correction should be made to this sentence?

    (1) change *were* to *was*
    (2) remove the comma after *abundant*
    (3) change *can* to *could*
    (4) change the spelling of *easily* to *eazily*
    (5) replace *costs by* with *costs. By*

44. Sentence 3: <u>**Furnaces also** fuel wasters.</u>

    Which of the following is the best way to write the underlined portion of this sentence? If you think the original is the best way, choose option (1).

    (1) Furnaces also
    (2) Furnaces
    (3) Furnaces being also
    (4) Furnaces were also
    (5) Furnaces that were

45. Sentence 4: **In fact, 30 percent or more of the heat produced went strait up the chimney.**

    What correction should be made to this sentence?

    (1) remove the comma after *fact*
    (2) insert a comma after *percent*
    (3) change *went* to *gone*
    (4) change the spelling of *strait* to *straight*
    (5) no correction is necessary

46. Sentence 5: **During the 1970s, political and economic events in the Middle East raised the price of oil imported from Arab countries, and suddenly energy conservation became important.**

    If you rewrote sentence 5 beginning with

    Energy conservation suddenly became important during the 1970s

    the next word should be

    (1) when
    (2) if
    (3) until
    (4) although
    (5) unless

47. Sentence 7: **They discover that weatherstripping around windows and doors reduced both drafts and fuel bills.**

    Which of the following is the best way to write the underlined portion of this sentence? If you think the original is the best way, choose option (1).

    (1) They discover
    (2) They discovered
    (3) They will discover
    (4) They have been discovered
    (5) Discovering

48. Sentence 8: **Adding an extra layer of insulation in the attic kept homes warmer in Winter and cooler in summer.**

    What correction should be made to this sentence?

    (1) insert a comma after *attic*
    (2) change *kept* to *keeped*
    (3) change *Winter* to *winter*
    (4) change *summer* to *Summer*
    (5) no correction is necessary

(1) An experienced renter considers far more than monthly rates when you're searching for a new apartment. (2) He checks the location of the unit to determine whether its close to his work or to a public transportation system. (3) Availability of stores and recreational facilities, is another consideration. (4) To find out if parking spaces are regularly available. (5) He visits the street at various times of the day and night. (6) Of course, the apartment building and the actual rental unit are closely inspected, are the entryway and hallways well maintained and well lit? (7) Most important, the renter makes a point of talking to the landlord or manager of the building. (8) Does the person seem interested and helpful? (9) Does the person seem bored and impatient? (10) It may be a good predictor of the response a tenant with a complaint will get.

49. Sentence 1: **An experienced renter considers far more than monthly rates when you're searching for a new apartment.**

What correction should be made to this sentence?

(1) change the spelling of *experienced* to *expirenced*
(2) change *considers* to *consider*
(3) insert a comma after *rates*
(4) replace *you're* with *he's*
(5) insert a comma after *searching*

50. Sentence 2: **He checks the location of the unit to determine whether its close to his work or to a public transportation system.**

What correction should be made to this sentence?

(1) insert a comma after *unit*
(2) replace *whether* with *weather*
(3) replace *its* with *it's*
(4) insert a comma after *work*
(5) no correction is necessary

51. Sentence 3: **Availability of stores and recreational facilities, is another consideration.**

What correction should be made to this sentence?

(1) change the spelling of *Availability* to *Availibility*
(2) insert a comma after *stores*
(3) change the spelling of *facilities* to *facilitys*
(4) remove the comma after *facilities*
(5) change *is* to *are*

52. Sentences 4 and 5: **To find out if parking spaces are regularly available. He visits the street at various times of the day and night.**

Which of the following is the best way to write the underlined portion of these sentences? If you think the original is the best way, choose option (1).

(1) available. He
(2) available, so he
(3) available he
(4) available, he
(5) available, and he

53. Sentence 6: **Of course, the apartment building and the actual rental unit are closely inspected, are the entryway and hallways well maintained and well lit?**

    What correction should be made to this sentence?

    (1) remove the comma after *course*
    (2) replace *are closely* with *is closely*
    (3) replace *inspected, are* with *inspected. Are*
    (4) insert a comma after *hallways*
    (5) no correction is necessary

54. Sentences 8 and 9: **Does the person seem interested and helpful? Does the person seem bored and impatient?**

    The most effective combination of Sentences 8 and 9 would include which of the following groups of words?

    (1) helpful although does
    (2) helpful, but does
    (3) helpful, and does
    (4) helpful, or he seems
    (5) helpful or bored

55. Sentence 10: **It may be a good predictor of the response a tenant with a complaint will get.**

    Which of the following is the best way to write the underlined portion of this sentence? If you think the original is the best way, choose option (1).

    (1) It may be
    (2) This may be
    (3) This being
    (4) This general attitude being
    (5) This general attitude may be

ANSWERS ARE ON PAGES 303–304.

WRITING SKILLS POSTTEST, PART 2

Directions: This part of the test is designed to find out how well you write. The test has one question that asks you to present an opinion on an issue or to explain something. In preparing your answer for this question, you should take the following steps:

1. Read all of the information accompanying the question.
2. Plan your answer carefully before you write.
3. Use scratch paper to make any notes.
4. Write your answer on a separate sheet of paper.
5. Read carefully what you have written and make any changes that will improve your writing.
6. Check your paragraphing, sentence structure, spelling, punctuation, capitalization, and usage and make any necessary corrections.

Take forty-five minutes to write on the assigned topic. Write legibly and use a ballpoint pen.

Topic

Every year, companies spend billions of dollars to advertise their products and services. We see advertising everywhere we look—on television, in magazines, on signs.

Write a composition of about two hundred words describing the effect of advertising on modern life. You may describe the positive effects, the negative effects, or both. Be specific and use examples to support your view.

INFORMATION ON EVALUATING YOUR ESSAY APPEARS ON PAGES 304–305.

POSTTEST ANSWER KEY

PART 1

1. (3) The possessive form must be used to show that a patient has a body.

2. (2) The verb must agree with the compound subject *machine* and *computer*. Since the subjects are joined by *and*, the verb must be plural to agree in number: *They have.*

3. (4) The new sentence is formed by shortening Sentence 5 into a modifying phrase that shows how the equipment works. The complete sentence would be "The new equipment produces three-dimensional images by taking a series of X-ray scans and reassembling them for viewing."

4. (2) By crossing out the interrupting phrase *of this technology*, we see that the subject of this sentence is the plural noun *versions*. The plural verb *take* agrees with this subject.

5. (2) The original word group is a fragment because it lacks a complete verb. The helping verb *are* provides the rest of the sentence skeleton. *Surgeons* is the subject, and *are pleased* is the verb.

6. (3) Use a comma to separate an introductory phrase from the main part of a sentence.

7. (3) The pronoun *This* is vague in the original sentence because it lacks an antecedent. Adding the word *procedure* makes clear what *this* refers to.

8. (3) From Sentence 3 on in this paragraph, present-tense verbs are used: *have been combined, produces, take, can reduce, saves.* Therefore, the verb in this sentence should also be present tense.

9. (3) The rule that applies is *I before E except after C.*

10. (4) The phrase *with infants and toddlers* should be placed directly after the word it modifies, *women.*

11. (1) Use commas to separate transitional words and phrases from the rest of the sentence.

12. (5) The two clauses in the original sentence were linked by the conjunction *although*, which shows contrast. The new sentence also needs a linking word to show contrast. It should read, "In many European countries, businesses routinely grant such leaves; however, they are expensive to employers because of the costs of finding and retraining temporary replacement help."

13. (2) The verb must agree with the plural subject *opponents: They insist.*

14. (2) The sentences can be combined by using the relative pronoun *which* to introduce a clause describing the law. Since the antecedent *law* is nonhuman, *which* must be used instead of *who*. The new sentence should read, "One compromise may be to develop a law guaranteeing parental leaves, which would allow either mothers or fathers to spend time with their new babies."

15. (3) Capitalize words that refer to specific places, like *American*, not general words like *national.*

16. (5) The sentence is correct as written.

17. (1) Except for the first sentence, every sentence in the paragraph is written in the present tense. Notice such present-tense verbs as *has caused, grant, are, occupy*, and *affects*. These verbs, as well as the other verb in Sentence 10, *want*, are clues that a present-tense verb must be used.

18. (1) The sentences can be combined by turning Sentence 2 into an introductory phrase that modifies *quality circle programs* in Sentence 1. The new sentence should read, "Originally used in Japan, quality circle programs have been adopted in a number of American businesses and industries in the last ten years."

19. (2) The passive form is used to show that someone designs these programs. This form requires the past participle of the main verb: *designed.*

20. (2) The word that fits the meaning of the rest of the sentence is *principle*, meaning "theory" or "basic idea."

21. (1) Other verbs in the paragraph, such as *operate* and *choose*, as well as the other verb in this sentence, *meet*, are clues that the present tense is needed to show a general truth.

22. (4) For parallel structure, use the same word form for compound elements: *attack, identify, test*, and *consider.*

23. (1) The sentence is correct as written. The conjunction *when* in the first clause links the two parts of the sentence. No other linking word is needed.

24. (3) To avoid a comma splice, use a semicolon to separate two independent clauses connected by a linking word or phrase like *in addition.*

25. (1) The rest of the paragraph uses plural pronouns to refer to the employees: *they choose, they consider, they make.* The plural pronoun *their* fits the same pattern.

26. (1) Don't use commas before phrases that follow the word they modify.

27. (5) The sentence is correct as written.

28. (5) The sentences can be combined by turning Sentence 4 into a renaming phrase that describes *walking*. The complete sentence should read, "If so, consider walking, an equal opportunity sport."

29. (3) The present-tense verb *cool* matches the other verb in the dependent clause, *stretch.*

30. (4) The second-person pronoun *your* must be used because the rest of the paragraph is written in the second person: *you stretch, you live, you may prefer.*

31. (2) The first clause in this sentence shows under what conditions the second clause will be true, so the logical link between the two clauses is *If.*

32. (4) The word *quiet*, meaning "silent," fits the meaning of the whole sentence. *Quite*, meaning "very," makes no sense in this context.

33. (1) When the verb in the independent clause is in the future tense *(will be)*, the verb in the dependent clause is in the present tense.

34. (4) For parallel structure, use the same word forms for compound elements: *coal supplies dwindle* and *available farmland shrinks.*

35. (4) Capitalize the name of a geographical feature when it is part of the name of a specific place.

36. (4) To show a general truth, the verbs in both the independent clause *(turns)* and the dependent clause *(boils)* must be in the present tense.

37. (3) Place a comma before *and* when it joins two independent clauses.

38. (2) The original word group is a fragment because it lacks a complete verb. The helping verb *are* makes the idea complete.

39. (1) The sentence can be rewritten by turning the second clause into a renaming phrase describing *abalone*. The complete sentence should read, "This environment is ideal for growing abalone, a shellfish considered a seafood delicacy."

40. (5) Since the pipes were *placed* in strawberry fields, a form of the verb *lay* must be used. The past participle form is needed here: *laid.*

41. (2) The unaccented vowel *e* in this word can cause spelling problems.

42. (5) The sentence is correct as written.

43. (3) Because the verb in the dependent clause, *were*, is in the past tense, the independent clause must also contain a past-tense verb.

44. (4) The original word group is a fragment because it lacks a verb. Choice (4) adds the verb *were.*

45. (4) To fit the meaning of this sentence, *straight*, meaning "directly," must be used. A *strait* is a narrow channel of water.

46. (1) The linking word *when* shows the time relationship between the two clauses. The complete sentence should read, "Energy conservation suddenly became important during the 1970s when political and economic events in the Middle East raised the price of oil imported from Arab countries."

47. (2) Because the rest of the paragraph is written in the past tense *(became, kept, wore, were replaced)*, a past-tense verb should also be used in this sentence.

48. (3) Don't capitalize the names of seasons.

49. (4) The pronoun must agree with its antecedent in person. Since the antecedent in this sentence is *renter*, the third-person pronoun *he* is correct.

50. (3) By substituting *it is* in the sentence, you can see that the contraction *it's* makes sense, not the possessive pronoun *its.*

51. (4) Don't separate the subject from the predicate with a comma.

52. (4) Sentence 4 is a fragment lacking both a subject and a verb. It should be attached to Sentence 5 as a modifying phrase and separated by a comma because it appears before the main part of the sentence.

53. (3) Sentence 6 is a comma splice consisting of two complete thoughts not joined by a coordinating conjunction. These ideas can be written correctly as two separate sentences.

54. (5) The conjunction *or* shows that alternatives are being presented. *Bored and impatient* is parallel in form to *interested and helpful*. The complete sentence should read, "Does the person seem interested and helpful or bored and impatient?

55. (5) In this sentence, *it* is a vague pronoun with no clear antecedent. *What* is a good predictor? The phrase *This general attitude* makes the meaning clear.

PART 2
Evaluating Your Essay

If at all possible, ask your instructor to read and evaluate your essay. At this point some advice from an experienced reader would be a great help to you! However, if you don't have access to an instructor, you might want to ask a friend or relative to read your paper. Choose someone whose reading and writing skills are at least as strong as yours—perhaps another member of your GED class who's been studying this book too.

A third possibility is to evaluate your essay yourself. This is a very difficult task, since it's hard to be objective about your own writing. If you do choose this alternative, be sure to set your work aside for a couple of days so that you can look at it from a fresh point of view.

Although the readers on the actual GED Writing Skills Test will have no specific set of questions to use as grading standards, the following evaluation checklist should help you or another reader predict the general range of scores in which your paper might fall.

Essay Evaluation Checklist

Yes	No	
_____	_____	1. Does the essay answer the essay question?
_____	_____	2. Does the main point of the essay stand out clearly?
_____	_____	3. Does each paragraph contain specific examples and details that help prove the main point?
_____	_____	4. Can you follow how the writer has arranged and linked the ideas in paragraphs and sentences?
_____	_____	5. Are errors in sentence structure, word choice, and mechanics (punctuation, capitalization, and spelling) minor enough and few enough that they don't distract you from the ideas in the essay?

If you or your reader can answer yes to these five questions, your essay would probably earn an upper-half rating (4, 5, or 6) in the Writing Skills Test. You should be ready to try the actual test. Good luck!

A *no* on one or more of these questions indicates that your essay might earn a lower-half rating (1, 2, or 3). If you receive any *no* answers, study your essay carefully to see how you could strengthen it. You may also want to review sections in the text related to problem areas in your essay:

- Essay organization—Chapter 5
- Unifying statements—Chapter 5
- Paragraph development—Chapters 3 and 4
- Linking paragraphs and sentences—Chapter 6
- Sentence Structure—Chapters 2, 4, and 5
- Punctuation—Chapters 2, 4, and 5
- Capitalization—Chapter 6
- Spelling—Chapters 2, 3, and 6

If you need more practice in essay-test writing, choose one or more of the topics from the list on page 286. Write your essay under timed conditions and apply the evaluation checklist to your finished product. With each practice session, you should feel more and more confident that you can pass this section of the GED Writing Skills Test.

Here are two sample essays that show how different writers might have responded to the posttest essay topic.

Sample Essay A

Like so many other complex issues, advertising has both good and bad effects on society. Advertising can provide you with information, and it also helps publishers and television stations stay afloat financially. However, advertising may also glamorize activities that could be harmful to you.

How did you discover your favorite kind of beer? Maybe you saw it in a television commercial. How did you know where to go to get your toaster on sale at 50 percent off? You probably saw an ad in the paper. Advertising gets information to you, whether a new product is coming out or an old product is being marked down. In addition, the television show and the newspaper that brought you those ads wouldn't be there without the ads. Advertising revenue brings you the six o'clock news, your favorite comedy, and Monday night football. It also pays newspaper reporters and editors whose job is to keep you up to date on the world around you. And what about your magazines? Your subscription or the price you pay in a store doesn't begin to cover the cost of those glossy publications.

However, advertising is not always performing a service to society. In fact, some advertising may be downright harmful. Ads for alcoholic beverages, for example, give you the impression that everyone drinks and that you are part of the "in" crowd if you drink, too. However, this impression may add to the problems of alcoholism and drunken driving that hurt so many people. Similarly, cigarette advertisements are de-signed to encourage you to smoke. You can be a macho Marlboro man, a liberated Virginia Slims woman, or any other brand you choose. However, the cigarette ads would rather not tell you that smoking is a proven health hazard to both smokers and non-smokers. These and other advertisements for harmful or useless products encourage you to do damage to yourself and others and waste your money.

While there may be some good reasons to sing the praises of advertising, you should always look at ads with a critical eye. Use them as a good source of information and appreciate them for the services they make possible, but don't get seduced by the pretty pictures.

Sample Essay B

Every day, advertising shows us everything we need to lead the good life. We see new cars, exotic foods, gorgeous women, and handsome men, but these desirable things are not ours. They are in the ads. Advertising makes us less appreciative of the things we have and of the people around us. We can't escape the effects of its influence. Advertising may well hurt both our pocketbooks and our relationships with one another.

We have all seen a child throwing a temper tantrum because she can't have some new toy. No matter how many Barbie outfits a little girl already has, she must have the newest one, too. Advertising robs children of their pleasure in toys they already own by telling them they need new and different ones. It also strains the parent-child relationship, forcing the parent either to anger the child by saying "no" or to give in to expensive whims and spoil the child.

This problem is not limited to children. In a similar fashion, we adults see a new kind of lawnmower or a new clothing style advertised in our favorite magazine. Suddenly, no matter what condition our old lawnmower or old clothes are in, they look outdated. As a result, we often buy items we can't afford.

Perhaps the worst aspect of advertising is that it constantly bombards us with images of beautiful people. It's hard to appreciate a plain-looking but friendly and hard-working receptionist after staring at the sex goddess in a Seagram's ad. Seeing the beautiful people in the ads may also make us more self-conscious and less confident in relationships. After all, the ads tell us that we need the right cologne, the right clothes, and the right car in order to be attractive. We may throw away chances to meet people or make friends because we're afraid we don't measure up.

All in all, we may never be able to really measure the influence of advertising on our society. However, advertising clearly places many strains on both our bank accounts and our mental health. We would be better off without it.

Posttest Evaluation Chart

Skill Area	Item Number	Review Pages	Number Correct
Fragments	5, 38, 44, 52	30–35	/4
Parts of a sentence	51	35–43	/1
Nouns	1	44–49	/1
Pronouns	50	50–56	/1
Verb tense/form	8, 17, 19, 21, 29, 33, 36, 40, 43, 47	71–92, 152–53	/10
Subject-verb agreement	2, 4, 13	92–104	/3
Independent clauses	12, 24, 37, 53	127–39	/4
Dependent clauses	23, 31, 46	139–47	/3
Modifiers	3, 6, 10, 18 26, 28, 39	183–91	/7
Parallel structure	22, 34, 54	191–95	/3
Pronoun reference	7, 14, 25, 30, 49, 55	195–205	/6
Sentence and paragraph links	11	226–28	/1
Capitalization	15, 35, 48	237–41	/3
Spelling	9, 20, 32, 41, 45	241–58	/5
No error	16, 27, 42		/3

Your score: _____ out of 55 correct

If you got fewer than 40 items correct, go back and find the areas in which you had the most difficulty. Then review those pages that you need additional work in.

ANSWER KEY

CHAPTER 2

Exercise 4: Identifying Sentence Fragments
page 34

Part A

1. F This group of words does not contain a subject. *Who* hunted?
2. F This group of words does not contain a predicate. *What* did the teenager do?
3. ?
4. .
5. F This group of words does not contain a predicate. *What about* the greatest movie ever made?
6. F This word group lacks a predicate. *What about* pink and purple plaid?
7. !
8. .

Part B

1. ?
2. F This group of words has no predicate. *What about* divided opinions?
3. .
4. F The word group has neither a subject nor a complete predicate. *What comes* from a balanced diet?

5. F The word group is a list of items lacking a subject and a complete predicate. *What* includes several servings of these foods?
6. .
7. .
8. F This group of words has no subject. *Who* substitutes empty calories?
9. F This word group is a list of items. It needs either a predicate (*what about* candy, cookies, and soft drinks?) or a whole sentence to be attached to.
10. ?

Part C

1. ?
2. .
3. .
4. F This word group lacks a subject and a complete predicate. *What happens* in the parking lot?
5. .
6. F The group of words lacks a subject. *Who* needs to learn?
7. F This word group lacks a subject and a complete predicate. *What happens* for stop signs and traffic lights?

Exercise 5: Writing Complete Sentences
page 35
Part A

Here is one possible way to correct each of the fragments. Check to make sure your new sentences are complete, containing both a subject and a predicate.

1. Gary frantically hunted for his billfold.
2. The teenager gossiped on the phone for hours.
5. *King Kong Eats Rhode Island* is the greatest movie ever made.
6. Pink and purple plaid clashes with orange.

Parts B and C

Here is one way to rewrite the paragraphs in order to eliminate fragments. Check to be sure that each of your sentences is complete, containing both a subject and a predicate.

Do most Americans need to take vitamin pills? Opinions are divided on this question. Some nutritional experts say that we can easily get all the vitamins we need from a balanced diet, including several servings of bread and cereals, fruits and vegetables, dairy products, and meat. Others feel that many Americans don't eat properly. They skimp on vegetables. They substitute empty calories from junk food like candy, cookies, and soft drinks. Could both sides be correct?

What mistakes are typical of beginning drivers? One important error is misjudging distances. It takes practice for a driver to estimate correctly how far his car is from the one beside him in the parking lot. A related error is misjudging braking distance. A driver needs to learn how to slow down smoothly for stop signs and traffic lights.

Exercise 6: Identifying Sentence Parts
pages 40-41

1. *program is*
2. *truck hit*
3. *snake slithered*
4. *(you) leave*
5. *newspaper is*
6. *Milk is*
7. *bills were*
8. *Statue of Liberty is*
9. *you Did see*
10. *baby slept*
11. *Mr. and Mrs. Garcia own*
12. *party lasted*
13. *President Roosevelt did die*
14. *Hurricane Elsa pounded*
15. *Martin Luther King was*

Exercise 7: Using Compound Elements
page 43
Part A

1. Do you want **scrambled eggs, oatmeal, or grits** for breakfast?
2. **Torrid romances and fatal illnesses** are featured in soap operas.
3. **Sam Abramowitz and Donna Tatum** are studying to become lawyers.
4. The batter **swung blindly, connected, and sprinted** for first base.
5. The food at Bob's Greasy Spoon is **filling but tasteless.**
6. He printed his name at the top of the application form **and began to list his qualifications.**

Part B

You might have answers similar to the examples below. Check to make sure that your sentences are complete and punctuated correctly.

1. On weekends I enjoy sleeping late, working on my motorcycle, and bowling.
2. Two of my favorite television programs are "Your Moment in Court" and "Rancid Romances."
3. I would go to China, Norway, and Brazil.
4. Brian Madden and Jorge Garcia live near me.
5. Writing skills, social studies, science, literature, and mathematics are covered on the GED tests.

Exercise 8: Recognizing Nouns
pages 44-45

The following words in each sentence are nouns.

1. plates, mugs, saucepan, vase, sink
2. hook, fights, round
3. earthquake, sections, Mexico City, rubble, thousands, people
4. boundary, United States, Canada, frontier, world
5. western, man, John Wayne
6. team, World Series, years
7. society, wisdom, courage, Americans
8. stare, Robert, marriage, trouble
9. Ace Manufacturing Company, plans, employees, month
10. Parenthood, patience, hope

Exercise 9: Spelling Plural Nouns
page 47
Part A

The rules referred to in these answers are on page 46.

1. countries (Rule 3)
2. needs (Rule 1)
3. homes (Rule 1)
4. businesses (Rule 2)
5. days (Rule 3)
6. nights (Rule 1)
7. cars (Rule 1)
8. trucks (Rule 1)
9. factories (Rule 3)
10. products (Rule 1)
11. fabrics (Rule 1)
12. people (Rule 6) or persons (Rule 1)
13. lives (Rule 4)

Part B

1. People
2. cities
3. wagons
4. highways
5. coaches
6. Lives
7. men
8. women

Exercise 10: Using Possessive Nouns
pages 49–50
Part A

The rules referred to in these answers are on page 48.

1. **The boy's friend** moved away. (Rule 1)
2. **James's friend** moved away. (Rule 1)
3. **The boys' friend** moved away. (Rule 2)
4. **The ladies' hats** are on sale. (Rule 2)
5. **The firemen's helmets** are worn for protection. (Rule 3)

Part B

1. My **dog's** favorite ball was out of reach behind her house.
2. In the last two seconds, the **team's** final chance to score appeared.
3. **Chicago's** skyscrapers now rival **New York City's** skyline.
4. **Men's** coats and **women's** sweaters are on sale this weekend only.
5. The **girls'** argument ended when their mothers called them for supper. (We can tell that the word *girls* is plural because of the clue words *their mothers* and *them*.)

6. **Lawyers'** and **doctors'** fees have skyrocketed in recent years.
7. **Caroline's** last letter arrived only yesterday.
8. The **newspaper's** headline this morning read "Plane Crash Kills 257."

Part C

Your sentences may be similar to the following examples. Check to be sure that your sentences are complete and that the possessive nouns are punctuated correctly.

1. **Women's** dresses have been on sale recently.
2. The **doctors'** fees in our clinic are much too high.
3. This **country's** biggest problem is unemployment.
4. The **world's** greatest athlete is King Kong Bundy.
5. Our **region's** major tourist attraction is Lake Ontario.

Exercise 11: Identifying Antecedents
page 51

3. John and Sarah
4. lake
5. John and Sarah
6. motorboat
7. John and Sarah
8. John and Sarah
9. John
10. John and Sarah

Exercise 12: Pronoun Form
page 53

1. *She*   The pronoun is the subject of the verb *is*.
2. *him*   *President Kennedy* should be replaced by an object pronoun since *leaders* is the subject of the verb *challenged*.
3. *My*   The possessive pronoun is required here to show that Susan has favorite vegetables.
4. *it*   No possession is shown in the sentence.
5. *They*   The pronoun is the subject of the verb *voted*.
6. *them*   An object pronoun is needed to replace *the senators*, since the subject of the sentence is *What*.
    their   The possessive pronoun is used to replace *the senators'* to show that the senators have actions.
7. *your*   Use the possessive form to show that the friends have trust.

8. *we*   The subject form is needed because it replaces *you and I*, the subject of *can make*.

9. *her*   The object form is used to replace *that woman* since the subject of the sentence is *weddings*.

10. *us*   The object is used to replace *my partner and me* since the subject of the sentence is understood to be *you*.

Exercise 13: Pronoun Form in Compound Elements page 54

1. *her*   Leaving *Jeremy and* out, we have *Keep an eye on her*. The object form is needed because the subject of the verb *Keep* is understood to be *you*.

2. *I*   Leaving *Bob and* out, we have *I plan to be married*. The pronoun is the subject of the verb *plan*.

3. *me*   Leaving *your father and* out, we have *Please let me know*. The object form is needed because the subject of the verb *let* is understood to be *you*.

4. *we*   Leaving *the Caswells and* out, we have *If we will be late*. The pronoun is the subject of the verb *will be*.

5. *she*   Leaving *Jessica and* out, we have *Where did she go?* The pronoun is the subject of the verb *did go*.

6. *him, me*   Using one pronoun at a time, we have *The flu hit him* and *The flu hit me*. The object forms are needed because the subject of the verb *hit* is *flu*.

7. *They*   Leaving *and their cousins* out, we have *They will hold a reunion*. The pronoun is the subject of the verb *will hold*.

8. *he*   Leaving *and Scott* out, we have *When he passed*. The pronoun is the subject of the verb *passed*.

9. *them*   Leaving *and their children* out, we have *The lottery winnings gave them a secure income*. The object form is needed because the subject of the verb *gave* is *winnings*.

10. *us*   Leaving *the Johnsons and* out, we have *They met us*. The object form is needed because

the subject of the verb *met* is *They*.

Exercise 14: Possessive Pronouns and Contractions page 56

Part A

1. *It's*   Use the contraction to show *It is past time*.

2. *Who's*   Use the contraction to ask *Who is hiding?*

3. *your*   Use the possessive pronoun to show that you had a childhood.
   you're   Use the contraction to say that *you are not going to believe*.

4. *theirs*   Use the possessive pronoun to show that they have a choice.

5. *its*   Use the possessive pronoun to show that America has a name.

6. *its*   Use the possessive pronoun to show that the commission had a report.

7. *your*   Use the possessive pronoun to show that you have a guess.

8. *Whose*   Use the possessive pronoun to show that someone has a name.

9. *Who's*   Use the contraction to ask *Who has been stealing?*

10. *There's*   Use the contraction to say *There is a stranger*.
    theirs   Use the possessive pronoun to say that they don't have a friend.

Part B

1. *its, it's*   Test each sentence you wrote by substituting *it is* or *it has*. If the sentence makes sense, you should have used *it's*. If it does not, you should have used the possessive pronoun *its*.

2. *theirs, there's*   Test each sentence you wrote by substituting *there is*. If the sentence makes sense, you should have used *there's*. If it does not, you should have used the possessive pronoun *theirs*.

3. *your, you're*   Test each sentence you wrote by substituting *you are*. If the sentence makes sense, you should have used *you're*. If it does not, you should have used the possessive pronoun *your*.

4. *whose, who's*   Test each sentence you wrote by substituting *who is* or *who has*. If the sentence makes sense, you should have used *who's*. If it does not, you should have used the possessive pronoun *whose*.

Exercise 15: Editing Practice Review
page 57

Janet's bedroom looks as though it's just been struck by a tornado. **Blouses**, sweaters, socks, and jeans form a crazy quilt pattern on the **floor**. A solid three-inch layer of old **newspapers** and magazines covers her desk. Half-empty pop cans and candy bar **wrappers** surround the overflowing wastebasket in the corner. **The bed is unmade**. Peeping out from under it are the moldy remains of a large pepperoni pizza that **she** and her best friend **shared two** weeks ago. Never in my life have I seen a room as messy as **hers**!

Exercise 16: Sentence Basics Review
pages 58–62

1. (1) The plural of *block* is *blocks*.
2. (2) Commas are used to separate the items in a series but not to separate a series from the rest of the sentence.
3. (3) Use the possessive noun to show that the driver had a fault.
4. (3) Leaving *John and* out, you can see that the pronoun *I* should be used as the subject of the verb *drove: I drove.*
5. (5) The sentence is correct as written.
6. (5) *Or lose them entirely?* is a fragment because it lacks a subject. *Who* was losing them? The fragment should be attached to the previous sentence with no comma because *or* connects only two items.
7. (4) The phrase *by it is incredible ugliness* doesn't make sense, so the contraction *it's* is incorrect. Use the possessive pronoun *its* to show that the monster had ugliness.
8. (3) Use commas to separate items in a series.
9. (1) The sentence is correct as written.
10. (4) The original is a fragment because it lacks a predicate. What about toxic wastes? Choice (4) adds the verb *are contaminating* to tell what the toxic wastes are doing.
11. (1) Leaving *You and* out, we have *I may picture*. Use the subject pronoun as the subject of the verb *may picture.*
12. (4) The original is a fragment because it lacks a predicate. What about the picture? Choice (4) rearranges the words and adds the verb *is* to make a complete thought.
13. (3) Don't separate the subject from the verb of a sentence with a comma.
14. (5) The original word group is a fragment because it lacks a subject. *What* is creating problems? Choice 5 adds the subject *family pattern* and the verb *is* to make a complete statement.
15. (1) Nouns ending in *y* preceded by a consonant are made plural by changing the *y* to *i* and adding *es.*
16. (2) Use the possessive noun to show that women have salaries.
17. (2) By substituting *there is*, which makes sense *(there is no doubt)*, you can see that the contraction *there's* is correct.
18. (1) The sentence is correct as written.

CHAPTER 3
Exercise 1: Matching Topic Sentences to Support
pages 65–66

Compare your topic sentences to the examples below. Be sure that each sentence is complete and that it states the central point of the paragraph.

1. Money from the property tax increase could benefit our town in many ways.
2. Different exercises strengthen different muscles.
3. Sharon is a reckless driver.
4. Thomas Grosso has a huge appetite.
5. People drink coffee for a variety of reasons.

Exercise 2: Providing Supporting Details
pages 67–69
Part A

1. Cross out *c.* Other examples might include Christmas wrapping paper displays in December and turkeys promoted before Thanksgiving.
2. Cross out *a.* Other examples might include *sew-so, there-their, way-weigh,* and *bear-bare.*
3. Cross out *c.* Other examples might include tacos from Mexico and lasagna from Italy.
4. Cross out *b.* Other examples might include daytime soap operas with laundry detergent commercials and baseball games with beer commercials.
5. Cross out *b.* Other examples might include test condition of brakes and check body for dents that indicate an accident.

Part B

Make sure that each sentence you added is a complete sentence and that it adds a specific detail to help prove the topic sentence. Possible answers appear below.

1. Cross out *The refrigerator and range were new.*
   Sample additional sentences:
   The windows were so filthy I couldn't see out. The door to the bedroom had been ripped off its hinges.
2. Cross out *She keeps an aquarium in her living room.*
   Sample additional sentences:
   She thinks nothing of borrowing a dozen eggs, which she never replaces. Every weekend she has a party that keeps us awake almost all night.
3. Cross out *Unfortunately, some adults are too embarrassed to admit that they never finished school.*
   Sample additional sentences:
   Some former dropouts want to get a higher-paying job that requires a high school education. Some return to school for the sense of accomplishment they'll feel when they have diplomas in their hands.

Exercise 3: Writing Paragraphs page 70

A sample response for each paragraph appears below. Make sure each of your paragraphs has a topic sentence that identifies the problem and several supporting sentences that provide specific details about the problem.

Paragraph 1

Marge Watson deserves an award for her many hours of volunteer service to the elderly. For the last five years, she's been helping two older women who no longer drive. She takes them to the grocery store, the bank, and the doctor whenever they need to go. Every Sunday she picks them up for church. Two years ago she contacted our local Girl Scout and Boy Scout troops to arrange for youngsters to do free yard work for senior citizens who request help. Last year she organized a weekly current events discussion group for retired people.

Paragraph 2

Greenbelt Park Road is fast becoming the most dangerous street in town. During good weather, joggers and bicyclists by the dozens use the road. Small children, too, ride their little bikes or rollerskate along the edge of the park. But these people have to compete with motor vehicles traveling at a posted speed limit of forty miles per hour—sometimes faster. I've seen motorcycles doing at least eighty down that road. The street is also a truck route, so there's often a parade of semis, cement trucks, and dumpsters heading toward the highway. It's pure luck that so far no one's been killed there in a traffic accident.

Exercise 4: Simple Tenses pages 73–74

1.	*satisfied*	The time clue *last night* tells you the verb should be in the past tense.
2.	*asked*	The past-tense verb *toddled* tells you this verb should be in the past tense, too.
3.	*arrives*	The time clue *every day* and the present tense verb *leaves* indicate that this verb should be in the present tense.
4.	*will picket*	The time clue *tomorrow* indicates the verb should be in the future tense.
5.	*travels*	The sentence states a general truth, so the verb must be in the present tense.
6.	*robbed*	The time clue *last year* tells you the verb should be in the past tense.
7.	*will perform*	The time clue *next week* tells you the verb should be in the future tense.
8.	*skips*	The time clue *usually* and the verb *makes* tell you that the sentence describes a usual action, so a present tense verb is needed.
9.	*wanted*	The time clue *an hour ago* tells you the verb should be in the past tense.
10.	*despise*	The time clue *now* tells you the verb should be in the present tense.

Exercise 5: Continuing Tenses page 75

| 1. | *will be flying* | The time clue *tomorrow at this time* indicates that the verb should be in the future continuing tense. |
| 2. | *am thinking* | The time clue *at present* tells you the verb should be in the present continuing tense. |

3. *were shivering* — The time clue *at this time last year* indicates that the verb should be in the past continuing tense.

4. *will be visiting* — The time clue *next winter* indicates that the verb should be in the future continuing tense.

5. *am steaming* — The time clue *still* indicates that the verb should be in the present continuing tense.

6. *was returning* — The time clue *yesterday afternoon* indicates that the verb should be in the past continuing tense.

7. *was feeling* — The time clue *last night* tells you the verb should be in the past continuing tense.

8. *are continuing* — The time clue *at the present* indicates that the verb should be in the present continuing tense.

9. *were chirping* — The time clue *yesterday* tells you that the verb should be in the past continuing tense.

10. *will be going* — The time clue *next fall* indicates that the verb should be in the future continuing tense.

Exercise 6: Perfect Tenses page 78

1. *had cleaned* — The time clue *by six o'clock last night* indicates that the action took place before a specific time in the past, so the past perfect tense is needed.

2. *has worked* — The time clue *since 1986* indicates that an action began in the past and is continuing. The present perfect tense is needed.

3. *had supervised* — The time clue *before retiring last year* indicates that the action took place before a specific time in the past, so the past perfect tense is needed.

4. *will have passed* — The time clue *by this time next year* shows that an action will be completed before a specific time in the future, so the future perfect tense is needed.

5. *have missed* — The time clue *for the past week* indicates that an action began in the past and is continuing. The present perfect tense is needed.

6. *will have started* — The time clue *by next fall* indicates that an action will be completed before a specific time in the future, so the future perfect tense is needed.

7. *had traveled* — The time clue *long before Columbus's voyage in 1492* indicates that an action occurred before a specific time in the past, so the past perfect tense is needed.

8. *had* — The time clue *before last week's race* indicates that an action occurred before a specific time in the past, so the past perfect tense is needed.

9. *has failed* — The time clue *in the past five years* indicates that an action began in the past and is continuing in the present. The present perfect tense is needed.

10. *had degenerated* — The time clue *last night* indicates that an action occurred before a specific time in the past, so the past perfect tense is needed.

Exercise 7: Passive Verbs page 80

1. *will be opened* — The time clue *tomorrow morning* indicates that an action will be performed, so the future tense is needed. The phrase *by the governor* is a clue that the passive form must be used.

2. *was tossed*   The time clue *yesterday evening* indicates that the verb should be in past tense. The phrase *by a passing motorist* is the clue that the passive form is needed to show that someone performed an action on the subject.

3. *was painted*   The time clue *in 1564* shows that the past tense is needed. The passive form is used to show that someone painted the masterpiece.

4. *was recorded*   The time clue *in 1983* shows that the past tense is needed. The phrase *by Chicago* indicates that the passive form must be used.

5. *will be offered*   The time clue *next month* indicates that the future tense should be used. The passive form is used to show that someone will offer an improved insurance package.

6. *are required*   The time clue *every year* shows that the present tense should be used. The passive form is needed to show that someone is requiring the staff to have an examination.

7. *is prohibited*   The present tense is needed to show a general rule. The passive form is used to show that someone prohibits smoking.

8. *will be monitored*   The time clue *for the next several hours* indicates that the future tense is needed. The phrase *by nurses* indicates that the passive form must be used.

9. *was awarded*   The time clue *in 1971* shows you that the verb should be in past tense. The passive form is used to show that someone awarded the medal.

10. *is closed*   The present tense is needed to show that a condition is true now. The passive form is used to show that someone has closed the plant.

Exercise 8: Regular Verb Review pages 82–83

Part A

1. *played*   Spelling rule 1. The time clue *last summer* indicates that the past tense is needed.

2. *hated*   Spelling rule 3. The helping verb *has* indicates that the present perfect tense is needed.

3. *earning*   Spelling rule 1. The present continuing tense is needed to show that the action is occurring now.

4. *carried*   Spelling rule 2. The time clue *in the past* indicates that the past tense must be used.

5. *stop or stopped*   Spelling rule 5. Either present or past tense could be used to show a regularly occurring action.

6. *hoped*   Spelling rule 3. The time clue *last month* indicates that the past tense should be used.

7. *permitting*   Spelling rule 5. The helping verb *are* shows you that the present continuing tense will be used.

8. *studying*   Spelling rule 2. The time clue *at the moment* tells you that the verb should be in the present continuing tense.

9. *comparing*   Spelling rule 3. The helping verb *were* indicates that the past continuing tense is used.

10. *referred*   Spelling rule 5. The past tense is needed to show that an action occurred at a specific time in the past.

Part B

1. *is filming*   The time clue *at this moment* tells you the verb should be in the present continuing tense to show that the action is occurring right now.

2. *will announce*   The time clue *tomorrow morning* indicates that the verb should be in the future tense.

3. *had gained*   The time clue *before 6:20* indicates the action occurred before a specific time in the past, so the past perfect tense is needed.

4. *has purchased*   The time clue *since 1980* indicates that the action began in the past and is still continuing. The present perfect tense is needed.

5. *will be earning*   The time clue *within six months* indicates that the action will occur in the future.

6. *drop-kicked*   The past tense verb *snarled* is a clue that this verb should also be in the past tense.

7. *overuse*   The sentence expresses a general truth, so the verb should be in the simple present tense.

8. *will be shipped*   The time clue *within two weeks* indicates that the action will occur in the future. The passive form is used to show that someone will ship the package.

9. *were loitering*   The time clue *last night* indicates that the action was occurring in the past.

10. *is picked*   The time clue *every Wednesday* indicates a usual action, so the verb should be in the simple present tense. The passive form is used to show that someone picks up the garbage.

11. *will have completed*   The time clue *by next week* indicates that the action will be completed before a time in the future, so the future perfect tense is needed.

12. *remark*   The time clue *often* indicates a usual action, so the simple present tense is needed.

Exercise 9: Must-Learn Verbs page 85

1. *gone*   The helping verb *have* indicates

that the past participle will be used.

2. *saw*   There is no helping verb.

3. *run*   The helping verb *have* indicates that the past participle will be used.

4. *brought*   You must memorize this irregular past tense.

5. *done*   The helping verb *have* (part of the contraction *I've*) indicates that the past participle will be used.

6. *came*   There is no helping verb.

7. *were*   Without a helping verb in the sentence, the simple past tense must be used.

8. *run*   The helping verb *has* indicates that the past participle will be used.

9. *seen*   The helping verb *have* (part of *I've*) tells you that the past participle will be used.

10. *come*   The helping verb *has* tells you that the past participle will be used.

11. *did*   There is no helping verb.

12. *went*   There is no helping verb.

13. *brought*   You must memorize this irregular past tense.

14. *did*   Because there is no helping verb, the main verb must be in the simple past tense.

15. *saw*   Because there is no helping verb, the main verb must be in the simple past tense.

Exercise 10: I-A-U Verbs page 86

1. *began*   Because there is no helping verb, the main verb must be in the simple past tense.

2. *swum*   The helping verb *has* indicates that the past participle form must be used.

3. *sang*   Because there is no helping verb, the main verb must be in the simple past tense.

4. *shrunk*   The helping verb *have* indicates that the past participle form must be used.

5. *rang*   Because there is no helping verb, the main verb must be in the simple past tense.

6. *sank*   Because there is no helping verb, the main verb must be in the simple past tense.

7. *begun*   The helping verb *has* indicates that the past participle form must be used.

8. *swum*   The helping verb *have* (part of *I've*) indicates that the past participle form must be used.

9. *rung*   The helping verb *has* indicates that the past participle form must be used.

Exercise 11: *En* and *N* Verbs page 87

1. *taken*   The helping verb *have* indicates that the past participle form must be used.

2. *chose*   The time clue *at our last meeting* indicates that the verb should be in the past tense.

3. *stolen*   The helping verb *has* indicates that the past participle form must be used.

4. *knew*   The past tense of *know* is irregular.

5. *grown*   The helping verb *has* indicates that the past participle form must be used.

6. *eaten*   The helping verb *have* (part of the contraction *we've*) indicates that the past participle form must be used.

7. *wrote*   Because there is no helping verb, the simple past tense must be used.

8. *broken*   The helping verb *have* indicates that the past participle form must be used.

9. *ate*   The verb *got* is a clue that the action occurred in the past.

10. *written*   The helping verb *has* indicates that the participle form must be used.

Exercise 13: Lie-Lay, Sit-Set, Raise-Rise pages 90–91

1. *lying*   The subject is resting alone.
2. *sit*   The subject is moving alone.
3. *raises*   The subject is moving an object (the flag).
4. *set*   The subject is moving an object (the cup).
5. *laid*   The subject moved an object (the money).
6. *rose*   The subject moved alone.
7. *lain*   The subject rested alone.
8. *sitting*   The subject is resting alone.
9. *laid*   The subject is moving an object (plans).
10. *lying*   The subject is resting alone.

Exercise 14: Verb Tense Review page 91

Before last night, neither the Mad Dogs nor the Spartans **had played** a good game all season. However, last night's football game **began** as a defensive battle and ended as a scoring free-for-all. During the first half, both teams ran the ball. The defensive lines on both sides **were** strong. At the end of the first half, the score was **tied** at 0–0.

In the second half, both teams **opened** with a new strategy. They passed the ball whenever they **saw** an opening. The quarterbacks **did** a superb job of setting up plays. The defensive lines, on the other hand, were **tiring**. They **weren't** blocking nearly as well. As a result, the final score **was** 47–39. By the end of that game, the Spartans **had won** their first victory of the season.

Exercise 15: Basic Subject-Verb Agreement page 95

Part A

1. *doesn't*   The subject, *Alice*, is singular.
2. *were*   The subject, *we*, is plural.
3. *move*   The subject, *daughters*, is plural.
4. *live*   The subject, *they*, is plural.
5. *doesn't*   The subject, *it*, is singular.
6. *were*   The subject, *they*, is plural.
7. *jogs*   The subject, *Jim*, is singular.
8. *runs*   The subject, *he*, is singular.
9. *don't*   The subject, *thunderstorms*, is plural.
10. *think*   The subject, *I*, does not take a verb ending in *-s*.

Part B

Compare your paragraph with the following example. Be sure that you have written at least five complete sentences in the present tense. No verb should end in *-s*, since the subject of each sentence is *I*.

Every day I <u>come</u> home from work exhausted. I <u>grab</u> a glass of iced tea. Then I <u>sink</u> down in an easy chair and <u>turn</u> on the TV. I <u>watch</u> the evening news. After that, I <u>switch</u> channels until I <u>find</u> a pro wrestling match. I always <u>cheer</u> for the underdog.

Part C

Compare your paragraph with the following example. Every verb should end in *-s* this time, because the subject of each sentence is *he* or *she*.

Every day he <u>comes</u> home from work exhausted. He <u>grabs</u> a glass of iced tea. Then he <u>sinks</u> down in an easy chair and <u>turns</u> on the TV. He <u>watches</u> the evening news. After that, he <u>switches</u> channels until he <u>finds</u> a pro wrestling match. He always <u>cheers</u> for the underdog.

Exercise 16: Compound Subjects
pages 97–98

1. *wants*   The subjects are connected by *nor*, so the verb agrees with the closer subject, *Saundra*.
2. *stop*   The subjects, *subway* and *bus*, are connected by *and*, so the compound subject is plural. *They stop.*
3. *checks*   The subjects are connected by *or*, so the verb agrees with the closer subject, *Dorothy*.
4. *provide*   Because *lock* and *burglar alarm* are connected by *and*, the compound subject is plural. *They* provide.
5. *contain*   Because *potatoes* and *carrots* are connected by *and*, the compound subject is plural. *They* contain.
6. *is*   The subjects are connected by *nor*, so the verb agrees with the closer subject, *Montana*.
7. *offer*   *San Francisco* and *Boston* are connected by *and*, so the compound subject is plural. *They* offer.
8. *stay*   The subjects are connected by *or*, so the verb agrees with the closer subject, *parents*.
9. *interfere*   *Spelling* and *handwriting* are connected by *and*, so the compound subject is plural. *They* interfere.
10. *appeals*   The subjects are connected by *nor*, so the verb agrees with the closer subject, *skiing*.

Exercise 17: Verbs Before Subjects
page 99

1. *are*   The subject, *sponges*, is plural.
2. *is*   The subject, *special*, is singular.
3. *is*   The subject, *sock*, is singular.
4. *Are*   The subject, *keys*, is plural.
5. *is*   The subject, *paper*, is singular.
6. *are*   The subjects, *apple* and *sandwich*, are joined by *and*, so the compound subject is plural. *They* are.
7. *are*   The subjects, *hat* and *coat*, are joined by *and*, so the compound subject is plural. *They* are.
8. *are*   The subject, *you*, never takes a verb ending in *-s*.
9. *are*   The subjects, *the Bulls* and *the Pistons*, are joined by *and*, so the compound subject is plural. *They* are.
10. *does*   The subject, *country*, is singular.
11. *Does*   The subject, *anyone*, is singular.
12. *Has*   The subject, *planet*, is singular.
13. *doesn't*   The subject, *doctor*, is singular.
14. *doesn't*   The subject, *government*, is singular.
15. *have*   The subject, *two*, is plural.

Exercise 18: Interrupters
pages 101–102

1. *is*   Crossing out the interrupter, *of butter cookies*, you see that *box* is the singular subject.
2. *knows*   Crossing out the interrupter, *with the aid of a multitude of spies*, you see that *Santa Claus* is the singular subject.
3. *have*   Crossing out the interrupter, *of the commission*, you see that the subject, *members*, is plural.
4. *were*   Crossing out the interrupter, *about John Kennedy*, you see that the subject, *specials*, is plural.
5. *have*   Crossing out the interrupter, *of the Central City Chamber of Commerce*, you see that the subject, *members*, is plural.
6. *are*   Crossing out the interrupter, *in this carton*, you see that the subject, *eggs*, is plural.
7. *blows*   Crossing out the interrupter, *on open farmlands*, you see that the subject, *snow*, is singular.
8. *makes*   Crossing out the interrupter, *together with a healthy bank account*, you see that *smile* is the singular subject.
9. *melt*   Crossing out the interrupter, *in an insulated glass*, you see that the subject, *cubes*, is plural.
10. *crunches*   Crossing out the interrupter, *of potato chips*, you see that the subject, *package*, is singular.

11. *takes*   Crossing out the interrupter, *loaded with five passengers*, you see that *car* is the singular subject.

12. *does*   Crossing out the interrupter, *as well as the team members*, you see that *coach* is the singular subject.

Exercise 19: Indefinite Pronouns
pages 103–104

1. *wants*   The interrupter is *in the club*. The subject is *everyone*. This pronoun is always singular.

2. *belong*   The interrupter is *of the marbles*. The subject is *none*. This pronoun may be singular or plural, depending on its antecedent. The antecedent of *none* in this sentence is the plural noun *marbles*.

3. *melts*   The interrupter is *of the ice from the polar caps*. The subject is *some*. This pronoun may be singular or plural, depending on its antecedent. The antecedent of *some* in this sentence is the singular noun *ice*.

4. *understand*   The interrupter is *of the listeners*. The subject is *most*. This pronoun may be singular or plural, depending on its antecedent. The antecedent of *most* in this sentence is the plural noun *listeners*.

5. *like*   The interrupter is *of our neighbors*. The subject is *few*. This pronoun is always plural.

6. *has*   The interrupter is *in the audience*. The subject is *someone*. This pronoun is always singular.

7. *wishes*   The subject of this sentence is *nobody*. This pronoun is always singular.

8. *is*   The interrupter is *of the cake*. The subject is *all*. This pronoun may be singular or plural, depending on its antecedent. The antecedent of *all* in this sentence is the singular noun *cake*.

9. *are*   The interrupter is *of the pieces of cake*. The subject is *all*. This pronoun may be singular or plural, depending on its antecedent. The antecedent of *all* in this sentence is the plural noun *pieces*.

10. *bites*   The interrupter is *of these dogs*. The subject is *one*. This pronoun is always singular.

11. *knows*   The interrupter is *with an ounce of brains*. The subject is *anyone*. This pronoun is always singular.

12. *attend*   The interrupter is *of my friends*. The subject is *many*. This pronoun is always plural.

Exercise 20: Subject-Verb Agreement Review
pages 104–105
Part A

1. *is*   Omitting the interrupter, *of my pet peeves*, you see that the subject is *one*. This indefinite pronoun is always singular.
   enter   The subject is the plural pronoun *they*.

2. *cause*   Omitting the interrupter, *like aspirin*, you can see that the subject is the plural noun *drugs*.

3. *is*   The compound subject is joined by *or*, so the verb agrees with the closer subject, *check*, which is singular.

4. *provide*   The subjects, *cotton* and *wool*, are joined by *and*, so the compound subject is plural. *They* provide.

5. *hopes*   Omitting the interrupter, *with a lottery ticket*, you see that the subject is *everybody*. This indefinite pronoun is always singular.

6. *do*   In this question, the verb comes before the subject. The subjects, *bride* and *groom*, are joined by *and*, so the compound subject is plural. *They* do.

7. *have*   Omitting the interrupter, *of the cookie crumbs*, you see the subject is *some*. This pronoun may be singular or plural, depending on the antecedent. The antecedent of *some* in this sentence is the plural noun

crumbs.

8. *are* In this sentence, the verb comes before the plural subject *cars*.
9. *makes* Omitting the interrupter, *wearing the huge plastic sunglasses*, you see that the subject is the singular noun *clown*.
10. *were* Omitting the interrupter, *after the storm*, you see that there is a compound subject, *tornado* and *streets*. Because these subjects are joined by *nor*, the verb agrees with the closer subject, *streets*, which is plural.

Part B

Are Americans becoming more interested in physical fitness? Evidence from a variety of sources **indicates** that they are. Jogging, swimming, or even brisk walking **is** becoming part of the daily routine of millions. In many offices, employees participate in exercise sessions offered by company wellness programs. Buying patterns also indicate an interest in fitness. Some of the most popular books on the market deal with dieting and nutrition. In grocery stores there **are** large displays of low-calorie meals. Apparently, both men and women in this country **hope** to live longer, healthier lives.

Exercise 21: Verb Review
pages 105–108

1. (4) The other verbs in the sentence, *slammed* and *shot*, indicate that the past tense of *throw* must be used. This is an irregular verb; its past tense is *threw*.
2. (1) This sentence is correct as written. The time clue *last night* indicates that the past tense of the verb should be used. Omitting the interrupter, *of the hottest rock groups in the country*, you see that the subject is *one*. The singular verb *was* agrees with this singular subject.
3. (5) The verb *is* in the first sentence is a time clue that the present tense is also needed in the second sentence. The verb *has* agrees with the singular subject *he*. Because the helping verb *has* is used, you need the past participle of the irregular verb *run* to form the present perfect.
4. (4) Drop the silent *e* on a verb before adding *ing*.
5. (2) The compound subjects, *Martha* and

brothers, are joined by *nor*, so the verb agrees with the closer subject, which is the plural noun *brothers*.
6. (3) The time clue *later this year* indicates that the verb should be in the future tense.
7. (2) Because there is no helping verb, the past tense of the verb *ring* is needed, not the past participle.
8. (3) The cat was resting alone, so the verb should be a form of *lie*, not *lay*.
9. (1) In this question, the singular subject *town* appears after the verb.
10. (3) The verb must agree with the singular subject *it*.
11. (5) The sentence is correct as written.
12. (3) Double the final consonant of a verb ending in a single vowel and a single consonant before adding *ing*.
13. (2) Omitting the interrupter, *of the suspects*, you see that the subject is the indefinite pronoun *neither*. This pronoun is always singular. When a verb ends in *y*, keep the *y* as you add *ing*.
14. (5) The time clues *at the moment* and *should be finished soon* indicate that the present continuing tense is needed to show an action going on right now.
15. (1) *Brought* is the past tense of the irregular verb *bring*.

Chapter 3 Cumulative Review
pages 109–110
Editing Practice (Part A)

As a child I loved having a yard full of trees. I climbed the smaller ones and **sat** for hours on the lower **branches munching** apples and reading. Often my friends and **I** used the trees for Wild West games. The outlaw **lay** in wait behind their broad **trunks and** prepared to spring out at unsuspecting settlers. During the long summer days, our laughter **mingled** with bird songs and the **chattering** of squirrels.

Now I stare out of my apartment onto a barren parking lot and **remember** those days with a sigh. **Are** some other children **having** the time of their lives in my old trees today?

Multiple-Choice Practice

1. (3) Subject and verb must agree in number. In this question, the verb appears before the plural subject *dogs*.
2. (5) The sentence is correct as written.
3. (2) The word group *Like hamsters and*

parakeets is a fragment, which must be attached to a complete sentence.

4. (3) When a verb ends in a single vowel and a single consonant and the accent falls on the last syllable, double the final consonant before adding -*ed*.

5. (3) Subject and verb must agree in number. Omitting the interrupter, *for the popularity of dogs*, you see that the subject of this sentence is the singular noun *reason*.

6. (1) The original word group is a fragment because it lacks a subject. Who follows the leader? By replacing *following* with *they follow*, you add a clear subject and verb to make a complete sentence.

7. (4) Because the rest of the paragraph is written in the present tense, a present-tense verb is needed in this sentence. The verb must agree with the singular subject *leader*.

8. (2) By substituting the words *it is* for the contraction *it's*, you can see that the sentence does not make sense. The possessive pronoun *its* is needed to show that a dog has a master.

9. (2) The time clue *today* tells you that the verb should be in the present tense. The passive form is used to show that someone or something located the farmland.

10. (1) Use commas to separate items in a series.

11. (4) A form of the verb *rise* must be used to show that the subject is acting alone. Because the compound subjects, *trees* and *silo*, are joined by *or*, the verb must agree with the closer subject.

12. (4) Form the plural of a noun ending in a consonant followed by *y* by changing the *y* to *i* and adding *es*.

13. (2) The word *ancestors* is a time clue that this sentence needs a past-tense verb.

14. (2) When adding -*ed*, double the final consonant of a verb only if the accent falls on the last syllable of the verb. In *covered*, the accent is on the first syllable.

15. (5) The sentence is correct as written.

16. (5) This section of the paragraph deals with conditions two hundred years ago. The other sentences provide clues that the past tense is needed.

CHAPTER 4

Exercise 1: Using Time Order
pages 115–16

1. b. 4
   e. 5
2. a. 5
   b. 2
   c. 1
   d. 3
   e. 4
   f. 6
3. a. 2
   b. 1
   c. 3
4. a. 5
   b. 3
   c. 1
   d. 4
   e. 2

Exercise 3: Cause-Effect Patterns
page 119

Here is a sample brainstorm list for topic 3.

3. Reasons for owning a car:
   protection from weather
   ~~cars are expensive to maintain~~
   can carry cargo/passengers
   desire for status symbol
   gives flexibility

Exercise 4: Writing Cause-and-Effect Paragraphs
pages 119–20

Here is a sample paragraph for topic 3 from Exercise 3. Make sure both of your paragraphs include a topic sentence that states the cause-effect relationship you are discussing. Then check to be sure all your supporting sentences are relevant to your topic sentence.

Many people want to own a car because of the advantages it gives them. Since it provides protection from the environment, a car allows them to carry out their business regardless of the weather. A car also allows them to carry extra passengers and cargo; therefore, they can make fewer trips to accomplish a task. Moreover, owning a car gives them the flexibility to go where they want, when they want. In addition to all these practical reasons, some people really want to own a car to impress the neighbors.

Exercise 5: Writing Comparison-Contrast Paragraphs
pages 122–23

Here is a sample chart and paragraph for the second topic.

Items to Discuss	Me	My Best Friend
1. Hobbies	playing piano	photography
2. How we both act	quiet, a loner	likes to be around people
	good listener	good listener
3. How we both look	tall; dark hair	tall; light hair
4. Background	urban	rural

My best friend and I have a few characteristics in common, but in many ways we're very different. She and I are both tall; however, her hair is almost blond while mine is very dark. We have different hobbies, too. She enjoys photography, while I prefer to play the piano. We are both good listeners, but I enjoy time alone while she loves to be in a crowd. Our backgrounds are quite different. She comes from a rural farm family; on the other hand, I was born and raised in the city. Despite our differences, we get along very well.

Exercise 7: Patterns of Organization in Test Questions
page 125

Pattern of Organization	Clue Words You Should Have Circled
1. Comparison-Contrast	more
2. Cause-Effect	Why
3. Time Order	Explain, how to
4. Cause-Effect	effect
5. Comparison-Contrast	Compare, advantages
6. Simple Listing	List

7. Simple Listing	examples
8. Cause-Effect	causes of
9. Time Order	Describe, incident
10. Cause-Effect	reasons for

Exercise 8: GED Writing Topic
page 126

Here is a brainstorm list used in writing the sample paragraph that follows it.

Topic: Effects of TV on my life

makes me less sociable (don't want to answer phone or talk to friends/family while engrossed in TV)

makes me less creative (vegetate in front of TV; don't play piano or read as much as when not watching)

watching TV makes me too passive — makes me feel sluggish

don't do things I need to (laundry, work, balance checkbook)

eat too much when watch TV

don't exercise enough (TV makes me passive)

Television has had a negative effect on ~~my life.~~ *by making me too passive for* ~~It has made me much more passive~~ *my own good. This passivity not only* ~~than when I'm not watching it, and there-~~ *affects me as I watch TV but* ~~fore has caused me to miss out on some~~ *infects other areas of my life as well.* ~~positive aspects of life.~~ For example, vege-

tating in front of the TV keeps me from

doing more creative and satisfying things

such as playing the piano, reading, or talk-

ing with friends. Moreover, the sluggish-

ness I feel ~~while during~~ *after* I've watched TV

for a period of time prevents me from ~~do-~~ *taking* ~~ing necessary tasks such as~~ *care of necessities like* laundry, work,

and balancing my checkbook. ~~(Maybe~~

~~that's why I do so much of it!)~~ Because of

my passivity from watching the tube, I'm

also less prone to exercise regularly like I
~~Combined with my tendency to~~ *Combined with my tendency to*
should. ~~In addition, I~~ nibble while I watch

TV, this has caused me to gain weight.

~~With these combined factors, I am noticing~~
Therefore,
~~that I gain weight. As a result of the above,~~

television has caused me to retreat from

the world in a negative way, which in the
has proven
long run ~~is~~ detrimental to my well-being.

Exercise 9: Compound Sentences with Conjunctions pages 130–31

Here are some sample answers. Does the conjunction you chose make sense in the new sentence? Make sure your sentences are punctuated properly. Also check each independent clause to make sure it has a subject and a predicate.

Part A

1. Color photographs are bright at first, but they begin to fade in a few years.
2. Do you want spaghetti for supper tonight, or would you prefer pizza?
3. X
4. The crowd roared its approval, and the cheerleaders jumped for joy.
5. The walls of the living room are magenta, and the carpet is daffodil yellow.
6. Andrea was afraid to dive off the high board, for she knew she would do a belly flop.
7. Neither Sam nor Barbara had finished high school, yet they managed to put their three children through college.
8. It was the first warm spring day, so Kelly begged to go outside.
9. X
10. We might look for work in the Minneapolis area, or we might move to Phoenix.

Part B

Your new sentences will vary. Below are some examples. Test the clauses you added to make sure each contains a subject and predicate and expresses a complete thought.

1. The Amadeos wanted a new car, but they couldn't afford to pay Slick Rick's prices.
2. I may decide to move to Texas, or I may stay right here in the Blue Ridge Mountains of Virginia.

3. He wanted to be respected, yet he insulted his employees.
4. Dr. Brady didn't make house calls, nor did he work on Saturdays.
5. Tua is studying computer science, for she wants to invent a new computer program that will make her rich and famous.
6. Mrs. Perez painted her bathroom, and her glasses got speckled with hot pink paint.
7. Frank Cataldo wants his son to do well in school, so he keeps the dog from chewing up his son's homework.

Exercise 10: Commas with And pages 132–33

1. Correct as written
2. A cup of coffee, a piece of toast, and an orange were all she ate that day.
3. Correct as written
4. Tom politely requested an application form, and after that he sat down to fill it out.
5. Julio plans to become a diesel mechanic, and Michael wants to play drums in a rock band.
6. Correct as written
7. Automatic transmission, power steering, and power brakes are standard on most models.
8. Job openings are available in restaurants, clothing stores, and lawn care.
9. Maria was watching her favorite soap, and Toni was studying a racing form.
10. The squirrel glanced up, froze momentarily, and darted for the tree.

Exercise 11: Compound Sentence with Connectors pages 135–36

Part A

For any connector you missed in the following sentences, go back and review the chart on pages 133–34. Study the meaning of both the correct answer and the connector you chose. Also check the punctuation in each of your sentences.

1. b The bus driver was frequently late to work; therefore, she lost her job.
2. a I can't stand your cooking; moreover, I despise your taste in music.
3. b The rear license plate was missing; however, the police officer didn't give Leon a ticket.
4. c Catch up on your child support payments by next month; otherwise, we'll garnishee your wages.
5. d Cynthia is sometimes forgetful; for

instance, once she bought three bags of groceries at the supermarket and drove home without them.

6. a   Popcorn is a tasty snack; moreover, it's more nutritious than candy.

7. c   Our ambassador spoke only English; consequently, he needed an interpreter with him at all times.

8. a   Eric was placed on probation for two years; in addition, he was ordered to pay back the money he stole.

9. d   She deeply distrusted his motives; nevertheless, she gave him her address.

10. c   We hate hot, humid weather; however, we plan to stay in tropical Florida.

Part B

Here are some sample answers. Make sure your sentences are punctuated correctly and make sense.

1. Shan loves to stay up late; however, she went to bed after dinner last night.
2. I want to earn $50,000 a year; therefore, I'm not going to volunteer for the Peace Corps.
3. Kelly bakes the best pies in town; moreover, her cakes take first prize at the local bazaar every year.
4. You should cut down on your drinking; otherwise, you're going to pickle your liver.
5. Theodore is the meanest kid on the block; for example, he pushed Mrs. Brantley off the curb instead of helping her across the street.

Exercise 12: Run-ons and Comma Splices
pages 138–39

Part A

Here are some sample answers. Make sure your ideas are connected properly, your sentences are punctuated correctly, and you used all three methods at least once each.

1. Harvey couldn't believe his eyes. There was an iguana in the bathtub.
2. He tried to trap the iguana in his old guitar case; however, it had other ideas.
3. Harvey stared thoughtfully at the iguana, and the creature stared back.
4. Suddenly Harvey slapped his forehead. Then he jumped up and ran out of the bathroom.
5. The iguana waited patiently for round two, for it was in no hurry to leave its porcelain palace.

6. Falling in love can be delightful, but it can also be total hell. 7. Women think they have to be gorgeous, and men spend all their time trying to be tough. 8. Some couples manage to give up the pretenses and just love each other. Those are the best relationships. 9. People need to learn to be themselves first; then they are ready to handle being in love. 10. Ready or not, people will probably always fall in love. It's just human nature.

Part B

Here is an example of how to rewrite the following paragraph. Remember that there is more than one way to correct the run-ons and comma splices. Make sure your sentences are punctuated correctly and make sense.

Used cars are fairly cheap to **buy, but they're** not always cheap to run. We bought a car with seventy thousand miles on the **odometer, and it** ran just fine for three **months. Then** our troubles began. The car began to gulp two quarts of oil a **week; in addition, there** was always a cloud of black smoke following us. Then the transmission started to **go, and we** had to swear at it to get it out of reverse. The electrical system was the last straw. We would turn the heater on, and the lights would go off. We'd had **enough, so we** sold our bargain to a junk collector for ten dollars.

Exercise 13: Choosing Subordinating Conjunctions
pages 142–43

For each conjunction missed, study its meaning in the chart on pages 140–41. Then reread the sentence to yourself, substituting the correct conjunction for the underlined words.

1. b
2. a
3. e
4. c
5. a
6. d
7. c
8. d
9. a
10. b

Exercise 14: Punctuating Complex Sentences
pages 144–45

1. C
2. When he tried to speak, he was pelted with rotten eggs.
3. After his constituents had booed him for the tenth time in fifteen minutes, he wadded up his speech and left the platform.
4. C

5. Although he had done his best, there was no chance for reelection.
6. C
7. While she waited for the store to open, she planned her shopping strategy.
8. Although she was the only customer waiting outside, she stayed close to the door.
9. C
10. Since this clearance sale happened only once a year, she was determined to take advantage of it.

Exercise 15: Dependent Clause Fragments
page 146

Part A

1. S
2. F
3. S
4. S
5. S
6. F
7. S
8. S
9. F
10. S
11. S
12. F
13. S

Part B

Riding the bus to work is an adventure in people watching. Each morning after I get on at 7:30, the same motley cast assembles. At the first stop after mine, a teenaged couple gets on. They hurry to the back of the bus so that they can hug and kiss undisturbed. Then the sports enthusiast appears. He sits across from the driver and talks nonstop about the latest game. If the driver tries to change the subject, he simply interrupts. My favorite character is the tiny old lady with the shopping bags. Although she never says anything, she observes the other passengers with as much interest as I do.

Exercise 16: Avoiding Double Signals
pages 147-48

Make sure you punctuated each of your sentences correctly.

1. a. After the last guest left, we cleaned the apartment.
   b. The last guest left; then we cleaned the apartment.

2. a. When the wind blows hard, the windows rattle.
   b. The wind blows hard; then the windows rattle.

3. a. Although Sue wants to lose weight, she can't resist buttered popcorn.
   b. Sue wants to lose weight; however, she can't resist buttered popcorn.

4. a. Because I'd left the headlights on all day, the car wouldn't start.
   b. I'd left the headlights on all day, so the car wouldn't start.

5. a. Dick wanted a new coat, but his budget wouldn't stretch any further.
   b. Dick wanted a new coat; however, his budget wouldn't stretch any further.

Exercise 17: Sentence Combining
page 149

Here are some possible ways you could have correctly combined these pairs of sentences. You should have written at least three combinations for each pair.

1. At fifty-six Leroy mastered fractions, decimals, and percents although he had had difficulty with math as a child.

   Leroy had had difficulty with math as a child, but at fifty-six he mastered fractions, decimals, and percents.

   Leroy had had difficulty with math as a child; however, at fifty-six he mastered fractions, decimals, and percents.

2. Harvey called the dogcatcher when an iguana climbed out of his bathtub.

   An iguana climbed out of Harvey's bathtub, so Harvey called the dogcatcher.

   An iguana climbed out of Harvey's bathtub; then Harvey called the dogcatcher.

3. Bridget has lost twenty-five pounds, and she is determined to lose fifteen pounds more.

   Although Bridget has lost twenty-five pounds, she is determined to lose fifteen pounds more.

   Bridget has lost twenty-five pounds; furthermore, she is determined to lose fifteen pounds more.

4. My children used a stepladder to get the brownies down after I put them on the highest shelf.

   I put the brownies on the highest shelf, but my children used a stepladder to get them down.

   I put the brownies on the highest shelf; however, my children used a stepladder to get them down.

Exercise 18: Rewriting Sentences
page 150

Here are some possible ways to rewrite the sentences. You should have rewritten each sentence three different ways.

1. Tom did not tell Jill about losing the airline tickets; therefore, she was angry with him.

    Jill was angry with Tom because he did not tell her about losing the airline tickets.

    Since Tom did not tell Jill about losing the airline tickets, she was angry with him.

2. Since Gigi needed to feed her cats, she was anxious to get home.

    Gigi needed to feed her cats; consequently, she was anxious to get home.

    Gigi needed to feed her cats, so she was anxious to get home.

3. After Sarah ordered lunch for the department, she made us all watch a soap opera.

    Sarah made the department watch a soap opera after she had ordered us lunch.

    Sarah ordered lunch for the department, and she made us all watch a soap opera.

4. Ann dialed a wrong number, and she got the city morgue.

    Ann got the city morgue when she dialed a wrong number.

    Ann dialed a wrong number; as a result, she got the city morgue.

Exercise 19: GED Practice
pages 151–52

1. (a) *After Joan put the baby to bed, she poured herself a cup of coffee.* Choices (b), (c), and (e) contain double signals. Choice (d) does not express the correct time order.

2. (e) *The grocery store was closed, so we couldn't buy more milk.* This answer is correct because it is the only choice that shows the cause-effect relationship indicated by the word *because* in the original sentence.

3. (a) *Although the vandals kicked in the door, they didn't steal anything.* Choice (a) expresses contrast and uses only one conjunction.

4. (c) *The clock struck twelve; then the guests decided to leave.* This is the only choice that shows the proper time order relationship.

5. (b) *The patient is in critical condition; however, the doctors expect him to recover.* Only this choice shows the contrast expressed in the original two sentences.

Exercise 20: Sequence of Tenses
pages 155–56

1. c Putting both clauses in the simple past shows two actions happening at the same time in the past.

2. a The sentence is correct as written.

3. b Putting both clauses in the present tense shows that the statement is always true.

4. a The sentence is correct as written.

5. c Putting both clauses in the present tense shows that the statement is always true.

6. b Putting the first clause in the past perfect shows that the action in the first clause happened before the action in the second clause.

7. e Putting both clauses in past continuing shows that both actions were happening at the same time.

8. b Putting the first clause in the past perfect shows that the action in the first clause happened before the action in the second clause.

9. e *Would* is incorrect in this sentence because it is past tense. The verb in the first clause is in the present tense, so the verb in the second clause must be in the present or future. See the list of special helping verbs on page 154.

10. d Putting both clauses in the present tense shows that the statement is always true.

Exercise 21: Writing Complex Sentences
page 157
Part A

Here are some sample sentences. Make sure your sentences use correct punctuation and the proper verb tense.

1. If we move next year, it will take three semis to transport all of our possessions.

2. His parents were divorced because they had discovered they couldn't get along.

3. Although the lake is shallow, we dive into it headfirst.

4. Hortense coughed whenever Archibald wore his cheap cologne.

5. After the alien spacecraft had landed, we invited the extraterrestrials in for dessert.

6. The nation will be in trouble if we elect those sleazy politicians on the ballot.

7. When David became furious, steam came out of his ears.

Part B

Here are some more sample sentences. Make sure that at least half of your sentences begin with a dependent clause. Check all your verb tenses to make sure they are correct.

1. Although I love to eat a spoonful of peanut butter, it makes my tongue stick to the roof of my mouth.
2. I'm afraid to go to the dentist because I always have a cavity.
3. Whenever my son practices his trumpet, the dog rolls over and plays dead.
4. I won't be able to finish my laundry if I run out of quarters.
5. He ran the marathon as though his life depended on it.
6. Despite the fact that she had butterflies in her stomach, Hildegarde was looking forward to the piano recital.
7. It's not wise to eat a big meal before you go swimming.
8. Until the cows come home, we won't have any milk for supper.

Exercise 22: Sentence Combining Review pages 158–62

1. (2) The ideas in this sentence are related by time, which eliminates choices (1), (4), and (5). Choice (3) does not make sense.
2. (5) This is the only choice that expresses the cause-effect relationship indicated in the original sentence.
3. (3) This choice is correct because you must use a comma after a dependent clause that begins a sentence.
4. (1) Correct as written
5. (4) This is the only choice that corrects the double signals in the original sentence.
6. (3) Only this choice correctly links the two ideas in the sentence.
7. (3) This choice corrects the comma splice in the original sentence.
8. (5) Correct as written
9. (1) Check: *If you have an inherited tendency toward a specific disease, there may be good news for you.* The other choices make no sense in the new sentence.
10. (5) This choice corrects the dependent clause fragment in the original passage.
11. (3) In the original sentence, *however* wrongly implies a contrast between the clauses. *In addition* tells you that the second clause adds information

to the first.
12. (2) This choice both corrects the run-on sentence and preserves its original meaning.
13. (2) No comma should follow a conjunction in a dependent clause.
14. (2) *For instance* shows that the second clause gives an example of the idea in the first clause.
15. (4) The second clause should be in the future tense. The sentence looks into the future with the action in the first clause occurring first.

Chapter 4 Cumulative Review pages 163–67
Editing Practice (Part A)

Do you remember when being a child meant **having red** measles, German measles, mumps, and whooping cough? If you **do, you're** probably at least thirty, for in the last few decades scientists **have** developed vaccines that immunize children against all of these diseases. Although many people thought they were **harmless, they** could actually be quite dangerous. If a pregnant woman **caught** German **measles, her** child might have severe birth defects. Another serious disease was **mumps. It** could cause sterility in adult males. Today **because** the medical community has worked so hard to eliminate them, these diseases are not likely to bother you or **your** children.

Multiple-Choice Practice

1. (5) The subject of this verb is *reputation and freedom*, a plural compound subject. *Were* agrees with a plural subject.
2. (1) *Seen* is a past participle and requires a helping verb. The correct simple past form is *saw*.
3. (4) The object pronoun *me* should be used because this pronoun is not the subject of a verb.
4. (3) This choice uses the proper punctuation for the connector *then*.
5. (5) Correct as written
6. (4) The original sentence is a fragment. Choice (4) is a complete sentence and uses the correct verb form.
7. (2) This choice separates with a comma the two compound elements *sworn in* and *questioned*.
8. (5) Correct as written
9. (1) This choice shows the contrast between the two original sentences.
10. (3) The verb tense in the first clause is in

the past tense, and the two clauses are happening at the same time. The helping verb *would* shows past tense.

11. (2) This choice corrects the misspelled plural *storys*.

12. (1) This choice correctly puts the verb in the past tense.

13. (3) Use a comma after a dependent clause that begins a sentence.

14. (1) Correct as written

15. (4) This choice corrects the misspelled verb form *writting*.

16. (1) Check: *When schoolteacher Christa MacAuliffe was chosen to be the second civilian in space in 1986, space travel became big news again.* The other choices do not express the relationship between the two original sentences.

17. (2) The subject of this sentence is *the crew, MacAuliffe, and the shuttle*, a plural compound subject. *Were* agrees with a plural subject.

18. (3) The time clue *for years to come* tells you the sentence should be in the future tense.

CHAPTER 5
Exercise 1: Outlining
pages 172–73

One possible outline for each set of items appears below. Your organization may be different. Be sure that your outline contains logical groupings with clear headings to cover the items in each group.

1. **Outdoor sports**
   I. Summer sports
      A. Water skiing
      B. Baseball
      C. Golf
      D. Tennis
   II. Winter sports
      A. Hockey
      B. Ice skating
      C. Cross-country skiing

2. **Transportation**
   I. Land—private
      A. Motorcycles
      B. Bicycles
      C. Cars
   II. Land—public
      A. Buses
      B. Trains
   III. Air
      A. Planes
      B. Helicopters

3. **How to Lose Your Job**
   I. Don't get along with others
      A. Argue with boss
      B. Get in fights with coworkers
      C. Treat customers rudely
   II. Cheat on work hours
      A. Regularly arrive late for work
      B. Take long breaks
      C. Leave work early
   III. Steal on the job
      A. Steal office supplies
      B. Steal store merchandise

Exercise 7: GED Writing Topic
page 181

This question asks you to choose *one* aspect of your life that you would like to change and to discuss the *effects* of that imaginary change on your life. The introduction of your essay should identify what you want to change, and the body should contain an explanation of the effects, grouped in a logical way. A sample essay in response to this question appears below.

Brainstorming
Married too young—if I'd married later in life, I would have developed a greater sense of independence.

1. didn't learn to budget my own money   *finances* ②
2. didn't make decisions on major purchases—car, home
3. ~~didn't develop my own hobbies—music~~
4. ~~no chance to travel~~
5. no chance to develop my talents in hair cutting   *career* ①

Essay
When I was eighteen, Jeff and I had been going steady for two years. My idea of living happily ever after was to get married right away, settle down in a house of our own, and start a family. That's exactly what we did. But now, ten years later, I'm convinced that marrying later in life would have given me a much greater sense of independence.

Marrying early kept me from having a career outside the home. For years, I'd wanted to go to barber school, but after we married there wasn't enough money for both schooling and house payments. When the twins were born, our finances became even tighter. I had no choice but to stay home.

Without the chance to earn my own money, I never got to practice money management. Jeff was the one with the full-time job, so he kept the checkbook and paid the bills. Whenever we made a major purchase, like a new car or a refrigerator, Jeff made the final choice. Without bringing home a paycheck, I never felt that I had the right to share in the financial decision making.

Some people say that getting married makes people grow up in a hurry. For me, though, an early marriage made it harder to grow up in terms of choosing a career and handling money. If I had it to do over again, I would still marry Jeff, but I would postpone that walk down the aisle for a few more years.

Exercise 8: Writing Sentences with Modifying Phrases pages 184–85

Possible answers appear below. Be sure that your sentences are punctuated correctly. All introductory phrases should be followed by commas.

1. **Smiling seductively,** Samantha sauntered toward Steve.
2. **In the middle of the president's speech,** a reporter shouted a question.
3. **To prevent looting after the shopping mall fire,** the governor called out the National Guard.
4. The campers were awakened by a bear **rummaging through the food supplies.**
5. Vandals smashed the windshields of twelve cars **in the vicinity of West High School last night.**
6. **Shouting and whistling their approval,** the crowd gave Slime Green a standing ovation.
7. The trucker drove an alternate route **to avoid the weigh station.**
8. Dick's Get 'n' Go was robbed **for the third time in less than a year.**
9. **To reduce the chances of catching a cold,** some people take large doses of vitamin C.
10. Smitty and Josh stared in fascinated horror at the tarantula **crawling across their sleeping friend's face.**

Exercise 9: Correcting Misplaced Modifiers pages 186–87

Sample corrections appear below. Be sure that your corrected sentences have commas following introductory modifiers and that all modifiers are placed near the words they describe.

1. *Stuck under his chair*
   Morris felt a large, moist blob of bubble gum **stuck under his chair.**
2. *Destroyed by hail*
   Larry Gunderson stared gloomily at his wheat field **destroyed by hail.**
3. *Swinging effortlessly from branch to branch*
   The children watched the chimpanzee **swinging effortlessly from branch to branch.**
4. *screaming for mercy*
   Screaming for mercy, the prisoner was escorted to Death Row by four guards.
5. *Gasping for air*
   The fans encouraged the marathon runner **gasping for air** to complete the last hundred yards.
6. *Hidden behind a layer of dense brown smog*
   We could barely see the outlines of the mountains **hidden behind a layer of dense brown smog.**
7. *with a neatly trimmed moustache and beard*
   A suave gentleman **with a neatly trimmed moustache and beard** strolled through the park.
8. *with a slight smile*
   With a slight smile, Sonja draped her boa constrictor around the trunk of the apple tree.
9. *Eager to recruit top athletes*
   Promising high school seniors are offered full scholarships by some colleges **eager to recruit top athletes.**
10. *Fuzzy and shriveled*
    We finally found the **fuzzy and shriveled** decaying orange in Will's top file drawer.

Exercise 10: Correcting Dangling Modifiers pages 188–89

Sample corrections appear below; your sentences might be different. Be sure that every modifier clearly describes a specific word in the sentence and that it is placed near the word it describes. In addition, be sure to place a comma after every introductory modifier or clause.

1. *Being the only guy she'd ever dated*
   Because he was the only guy she'd ever dated, she was desperate to get married right away.
2. *to keep from getting the flu*
   Some people wore garlic necklaces at all times to keep from getting the flu.
3. *Returning my library books two weeks*

late
Because I returned my library books two weeks late, the fine was $1.20.

4. *unaware of the road block*
Unaware of the road block, the driver of the getaway car sped down Highway 37.

5. *Eager to break for cocktails and dinner*
Because the members were eager to break for cocktails and dinner, the meeting was adjourned until eight o'clock the following morning.

6. *Stumbling over a fallen log*
As he stumbled over a fallen log, the rifle discharged.

7. *Despondent about losing his job and filing for bankruptcy*
Despondent about losing his job and filing for bankruptcy, Jim found suicide a tempting prospect.

8. *to prevent accidental poisoning*
Parents should lock cleaning fluids and medicines away from small children to prevent accidental poinsoning.

9. *Curious about the strange visitors and eerie music night after night*
Curious about the strange visitors and eerie music night after night, the police placed the house under surveillance.

10. *Giggling uncontrollably*
Giggling uncontrollably, I felt the room spin around me after my fourth glass of champagne.

Exercise 11: Using Renaming Phrases
pages 190–91

1. The Statue of Liberty, a gift from France, stands at the entrance to New York Harbor.

2. Bone strength depends on an adequate supply of calcium, a mineral found in dairy products and some vegetables.

3. This week's lottery winner, a mother of ten from the Bronx, will receive twenty thousand dollars a year for the next twenty years.

4. Use Dazzle, a revolutionary new detergent, to get your clothes sunshine clean.

5. Our store detective is Farley Finck, a man who can spot a shoplifter at fifty paces.

Part B

Sample sentences using renaming phrases appear below. Be sure that in your sentences the renaming phrases appear directly after the word they describe and that they are separated by commas from the rest of the sentence.

1. The movie being shown tonight is *Rocky*, **a film about a common man who makes his**

dream come true.

2. Unfortunately, my fiancé's favorite vegetable is cauliflower, **the one food I'm allergic to.**

3. Stephen King's novels, **fast-paced horror stories,** are popular with young adults.

4. Paula Hansen, **my next-door neighbor,** owns the hardware store on Second Street.

5. The plane, **a B-17,** crashed while attempting to make an emergency landing.

6. I've always wanted to visit New Orleans, **a city with a reputation for fine food and great jazz.**

7. Dr. Sidney Boldt, **a sour man with a persistent frown on his face,** had never developed a smooth bedside manner.

8. The band was playing "You Ain't Nothin' But a Hound Dog," **an old Elvis Presley hit**, when Angelo realized he'd forgotten to feed his poodle.

9. Our next speaker is Sharon Moser, **a woman with a keen sense of justice and a determination to protect the rights of all our citizens.**

10. Maggie may have been a Scot, but she refused to eat haggis, **a disgusting concoction of oatmeal and the vital organs of sheep.**

Exercise 12: Revising for Parallel Structure
pages 193–95

Part A

Your sentences may differ from the samples below. Be sure that all compound elements are written in the same form.

1. well coordinated, agile, *have strength*
A gymnast must be well coordinated, agile, and **strong.**

2. knitting, *to play*
Knitting nose warmers and **playing** Wahoo were Albert's hobbies.

3. brave, honest, *a compassionate man*
Mr. Bubany was brave, honest, and **compassionate.**

4. adding, subtracting, multiplication, dividing
We can solve arithmetic problems by adding, subtracting, **multiplying**, and dividing.

5. love, *she hates*
Why does Elizabeth love to cook but **hate** to do dishes?

6. took, drank, *she slept*
When Sue had the flu, she took aspirin, drank plenty of liquids, and **slept** a lot.

7. sipping, *if I listened*
Long ago I discovered that I could relax

by sipping a cup of hot tea or **listening** to soft music.

8. in the hallway, through the kitchen, *they got it on the living room carpet*
The kids tracked mud in the hallway, through the kitchen, and **on the living room carpet.**

9. stopped, *was scratching,* wondered
John stopped, **scratched** his head, and wondered what to do next.

10. to have, to care, *when you lose*
One of life's greatest sorrows is to have a child, to care for him lovingly as he grows, and then **to lose** him to drugs.

Part B

Possible answers appear below. Be sure that all items in each list use the same word form.

1. Three character traits that I admire in a person are **honesty, gentleness,** and **wit.**

2. **Nursing, repairing cars, banking,** and **drafting** are all careers that interest me.

3. In my spare time I like to **cook Chinese food** or **read westerns.**

4. I would like to find out **where my ancestors were born, why they left their homeland,** and **whether they were happier in America.**

5. Yesterday morning **I bought a sack of doughnuts, took them to work,** and **ate all but one.**

6. This country will be a better place to live when our citizens **stop carrying handguns** and **start trusting the police to enforce the law.**

7. An effective speaker talks **slowly** and **clearly.**

8. **Munching popcorn, watching TV, cleaning the attic,** and **talking on the telephone** are good ways to pass the time on a rainy Saturday.

9. Whenever I lose something, I look **in my jeans pockets, on the kitchen table,** and **under the car seat.**

10. An ideal spouse should be **steady, cheerful,** and **loving.**

Exercise 13: Eliminating Confusing Pronouns
pages 196–97

Sample answers appear below. If your sentences differ, be sure that your wording eliminates any confusion about which word a pronoun might refer to.

1. After **Sam** called **Ted** a liar, they got into a bitter argument.

2. As the dog approached the wounded bear, **the bear** was snarling menacingly.

3. I like November much better than February; **February** is such a dreary month.

4. Steven will probably never speak to James again now that **James** is a millionaire.

5. I can't decide whether to buy the brown shoes or the black ones; **the brown ones** are more expensive, but they'll probably last longer.

6. Although **Maria** wanted to maintain their friendship, Sonja never spoke to her again.

7. C

8. Just as **Tim** was about to step from the curb, Sean glanced up and shouted, "Tim, watch out!"

9. C

10. The country music fans and the rock fans never got along because **the country music fans** thought the others were stupid and crude.

Exercise 14: Eliminating Vague Pronouns
pages 198–99

Sample answers appear below. Be sure that the noun you've substituted in each incorrect sentence makes the meaning clear.

1. You should have seen the children chasing each other around the playground; **the scene** was hilarious.

2. With the growing importance of computers, **schools** need more qualified instructors at all levels.

3. Although the doctor lectured the teenagers on the dangers of smoking, **the warning** didn't stop them from experimenting.

4. **Some people** say that animals grow thicker fur before an unusually harsh winter.

5. When the father rocked and sang to his baby, **his voice** seemed to quiet the child.

6. We asked Laura to get some counseling, but she insisted that **counselors** do more harm than good.

7. Mr. Cutforth was notified last night that he'd won. **The news** excited him so much that he nearly passed out.

8. In the article **scientists** say that acid rain is endangering wildlife and forests in the Northeast.

9. C

10. Marian wanted to go into engineering because **engineers** have an excellent income.

Exercise 15: Choosing the Correct Relative Pronoun
page 200

	Antecedent	Relative Pronoun
1.	movie	that

2.	catcher	who
3.	Soccer	which
4.	birds	that
5.	redwood	which
6.	Lyndon Johnson	who
7.	dogs	which
8.	shift	which
9.	teller	who
10.	house	that

Exercise 16: Making Pronouns Agree in Number
pages 202–203
Part A

	Antecedent	Pronoun
1.	Germany	its
2.	woman	her
3.	Carter, Reagan (connected by *and*)	their
4.	cat, dogs (connected by *or*)	their
5.	dog, cat (connected by *and*)	their
6.	paper clip	It (weighs) its
7.	company	its
8.	finches	they
9.	all (members)	their
10.	man	he (begins)

Part B

Children are much less upset by hospital stays if **they have** been prepared properly for the experience. If possible, **they** should be taken on a tour of the hospital before **they are** admitted. Becoming familiar with these new surroundings will reduce **their** anxiety and help them adjust more quickly to being away from home.

Exercise 17: Making Sentences Agree in Person
page 205
Part A

	Antecedent	Pronoun
1.	our	we
2.	you	you ('re not)
3.	Jim	he
4.	farmers, workers (conncted by *and*)	their

Part B

As we neared the seacoast, the fog enveloped us so thickly that **we** couldn't see two feet in front of our car. **We** felt as if **we** were moving in outer space, with no signposts, no trees, not even a roadway to orient **us**. Even the sounds were muffled. An occasional car droned past us, its driver slowly feeling his way in the opposite direction. Most of the time, though, all **we** could hear was the dull throb of the waves on the beach and the mournful foghorns warning ships away from hidden rocks.

Exercise 18: Sentence Structure Review
pages 207–11

1. (2) Use commas to separate renaming phrases from the rest of the sentence.
2. (2) The pronoun *they* is unclear in this sentence because there is no antecedent for it. The noun phrase *some educators* tells you who says that children should spend less time on drill.
3. (4) The sentence contains a series of things that children should be taught to do. For parallel structure, the items in the series should have the same word forms: analyze, *select*, and decide.
4. (1) The complete sentence would read, "While the calculators perform the mechanical operations, the children will be able to concentrate on the real thinking skills." This wording avoids misplaced modifiers by making clear what the calculators do and what the children do.
5. (4) Previous sentences refer to *the children*. The pronoun that agrees in number and person with this antecedent is *they*.
6. (1) The human antecedent *children* requires the human relative pronoun *who*.
7. (4) In this sentence, *which* is a vague pronoun because it has no clear antecedent. What did Frank ignore? The correct version replaces *which* with the noun phrase *their advice*.
8. (5) For parallel structure, each item in a series should use the same word form: an expensive car, a television set, a trip.
9. (5) The sentence is correct as written.
10. (1) Use commas to separate renaming phrases from the rest of the sentence.
11. (2) The original sentence contains a dangling modifier. *Who* was confronted with a bill? Choice (2) makes clear that Frank was confronted and that he cut up the card.
12. (5) The sentence is correct as written.
13. (1) Separate an introductory modifier from the rest of the sentence with a comma.

14. (4) The combined sentence should read, "The higher we climbed, the faster my heart beat." The two parts of the sentence are parallel, because the same word forms are used: *the higher, the faster.*

15. (4) If a sentence begins with a modifying phrase, the next word should tell what the phrase describes. Otherwise, the sentence will contain a dangling or misplaced modifier. The complete sentence should read, "Upon finally reaching the peak, we decided that the view made our struggle worthwhile."

16. (3) The pronoun *we* used in earlier sentences indicates that first person pronouns should be used throughout the paragraph.

Chapter 5 Cumulative Review pages 212–16
Editing Practice (Part A)

Break-ins, muggings, and rapes **have** increased dramatically in our community since 1960. With this increase in street **crime, we** citizens have lost much of our freedom. **When we were growing up**, our front door was never locked. **We** simply didn't worry about someone walking in and stealing our property. **When I was eight years old**, my parents let me ride the bus downtown by myself. My **mother, always** a protective person, had no qualms about my safety. A few years later when I was in high school, my friends and I would often meet at five o'clock in the morning and walk six blocks to the **park to** play tennis. **We had no** reason to fear being robbed or raped.

My daughter, **who** is now ten, doesn't enjoy the same freedom I had. Our house is **equipped** with plenty of locks for the doors and a burglar alarm as well. We don't allow Cindy to take the bus alone or **walk** around the neighborhood after **dark. There** are too many reports of robberies and rapes for us to feel safe. For her and for most other children, the fear of crime has taken some of the fun out of childhood.

Multiple-Choice Practice

1. (3) The first word group is a dependent clause fragment. It should be attached to the second sentence with a comma because it is an introductory clause.

2. (4) All items in the series should be made parallel by using the same word forms: builds, increases, and *improves.*

3. (4) There is no clear antecedent for the pronoun *this,* so it should be replaced by a noun to eliminate confusion.

4. (5) The sentence is correct as written.

5. (2) The subject of the sentence, *injuries* and *concussions,* is plural, so the plural verb *are* must be used.

6. (2) The other verb in this sentence, *provides,* is the time clue that this verb should also be in the present tense. *Cheer* agrees with the plural subject *they.*

7. (3) The plural pronoun *their* must have a plural antecedent in this sentence. *Swimmers* chart *their* progress.

8. (2) The word *but* shows the contrast between not winning a ribbon and still feeling satisfied.

9. (5) The word *whereas* shows the contrast between the technology of the first half and that of the second half of the century.

10. (1) Use commas to separate renaming phrases from the rest of the sentence.

11. (1) If a verb ends in a consonant followed by *y,* change the *y* to *i* when adding *-ed.*

12. (2) Since the second sentence describes a noun in the first sentence, the sentences can be combined using a relative pronoun. The pronoun *that* must be used instead of *who* because it refers to an object, *computers.* The complete sentence should read: "Automobiles and trucks also contain computers that regulate their fuel and electrical systems."

13. (4) The plural verb *are* agrees with the plural subject *computers.*

14. (1) The sentence is correct as written. This version maintains parallel structure in the two parts of the sentence by using the same word forms: not only do they *write,* but they also *maintain.*

15. (4) Because the rest of the paragraph is written using present-tense verbs to discuss the use of computers (for example, *take, print, maintain*), this sentence should also use a present-tense verb. The plural verb *allow* agrees with the plural subject *tellers.*

16. (1) Because the main verb follows the helping verb *have,* the past participle form, *become,* must be used.

CHAPTER 6
Exercise 1: Using Specific Reasons
pages 220–21

The sentences that used circular reasoning in this exercise have sample answers. Make sure that your sentences include specific reasons and don't restate the first clause.

1. City life is more stressful than farm life because the city's extra noise, crowded conditions, and pollution make relaxing very difficult.
2. OK
3. Cigarette smoking is a harmful habit because it causes lung cancer, emphysema, and other life-threatening illnesses.
4. The automobile is one of the most useful inventions of this century; it has made transportation cheaper and more accessible to a broad cross section of the population.
5. OK
6. I believe that water pollution is a serious environmental problem in this country because it contaminates our drinking water and poisons our fish and wildlife.
7. OK
8. Elementary school children should be required to learn a foreign language because it teaches them about a culture other than their own.
9. College athletes should be paid for playing because ticket sales from games are an important source of money for colleges.
10. The minimum wage should be increased by at least one dollar per hour because the current wage does not take the rising cost of living into account.

Exercise 2: Adding Specific Examples
page 222

Here are some possible examples for each of the general statements.

1. I dropped out of high school because I wanted to earn money to help my mother, who was raising six kids on her own.
2. For instance, we could find out what happened in our families during the Great Depression of the 1930s.
3. For example, assembly line workers often find their work dull because they do the same thing over and over.
4. Day after day, you read stories in magazines and newspapers about rich film stars

getting divorced or being hooked on alcohol or drugs.
5. For example, fires can spread very fast when buildings are close together.

Exercise 3: Adding Specific Details
pages 224–25
Part A

Here are sample answers to the first five sentences. Make sure your sentences use specific nouns and verbs to show, not just tell, what's happening.

1. Standing in the ticket line of the downtown bus terminal, the elderly grandmother sobbed uncontrollably when she discovered that her wallet had been stolen.
2. Mrs. McGillicuddy's German shepherd, Matildabelle, lunged at her yesterday when she tried to pet the protective dog's newborn pups.
3. The increase in the number of abandoned buildings, vacant lots, and litter-covered streets in Laketown has caused many shopkeepers to move their businesses to better-kept areas of the city.
4. James was so nervous when he changed his newborn daughter Lisa's diapers that he almost poked her with the diaper pin.
5. Seventy-five percent of the apartment buildings in Laketown have been sprayed with graffiti over the last year.

Part B

Here is a sample paragraph. Make sure you have used specific examples to show what you mean.

Joe's Cafe is the worst place to eat in town. First of all, the place is filthy inside and out. When you drive into the lot, you have to dodge empty beer cans, trash, and broken bottles in order to park. Walking in the front door is no improvement. Flies swarm around your head, and cockroaches run for cover with every step you take on the frayed, threadbare carpet. The service is lousy, too. About an hour after you've been seated, Joe waddles out of the kitchen in his grimy apron to clear off the table and take your order. After another hour, he plops an unrecognizable cut of meat swimming in gravy under your nose. Not only does it *look* unappetizing, but it tastes terrible as well. However, the worst is yet to come—the check. Not only have you subjected yourself to horrible abuse, but you now have to pay a fortune for it!

Exercise 5: Using Transition Words
page 228

The following sentences contain sample transition words or phrases. Make sure you use a transition word that links or shows the relationship of the ideas in the two sentences. Also make sure that you use the correct punctuation with your transition word or phrase.

1. **However,** those frontier days are long past.
2. States like Arizona and New Mexico, **for example,** may run short of water for their new residents.
3. **First,** shake the can vigorously. **Next,** point it at your target before pulling the tab to open it. **Finally,** laugh your head off and run away.
4. **In addition,** they must adapt to unfamiliar interviewing practices.
5. The acting, **on the other hand,** is terrible.

Exercise 6: More Transition Words
page 230
Part A

The following paragraphs use sample transition words and phrases to make clear the relationship between ideas. Be sure to use the correct punctuation with your transitions.

1. You can make Tante Hanne's Apple Macaroons for dessert in forty-five minutes if you follow these simple directions. **First,** butter a pie tin and slice four or five medium apples into it. **Second,** cover the apples with half a cup of sugar and as much cinnamon as desired. **Next,** cream together four tablespoons of margarine and half a cup of sugar. **Then** beat in one egg. Mix in half a cup of flour and a dash of salt. **Finally,** spoon the batter over the apples and bake for half an hour at 350 degrees.
2. High school students should not be allowed to drive for several reasons. **First,** they're not mature enough to handle the responsibility. **For example,** every Friday night one seventeen-year-old I know downs a six-pack of beer and then challenges his classmates to drag race down Main Street.

   Second, cars detract from schoolwork. Most students who own cars work to pay for gas and insurance. **Therefore,** they spend less time on the schoolwork that should be their primary concern.

   Finally, cars give them too much freedom. Instead of cruising the streets looking for parties to crash or girls to pick up, they should be with their families, where more adult supervision is provided.

Exercise 7: Eliminating Repetitive Wording
pages 231–32

Here is a sample paragraph. Read your paragraph aloud to check for repetitive wording.

Frank was annoyed with Lisa because she never became angry with **him**. Whenever **he** complained to **her** about anything, Lisa apologized to **him** instead of **getting mad** in return. Frank found it impossible to have a good argument with **her** because **she** refused to **fight back**. Lisa's **unwillingness** to argue simply made Frank **more irritated** than **he** was to begin with.

Exercise 8: Tightening
pages 233–34
Part A

Here are some sample answers.

1. The dress is blue cotton.
2. OK
3. The chicken wings in the refrigerator can be warmed up for supper.
4. The sign that the vandals destroyed last night will cost a thousand dollars to replace.
5. We finally found a large but inexpensive apartment.

Part B

Here is one way to eliminate the wordiness in the original paragraph.

Today's heating costs are dangerously high for poor people. Retired people must rely on a fixed income. Their social security checks just aren't large enough to cover higher utility bills when the weather is cold. Congress should pass a bill to assist people in this situation.

Exercise 10: GED Writing Topic
page 236

Here is a sample essay. Notice how the writer has revised it by adding transition words and specifics and by tightening the wording.

Because drunken driving ~~is a serious~~ *claims countless lines* ~~problem~~ in the U.S., I believe something needs to be done *both* to get drunk drivers off the streets and ~~to impress on them the se-~~ *to try to treat this addiction to alcohol. But simply punishing them for* ~~rious nature of their crime. I don't how-~~ *their behavior won't solve the problem. Therefore,* ~~ever, believe that~~ the proposal to give a mandatory thirty-day jail sentence to those

convicted will *not* have a lasting effect in re-

ducing the incidence of drunken driving.

Statistics show that many drunk driv-

ers are repeat offenders. *Some have even* ~~some even having~~

spent *time* ~~several terms~~ in jail for their crime*, but*

without result. Doing time fails to keep
~~Yet such jail terms don't keep them from~~

them from driving while drunk because
~~going out on the road drunk again because~~

it doesn't address
~~they fail to solve~~ the underlying problems

, such as job- or family-related stressor
causing their dependence on alcohol*, feelings*
of inadequacy.

A more effective solution would be to

first-time offenders
require ~~those convicted of drunken driving~~

~~for the first time~~ to enter a residential

Such a pro-
drug/alcohol rehab program. ~~In the pro-~~

gram would enable these drivers to
~~gram, they would~~ get the assistance they

problems behind
need to deal with the ~~underlying causes of~~

their alcohol abuse. ~~such as job and family-~~

~~related stress, loneliness, feelings of inade-~~

Addressing
~~quacy, etc. Such attention to~~ these underly-

is the best way to bring
ing causes ~~would have longer lasting ef-~~

about a lasting solution to drunken
~~fects than a mandatory jail sentence.~~

driving.

Exercise 11: Capitalizing Specific Names
page 239

1. Although **Margaret** was born in **London**, her parents were **German** citizens.
2. The largest continent in both geography and population is **Asia**, but the highest standards of living are enjoyed by **Europeans** and **North Americans**.
3. What a different world this would be without the inventions of **Thomas A. Edison** and **Alexander Graham Bell**!
4. Thanks to vaccines, potentially dangerous childhood diseases like mumps and **German** measles have been almost eliminated in the **United States**.
5. The relations between this country and our **Latin American** neighbors have not always been friendly.

Exercise 12: More Capitalizing Specific Names
page 241

1. Last week a Laotian couple moved into the red brick house on Oakdale **Road**.
2. Our Independence Day is not an official **holiday** in England.
3. On Monday morning **Governor** O'Reilly will begin a campaign swing around the state.
4. An **Indonesian** restaurant offers diners rice dishes, peanut sauce, chicken and pork, and baked bananas for dessert.
5. When it's time for **spring** cleaning, Aunt Gladys and her neighbor roll up their sleeves and scour from attic to basement.
6. Two senators and a **judge** were indicted on April 26 for accepting bribes.
7. The Mississippi is the longest **river** in the United States, but not the longest in the world.
8. Both Hannukah and Christmas are **winter** holidays.
9. The Smoky **Mountains** of Tennessee are named aptly because of the haze that often covers them.
10. Turn right off the county road when you reach **Highway** 75 and drive five miles until you see the sign for Spring Lake Park.

Exercise 14: Using Spelling Rules
pages 249–50

Here is the correct spelling of the word you should have picked.

1. C
2. *newsstand* This correct spelling follows the rule of combining compound words: don't change the spelling of either word when you combine them.
3. *immediately* Follow the rule of keeping the silent *e* of the base word when you add a suffix that begins with a consonant.
4. *noticeable* This word keeps its silent *e* before adding a suffix beginning with *a* in order to keep the soft *c* sound.
5. C
6. *marriage* This word follows the rule of changing the *y* to *i* before adding any suffix other than one beginning with *i*.

7. *occasional* — This word follows the general suffix rule of not changing the spelling of the suffix or the base.

8. *mournful* — Look at the correct spelling of the suffix *ful* in the chart on page 246.

9. *disapprove* — When adding a prefix to a word, don't change the spelling of either the prefix or the base word.

10. *arrangement* — This word follows the rule of keeping the *e* before adding a suffix beginning with a consonant.

11. *friend* — *I* before *E* except after *C*.

12. *believe* — *I* before *E* except after *C*.

13. *foreign* — This word is one of the exceptions (found in the nonsense sentence on page 249) to *I* before *E* except after *C*.

14. *bicycle* — The base word is *cycle*, the prefix is *bi*.

15. *careless* — In general, don't change the spelling of the suffix or the base.

Exercise 15: Using Soundalike Words
pages 253–54

If you missed any of these, go back and restudy the meanings.

1. quite, principal
2. write, personnel
3. already, accepted
4. thorough, heroin
5. lesson, break, your
6. whole, weak
7. too, lose
8. dessert, sweet, rolls
9. hoarse, breath, their
10. It's, past, dinner
11. advice, whether, break
12. They're, wasting, their, dessert
13. all right, board, there, later
14. know, desert, plane, week
15. sole, advice

Exercise 16: Spelling Review
pages 257–58
Part A

1. *advertise* — You must memorize this spelling.

2. *weigh* — This spelling follows the rule that says "*e* before *i* when sounding like *a* as in neighbor and weigh."

3. *associated* — You must memorize this spelling.

4. *cemeteries* — To make plural a word that ends in *y* preceded by a consonant, drop the *y* and add *ies*.

5. *February* — This word is commonly misspelled because the first *r* is often not pronounced when the word is spoken.

6. *disappointed* — When you add a prefix, don't change the spelling of either the prefix or the base word.

7. *siege* — *I* before *E* except after *C*.

8. *succeed* — You must memorize this commonly misspelled word.

9. *there* — This word is commonly mistaken for *their* and *they're*.

10. *principal* — In this phrase, *principal* means "main."

11. *dinner* — This word is commonly confused with *diner*, which means "coffee shop."

12. *waist* — This word sounds just like *waste*, meaning "garbage."

13. *mysterious* — See the suffix rules on pages 247–48. *Mystery + ous = mysterious*.

14. *role* — *Role* and *roll* are commonly confused soundalike words.

15. *acceptable* — You must memorize this spelling.

Part B

Organizing a **surprise** party for a **friend** requires **a lot** of **planning**. You'll need to attend to **usual** matters like **invitations** and refreshments, but you'll have to keep your **activities** a secret. To prevent the guest of honor from **guessing** that anything's up, you must **decide** on a logical **reason** for inviting her to the place where the party will be held. **Another** concern is how to hide the rest of the guests until the proper moment. For the party to be **successful**, **your timing** must be perfect.

Exercise 17: Capitalization and Spelling Review
pages 259–62

1. (1) This choice replaces the incorrect possessive pronoun *its* with *it's*, the contraction for *it is*.

2. (4) The word *nations* in this sentence is general, so it should not be capitalized.

3. (3) The specific name *Ohio River* should

be capitalized.

4. (2) Drop the silent *e* when adding a suffix beginning with a vowel.

5. (2) To form the plural of a word ending in *y* preceded by a vowel, drop the *y* and add *ies*.

6. (3) *Their* and *there* are commonly confused.

7. (1) You need to memorize this commonly misspelled word.

8. (4) Do not capitalize names of the seasons.

9. (3) To form the plural of a word ending in a hissing sound, add *es*.

10. (3) You need to memorize this commonly misspelled word.

11. (5) Correct as written.

12. (3) Drop the silent *e* when adding a suffix that begins with a vowel. Do not double the consonant.

13. (2) This choice replaces the incorrect use of the word *hole*, meaning "a gap," with *whole*, meaning "total."

14. (2) You need to memorize this commonly misspelled word.

Chapter 6 Cumulative Review pages 263–66

Editing Practice (Part A)

Some **psychologists** suggest that **people** can reduce tension by imagining themselves in a peaceful setting. Whenever I use this **advice, I remember** Cave Point, a **park** in Wisconsin on the shore of **Lake** Michigan. I picture myself sitting on top of a cliff overlooking the water. Despite the cool lake breeze, the sun **shining** on my back makes a sweater **unnecessary. Closing** my **eyes, I** soak in the warmth and listen to the **rhythmical** thumping of water in the limestone caves carved by centuries of waves. Once **again** this oasis of **calm works** its **magic, and I** can return to the hassles of everyday life with renewed inner **strength**.

Multiple-Choice Practice

1. (1) The subject of the sentence, *citizens*, requires a plural verb, *do*.

2. (3) A word derived from the name of a specific place must always be capitalized.

3. (1) The sentence is correct as written. The singular indefinite pronoun *each* takes a singular verb, *has*.

4. (3) A modifying phrase at the end of a sentence is not set off by a comma.

5. (5) Adding the verb *is* makes this fragment a complete sentence.

6. (2) Sentences 3, 4, and 7 use the first person pronouns *we* and *our*, so this

pronoun should also be in first person.

7. (3) This choice uses a connector that correctly shows the contrast indicated by *Although* in the original sentence.

8. (1) Check: *Because of the prejudice of people who have forgotten their immigrant roots, each new group has had to face discrimination in housing, education, and jobs.* This sentence shows the cause-effect relationship.

9. (1) This word is often misspelled because many people don't pronounce the second syllable.

10. (2) Don't separate the subject of the sentence from the predicate with a comma.

11. (4) A comma must precede the conjunction *and* when it connects two independent clauses.

12. (1) A transition word like *however* needs to be set off from the rest of the sentence.

13. (5) Check: *Some patients lie in comas for years, unable to respond to their environment.*

14. (1) This sentence calls for the possessive pronoun *their*.

15. (5) The passage is written in the present tense.

16. (3) This choice corrects the comma splice in the original sentence.

CHAPTER 7

Exercise 1: Planning Your Essay page 283

A sample brainstorming list for the third topic appears below. Your ideas may be completely different. Check to be sure that you have a clear unifying statement, that your details will help explain your point to your reader, and that they are logically arranged.

Unifying statement: Rituals give participants a sense of belonging, importance, and control.

3 **gives sense of control over natural forces**
birth—christening
death—funeral
~~aggression—sports~~

1 **unifies participants who come together**
singing National Anthem at game
saying prayer together in church

2 **adds to sense of importance of an occasion**
music, oath of office for president
official awarding of medals at Olympics
exchange of vows in wedding ceremony

Exercise 2: Writing Your Essay page 284

The sample essay below builds on the brainstorming list from Exercise 1. It still needs work on revising and editing.

Why don't more people just move in together instead of having a wedding ceremony? Why did teams hold opening ceremonies for athaletic games instead of just starting to play? Why does a president have an inauguration instead of simply moving into the Oval Office? Ceremonies are an important part of our lives. We use these rituals to create a sense of belonging to emphasize the importance of events, and to give ourselves a feeling of control.

Ceremonies help to unify the participants in an event. For the time that the National Anthem is sung before a baseball game, the crowd and the players are performing as a unit, in the same way, the congregation in a church are brought together when they sing a hymn or recite a prayer. Performing a ritual together gives you a sense of belonging.

Ceremonies also add to the sense of importance of an occasion. Couples which repeat wedding vows making a public, solemn statement of their intention to live together permanently. There decision seems much more significant than an offhand "Let's share an apartment" would be. In the same way, when a president swears in public that he will uphold the Constitution of the united states the whole country realizes the importance of the job and of his commitment to it.

Finally, at a basic level, rituals give people a sense of control over their lives, and this function is especialy evident in funerals. We can't prevent the death of a loved one, but we can organize a ceremony to mark the event. This ritual helps us feel that we are not totally at the mercy of natural forces.

On the surface, ceremonies may seem like a waste of time, empty words repeated unthinkingly. But rituals do have underlying importance. By serving such basic human needs as the desire to belong, to see our actions as important, and to feel in control of our world, these rituals have a real function in our lives.

Exercise 3: Revising and Editing page 285

Here is a revised and edited version of the sample essay from Exercise 2.

Why don't more people just move in together instead of having a wedding ceremony? Why **do** teams hold opening ceremonies for **athletic** games instead of just starting to **play**? Why does a president have an inauguration instead of simply moving into the Oval Office? Ceremonies are an important part of our lives. We use these rituals to create a sense of **belonging, to** emphasize the importance of events, and to give ourselves a feeling of control.

Ceremonies help to unify the participants in an event. For the time that the National Anthem is sung before a baseball game, the crowd and the players are performing as a **unit. In** the same way, the congregation in a church are brought together when they sing a hymn or recite a prayer. Performing a ritual together gives **people** a sense of belonging.

Ceremonies also add to the sense of importance of an occasion. Couples **who** repeat wedding vows **are making** a public, solemn statement of their intention to live together permanently. **Their** decision seems much more significant than an offhand "Let's share an apartment" would be. In the same way, when a president swears in public that he will uphold the Constitution of the **United States, the** whole country realizes the importance of the job and of his commitment to it.

Finally, at a basic level, rituals give people a sense of control over their **lives. This** function is **especially** evident in funerals. We can't prevent the death of a loved one, but we can organize a ceremony to mark the event. This ritual helps us feel that we are not totally at the mercy of natural forces.

On the surface, ceremonies may seem like a waste of time, empty words repeated unthinkingly. But **they do have a deeper meaning**. By serving such basic human needs as the desire to belong, to see our actions as important, and to feel in control of our world, these rituals have a **valuable** function in our lives.

INDEX